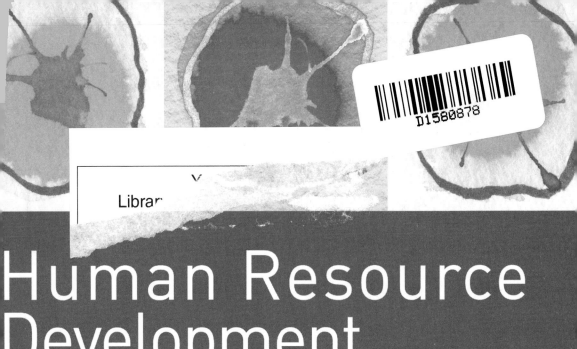

Human Resource Development

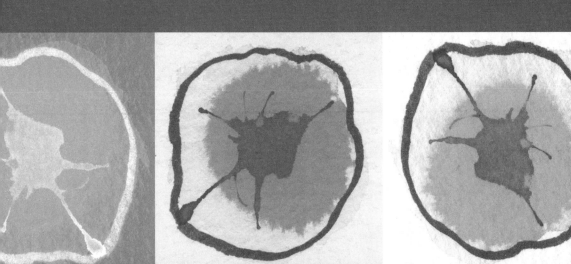

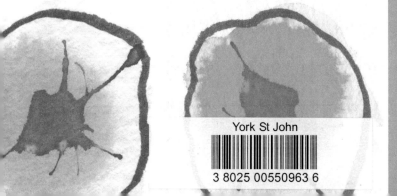

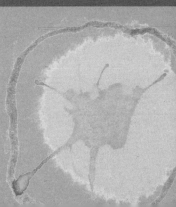

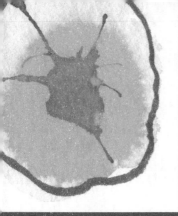
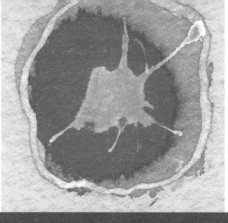
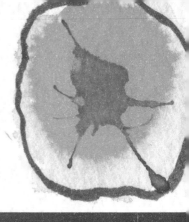

Human Resource
Development

Theory and Practice

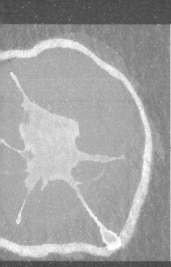

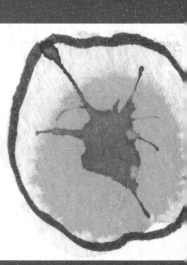

David McGuire and Kenneth Mølbjerg Jørgensen

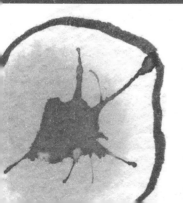

⑤SAGE

Los Angeles | London | New Delhi
Singapore | Washington DC

Editorial arrangement © David McGuire and Kenneth Mølbjerg Jørgensen 2011

Chapter 1 © David McGuire 2011
Chapter 2 © David McGuire 2011
Chapter 3 © David McGuire 2011
Chapter 4 © David McGuire 2011
Chapter 5 © Peter Cleary 2011
Chapter 6 © Robin Grenier and David McGuire 2011
Chapter 7 © David McGuire 2011
Chapter 8 © Ulla Thøgersen and Kenneth Mølbjerg Jørgensen 2011
Chapter 9 © Kenneth Mølbjerg Jørgensen 2011

Chapter 10 © Lars Bo Henriksen, Dorte Sveistrup and Hanne T. Andersen 2011
Chapter 11 © Kenneth Mølbjerg Jørgensen and Lars Bo Henriksen 2011
Chapter 12 © Kenneth Mølbjerg Jørgensen 2011
Chapter 13 © David McGuire 2011
Chapter 14 © David McGuire 2011
Chapter 15 © David McGuire 2011
Chapter 16 © David McGuire 2011

First published 2011

SAGE Publications Ltd
1 Oliver's Yard
55 City Road
London EC1Y 1SP

SAGE Publications Inc.
2455 Teller Road
Thousand Oaks, California 91320

SAGE Publications India Pvt Ltd
B 1/I 1 Mohan Cooperative Industrial Area
Mathura Road
New Delhi 110 044

SAGE Publications Asia-Pacific Pte Ltd
33 Pekin Street #02-01
Far East Square
Singapore 048763

Library of Congress Control Number: 2010924844

British Library Cataloguing in Publication data

A catalogue record for this book is available from the British Library

ISBN 978-1-4129-2298-2
ISBN 978-1-4129-2299-9 (pbk)

Typeset by C&M Digitals (P) Ltd, Chennai, India
Printed in Great Britain by MPG Books Group, Bodmin, Cornwall
Printed on paper from sustainable resources

Mixed Sources
Product group from well-managed forests and other controlled sources
www.fsc.org Cert no. SA-COC-1565
© 1996 Forest Stewardship Council
FSC

Contents

Tables and Figures

Contributors

David McGuire, PhD is lecturer in human resource development at Queen Margaret University, Edinburgh, Scotland. A graduate of the University of Limerick and National University of Ireland, Galway, David teaches undergraduate and postgraduate classes in the areas of HRD, leadership and managing diversity. A former Fulbright and Government of Ireland scholar, David sits on four editorial boards (*Human Resource Development Quarterly*, *Advances in Developing Human Resources*, *Journal of Change Management*, *Journal of European Industrial Training*) and is book reviews editor for the *Journal of European Industrial Training*. In 2008, David received the Early Career Scholar award from the Academy of Human Resource Development. His email address is: dmcguire@qmu.ac.uk.

Kenneth Mølbjerg Jørgensen, PhD is Associate Professor at The Department of Education, Learning and Philosophy at Aalborg University in Denmark. He conducts research and teaching in the areas of organisational change and organisational learning. His research interests include power, language and identity in organisations. His current interests are centred on narrative and storytelling in relation to organisational learning and management education. He has been involved in numerous projects on organisational change and learning. Kenneth has authored and co-authored numerous books, book chapters, journal articles, conference papers. His recent international authored book is *Power without Glory – A Genealogy of a Management Decision* published by Copenhagen Business School Press. Currently, Kenneth is involved in projects on human resource development in public organisations and on educational leadership and management. His email address is: kmj@learning.aau.dk.

Hanne Toft Andersen, MA in Learning and Innovative Change, is Head of HR at Global Wind Power, which is an international developer of wind turbine projects. Hanne works within various aspects of human resource development. Her current area of interest is primarily the use of narrative approach in maintaining feelings of shared organisational culture in an international, expanding company. Another area of interest is improving structural and traditional elements within the HR field to create a strategic coherence between these elements and the company strategy. Her email address is: hta@globalwindpower.com.

Peter Cleary, PhD lectures in Management Accounting and Financial Accounting at University College Cork (UCC), Ireland at undergraduate, postgraduate and executive education levels. A graduate of UCC, Peter has worked for organisations in accounting roles in both Ireland and the USA. He completed his doctoral dissertation at the University of Limerick (UL), Ireland in 2007 which focused on the relationship between Management Accounting and Intellectual Capital in the Irish Information and Communications Technology (ICT) sector. His other research interests include: the role of the Chief Financial Officer (CFO) in e-business, corporate governance in Irish ICT firms and employee stock-options in knowledge-intensive firms. Peter has published his research findings in a range of international journals including the *Journal of Intellectual Capital*, the *International Journal of Accounting, Auditing and Performance Evaluation* and the *Journal of Human Resource Costing and Accounting*. Furthermore, Peter has also presented papers at both national and international conferences. A qualified Chartered Management Accountant (CIMA), Peter is currently the Academic Course Director for the BSc (Accounting) degree programme at UCC. His email address is: p.cleary@ucc.ie.

Robin S. Grenier, PhD is an Assistant Professor of Adult Learning in the Department of Educational Leadership, at the University of Connecticut. In the Neag School of Education she teaches graduate courses in adult learning theory, organisational and workplace learning, and qualitative research. Robin earned her PhD in Adult Education from the University of Georgia, as well as a Certificate in Qualitative Inquiry. Before moving to higher education, she worked as a high school English teacher in Tampa, Florida and a training and educational consultant for school districts and non-profit organisations throughout the United States. Her research interests include: expertise development, informal and experiential learning in the lives of adults, museums as places of life-long learning, and qualitative inquiry. Her email address is: robin.grenier@uconn.edu.

Lars Bo Henriksen, PhD is Associate Professor at The Department of Development and Planning Philosophy at Aalborg University in Denmark. He does research and teaches within the area of organisational change and engineering education. His research interests include organisational sociology, language and the philosophy of technology. His current interests are centred on narrative and storytelling in relation to engineering education and engineering in everyday life. He has been involved in numerous projects on organisational change and learning. Lars Bo has authored and coauthored books, book chapters, journal articles, conference papers. His recent international authored book is *Dimensions of Change* published by Copenhagen Business School Press and Engineering Science, Skills and Bildung, published by Aalborg University Press. Currently, Lars Bo is involved in projects on the everyday life of engineers. His email address is: lbh@plan.aau.dk.

Dorte Sveistrup, MA in Learning and Innovative Change, is a process consultant at the Department for Young Children in Aalborg, Denmark. She works in the fields of organisational learning and organisational change, looking at the care and learning support provided within children's institutions in Aalborg. Her approach to this work is narrative with an emphasis on the significance of language, and on joint conceptualisation concerning values and action in the individual institution as well as among all involved authorities. Her email address is: svei-fb@aalborg.dk.

Ulla Thøgersen, PhD, is Assistant Professor at the Department of Education, Learning and Philosophy, Aalborg University, Denmark. She has a background in philosophy and communication studies. Her current interests are centred on phenomenological philosophy and reflections on body, desire and speech in relation to workplace learning and organisation studies. Previously she has been engaged in the EU-funded development and research project 'Competence development in fringe areas' which is focused on issues concerning workplace learning. Currently she is engaged in a research project investigating coaching as a specific learning method in organisations. Her email address is: ulla@learning.aau.dk.

Acknowledgements

David McGuire: I wish to thank my gorgeous wife, Fiona for her constant love and encouragement during the writing of this book. I am also grateful to the McGuire and Baxter families for their kindness, support and friendship. I would like to acknowledge the advice and insights provided by colleagues at Queen Margaret University and former colleagues at Edinburgh Napier University and Oakland University, Michigan. I would like to record a note of appreciation to Dr Thomas Garavan (University of Limerick), David O'Donnell (Intellectual Capital Institute of Ireland) and Professor Maria Cseh (George Washington University) for being mentors to me and introducing me to the field of HRD. In relation to chapter contributions, I wish to thank Peter Cleary and Robin Grenier and all our Danish colleagues for their valuable inputs to the text. Thanks also must go to Kiren Shoman and Alan Maloney at Sage Publishing for their tireless patience in seeing this project to a conclusion. Finally, a word of gratitude to my friends and colleagues within the AHRD and UFHRD for the hand of friendship offered to me over the last decade. You are a great bunch of people!

Kenneth Mølbjerg Jørgensen: This book could not have come to fruition without the guidance and assistance received from many people, organisations and institutions. Special thanks to David McGuire, who offered his close collaboration and who has handled all communication with the publisher. Special thanks also to my colleagues at The Department of Education, Learning and Philosophy who have supported me both financially and intellectually. In particular I want to thank the co-authors on some of the chapters in the textbook, Ulla Thøgersen and Lars Bo Henriksen for many interesting debates and discussions. Thanks to Hanne Dauer Keller for previous discussions on communities of practice in relation to human resource development and thanks to the whole group concerned with organisational learning at the department. Apart from Hanne and Ulla, this includes Erik Laursen, Thorkil Molly Søholm, Søren Willert, Kristian Lange Østergaard, Kaveh Shamshiri, Lene Østergaard Johansen, Tina Bering Keiding and Karin Højbjerg. Other people have had important contributions in regard to particular subjects in the book. They include Palle Rasmussen and Lennart Nørreklit from the department and David O'Donnell from The Intellectual Capital Institute of Ireland. Deep felt thanks go to David M. Boje, New Mexico State University, for his friendship and intellectual support and to whom I am particularly indebted in regard to the chapters on identity and human resource development and futures and strategic learning. Finally, and most importantly, I thank Anette and our four children Ahndus, Alexander, Mikkeline and Marcus for their invaluable home support and patience.

Preface
David McGuire

Human resource development (HRD) is an evolving, dynamic, ever-changing field. It is shaped by the global environment and the people and organisations that work within it. To comprehensively capture the field of HRD within the confines of one book is an impossible task – so herewith is a snapshot of the field, opening up to you, the reader, opportunities and possibilities for further investigation and research.

This textbook seeks to introduce readers to the key debates and challenges within the field of HRD. It aims to cover the important aspects of the field and provide a useful synthesis of research across 14 disciplinary areas. While the textbook is principally oriented towards research and a critical viewpoint, there is much within the text to satisfy the interests of practitioners. To this end, the textbook should inform evidence-based practice and offers up a menu of possibilities for advancing organisational practice.

Chapter 1 sets out to unearth the foundations of human resource development. It traces the origins of HRD and looks at the early struggles to clearly define and demarcate the field. In doing so, it explores the multidisciplinary nature of the field and examines differences in emphasis between the US and Europe. It identifies the practical challenges facing the field and identifies the need for HRD to develop its empirical base as well as providing practitioners with useful tools to strengthen the competitiveness of organisations. Finally, the chapter discusses critical dimensions of HRD – a theme that is followed up in subsequent chapters.

Chapter 2 examines one of the core aspects of human resource development – namely training and development. Rather than review a range of training interventions in isolation, this chapter seeks to compare a selection of commonly used interventions across eight separate training dimensions: learning theory; knowledge-skills mix; training transferability; degree of learner involvement; locus of initiation; degree of reflection; individual/social interaction and cost. This approach is designed to help practitioners make a more informed choice in their selection of training interventions.

Chapter 3 reviews the literature on training evaluation. It assesses the core function of evaluation as one of understanding cause-and-effect in making more effective organisational decisions. It briefly considers evaluation from ontological and epistemological perspectives and moves on to look at commonly used evaluation models in the literature. The final two sections of the chapter examine the concepts of bench-marking and the balanced scorecard and highlights the value of these approaches to practitioners.

Chapter 4 embarks upon an analysis of the role of HRD in performance management. It investigates the emergence of strategic HRD and the adoption of competency-based approaches to managing learning and development in organisations. It then looks at the role of line managers and assesses the range of responsibilities falling upon line manager shoulders in downsized and devolved organisations. The chapter then briefly examines the three concepts of coaching, mentoring and employee counselling before exploring how leaders can positively affect the performance management process.

Chapter 5 looks at the under-researched area of human resource accounting. It seeks to address the question of how one can accurately assess the value of employee contribution and reflect it in an organisation's balance sheet. The chapter looks at the origins of the human resource accounting movement and identifies the challenges associated with valuing intangible assets in today's knowledge economy. It reviews recent developments in the area of financial accounting, including the introduction of International Accounting Standards for public firms operating in the European Union in 2005. It also looks at how intellectual capital contributions are captured in management accounting terms and issues a challenge to the accountancy profession to do more in collecting and reporting on the value and contribution of intangible assets, lest the accountancy function lose its privileged status as a primary information provider within organisations.

Chapter 6 recognises the importance of creativity in human resource development. It examines barriers to employee creativity in the workplace and outlines a frame-work for fostering creativity around the three dimensions of positionality, perspective and perception. Positionality considers the situatedness of creativity and its connect-edness to individual identity and historic and cultural context. Perspective acknowl-edges that creativity is an outcome of one's cognitive style, experiences and risk-taking disposition, while perception sees creativity as being influenced by the work environment, level of leader support and employee motivation. The chapter concludes that further research needs to focus on how to empower employee creativ-ity and investigate group and team creativity in more depth.

Chapter 7 explores how adults learn. It provides a synopsis of the three key schools of learning, namely cognitivism, behaviourism and humanism. It reviews the key tenets underpinning each of the three schools, examining the learning and develop-ment implications that emerge. The final section examines critical theory approaches to learning and critiques the role of individuals, educationalists and professional bodies in the learning process.

Chapter 8 covers workplace learning and its contribution to human resource devel-opment goals in the workplace. Through the use of a specific case study, the authors identify and discuss the challenges involved in work-based learning and embedding such learning within new practices and processes. It examines the need for workplace learning to engage with the organisational environment and to recognise the learning needs and preferences of participants. This chapter also examines differences between organisational learning and organisational development as well as exploring links to lifelong learning and continuing education.

Chapter 9 examines the relationship between organisation learning and HRD. In particular, the chapter argues that organisational learning is often constructed through designed dialogues. It suggests that language provides a medium for the construction of experience allowing individuals to shape and be shaped by organisational forces. Systems approaches, situated learning and communities of practices are explored as perspectives on organisational learning. The chapter concludes that organisational learning provides an important nexus for linking organisational development and individual learning.

Chapter 10 analyses the links between organisational development and HRD. Using the vehicle of a case example, the chapter explores the nature of organisational culture and the processes, images, symbols and rituals that define the shared beliefs and values of organisational members. It highlights the central importance of understanding organisational culture before embarking on widespread organisational change. It concludes that organisational development can often be a painful and difficult process requiring both time and resources to be successful and that cultural change should take precedent over structural change.

Chapter 11 discusses the issue of identity and HRD. It follows on the discussion from Chapter 10 and looks at experience as polyphonic, plural, multilayered and fragmented. The chapter argues that the multiplicity of language is a source of continuous challenge to rational management concepts which can be counterpointed and brought to order by strong organisational narratives. Identity thus becomes an issue of projection, which is the outcome of a learning process. In this sense, the human experience (and the learning derived from it) is described as always being inter-subjective, plural, ambiguous, open-ended and emergent. Such issues become important in relation to HRD and organisational development initiatives. Employee involvement in change programmes allows integration of new values and processes with existing professional identities and values of employees – thus, if employees are to own change initiatives, they need to understand, accept and embed the logic behind such change.

Chapter 12 challenges the linear simplistic logic underpinning strategy formation in a chapter entitled 'Futures and Strategic Learning'. It argues that complex organisations demand complexity in strategy formulation to ensure plural, inconsistent and contradictory demands and goals. It also maintains that core competencies are not static entities, but ones which must continuously develop and change to meet and satisfy market trends and challenges. The chapter examines relations between narrative, strategy and learning and looks at the importance of reflective and reflexive learning in determining the future direction of the organisation.

Chapter 13 provides a synthesis of the literature on leadership development. The chapter reviews research on four prominent leadership approaches (trait, behavioural, contingency, transformational) looking specifically at the developmental implications flowing from each leadership approach. The chapter argues that to date, much discussion on leadership theories has clearly distinguished various traits and characteristics that effective leaders need to have, but has provided little detail on how such traits and characteristics should be developed. The chapter concludes that leadership remains an elusive concept, being shaped and affected by a range of forces. In turn, leadership development is thus a complex process necessitating leadership development consultants to work across all four leadership approaches in developing and delivering well-rounded and effective interventions.

Chapter 14 recognises the importance of diversity issues in HRD. For too long, the field of HRD has neglected employee differences and this chapter provides a useful commentary on the role that HRD can adopt as a diversity champion in the workplace. In particular, the chapter explores the obstacles faced by employees arising from their gender, race or sexuality and identifies interventions that can be used to promote openness to diversity in the workplace.

Chapter 15 focuses on the emerging field of international HRD. It examines the cross-cultural applicability of HRD concepts and how HRD interventions can be usefully exported across national boundaries. It presents a framework for examining international HRD, identifying four separate phases in the internationalisation process (multi-domestic, international, multinational and transnational). For each phase, the framework explores the characteristics of the organisation under the headings of structural issues; cultural issues and HRD issues. The chapter concludes that HRD has an important role to play in the internationalisation process and in ensuring the maximisation of organisational efficiencies.

Chapter 16 presents some concluding thoughts on the state of the field of HRD. It identifies six grand narratives (definitional; training; performance; learning; identity and international) as shaping research and practice within the field. It argues that HRD is in a constant state of evolution, responding to organisational and environmental change. It identifies a need for the field to develop its empirical base and to continue to foster dynamism and promote diversity of thought.

In conclusion, human resource development is a powerful tool empowering individuals, organisations and societies to compete effectively in a global marketplace. It harnesses the latent capabilities of individuals helping them achieve real progress in the organisations, communities and societies where they live. In so doing, HRD practitioners through the application of their skills and talents can make a real difference to the lives of people across the world.

1 Foundations of Human Resource Development

David McGuire

■ ■ Chapter objectives ■

The objectives of this chapter are to:

- investigate the historical origins of human resource development and its interdisciplinary roots;

- explore the various ways in which HRD has been defined;

- review the criticisms levelled at the theory and practice of HRD;

- examine the emergence of critical HRD.

Introduction

Human Resource Development (HRD) is in a state of becoming. With these words, Lee (2001) describes the emerging field of HRD. From its origins (Harbison and Myers, 1964; Nadler, 1970), HRD has evolved as a field of theory and practice with a distinctive tripartite agenda of human betterment, organisational enhancement and societal development. The transformative power of HRD lies in its capacity to empower the creation of innovative and radical solutions to real world problems.

HRD has evolved to meet the changing individual, organisational and societal environment it inhabits. Its historical development has mirrored changes in the nature of work and reflects the diverse cultures and values it occupies (Alagaraja and Dooley, 2003). They trace the development of HRD to the work of the toolmaker in constructing human axes leading to the development of agriculture and animal husbandry in the era 5 million to 3000BC. Swanson and Holton (2001) trace the roots of HRD back to the legacy of the Greeks and Romans (100BC–AD300), while Ruona (2001) identifies the Training Within Industry (TWI) agency in the 1940s as being pivotal to the emergence of contemporary HRD. McGuire and Cseh (2006) highlight some of the more recent key milestones in the development of the field as the publication of Malcolm Knowles' *The Modern Practice of Adult Education: From Pedagogy to Andragogy* (1988); the publication of Nadlers' *Developing Human Resources* (1970) and the foundation of the Academy of Human Resource Development.

Founded upon the long-established fields of training, education and development, HRD has grown to encompass new emerging fields of knowledge including social capital, knowledge management and the learning organisation (McGoldrick et al., 2002a). By embracing new thinking and focusing on activities and processes intended to improve individual and organisational learning, HRD will inform, shape and remain relevant to professional practice. Notwithstanding these benefits, HRD currently suffers from a limited empirical base and much HRD research has focused on particular organisational contexts (Hamlin, 2002).

This opening chapter explores how HRD is defined and how the shape and nature of HRD has changed over time. It examines its disciplinary origins of the field and explores briefly the role played by HRD practitioners. An examination of criticisms levelled at the field is undertaken and this is followed by an exploration of critical approaches to HRD. The chapter concludes by summarising the key points and assessing the overall potential of the field to add value to individuals and organisations.

Defining HRD

Despite numerous attempts to define the field of HRD, consensus does not yet exist on a specific definition for what HRD is and includes. Attempts to define HRD have preoccupied HRD academics for many years and have led to much debate in journal writings (McGuire and Cseh, 2006; McLean and McLean, 2001; Ruona, 2000; Weinberger, 1998). This led Ruona (2000) to suggest that a major barrier to HRD is that the work of HRD academics and professionals and what HRD stands for is not yet well understood by others. She maintains that the HRD community have not done a good job of working to identify who we are, what we stand for and what we can do for those we serve. It is arguable that the lack of clarity regarding definitional boundaries and conceptual underpinnings may be due to the multidisciplinary and omnivorous nature of the field. In support of this view, Lincoln and Lynham (2007) maintain that HRD calls upon and integrates existing theories to create its unique disciplinary theory and that good theory is imperative to sound, informed practice and the continued development and maturity of a discipline.

The multidisciplinary nature of the field of HRD has been long established. Chalofsky (2004) argues that HRD has been long considered to have an interdisciplinary foundation and maintains that human and organisation studies may describe more accurately the content and substance of HRD. Similarly, Hatcher (2006) maintains that we cannot become complacent about defining such a complex, multi-disciplinary field such as HRD. He argues that the strength of the field of HRD lies in its multi-dimensional nature and that while one-dimensional approaches may solve immediate problems, they exacerbate long-term needs. Meanwhile, Swanson and Holton articulate what they see as the core foundational tenets of HRD, namely 'a strong belief in learning and development as avenues to individual growth; a belief that organisations can be improved through learning and development activities; a commitment to people and human potential; a deep desire to see people grow as individuals and a passion for learning' (2001: 145–146).

Several authors have refused to define HRD. Blake (1995) argued that the field of HRD defies definition and boundaries. He argues that it has become difficult to put in a box and has become so large, extensive and inclusive that it is now greater than all outdoors. Lee (2001) refuses to define HRD as she argues that to proffer definitions of HRD is to misrepresent it as a thing of *being* rather than a process of *becoming*. She also argues that defining the field runs the risk of disengaging from the moral dimension of HRD. McGoldrick et al. (2002b) posit that attempts to define HRD have proved frustrating, confusing and elusive. Specifically, they state that the process of defining HRD is frustrated by the apparent lack of boundaries and parameters, elusiveness is created through the lack of depth of empirical evidence of some conceptual aspect of HRD and confusion arises over the philosophy, purpose, location, and language of HRD. An earlier contribution by Stewart and McGoldrick (1996) maintain that while no definitive consensus has been reached on the composition of HRD, it comprises of strategic and practical components. In addition, they propose that HRD is implicit in organising and managing and concerns itself with leadership, culture, organisational learning and development and change. Moreover, McLean and Wang (2007) suggest that for some commentators, HRD appears to be inwardly directed and without substantial impact. They question whether the lack of definitional consensus is harmful to the field and could potentially lead to the collapse of the field itself.

An examination of the literature also reveals that HRD has been developed from different traditions in Europe and the US. Woodall (2003) argues that in a UK context, there tends to be a close alignment of HRD with HRM programmes which contrasts strongly with the close association of HRD with adult education within the US. Such differences invariably lead to variation in the focus, direction and overall purpose and goals for HRD. Similarly Hilton and McLean (1997) maintain that the definition of HRD varies from one country to another and national differences are a crucial factor in determining the way in which HRD professionals work.

Table 1.1 presents a collection of definitions of HRD found in the literature. Examining these definitions provides an insight into the development of the field over time and the interests served by HRD. The earliest definition by Harbison and Myers (1964) acknowledges the role HRD plays at an economic and societal level. It views HRD as a vehicle for the modernisation and advancement of society as a whole. This definition contrasts with the emphasis placed by later definitions which tend to focus upon the interests of individuals or organisations. There is some evidence of recent expansion of the boundaries of HRD (McLean and Wang, 2007). For their part, Donovan and Marsick (2000) maintain that HRD now includes organisational leadership, organisational values, workforce development and labour economics. Dilworth (2003) includes strategic change management, knowledge management, insourcing and outsourcing of training, team-building and leadership development within the boundaries of HRD.

Several criticisms have been directed at the manner in which HRD has been defined. Nair et al. (2007) argue that current definitions of HRD are limited in scope solely focused on organisations to the exclusion of individuals and society. Swanson and Arnold (1997) highlight the overemphasis placed on the organisational perspective and suggest that it is difficult to find an article on HRD that does not make some reference to the relationship between HRD and organisational strategy. A second criticism levelled at how HRD is defined is the predominance of UK and US definitions of HRD. McLean and McLean (2001) argue that this trend is unsurprising simply because many students of HRD receive their education in the US. They maintain that there is a need to broaden the debate about HRD to consider how HRD is viewed in other countries, specifically in Asia and Continental Europe.

Table 1.1 Definitions of human resource development found in literature

Author	Definition
Harbison and Myers (1964)	HRD is the process of increasing the knowledge, the skills, and the capacities of all the people in a society. In economic and terms, it could be described as the accumulation of human capital and its effective investment in the development of an economy. In political terms, human resource development prepares people for adult participation in political processes, particularly as citizens in a democracy. From the social and cultural points of view, the development of human resources helps people to lead fuller and richer lives, less bound by tradition. In short, the processes of human resource development unlock the door to modernisation.
Nadler (1970)	HRD is a series of organised activities conducted within a specific time and designed to produce behavioural change.
Craig (1976)	HRD focuses on the central goal of developing human potential in every aspect of life-long learning.
Jones (1981)	HRD is a systematic expansion of people's work-related abilities, focused on the attainment of both organisation and personal goals.
Chalofsky and Lincoln (1983)	The discipline of HRD is the study of how individuals and groups in organisations change through learning.
Smith (1988)	HRD consists of programmes and activities, direct and indirect, instructional and/or individual that possibly affect the development of the individual and the productivity and profit of the organisation.
Gilley and Eggland (1989)	HRD is organised learning activities arranged within an organisation to improve performance and/or personal growth for the purpose of improving the job, the individual and/or the organisation.
McLagan (1989)	HRD is the integrated use of training and development, career development and organisational development to improve individual and organisational effectiveness.
Bergenhenegouwen (1990)	HRD can be described as training members of an organisation in such a way that they have the knowledge and skills needed within the context of the (changing) objectives of the organisation.
Garavan (1991)	HRD is the strategic management of training, development and management/professional education intervention, so as to achieve the objectives of the organisation while at the same time ensuring that the full utilisation of the knowledge in detail and skills of the individual employees.
Chalofsky (1992)	HRD is the study and practice of increasing the learning capacity of (1992) individuals, groups, collectives and organisations through the development and application of learning-based interventions of the purpose of optimising human and organisational growth and effectiveness.
ITD (1992)	HRD is the process whereby people develop their full potential in life and work.
Megginson et al. (1993)	HRD is an integrated and holistic approach to changing work-related behaviour using a range of learning techniques.
Horwitz et al. (1996)	HRD is concerned with the processes whereby the citizens of a nation acquire the knowledge and skills necessary to perform both specific occupational tasks and other social, cultural, intellectual and political roles in a society.
Stead and Lee (1996)	HRD is a holistic societal process of learning drawing upon a range of disciplines.

Table 1.1 (Continued)

Author	Definition
Stewart and McGoldrick (1996)	HRD encompasses activities and processes, which are intended to have impact on organisational and individual learning. It assumes that organisations can be constructively conceived of as learning entities and that the learning processes of both organisations and individuals are capable of influence and direction through deliberate and planned interventions.
Watkins and Marsick (1997)	HRD is the field of study and practice responsible for the fostering of a long-term, work-related learning capacity at the individual, group and organisational levels. As such, it includes – but is not limited to – training, career development and organisational development.
Armstrong (1999)	HRD is concerned with the provision of learning, development and training opportunities in order to improve individual, team and organisational performance. It is essentially a business-led approach to developing people with a strategic framework.
Gourlay (2000)	HRD focuses on theory and practice related to training, development and learning within organisations, both for individual and in the context of business strategy and organisational competence formation.
McCracken and Wallace (2000)	HRD is the creation of a learning culture, within which a range of training, development and learning strategies both respond to corporate strategy and also help to shape and influence it.
McLean and McLean (2001)	HRD is any process or activity that, either initially or over the long term, has the potential to develop adults' work-based knowledge, expertise, productivity, and satisfaction, whether for personal or group/team gain, or for the benefit of an organisational community, nation, or ultimately, the whole of humanity.
Nyhan (2002)	HRD refers to educational training and development activities related to working life. It relates to development and learning activities for those who are at work and have completed their basic professional or vocational education and training.
ESC Toulouse (2002)	HRD encompasses adult learning at the workplace, training and development, organisational development and change, organisational learning, knowledge management, management development, coaching, performance improvement, competence development and strategic human resource development. Instead of being a sub-discipline of HRD, HRD is becoming a 'multi-disciplinary' or 'trans-disciplinary' field in its own right.
Vince (2003)	HRD should be conceptualised as an approach that supports the impact that people can have on organising. The focus of HRD is on action, on developing the capacity to act, on generating credibility through action and on influencing and working with others in situations loaded with emotion and politics. The HRD function should be about discovering how an organisation has managed to become set in its ways, how to organise opportunities for change that can challenge a tendency to resist change and how to imagine and deliver processes that can underpin organisational development and transformation.
Slotte et al. (2004)	HRD covers functions related primarily to training, career development, organisational development and research and development in addition to other organisational HR functions where these are intended to foster learning capacity at all levels of the organisation, to integrate learning culture into its overall business strategy and to promote the organisation's efforts to achieve high quality performance.

Source: Adapted from Weinberger (1998)

Figure 1.1　McLagan's Human Resource Wheel

Disciplinary origins of HRD

As a discipline, HRD has been shaped by a wide number of disparate forces. In the 1970s and 1980s, Gilley and Eggland (1989) argue that management began to realise the importance of human resources in face of increased competition. Their work coincided with the publication of the McLagan HR wheel. McLagan (1989) maintains that HRD is comprised of training and development, organisation development and career development. Consequently, HRD is focused on the three elements that contribute to individual performance improvement. For their part, Woodall et al. (2002) see the key contribution of McLagan's HR wheel as distinguishing HRD from other HR functions.

The publication of Hamel and Prahalad's (1994) *Competing for the Future* brought with it the realisation that the competitiveness of firms is closely linked to the possession of core competencies. They postulated that organisations can possess unique clusters of factors that allow the firm to be competitive and the skills possessed by employees is one of those factors. Likewise, Cappelli and Singh (1992) maintain that employees can potentially create competitive advantage, where competencies attained are firm specific and difficult to imitate. This led to greater emphasis on the resource-based view where an organisation is identified as a collection of competencies and issues such as learning, knowledge management and experience take priority.

For his part, Van der Veen (2006) identifies two distinct stages in the development of HRD. Firstly, he views the emphasis on facilitation and learning of communication as being critical to the increasing level of specialisation of employees within organisations and the need to engender greater levels of collaboration among such specialists. Aligned with the development of expertise has been a focus on reflection and transformative learning. The fostering of reflection involved attempts to engage employees in learning the mistakes of the past and moving beyond purely task achievement to systems improvement and enhancement. In this environment, increasing organisational effectiveness became a priority enabling organisations to compete effectively and on a global scale. Secondly, he highlights the greater autonomy of employees and development of creative thinking skills as furthering the growth of the field of HRD. Through this avenue, HRD embraces elements associated with adult learning such as mentoring and coaching and widens its scope in making use of new technologies and techniques for learning.

Practical aspects

The relationship between theory and practice is of particular relevance to the field of HRD. At its heart, HRD is an applied discipline and seeks to solve real world problems through adopting a multidisciplinary approach. Owing to its origins and the fact that its development has primarily been driven by the Academy of Human Resource Development (US) and the University Forum for Human Resource Development (Europe), bodies populated primarily by academics, much work remains in bridging the gap between academics and practitioners. Kuchinke (2004) acknowledges this fact and argues that HRD seeks particular proximity between theory and practice, but recognises that much remains to be done to achieve this proximity. Sambrook and Stewart (2002) describe the reality in organisations that the term HRD is rarely encountered in the workplace and even when the term is used, the function described corresponds to little more than training activity. In agreement, Harrison and Kessels (2004) assert that in real life, stakeholders have little patience with HRD professionals who are confused about the function, yet claim it to be crucial to their organisation's success. They posit that there needs to be greater clarity regarding the field's organisational purpose and that this clarity matters more than agreement about whether the field should be called 'human resource development' or 'learning and development' or any number of other associated terms.

The value-added role of HRD has attracted much attention in the literature. Ruona et al. (2002) argue that one of the core challenges facing HRD has been and continues to be that HRD professions must better demonstrate strategic and bottom-line impact. In a survey of CEOs and senior management at a future of HRD conference, Bing et al. (2003) report that those assembled agreed that the most effective way for HRD practitioners to establish themselves as key players in the development of organisational strategy is to demonstrate how what they do correlates with the productivity and welfare of the company. However, the challenge of demonstrating the utility and value-added nature of HRD is a significant one. Ty (2007) argues that in many organisations, HRD is practised indirectly, unintentionally and intuitively. He maintains that there is a lack of systematic application of strategic planning and decision-making throughout the organisation, resulting in organisational learning for lower echelon employees becoming incidental and anecdotal.

There exists some evidence to suggest that the role of the HRD practitioner is becoming more clearly defined. Mavin et al. (2007) ascribes three critical roles to HRD practitioners: firstly, they act as problem makers who identify and name the development challenges facing an organisation; second, they may be agents of organisational change, internal consultants or experts in uncertainty and finally, they work in partnership with managers to support business operations. Likewise, Swart et al. (2005) argue that the role of HRD practitioners in the twenty-first century is shifting from training to learning and must be more heavily involved in managing and disseminating knowledge across the organisation more effectively.

Criticisms levelled at the field of HRD

It is clear that for a young field there is significant discussion regarding the direction and ambitions of the field. Some of this discourse can be labelled as criticisms – however, it can be argued that it is through valid critique and constructive argument that the foundations of the field become solidified and more widely accepted. Indeed, HRD stakeholders are more likely to take ownership of the field if they are involved and participate in such debates. A moderate position in line with this view is taken by Kuchinke (2007) when he states that the apparent dilemma between maximal inclusiveness (Lee, 2001) and the need for definition (McLean and McLean, 2001) may be better understood as a creative tension where the two positions are not mutually exclusive, but are constitutive of each other.

In terms of criticisms related to the very nature of the field, these have focused on the under-developed empirical and theoretical base and its relationship to HRM. The under-developed empirical and theoretical base of HRD has been acknowledged by several commentators. Stewart (2007) argues that one of the key weaknesses inhibiting the growth of HRD as a field of research and practice is the willingness to engage in esoteric argument and debate over theoretical concepts. He also identifies a high degree of insularity, both geographic and conceptual that exists in the HRD research community. An older study by Lowyck (1995, cited in Kessels, 2007) argues that HRD research suffers from two major weaknesses: firstly, he suggests that a lack of rigour is exhibited in carefully building a coherent cycle of empirical research in HRD and secondly, he argues that HRD research jumps clumsily from descriptive studies to prescription. A broader criticism of HRD which appraises the poor development of the field is forwarded by Vince who states:

> **HRD is based on people development and rational planning; it is rooted in standardised products and services; driven by competencies, defined by professional bodies and focused on predictability and consistency. There are too many organisations whose approaches require staff members to learn mechanistically, and only a very small number of models of development that are used (the top three are the training cycle; Kirkpatrick's evaluation ladder and**

Kolb's learning cycle). HRD has been weak strategically, placing the emphasis on individuals to learn and change, and largely ignoring the wider politics of organising in which HRD exists and can have an impact. (Vince, 2003: 560)

The relationship of HRD with HRM has attracted some comment – although a consensus is emerging regarding the separate and distinct identity of HRD. Traditionally, both fields concentrated on the 'human resource' component and organisations often did not appreciate the need for separate departments. As Mankin (2001) argued, HRD roles were often subsumed within the HRM or personnel department where the individuals involved often had very little background or training in HRD. He maintained that this situation resulted from the ambiguous and problematic nature of the concept of HRD, where the relationship between HRM and HRD was not clearly defined. However, he argued that while both concepts have their own identities, they depend upon each other for mutual success and the maximisation of human resource potential within organisations.

It would be foolish to deny that there are not links between HRM and HRD. However, current trends in globalisation and the importance placed on technological advances, knowledge management and value-added creativity have established the critical need for HRD interventions. For his part, Friedman (2005) argues that organisations are emphasising individual customer relationships and product customisation in order to differentiate themselves from their competitors. As he so eloquently puts it, 'There is no money in vanilla' – meaning that standardised products are so easy to replicate that they will no longer form a viable business model. The challenge for HRD then is to find ways to promote creativity thinking and risk-taking amongst employees as well as fostering individual autonomy and self-management and development.

Arriving at a critical understanding of HRD

Critical approaches to HRD render as problematic the 'resource' aspect of HRD as suppressing employee voice. Only in recent years have critical approaches begun to be applied to HRD. Callahan (2007) argues that HRD contains very little critique of the workplace and even less critique of society. She maintains that the non-critical orientation of the field emphasises performativity which serves to subordinate knowledge and truth to the production of efficiency. She posits that those who would work in the interests of workers must make a Faustian bargain when they try to appeal to both worker and employer as the very structures within which they work are controlled by those in power and historically, those in power are wont to share it. Likewise, Fournier and Grey (2000: 17) argue that a non-critical orientation focuses primarily on 'the principle of performativity which serves to subordinate knowledge and truth to the production of efficiency'. They maintain that critical and non-critical works may be differentiated along three dimensions: performativity, deneutralisation and reflexivity. For her part, Fenwick (2004) shares some of the aforementioned concerns and is critical of the prevailing performance paradigm within HRD as it focuses little on social justice.

Sambrook (2004) views the emergence of critical HRD as a means of challenging traditional approaches to HRD. She argues that the shortcomings of traditional HRD approaches include a neglect of political factors, a reluctance to explore the views of those marginalised or oppressed and an unwavering adhering to conventional research methodologies. Critical HRD is therefore viewed as embracing a broad agenda taken to include examinations of power, politics, ideology, and status (Githens, 2007; Fenwick, 2004; Trehan, 2004). Ty (2007) argues that critical HRD, explores the foundation and structure of power relations within an institution and examines questions of social justice and equality. He suggests that critical HRD does not look towards maintaining power relations, but seeks to build power from the bottom and empower workers. Consequently, he provides the following definition of HRD from a critical theory perspective:

> **As a product of clashing social forces and ideologies, human resource develop- ment (HRD) is a pro-active, forward-looking process that responds to social forces as well as overhauls organisational and social structures. It taps inter- individual human potentials and talents as well as takes into consideration gender, ethnicity, class, environment and other critical issues, thereby paving the way for a new transformed organisational and social order that promotes social justice and lasting peace. Critical HRD takes into account social justice, where all persons in an organisation are engaged in participatory collabora- tion, are treated fairly, receive just share in the benefits of the organisation, and are equally recognised for all their contributions to the development of the organisation. (Ty, 2007: 132)**

Critical approaches to HRD need to be conscious of the need to provide practical workable solutions to identified problems. As Valentin (2006) points out, critical theory seeks to 'problematise' rather than solve problems and can therefore be justi- fiably censured for its lack of practical application. Similarly, Fenwick (2004) argues that without due attention to the practical application of critical theory, the movement may become isolated, lack impact and may become considered as elitist. Therefore, in recognising the relativity of employees in relation to their level of economic wealth, political power, and cultural dominance, critical approaches should identify clear pathways for guiding employees towards emancipation.

In summary, critical approaches to HRD offer an important vehicle for questioning taken-for-granted assumptions and prevailing methodologies for generating and disseminating knowledge. As Ty (2007) argues, critical HRD does not accept the universality of virtues and ethics but realises the subjectivity and constantly shifting nature of employees' relationship with the organisation. Certainly HRD professionals need to face the reality that they serve two masters and must in some way reconcile the inherent duality and conflict that may exist within their positions (Callahan and Dunne de Davila, 2004). Indeed as Short et al. (2003) point out, organisations in general need to demonstrate greater corporate accountability beyond shareholders to communities and societies.

Conclusions

The development of the field of HRD charts an interesting and exciting course. As a discipline, HRD has evolved and changed over time to maintain its relevance to individuals and organisations. From its earliest inception by Harbison and Myers, HRD has been connected to the concepts of skill acquisition, self-actualisation and modernisation. Though the emphasis of various definitions have differed, the core of HRD has centred upon improving individuals, organisations and society through a developmental process seeking to maximise individual potential.

From a disciplinary perspective, there remains broad support for McLagan's conceptualisation of HRD as encompassing three separate foci, namely training and development, career development and organisational development. HRD can be viewed as the synergetic combination of all three foci, bringing about greater organisational efficiencies and effectiveness through more fully engaged and skilled employees whose performance and work outputs are congruently linked to the goals of the organisation. In so doing, commitment to learning and development becomes the vehicle through which the dual ambitions of the individual and organisation become realised.

Several criticisms have been levelled at the HRD concept. For starters, the relationship of HRD to HRM has come under much scrutiny. While both concepts acknowledge the importance of human resources, it is clear that a strong case can be made for the contribution of HRD to individuals and institutions. Current trends in globalisation, technological advances and the need for creative innovative employees who can add value to organisations underscores the need for developing employee knowledge and skills. Indeed, there is a clear need to develop the underlying theoretical and empirical foundations of the field to demonstrate the real contribution HRD can make to individuals and organisations.

The emergence of critical approaches to HRD has focused attention on the perceived shortcomings of HRD. It is argued that HRD has uncritically accepted the performance agenda without questioning the consequences for employee subordination and oppression. The lack of attention in traditional HRD discourse to political and power dimensions and an unwillingness to engage with minority or suppressed viewpoints has led to suggestions that HRD has aligned itself closely with capitalist imperatives. Indeed, critical HRD questions how HRD practitioners may be simultaneously agents for both employees and management and posits that employees should be involved more fairly and equitably in the organisational system. However, to date, critical HRD has been criticised for its lack of practical application with the associated implicated that it is 'all talk and no action'.

 Discussion questions

- From the 25 definitions of HRD listed in Table 1.1, what do you consider to be the key components of HRD?

- How does HRD balance the needs of employees, organisations and society?

- Discuss how HRD fulfils an important function in the workplace.

- What are the challenges facing the field of HRD?

2 Assessing the Effectiveness of Training Solutions

David McGuire

■ ■ Chapter objectives ■

The objectives of this chapter are to:

- examine the learning theories underpinning particular training interventions;

- look at the knowledge/skills mix associated with training interventions;

- review Baldwin and Ford's model in relation to training transferability;

- present a framework for examining training interventions across a number of important dimensions.

Introduction

The provision of training and development programmes in organisations realises a number of important benefits for individual employees, their work departments and the organisation as a whole. Elangovan and Karakowsky (1999) argue that organisations gain from training programmes through the improved performance and increased productivity that accompanies employee development, while employees enjoy extrinsic and intrinsic rewards associated with skill development and performance improvement. As an expensive investment in an employee's future (Cheng and Ho, 2001), organisations are constantly seeking to improve on the effectiveness and return on their investment. Consequently, much attention has been devoted towards optimising training design and facilitating greater transfer of training back to the workplace (Holton and Bates, 2000). However, critics have argued that much research on training effectiveness is both atheoretical and faddish (Baldwin and Ford, 1988; Clark and Dobbins, 1993). In particular, Clark and Dobbins state:

> **Researchers have frequently attempted to increase the effectiveness of training by focusing on training techniques. Special attention has also been paid to the arrangement of training environments. But without a theoretical basis for studying the techniques and training environments, researchers are often at a loss either to explain why they are effective or to predict their effectiveness in other settings or for other trainees. (1993: xx)**

In recognising the criticisms levelled at research on training effectiveness, we have decided in this chapter not to simply review a selection of commonly used training interventions, but rather, we examine these training interventions across eight separate training dimensions: learning theory; knowledge-skills mix; training transferability; degree of learner involvement; locus of initiation; degree of reflection; individual/social interaction and cost. Employing this approach permits a more detailed analysis of the strengths and weaknesses of each intervention, allowing the reader to make a more considered choice of intervention to fit their particular circumstances.

Learning theories

It is widely acknowledged that there has been something of a 'language turn' in contemporary discourse on education, training and development (Honey, 1998; Holmes, 2004). This emphasis on learning asserts that the individual learner should take responsibility for learning and determine the 'what' and 'where' of learning as well as adjudicating the effectiveness of the learning process. Garavan (1997) argues that increasing an individual's capacity to learn and their involvement in the learning process is critical to ensuring its effectiveness. Training provision should therefore be sensitive to the learning needs and styles of participants. Despite arguments by Swieringa and Wierdsma (1992) that training is one of the most important interventions to nurture the learning process, both Robotham (2003) and Berge and Verneil (2002) maintain that training focuses too much on the trainer, while in learning, the focus is on the learner.

Selecting particular training interventions to fit the learning styles of participants is a common method used by trainers. Hayes and Allinson (1996) suggest that it is unclear whether once having identified an individual's learning style, it is then more effective to match the training style used to that particular learning style or to aim for a deliberate mismatch between training and learning styles. Whichever approach is adopted, it is important to have a detailed understanding of the learning theories underpinning training interventions.

Lectures are the most common form of training intervention and are used by 93 per cent of organisations in training employees (Froiland, 1993; Communications, 2001). Although less common, distance learning also concerns the presentation of material in a structured logical manner. Based upon cognitivist approaches to learning, the use of lectures and distance learning assumes that individuals are capable of structuring and arranging information in order for it to make sense. Anderson (2000) distinguishes three categories of information – procedural, declarative and episodic. He suggests that procedural information relates to routines and sequences, while declarative information involves the accumulation of facts, concepts and principles. Finally, episodic information entails the recall of different events. Cognitivism assumes that individuals are capable of encoding these types of information for future recall and utilisation (Silber, 2002).

The use of role-plays, case studies and simulations constitute useful methods for developing skills through practice, changing employee attitudes and increasing diagnostic and problem-solving skills (Carter, 2002). Based upon a constructivist view of learning, these methods require participants to interact with material in a specified context. Both Hwang (1996) and Bednar and Cunningham (1991) advocate a constructivist view of learning and argue that learners build an internal representation of knowledge as well as a personal and social interpretation of such experiences.

Such views ascribe to human knowing as a relational phenomenon (Patriotta, 2003), with Bramming (2004) arguing that individual and organisation are mutually constitutive, meaning that they are always producing each other and at the same time are the products of each other.

The use of group discussions, workshops and outward-bound training engages participants in experiential learning. Following Piaget's (1970) dialectic of cognitive organisation and cognitive adaption, experiential learning theory is viewed as an action-oriented process actively shaping the attitudinal and belief system of individuals through experiencing specific situations. In this regard, Holman and Pavlica (1997) argue that the social relationships that individuals form are of critical importance to learning. The construction of meaning is considered to be both an internal and external activity and collaboration with others can form the basis of learning as much as argument and debate with oneself.

Knowledge/skills mix

Determining the correct mix of knowledge and skills is critically important in deciding upon the content of training programmes. Increasingly, knowledge is becoming a key organisational resource impacting on the competitiveness of firms. Leonard-Barton (1992) argues that managing knowledge is a skill and managers who understand and develop it will dominate competitively. Within the firm, Itami (1987) emphasises the embodied nature of knowledge and its importance in determining an organisation's competitive power. Nelson and Winter (1982) argue that firms constitute a 'repository of knowledge' whose past and present ways of organising and managing stimulate or inhibit knowledge creation. Both Kessels and Harrison (2004) and Russell and Parsons (1996) maintain that research into knowledge-intensive organisations provides support for an emphasis that is less on devising management systems to 'control' learning or to 'manage' knowledge and more on finding new ways to encourage people to think creatively and feed their thoughts back into the organisation.

At its base, an individual's knowledge system has an explicit and implicit component (Table 2.1). This classification acknowledges the fact that individuals possess a high level of knowledge of which they are not consciously aware. The importance of implicit/tacit knowledge lies in the fact that it is a local informal subjective form of knowledge, which is automatic, requiring little or no time or thought (Smith, E.A., 2001). It is essentially a product of socialisation processes and is embedded in local cultural and organisational value systems. According to Sternberg (1997), cognitive tacit knowledge incorporates implicit mental models and perceptions that are so ingrained they are taken for granted. van Zolingen and Streumer (2001) argue that the primary mechanism for tacit knowledge sharing is to connect people in a dialogue – getting people to talk face-to-face, or at least through video-conferencing or some

Table 2.1 The effect of knowledge systems on cognitive schemas

	Individual	Social
Explicit	Conscious	Objectified
Implicit	Automatic	Collective

interactive media. They argue that during dialogue, experiences, mental models and skills are shared and a collective intelligence is created and people arrive together at a shared understanding of a problem and a collective solution that combines the ideas of many people.

Reber (1993) distinguishes between social knowledge that is explicit and social knowledge that is implicit. Where the social knowledge is implicit, knowledge is acquired through the process of socialisation. Baumard (1999) terms this process 'the articulation of tacit knowledge' involving both endogenous methods (imagination, induction, mental elaboration) and exogenous methods (socialisation, non-formalised interaction, observation, sensation). This type of knowledge is characterised as furtive, discretionary and simultaneous. In contrast, social knowledge that is explicit provides the basis for the ordering of societal activities. Objectified social knowledge is regarded as universal generalisable knowledge and can often take the form of rules, laws and regulations. Such knowledge is inevitably formed from an explicitation of collective implicit knowledge acquired through socialisation. Objectified social knowledge provides a platform for individual interaction in society through the wide dissemination of socially accepted norms, rules and procedures. In agreement, Habermas (2001) argues that cultural values and motives interpenetrate in social orders, whereby these orders in turn lend reality to normative patterns by specifying values with regard to typical situations. In essence, objectified social knowledge creates an institutionalised social order based on a pre-established consensus on a set of intersubjectively recognised values.

In relation to skills, many studies have focused on highlighting the significant gaps between current workforce skills and organisational skill requirements (Saunders and Skinner, 2005). Increasingly, skills have been usurped into the language of competencies, which seeks a stronger linkage to overall organisational strategy. Empirical evidence exists to suggest that the competency movement has taken hold in a number of countries, among them Australia, the US, the UK, the Scandinavian countries, and Israel (Boyatzis and Kolb, 1995; Garavan and McGuire, 2001). Competencies have been conceptualised in a number of different ways: as characteristics of individuals, as characteristics of organisations and as a mode of discourse between education and the labour market (Garavan and McGuire, 2001). The transition from skills to competencies is marked by recognition of the importance attaching to the knowledge economy and the role of skills in supporting knowledge creation and dissemination.

Dick and Carey (2001) distinguish three categories of skills that can form the basis of training programmes, namely, verbal skills, intellectual skills and psychomotor skills. Within the realm of verbal skills, they argue that these skills require learners to provide specific responses to relatively specific questions. These skills do not require symbolic manipulation of application of rules and procedures. The second category, intellectual skills require learners to apply their cognitive capabilities towards solving a problem or in manipulating information. The increasing intellectualisation of work arising from modern integrated production systems demands that employees have the capacity to detect, identify and solve problems (Svensson and Ellstrom, 2004). Finally, psychomotor skills involve the co-ordination of mental and physical activity (Dick and Carey, 2001). In a training context, there is evidence to suggest that video-based training is an easier medium for learning psychomotor skills than traditional classroom methods (Marx and Frost, 1998). Indeed, further research by Ginzburg and Dar-El (2000) indicates that forgetting is quicker in relation to intellectual skills and concerning psychomotor skills.

The successful transfer of skills and knowledge from the training room to the workplace is one of the key challenges facing instructors and organisations. A study by Georgenson (1982) suggests that employees transfer less than 10 per cent of training expenditures back to their workplaces. Kelly (1982) argues that one of the reasons for a low rate of training transfer relates to the isolated and peripheral nature of the training function and the fact that training transfer is not 'built into' the training programme. Not only does such research pose problems for investing organisations eager to expand production and increase profits, but it also undermines the reputation of the training profession and its perceived utility. Eraut (2004) maintains that training transfer is particularly difficult because of the differences in context, culture and modes of learning. In this subsection, we examine the characteristics of trainees, explore similarities in the learning-performance context and consider the work community and support provided to the learner in facilitating transfer of training.

Baldwin and Ford (1988) define training transfer as the application of knowledge, skills and attitudes learned from training on-the-job and subsequent maintenance of them over a period of time. In their seminal model, they identify trainee characteristics (personality, trainee ability, motivation effects), training design (principles of learning, sequencing and training content) and work environment (supports-in-organisation, continuous learning culture, task constraints) as factors affecting the transfer of training process (see Figure 2.1).

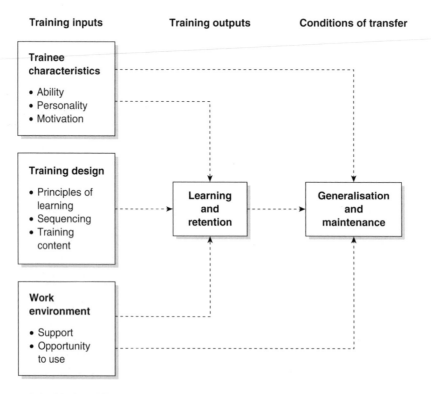

Figure 2.1   Model of Training Transfer Process (Baldwin and Ford, 1988)

The personality, ability and motivation of trainees is an important factor in determining the level of training transfer. A study by Oakes and Ferris (2001) found that personality factors can influence skill acquisition, which in turn can influence the level of job performance. From a Jungian personality perspective, Myers and McCauley (1986) argue that variations in behaviour are actually quite orderly and consistent, being due to differences in the way individuals prefer to use their perception and judgement. In this regard, Smith (2005) argues that the degree to which an individual is sensing or intuitive and thinking or feeling will affect how we perceive and take in information. Humphreys (1979) states that ability is an important factor in determining both the success of training and its effective transfer back to the workplace. Indeed, Schmidt and Hunter (1992) argue that cognitive ability represents the most valid predictor of job learning and performance. As an innate quality of an individual, cognitive ability determines the speed of acquisition of new skills and knowledge. The motivation of individuals plays a key role in the success of the training programme. Thomson and Mabey (2001) argue that trainees are often very instrumentalist in relation to undertaking training and development activities, and often are preoccupied with the 'exchange' value of qualifications rather than their actual 'use' to the organisation. Furthermore trainers need to be aware of the anxiety levels of participants as these can affect feelings of self-efficacy and the conviction of individuals that they can master a given task (Wexley and Latham, 1991). Both Brown and Morrissey (2004) and Brown and McCracken (2004) argue that verbal self-guidance, where people learn to overcome negative self-statements that inhibit transfer, can improve transfer in terms of self-efficacy.

The degree of similarity between the learning and performance contexts is critical to effective training transfer. A number of studies on training transfer have concluded that transfer increases with the similarity between the training context and performance context (Bruce, 1933; McKinney, 1933; Gibson, 1941). Stein (2001) argues effective learning requires the building of an instructional environment sensitive to the tasks trainers must complete to be successful in practice. In this regard, Kim and Lee (2001) distinguish between near transfer, where a high degree of similarity exists between training and task content and far transfer where there exists an approximate match between training and task content (see Table 2.2).

Both Clark and Blake (1997) and Nitsch (1977) argue that it is important that training be demonstrated in varied contexts in order to enhance training transfer, in particular far transfer.

Table 2.2 Transferability of training

	Near transfer	Far transfer
Relationship between the training content and work task	Close match such that the training content and outcomes relate to one work task	Approximate match such that the training content and outcomes relate to a set of related work tasks
Training design	Specific concepts Procedures Problem-solving Decision-making	General concepts Broad principles Problem-solving rules Decision-making rules

Source: Kim and Lee (2001)

The degree of support and encouragement offered to trainees will affect the rate of training transfer. Clark and Dobbins (1993) report that the expected training transfer climate will affect the perceived job utility of training. They found that trainees were more motivated to learn when they perceived that their training was related to performance in their current job or would provide them with an opportunity for future advancement. They also found that the level of supervisory support will affect trainee motivation and where supervisory support is low, trainees will place a low utility value on training. MacNeil (2004) argues that there is a need for supervisors to move away from managing in a command and control style, which is inadequate for the facilitator role of enabling trust, for tacit knowledge sharing in teams.

Individuals need to be provided with an opportunity to practise learned skills when they return to the work environment. Relapse prevention strategies, which may involve practice opportunities and assessment strategies can be used to reinforce learning outcomes. Research has shown that relapse prevention strategies, which help minimise skill erosion among trainees, can positively affect levels of training transfer (Wexley and Nemeroff, 1975; Tziner and Haccoun, 1991). Likewise, Duncan (1984) argues that the amount of training transfer increases with an increasing amount of practice and secondly, that variation in training techniques increases the level of training transfer.

Degree of learner interaction

The degree of learner interaction in the learning process is crucial to the success of the training event and ownership of learning. Verdonschot and Kwakman (2004) argue that contact and interaction between people are key ingredients for learning and knowledge construction to take place.

Hillman and Willis (1994) distinguish four forms of interaction: learner–teacher, learner–learner, learner–content and learner–technology. In the first two listed forms of interaction (person-to-person contact), Patel (2003) considers the interaction between a trainer and student to be a social act that needs to encompass the personal, professional, social and human needs of the learner. He argues that these needs are not merely to learn knowledge but to be heard, praised and accepted within a community of learners. Person-to-person encounters also present other advantages for ensuring beneficial learning occurs. Firstly, direct interactional relationships encourage bonds of respect and friendship to be formed among training participants. Von Krogh (1988) argues that such bonds are manifested in behaviours such as mutual trust, empathy, access to help and co-operation and leniency in judgement. Secondly, Duncan (1972) argues that with face-to-face conversations, there is a constant back-channeling process, during which participants respond to each other and constantly reinforce each other's contribution with simple gestures, eye contact, nodding of a person's head and short verbal exchanges. Sacks and Schegloff (1974) agree that in face-to-face encounters, there is a turn-taking system in action.

In learner–content situations, learners are required to display greater self-discipline and motivation to learn. In contrast to previous forms of interaction, Thompson and Thompson (2004) describe learner–content methods (for example distance education) as instructional delivery in which learners and teachers are separated during the learning process by time and/or space. As a training method, distance learners may suffer from diminished access to social networks and support through shared experience usually found within educational environments, but may provide learners with the freedom to become self-directed in their learning. Patel (2003) defines self-direction in interaction terms as marked by a situation where the student takes ownership of knowledge and the methods of establishing knowledge and develops responsibility for it. Knowles et al. (2005) describe the difficulties of developing self-directed learners and decries the instructor dependency culture that arises the minute adults walk into traditional education and revert back to the conditioning of their previous passive school experience. They argue more generally that trainers need to acknowledge and respond to adults' need for self-direction. For their part, Cho and Kwon (2005) maintain that organisations are increasingly looking to self-directed learning to increase flexibility in the delivery of training programmes and reduce training costs.

In learner–technology situations, learners are expected to have an advanced level of technical ability prior to commencing instruction. Benjamin (1994) argues that e-learning frees learners from rigid schedules and physical limitations and passes control for learning back to the learner. The anonymity and security of the internet may also empower certain learners to become more involved than in a traditional face-to-face situation. However, Vrasidas and Zembylas (2003) argue that online interaction suffers from reduced speed of communication and lacks continuity, richness and immediacy when compared to face-to-face interaction. They argue that the absence of non-verbal cues and the often-disjointed nature of online communication interrupts the continuity of conversation and can create obstacles to learning for students inexperienced in technology-mediated interaction.

In summary, the degree of learner interaction plays an important role in encouraging learners to become more actively involved and to take more ownership for their learning. Streibel (1991) comments that a training system should encourage discourse practices involving collaboration and interaction to produce more effective learning. If the goal of such a system is self-directed learners, then Kerka (1999) argues that self-directed learners are neither independent or dependent, but interdependent, forming new understanding through dialogue, feedback and reflection with others.

Locus of initiation

The degree of formalisation of training courses and the structure attaching to both organisations and programmes can have a significant impact on the effectiveness of the training itself. Merx-Chermin and Nijhof (2004) argue that it is necessary in work organisations to configure work-learning environments to facilitate processes of knowledge retrieval, development of new knowledge combinations and the sharing of knowledge across departmental boundaries. Maxwell and Watson (2004) recognise the importance of organisational culture as enabling greater dissemination and dispersal of training throughout the organisation. They argue that learning is a means of transmitting and changing culture as well as a product of it.

Some commentators however have suggested that organisations need to re-examine training approaches. Bryans and Smith (2000) argue that there is a need for organisations to move beyond the narrowness of training, while avoiding the decontextualisation of development. They suggest that individuals should form dialectical relationships with organisations which are richer and more responsive to the conditions of a knowledge economy. This involves recognising and removing barriers to knowledge sharing and facilitating inclusion and open communication within the organisation. McCracken (2005) argues that key to the creation of a learning culture is the strategic recognition of training and HRD by top management. Likewise, Sambrook and Stewart (2000) advocate greater involvement of line managers and employees in order to create an open learning culture within the organisation.

Degree of reflection

In line with broader moves within professional associations to develop more reflective practitioners, this section examines the degree of reflection associated with training interventions. Childs (2005) argues that the quest to become a reflective practitioner is marked by means and ways whereby thought-action becomes deliberately and deliberatively linked as an iterative process. She maintains that critical reflection aims to stimulate not thought alone, but reflected actions, whereby the individual examines his/her behaviour and the lessons to be learned from it. Likewise, Swieringa and Wierdsma (1992) argue that it is through reflection that both individuals and groups can make a 'leap' in their learning process.

In defining critical reflection, Dewey (1933) argues that reflective thinking is characterised by a state of doubt, hesitation, perplexity or mental difficulty in which thinking originates, and searching and enquiring to put an end to doubt and uncertainty. Later work by Schön (1983) draws an important distinction between 'reflection in action' and 'reflection on action'. He describes the former concept as 'a reflective conversation with a unique and uncertain situation'. Jones and Kriflik (2005) argue that it represents a spiral integrating elements of appreciation, action, and reappreciation allowing managers to think creatively and permit them to reframe problems and experiences. In relation to the latter concept, Schulz (2005) argues that reflection on action allows employees to bridge practical knowing and theoretical knowledge about practice. This encourages a deeper understanding of system and product processes and greater awareness of differences in rhetoric and reality.

Stein (2000) maintains that reflection leads to new understanding through surfacing social, political, professional, economic and ethical assumptions, which are influencing a particular course of action. Clearly, an understanding of such assumptions can lead to new thinking and innovation, which has benefits for both the individual and organisation. In this regard, Reynolds (1998) suggests that critical reflection involves an analysis of power and control and an examination of the 'taken-for-granted' world within which the task or problem is situated. However, both Densten and Gray (2001) and Reynolds (1999) argue that engaging in reflection can cause individual discomfort and dissonance. They argue that three attributes are needed for critical reflection; namely open-mindedness, responsibility and wholeheartedness.

Likewise, Robotham (2003) sees an important role for trainers in leading by example and promoting reflective practice. However, he argues that unless trainers are able to engage actively in introspection on their own learning processes, then they will be less able to promote such engagement in others.

Cost

The issue of cost is critical to determining commitment to employee training programmes. As a needs-based investment, Wright and Belcourt (1995) argue that training and development has long struggled between those who regarded it as a cost (input-based) and those who viewed it as a benefit (output-based). Training is an expensive activity and as Palmer and Smith (1999) argue, the majority of training programmes have produced disappointing outcomes in relation to the level of money invested. Underpinning investment in training has been the traditional assumption that organisations support training because it shows concern for employees and there is an assumption that the benefits will exceed the cost (Campbell, 1994). Moreover, the success of training programmes has often relied on subjectively perceived quality as adjudged through 'happy-sheets' from participants.

Research has shown that the most successful SMEs (small and medium sized enterprises) provide much more training than average (Competitiveness, 1996). However the cost of training is considered to be greater for SMEs due to the absence cost of managers and the fact that training costs are spread over a small group of employees (Storey and Westhead, 1997; Loan-Clarke and Boocock, 1999). Moreover the direct financial costs of training include annual registration fees, costs of books and journals, costs of attending events, programme documentation and research. Some less direct costs include time, networking activities, committee membership by legal professionals and other voluntary meetings. Table 2.3 summarises the key dimensions associated with commonly used training interventions.

Conclusions

Exposing training interventions to an underlying set of dimensions illustrates the underlying purpose and structure that can have a critical impact on training outcomes and effectiveness. Training is an expensive activity, hence it is crucial that training expenditure can be soundly justified and fits with the organisational vision and strategy. The dimensions examined in the chapter allow the reader to make an informed choice to fit the overall objectives being pursued. Moreover, by drawing on research findings, the reader will have a clearer understanding of the impact that effective training can have on employee participation, commitment and organisational effectiveness.

Getting the right mix of training intervention is as much an art as a science – however, training practitioners need to carefully consider the overall training objectives and look at a range of dimensions (such as learner interaction, transferability, degree of reflection) in developing an overall training programme. Such attention to detail will invariably improve the effectiveness of training interventions and benefit the organisation as a whole.

Table 2.3 An examination of the dimensions of commonly used training interventions

Intervention	Learning theory	Knowledge-Skills mix	Training Transferability	Degree of Learner interaction	Locus of Initiation	Degree of Reflection	Cost
Lecture	Cognitivism (Expository Teaching)	Predominantly knowledge driven	Low level of similarity between learning and performance context	Large number of participants	Formal, planned and highly structured	Reflection on action	Generally low
Role play	Constructivism (Simulation)	Both knowledge and skills based	High level of similarity between learning and performance context	One-to-one exercise with observers	Structured activity	Reflection in action	Medium
Group discussion	Collaborative Learning Experiential Learning Theory	Can be knowledge or skills based	Medium degree of transferability as discussion tends to be specific	Involves a number of participants	Loosely structured activity	Reflection on action	Low
Workshops	Collaborative Learning Experiential Learning Theory	Can be knowledge or skills based	Medium degree of transferability as discussion tends to be specific	Involves facilitator and number of participants	Highly structured activity – facilitator led	Reflection on action	Medium
Case study	Constructivism (Simulation)	Can be knowledge or skills based	Medium degree of transferability as discussion tends to be specific	Individual activity	Structured non-directed activity	Reflection on action	Low
Projects	Constructivism	Tends to be knowledge based	High level of applicability to performance context	Individual activity	Self-directed activity which typically follows a set structure	Reflection on action	Low
Distance Learning including e-learning	Cognitivism	Predominantly knowledge driven	Low level of similarity between learning and performance context	Individual activity – limited interaction	Structured activity in an informal setting	Reflection on action	Medium-High
Learning Logs	Reflective Learning	May relate to both knowledge and skills	High level of applicability to performance context	Individual activity	Informal, self-directed activity	Reflection on action	Low
Mentoring/ Apprenticeship	Experiential Learning Theory	May relate to both knowledge and skills	High level of applicability to performance context	Individual activity	Structured activity facilitated by experienced individual	Reflection on action	Medium
Outward Bound Training	Experiential Learning Theory	May relate to both knowledge and skills	Medium degree of transferability as discussion tends to be specific	Individual or Group activities	Planned and highly structured set of activities	Reflection in action	High

- Given that lecture format is used in 93 per cent of training instances, what learning outcomes is a lecture-style classroom format most suited to?

- Too often, training interventions are selected because of trainer preferences – rather than learner preferences. How important is learner-focused training? Why?

- What factors need to be examined to improve training transferability?

- Technology is changing the relationship between trainers and learners. What are the benefits of technology-mediated training?

3 Evaluating Training Outcomes
David McGuire

───────■ ■ **Chapter objectives** ■──────────────

The objectives of this chapter are to:

- briefly examine the evaluation process in ontological and epistemological terms;

- review the Kirkpatrick four-levels typology and criticisms associated with it;

- explore the usefulness of benchmarking and different forms of benchmarking;

- consider the importance of the balanced scorecard to delivering a complete picture of organisational performance.

──────────── **Introduction**────────────────────

In an increasingly competitive environment, organisations are looking to HRD programmes to add value and increase employee capability. There is increasing evidence that organisations in a knowledge economy are relying upon and investing large sums of money in HRD programmes and are looking to evaluation to determine the degree of success of such programmes and return on investment arising from them. While many organisations continue to invest large sums of money in evaluation interventions, some organisations now take the view that the level of return may not be worth the investment.

The primary purpose of evaluation is to assist organisational decision-making. In essence, it represents a serious attempt to understand the process of cause-and-effect and how training can affect individual behaviour, group and departmental targets and organisational efficiency. Preskill and Torres (1999) maintain that evaluation is a process of enhancing knowledge and decision-making within organisations and communities. They argue that evaluation is a means for understanding the effect of our actions in a work environment and a process for measuring and promoting shared individual, team and organisational learning. For his part, Swanson (2005) identifies one of the functions of evaluation as being that of discrimination: being able to make judgements based upon the information provided and surrounding circumstances.

Too often however, evaluation has been considered in simplistic terms, thus ignoring the wider implications and factors affecting evaluation processes. It is worth noting that evaluation is inherently a political activity that occurs in a fluid complex environment. Weiss (1987) argues that politics and evaluation are connected in that training programmes are creatures of political decisions and evaluation itself feeds into the decision-making and resource-allocation model. Likewise Newby (1992) maintains that evaluation data can be used as a source of power and argues that this may account for much of the defensiveness of training practitioners when faced with proposals for evaluation.

Many of the shortcomings of evaluation can be traced back to HRD practitioners themselves. According to Russ-Eft and Preskill (2005), most HRD practitioners lack an in-depth knowledge of evaluation approaches and few HRD evaluations consider their work within the context of organisational learning, performance and change. Indeed, Preskill (2007) argues that the field of HRD has been painfully slow to recognise that there is a rich and relevant set of evaluation theories beyond Kirkpatrick's four-levels evaluation taxonomy. A further shortcoming arises from a narrow instrumentalist view of evaluation. Michalski and Cousins argue that training providers often view the purpose of evaluation as 'mostly to highlight training merit and worth and to sustain and expand training budgets' (2001: 37). This restrictive view of evaluation has led to calls that organisations need to move beyond the bottom line to look at a wider set of evaluation criteria, such as organisational culture change and contribution to community and society (Newby, 1992).

A number of factors have been identified by Lewis and Thornhill (1994) to explain why organisations do not engage HRD programmes. Firstly, they identify the 'confounding variables effect' where organisations refuse to evaluate because of the difficulty of disentangling training from other stimuli. Second, they recognise the 'non-quantifiable effect' where the effects of training are difficult to quantify. Third, many organisations do not evaluate training due to the 'cost outweighing the benefits effect'. In this regard, research by Brinkerhoff (2006) argues that for many organisations the cost of evaluation is not worth the benefit with the impact from training usually less than 15 per cent. Fourth, the 'act of faith effect' occurs when organisations suppose that training must bring about beneficial effects and negates the need for evaluation. The 'trainer sensitivity' effect discounts evaluation due to the possible negative feedback that could arise and affect the confidence of the trainer. Finally, the 'organisational political effect' arises when conducting training evaluation may have adverse political consequences for the HR department or senior management.

Conducting training evaluations can be expensive, consequently, it is important to identify occasions where it is best not to evaluate. It is arguable the occasions not to evaluate HRD programmes include: when the programme is low in cost, compared to the cost of evaluation; when it's a once-off programme; when results won't influence decision-making and when no one is interested or competent enough to carry out the evaluation. In the following sections, we examine the concept of evaluation in ontological and epistemological terms. We probe Kirkpatrick's four-levels taxonomy and consider other common evaluation models. We investigate the incidence of benchmarking and how it is conducted. Finally, we analyse the importance of the balanced scorecard and how it assists organisations in strategic planning and priority setting.

Examining evaluation in ontological and epistemological terms

In order to evaluate an HRD programme, a wide range of information is needed. Organisations will seek to establish the number of participants, how well they did, what participants learned, the quality of the trainer and training and the estimated return on investment. An effective evaluation therefore requires both descriptive and judgemental information indicating facts and figures about the HRD programme, but also opinions and beliefs regarding aspects of the programme. Concerns regarding validity and reliability affect both perceptions and approaches towards evaluation. HRD practitioners seek out evaluation instruments and approaches that accurately and fairly measure what they are intended to measure, but also exhibit preciseness in measurement over time. They must understand what is being measured and how it is being measured. While factual knowledge is often easy to collect, assessing the level of learning, the effectiveness and transferability of such learning and attitudes towards the programme itself requires consideration of issues of ontology and epistemology.

The concept of ontology is measured on a continuum from realist to constructivist. A realist ontology views reality as an objective entity independent of the observer capable of determination through a positivist methodology. According to Morgan and Smircich (1980) realist ontologies take an objectivist view of the social world as an independent concrete structure. They argue that through the adoption of a realist ontology, evaluation attempts to freeze the world into structured immobility where individual actors are influenced by a set of more or less deterministic forces. This allows the clear identification of HRD programme strengths and weaknesses. The use of a positivist epistemology through quantitative evaluation instruments and approaches such as Likert scale attitudinal measures is indicative of this approach. Indeed, Stewart (1999) contends that most evaluation processes adopt a functionalist realist position supporting a view of evaluation as an objective process. However, he criticises realist approaches to evaluation for their adherence to semblances of objectivity and their reluctance to recognise that knowledge is inherently personal and is constructed by participants in educational and training environment.

Constructivist ontologies recognise that knowledge is interactionally constructed, socially transmitted, historically sedimented, institutionally congealed and communicatively reproduced (Gunnarsson et al., 1997). It embraces the notion of multiple realities and argues that people use language to describe, explain or construct versions of the world in which they live (Chimombo and Roseberry, 1998; Gergen, 1985; Hill and McGowan, 1999). HRD evaluations recognising constructivist principles place importance on the uniqueness of training for each individual and emphasise that training builds upon prior experience and distinctive skill sets that each person possesses and therefore training outcomes will differ for each person taking part. The use of a phenomenological epistemology through qualitative approaches such as interviewing and focus groups supports a constructivist ontology. It seeks to understand the progress made by individuals through their participation in training and identify the obstacles and barriers they encountered. Constructivist approaches have been criticised for their lack of generalisability and the openness of the data to bias (halo/horn effects amongst others). Indeed, Ardichvili and Kuchinke (2002) argue that while constructivist researchers pride themselves on their ability to report a more accurate, realistic picture of people's lives, they often fail to do just this.

In summary, knowledge of realist and constructivist ontologies and their associated epistemological approaches will provide HRD practitioners with a valuable insight into the relative merits of each paradigm. It will allow HRD practitioners to identify an evaluation methodology best suited to their needs and the outcomes they wish to achieve. Moreover, a combination of approaches may be selected by HRD practitioners to overcome weaknesses of each paradigm and provide more accurate holistic feedback on the training intervention.

Getting to grips with evaluation – Kirkpatrick and other models

Being serious about training evaluation requires more than the allocation of resources to summatively appraising a training programme. Organisations need to recognise that evaluation is more than a closing after-thought or concluding period of a training programme but needs to be systematically integrated into a training programme. As James and Roffe (2000) point out, evaluation should be an ongoing progressive activity, comparing the actual and real to the predicted or promised. They see the real value of evaluation as highlighting good and bad practice, detecting errors and correcting mistakes, assessing risk, maximising investment and optimising individual and organisational learning. In this regard, Campbell (1998) advocates preparing an evaluation schedule involving a wide range of stakeholders so that lines of responsibility and accountability can be clearly established and potential conflicts can be more easily resolved.

Without doubt, Kirkpatrick's four-levels taxonomy is currently the most commonly used method for evaluating training interventions. Although developed in 1967, it remains to this day a highly influential model and underpins the UK investors in people model (Santos and Stuart, 2003). The Kirkpatrick Taxonomy proposes evaluation along a hierarchy of learning outcomes (reactions, learning, transfer and results). Russ-Eft and Preskill (2005) characterise Kirkpatrick's taxonomy as a conceptually simple approach to evaluation but nonetheless attest to its standing over time and its apparent straightforward appeal with practitioners. In a critique of Kirkpatrick's work, Holton (1996) argues that despite its dominance as the leading training evaluation taxonomy, the four-levels approach has received little research and is seldom fully implemented in organisations. Figure 3.1 explains Kirkpatrick's Four Level Taxonomy in greater depth.

Evaluating participant reactions is the most common form of training evaluation. As Lanigan and Bentley (2006) point out, reactionnaires (or so-called 'smile sheets') are effortless to create, simple to administer and easy to store in a cabinet drawer. Reports on the use of reactionnaires shows that 2 per cent of companies evaluate at the results level, 11 per cent at the behaviour/transfer level, 29 per cent at the learning level and 89 per cent at the reactions level (Bassi and Van Buren, 1999). However, much research casts doubt on the highly questionable assumption that because trainees were satisfied with the training, that it was effective (Burrow and Berardinelli, 2003; Collins, 2002). Indeed, Preskill and Russ-Eft (2005) argue that at best, reliance on reactionnaires limits the amount and usefulness of information obtained and at worst, inhibits HRD professional's involvement with the strategic operations of the organisation. To be anyway effective Pershing and Pershing (2001) argue that HRD

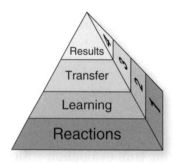

Level 1: *Reactions:* The responses of trainees to the content and methods of the programme are elicited. Feedback sheets (sometimes called reactionnaires or happy sheets), oral discussions and checklists are used. This level constitutes a formative evaluation.

Level 2: *Learning:* The actual learning of trainees is measured and an assessment is made regarding how well trainees have advanced in their level of knowledge and skills. This is achieved through the use of tests, projects, portfolios and learning logs. This level constitutes a formative evaluation.

Level 3: *Transfer:* The effect of the training programme on the behaviour of the trainee in the workplace is measured. Observation, interviews, critical incident technique and post-programme testing are often used to assess the level of training transfer. This level constitutes a summative evaluation.

Level 4: *Results:* The impact of the training on the performance of the employee is examined. Workplace metrics (such as productivity, levels of waste, throughput) and cost–benefit analysis can be used here, however, it is often difficult to establish casual linkages to the improvement resulting from training. This level constitutes a summative evaluation.

Figure 3.1   Kirkpatrick's Four Level Taxonomy

practitioners designing reactionnaires must pay careful attention to issues of structure and content.

Assessing the overall level of trainee learning is a difficult process and can be affected by a number of factors. Some of these factors include: trainee motivation, training design, prior trainee experiences, training delivery and perceived relevance of the training material. For his part, Dionne (1996) argues that any HRD programme evaluation needs to take account of the relationship between the learning to be acquired, the design of the training and the teaching strategies used. In a similar vein, Holton (1996) maintains that the level of learning will be affected by readiness for training, job attitude, ability level and trainee personality. Too often, HRD practitioners use simple tests to assess the level of learning without taking full account of the range of factors affecting the learning of trainees. Indeed, it can be argued that the level of trainee learning will be affected by whether trainees adopt a surface or deep approach to learning (Biggs, 2003). Surface approaches indicate an intention to get training out of the way with minimum trouble, yet fulfilling course requirements, while deep approaches signal a meaningful engagement with the training in fulfilment of personal need or interest, self-actualisation or professional curiousity. Consequently, deep learning may be affected by the degree to which trainers stimulate learner curiousity and self-interest and build upon the previous experiences of learners.

Determining the level of transfer from the training site back to the workplace is a difficult task. As we have already seen, transfer is an important element in ensuring the programme adds value to the organisation. Unless transfer is handled effectively, trainees will gradually lose the information gained on the training programme (Velada and Caetano, 2007). Research by Wexley and Latham (2002) suggests that 40 per cent of training content is transferred immediately and this level of transference falls to 25 per cent within six months and 15 per cent over a year. Two key factors appear highly significant in influencing training transfer: firstly, the level of training transfer may be increased by improving the connection between the training context and performance context (Vermeulen, 2002) and secondly, by enhancing the level of social support that employees receive upon returning to the workplace, particularly from their supervisors (Nijman et al., 2006).

Establishing the impact of training is critical to assessing the overall effectiveness of training programmes. Many authors have argued that this element of the process is just too complex and too difficult to be done (Smith, 2004) and the benefits of training are often subjective and difficult to quantify and express in monetary terms (James and Roffe, 2000). Jack Phillips (1991) added a fifth level of return on investment (ROI) to Kirkpatrick's four-level evaluation. As Kline and Harris (2008) point out, establishing the ROI of training promotes justification of current and future budgets; improves training programme selection; impacts positively the tracking of costs, increases the prediction of revenue based on improved service and product selection and improves the awareness of the level of accidents, turnover and absenteeism.

Apart from Kirkpatrick's four-levels taxonomy, several evaluation models have appeared in the training literature. Hamblin's model bears some similarities to that of Kirkpatrick's but places greater emphasis on the results stage – breaking this up to look at the effect at the departmental level and organisational level. Other models by Warr et al. (1976) and Easterby-Smith (1986) trace their roots to systems theory looking at context, inputs and outputs. A new model by Chartered Institute of Personnel and Development (CIPD) and developed by Valerie Anderson (2007b) identifies internal (learning, return on investment) and external aspects to evaluation (benchmarking and capacity indicators). She also recognises the subjective aspects of evaluation through examining return on expectations.

Benchmarking

Understanding how an organisation is performing in relation to its competitors is critical to an organisation's survival and long-term growth. Aligning an organisation with industry standards is an important method of preserving good practice. In addition, benchmarking identifies strengths and weaknesses and empowers organisations to examine their internal processes and systems and prioritise areas for improvement. Yasin (2002) argues that benchmarking is a multi-faceted technique that can be utilised to identify operational and strategic gaps and search for best practices that would eliminate such gaps. It allows an organisation to examine its performance against established standards and can help promote a culture of continuous improvement within the organisation. Kumar and Chandra (2001) argue that benchmarking may be considered a form of backward engineering which encourages organisations to develop customised processes and methods to achieve desirable end goal standards.

The process of emulating successful organisations has fostered high levels of creativity and innovation amongst employees and managers and led to significant change in products, processes and practices. Product benchmarking involves the comparison of an organisation's product against a similar offering by a competitor. The analysis of both products is done with reference to a specific set of criteria, such as product characteristics, functionality, performance and environmental feature. As Wever et al. (2007) point out, effective product benchmarking can contribute to product improvement and lead to significant cost reductions. As such, product benchmarking provides hard data and facts about a product; however, with product life cycles shortening, this information often becomes obsolete quite quickly (Kumar and Chandra, 2001)

Process benchmarking seeks to identify activities where the firm has superior performance or cost advantage relative to competitors which can be used for building competitive advantage (Ralston et al., 2001; Anderson, 1999). In this regard, Delpachitra and Beal (2002) consider process benchmarking as an indirect measure of operational efficiency as it examines budgets, work systems, administration, technology and human resources. They argue that it is often difficult to get organisations to participate in this form of benchmarking as it often involves divulging commercially sensitive or confidential information.

Best practice benchmarking involves seeking out organisations regarded as superior performers in specific functional areas and developing benchmarks against these particular areas of expertise. In this regard, best practice cannot simply be copied – it must be adapted to the specific style and context of the organisation (Bhutta and Huq, 1999). Indeed, the organisation must not simply transfer the practice, it needs to understand the drivers for such a practice, the prevailing culture and skill set needed before the practice is integrated into the organisation.

In spite of the obvious benefits to be derived from benchmarking, most organisations do not engage in benchmarking. A study by Davies and Kochhar (1999) identifies several reasons why British companies do not engage in effective benchmarking. Firstly, they identify a preference for company visits among executives (so-called 'Industrial Tourism'); however, they found that these visits tended to be superficial and did not lead to substantial change. Second, they identified a preoccupation among executives with metrics rather than the practices behind superior performance. Third, many organisations believed their organisations were unique and would not benefit from benchmarking. Fourth, a lack of planning led to suboptimal benchmarking results for many organisations. Fifth, they found that three-quarters of all companies believed they were better than they actually were and did not need to engage in benchmarking. Finally, some companies reported having difficulty in finding benchmarking partners. Hinton et al. (2000) confirm this problem and report that accessing suitable comparable partners was the most common difficulty experienced with benchmarking.

Balanced scorecard

Widely regarded as one of the most important innovations in strategic change management and performance measurement, the balanced scorecard has become the management tool of choice for organisations worldwide (Pangarkar and Kirkwood,

2008). Developed by Robert Kaplan and David Norton in 1996, the balanced score-card seeks to provide organisations with a range of organisational metrics necessary for the effective strategy development and implementation. In essence, the balanced scorecard works as an organisational dashboard and includes a range of real-time measures that give management a quick view of how the organisation is faring across a range of key performance indicators (DeBusk et al., 2003). The appeal of the balanced scorecard lies in the ability to manage a range of metrics rather than focusing on a single measure of performance.

Traditionally, organisations have overemphasised financial measurement at the expense of some of the drivers of financial measures. Maltz et al. (2003) argue that traditional financial measures can give misleading signals for continuous improve-ment and innovation and are not relevant to the skills, knowledge and competencies required in today's competitive environment. Likewise, Chakravarthy (1985) found that financial measures are incapable of differentiating levels of organisational performance and that such measures only record the history of a firm. For this reason, the balanced scorecard aligns financial and non-financial measures to give a more complete overview of the organisation's performance.

As a holistic, multi-dimensional performance measurement tool, the balanced scorecard brings together a wide range of financial and non-financial data to create a complete picture of the organisation's status. Kaplan and Norton (1996) argue that the balanced scorecard addresses a serious deficiency in traditional management systems: their inability to link a company's long-term strategy with its short-term actions. In this sense, the balanced scorecard focuses on better understanding the causal relationships and links between inputs and outcomes and the levers that can be used to improve organisational effectiveness (Dye, 2003).

Providing organisational decision-makers with more complete information about the organisation will enable better decision-making and more targeted training and develop-ment interventions. For their part, Kaplan and Norton (1996) argue that the balanced scorecard permits 'a balance between short-term and long-term objectives, between outcomes desired and the performance drivers of these outcomes and between hard objective measures and softer subjective measures'. They identify four perspectives through which the organisation's activity can be examined (see Table 3.1).

Table 3.1 Balanced scorecard dimensions

Financial perspective: This examines the market share, return on equity, financial results and cash-flow of the organisation. It provides an indication of the financial health of the organisation.

Customer perspective: This explores the target market of the organisation, customer profile, the degree of penetration, performance delivery targets, customer loyalty, satisfaction and retention. It highlights the strength of the relationship between the organisation and its customers and is an important indicator of how well the organisation is doing in the market.

Internal process perspective: This provides data on the operational effectiveness of the organisation. It looks at the level of automation, throughput, quality, cost and order fulfilment. This highlights how well the organisation is functioning internally.

Learning and growth perspective: As the organisation represents a combination of people and process, it is important to collect data on the skill sets of employees, the training and development opportunities available, employee satisfaction, employee turnover and level of internal promotions. This perspective reflects the priority placed on people issues in the organisation.

Not only does the balanced scorecard provide accessible information to managers, it represents a useful device for communicating with employees. Mooraj et al. (1999) maintain that the balanced scorecard may be used to define and disperse an organisation's core values, through making employees aware of the mission, vision and major strategic goals. It also enables employees and departmental teams to identify development priorities necessary to fulfil the identified strategic goals.

Despite its widespread appeal, several criticisms have been levelled at the balanced scorecard. Olve et al. (1999) argue that the seeming simplicity of the balanced scorecard leads to an underestimation of the difficulties in implementing it within an organisation. Indeed, recent research has shown that as many as 70 per cent of balanced scorecard initiatives fail due to difficulties in implementing certain aspects of the process (Othman, 2008; Atkinson, 2006). The balanced scorecard has also been criticised for failing to take account of key stakeholder interests (Chang, 2007; Neely et al., 1995).

While the theory underpinning the balanced scorecard argues for the need to measure performance and the drivers of performance, the balanced scorecard does not include a casual model depicting cause–effect relationships across the four perspectives, although Kaplan and Norton (1996) do recommend development of this model. Indeed, research studies have shown that many of the popular performance measures used (customer service, productivity, market share) exhibit weak correlativity (Malmi, 2001). Indeed some organisational measures may work in a converse-expectancy manner (for instance, profitability and customer service levels may on occasions have an inverse relationship). Finally, with the large volume of data to be collected, Othman (2006) cautions that the balanced scorecard may become an exercise in developing more paperwork than one having any strategic impact.

Conclusions

Evaluation remains an important aspect of the training process. Without evaluation, there is no mechanism for establishing the changes to be made to the training programme, the degree of learning attained by participants and the effectiveness of training along both financial and non-financial metrics. In terms of general observations from the research data, it appears that HRD practitioners are not very knowledgeable about evaluation processes and often employ evaluation in a strategic manner to both satisfy political motives and justify training expenditures. These factors will affect how the evaluation is structured and the results obtained from the implementation of the process.

A knowledge of ontology will provide HRD practitioners with an understanding of the evaluation choices available to them and the methods (qualitative and quantitative) through which the data should be collected. Too often, organisations rely solely on reactionnaires (smile sheets) to gain instant feedback on participant satisfaction with training. Such practices ignore the rich tapestry of evaluation information that can be collected through a considered and planned evaluation methodology. Employing a variation and combination of evaluation techniques will provide organisations with more accurate and detailed information leading to the more effective selection of participants, tailoring of teaching styles and individualising the learning experience.

The Kirkpatrick four-levels taxonomy remains the most consistently used method for evaluation training. Its conceptual simplicity makes it attractive to HRD practitioners; however, all four levels are rarely implemented by organisations. The reactions level measures contentedness of participants with training content, training structure, instructor style and assessment type. The learning level examines the knowledge and skill progression of participants arising from the training course. The transfer level assesses how well learning is employed in the workplace. Finally, the results level gauges the impact of training on organisation metrics such as productivity and profitability. A key criticism of the Kirkpatrick four-levels taxonomy relates to the lack of correlation among each of the levels. Furthermore, HRD practitioners need to be aware of other evaluation models, beyond that of Kirkpatrick, which may be more appropriate to their needs.

As a process, benchmarking enables an organisation to measure its achievements against industry standards and identify strategic gaps in its operations. Three types of benchmarking are commonly in operation: product benchmarking enables organisations to conduct an analysis of their product versus a competitor offering along a specific set of criteria such as functionality, design, performance and environmental features. Process benchmarking compares the effectiveness of work systems and practices and identifies areas where further improvements can be made. Finally, best practice benchmarking ascertains centres of excellence across organisations where specific practices are widely admired and propel superior performance. These practices are then adapted and incorporated into the host organisation to improve overall efficiency and effectiveness.

The balanced scorecard offers organisations an opportunity to manage their operations more effectively through examining performance across a range of metrics, rather than solely relying on traditional financial measurements. The balanced scorecard allows organisations to look at outputs and the drivers of those outputs. In so doing, it allows management to set a range of priorities for the short, medium and long-term to align the organisation with the external environment. Through the four perspectives of financial, customer, internal process and learning and growth, a more complete picture of the state of the organisation is provided and such an analysis can be easily communicated to employees. Some research on the balanced scorecard questions its overall effectiveness and there is evidence to suggest that weak levels of correlativity exist among some of the metrics used in the balanced scorecard.

 Discussion questions

- Identify and discuss occasions when evaluation is 'an unnecessary waste of resources'.

- Kirkpatrick's four-levels typology continues to be the most commonly used evaluation model. Why is this the case? What are the merits associated with the Kirkpatrick model?

- What are the benefits associated with the proper use of benchmarking?

- Does the balanced scorecard involve too much measurement?

Table 3.2 Other common evaluation models and approaches

Hamblin Evaluation Framework (1974)

Reaction level: Measures employee opinions regarding the nature of the training programme. It examines usefulness of training, perceptions in relation to content and trainers.
Learning level: Measures the content of what trainees have learned, particularly in relation to knowledge, skills and attitudes.
Job behaviour level: Measures the impact of the HRD programme on the behaviour of employees in the workplace. It seeks to establish the level of training transfer.
Department level: Measures effect of learning on departmental metrics and examines how changes in job behaviour have impacted upon the department.
Organisation level/ultimate value: Measures how the organisation has benefited from the HRD programme. This will be examined in terms of metrics such as growth, profitability and productivity.

Warr, Bird and Rackham Evaluation Matrix (1976)

Context: Focuses on factors such as identification of training needs and objective-setting in relation to organisation culture and climate.
Input: Examines the design and delivery of the training activity and how individual interventions are framed.
Reaction: Explores the process of acquiring and using the feedback received in relation to individual trainee experiences.
Output: Measures training outcomes along three dimensions: immediate post-intervention changes, training transfer back to the workplace and impact on departmental and organisational performance.

Easterby-Smith Evaluation Framework (1986)

Context: Examines factors surrounding the HRD programme, such as organisational culture, climate, values, provision of support and availability technology.
Administration: Examines how the HRD programme is marketed and communicated to employees. Looks at pre-programme instructions, location of programme and expectations communicated to trainees.
Inputs: Examines the various elements to comprise the training programme – such as training techniques to be used, topics to be covered, format of training room etc.
Process: Examines the content of the HRD programme and the means by which the content is delivered. Focuses on how learning is structured and the experiences of participants.
Outputs: Examines the changes that occur as a result of the HRD programme. At the individual level, this focuses on the knowledge, skills and attitude changes.

CIPD Model of Value and Evaluation (2007)

Evaluation is considered across four dimensions:

Learning function measures: Focuses on the effectiveness and efficiency of the learning function. It examines the provision of training and competence of personnel within the function.
Return on expectation measures: Looks at the anticipated benefits of the training programme and whether these have been achieved. Attempts to establish what changes have occurred as a result of the programme.
Return on investment measures: Examines the benefits resulting from the training programme relative to the costs incurred over a specific period of time. Explore how learning is contributing to the attainment of key performance targets.
Benchmark and capacity measures: Compares the programme to a set of internal and external standards. Seeks to promote good practice and a culture of continuous improvement.

4 Performance Management and HRD
David McGuire

████ ██ **Chapter objectives** ██

The objectives of this chapter are to:

- examine the importance of strategic HRD and the role of competency frameworks within organisations;

- consider the role of line managers in performance management in increasingly devolved organisations;

- look at developmental relationships such as coaching, mentoring and employee counselling;

- explore the role of leaders in the management of performance in organisations.

Introduction

Getting employees to achieve optimum level work performance is a long-standing challenge facing HRD professionals. Gradually, organisations are recognising that greater effectiveness can be achieved through strategic HR and performance management initiatives. This slow realisation is moving organisations beyond operational and technological fixes towards greater engagement with employees. Krinks and Stack (2008) report that the three most critical challenges facing organisations are developing and retaining employees; anticipating and managing change and enhancing operational effectiveness through becoming a learning organisation and transforming HR into a strategic partner. For her part, Bierema has lamented the 'machine mentality in the workplace which has created a crisis in individual development' (1997: 23). She argues for an expansive development focus for employees that is not restricted to productivity metrics, but which treats employees are more than mere machines and equips them to meet broader workplace and societal challenges. However, Hassan (2007) reports that to date, most organisations do not yet recognise the importance of HR and fail to include HRD personnel in the strategic planning process.

The performance paradigm has for a long time been the driving force behind theory and practice in the field of HRD; concerning itself with how employees can be more effectively developed, how resources utilisation can be optimised, how quality is enhanced and how employees can be more effectively engaged in the organisation (O'Donnell et al., 2006; Beaver and Hutchings, 2004; Rummler and Brache, 1995). In this regard, Holton (2002) views the purpose of HRD as to advance the organisation's efforts by improving both individual capabilities and the overall work system. For her part, Holbeche (2008) cites research studies showing that 80 per cent of performance needs are due to factors about the structure and defini-tion of the job with the remaining 20 per cent of performance improvement needs due to knowledge or skill requirements. Such studies underscore the need for HRD professionals to examine job structures and systems as well as providing skill development programmes.

Differences in approach to HRD's role in performance management are evident in the US and UK literatures. As Simmonds and Pedersen (2006) point out, a clear dichotomy exists between the US performance outcomes paradigm which is under-pinned by coaching, mentoring and leadership development and the UK learning and development paradigm emphasising training, education and development. Indeed such differences in emphasis illustrate the tension between learning and performance as the primary outcome of HRD. However, Ruona (2000) argues that both learning and performance should be viewed as central goals of HRD, given the interactive relationship that exists between them. Indeed, she suggests that improved perform-ance may be the ultimate outcome, with learning the crucial motivator towards achieving this outcome. In spite of the differences and tensions that exist there exists one overriding imperative: namely that to be viable, HRD must contribute to the attainment of organisational goals and bottom-line performance in a cost-effective manner.

This chapter examines the role of HRD in performance management. It looks at the evolution of strategic HRD and how environmental changes have moved strategic HRD modelling from the prescriptive to the descriptive. With the increasing use of devolvement to line managers, the chapter examines the challenges and difficulties faced by frontline supervisors and managers in combining traditional operational responsibility with new HR tasks. Coaching, mentoring and employee counselling are explored as mechanisms for supporting employees to achieve high-level performance. The role of leadership in performance management is then discussed followed by some tentative conclusions on the role of HRD in performance management.

Strategic HRD

The management of learning and knowledge is increasingly being regarded as critical to the strategic well-being of organisations. In the knowledge economy, the traditional development model of 'Training, Education and Experience' is being replaced by a contemporary emphasis on learning and development. This highlights an increased recognition of the role of tacit knowledge and skills in the modern economy and a realisation that the exploitation of ideas and creative insights will give organisations a crucial edge in a competitive market. As Rainbird (1995) points out, competitive advantage is secured when organisations have skills and capabilities that are unique and difficult to replicate and imitate by competitors. The goals of out-learning the competition and staying ahead of the game has placed a premium on tailored customised HRD strategies that satisfy the dual goals of structuring and aligning learning to organisational goals, but providing space for learning to move in new and innovative directions.

For the past two decades, competency frameworks have been employed as an effective means of structuring development processes within organisations. As Hafeez and Essmail (2007) point out, much discussion has taken place on the distinction between competences and competencies. They propose that competences refer to the activities that an organisation must excel at to outperform competitors, whereas competencies relate to individual knowledge, skills and attributes necessary to carry out a function effectively. For his part, Post (1997) argues that competences are created when distinctive activities are executed through application of a range of individual competencies. Employee knowledge and skill specialisation and its combination in an organised structured form will generate collective learning and are likely to lead to processes and products that are unique and add value. In the mid-1990s as the information age took hold, competency frameworks began to emphasise the importance of knowledge and learning in a more substantial way. There was also a realisation that with more complex roles, effective performance was more likely to be driven by tacit intangible skills than explicit characteristics (Garavan and McGuire, 2001). The recognition of 'tacit' and 'explicit' knowledge by Nonaka and Takeuchi (1995) opened up the field of knowledge management through recognising the importance of highly subjective insights, intuitions and ideals. As Boud and Garrick (1999: 48) put it, the current and future wealth of organisations exists principally in the heads of employees and 'walks out of the office building every day'. Building upon Senge's (1990) work on the learning organisation emphasising the importance of shared mental models and systems thinking, Nonaka and Takeuchi recognised the importance of sharing personal knowledge through frequent interaction and transcending traditional boundaries. Indeed, such has been the widespread adoption of competency frameworks and the premium now placed on knowledge that Garavan (2007) classifies competency-based systems as a traditional HRD activity, citing knowledge management and business partnering solutions as transformational activities.

In the search to make HR more strategic and relevant to contemporary organisations, HR systems have become more complex and multi-layered. Responding to criticisms from Caldwell and Storey (2007) that the drive to increase value through HR improvements has led to more disorder and fragmentation in HR processes leading to confusion and frustration amongst internal customers, Ulrich (cited in Crabb, 2008) maintains that the HR profession must learn to live with increasing complexity and must get comfortable with being strategic and administrative at the same time. Such thinking has lead to the creation of HR business solutions managers, marking the transformation of HR from a linear, subject-matter oriented administrative function to a outward looking service leading change and innovation through the organisation. It also marks a dismantlement of boundaries between HRD and organisational development and establishes a new vision for HRD as being tasked with not only human resource optimisation, but also focused on improving the interaction between human capital and the overall system. In this regard, HRD plays an important role in work system design and in the improvement of the human–technology interface. IT solutions must be accessible, needs-driven, fit for purpose and capable of unleashing and disseminating knowledge quickly and effectively. Moreover, HRD professionals must work to ensure that both human and technological processes work effectively and in alignment with the overall business strategy.

So, what becomes of strategic HRD? As Garavan (2007) articulates, strategic HRD is a multi-level concept which enables an organisation to combine different knowledge elements, connect prior and new knowledge and merge internal and external knowledge to ensure sustained competitive advantage. He argues that strategic HRD creates core capabilities which make an organisation more change-ready and adaptive to change. In various contributions (see Garavan, 1991, 2007; McCracken and Wallace, 2000; Gilley and Maycunich, 2000), strategic HRD has moved from a prescriptive set of practices to a more descriptive and holistic approach to achieving internal and external alignment and promoting an organisational learning culture. In so doing, HRD professionals must connect with customers both internally and externally through formulating solutions that deliver practical and measurable business results.

'Doing' strategic HRD requires knowledge of five key underpinning assumptions. As Garavan (2007) articulates, strategic HRD must recognise the context, the importance of multiple stakeholders and partnerships and the development of vertical and horizontal linkages across the organisation. He argues that to achieve a vertically aligned and horizontally integrated set of learning and development activities, strategic HRD must satisfy five conditions. First, alignment must be achieved between the organisational mission, corporate plans and HRD vision. Tseng and McLean (2008) recognise the importance of integrating strategic HRD into every aspect of the organisation, such that it encourages proactive behaviour that fits with the internal and external environment. Second, environmental scanning should be regularly conducted and reflected in the shape of corporate strategy and HRD. In agreement, Tseng and McLean (2008) argue that the environment may pose a threat to the HRD function and consequently HRD strategy needs to be well-positioned in the business context. Third, HRD planning should be formal, systematic and integrated with both corporate and HRM planning. Indeed, Luoma (2000) suggests that the HRD function may itself facilitate the planning process for the organisation by seeing it as a set of learning experiences related to problem-solving and interaction. Fourth, HRD solutions must be appropriate to the problems faced and must add value. Garavan (2007) argues that HRD must not be seen as a panacea to cure all organisational problems but should be deployed in a responsible effective manner. Finally, sharing ownership of HRD is critical to adding value to the organisation. Crucially, Tseng and McLean (2008) argue that line managers are best placed to assess training needs, facilitate training routes and provide counselling, support and advice to employees. In the next section, we examine in greater depth the evolving role of line managers.

The role of line managers in performance management and employee development

With HRD professionals adopting more strategic roles and becoming more fully involved in change and innovation processes, much responsibility for traditional HRD practices has been devolved to line managers. Getting line managers involved in HR follows Guest's avocation to HR departments that, 'If HR is to be taken seriously, personnel managers must give it away' (1987: 510). For their part, Larsen and Brewster (2003) identify devolution to the line manager as a growing global trend, but one which has widespread implications for the organisation's capacity to develop, implement and administer HR policies across the entire firm. Indeed, 'giving away

HR' has resulted in HRD professionals encountering a number of problems, including: having less interaction with the line manager; experiencing difficulties in defining new HR roles; having to overcome resistance to change amongst employees and line managers; and dealing with skills gaps and resource deficiencies amongst line managers (CIPD, 2007a).

One of the most vaunted advantages for devolving HR has been the closeness of line managers to frontline employees and a greater understanding of the difficulties faced at shopfloor level. Indeed, Beattie (2006) argues that in recent years, there has been a resurgence in recognition of the workplace as a site of natural learning and an increasing awareness of the need to consider the developmental responsibilities of line managers. Hales (2005) maintains that the spread of more participative forms of management means that line managers are taking on the roles of 'coach', 'conductor' or 'leader' and that the process of HR devolvement means that line managers are becoming 'mini-general managers'. Budgetary cuts also mean that line managers' responsibilities are being stretched to include traditional HR functions including grievance and discipline handling. As McGuire et al. (2008) argue, such widespread devolvement may represent a lack of appreciation of the workloads, priorities, time pressures and skills sets of line managers jeopardising HR standards and effective delivery. In this regard, attention should be paid to the findings of the UK National Skills Task Force (2000) who argue that the capability and commitment of line managers is one of the most important factors in determining the effectiveness of workplace learning.

Getting line managers interested in taking on HR responsibilities has presented an ongoing challenge to HRD practitioners. On the one hand, Harris et al. (2002) argue that providing greater authority to line managers and encouraging initiative taking may address a long-standing criticism levelled at HR departments; namely a lack of appreciation of the immediacy of the line manager's problems. However, research indicates that many line managers view HR issues as secondary to more immediate business goals and consequently devote less time to HR issues (Perry and Kulik, 2008; Cunningham and Hyman, 1995). A lack of training for line managers in handling HR issues has also been cited as a key factor in the inconsistent application of HR policies on the shopfloor level with Longenecker and Fink (2006) arguing that management development is not a priority for the top management with reliance placed on the notion of 'trial and error'. Some organisations however have recognised the need to equip line managers for their new responsibilities with O'Connell (2008) reporting that many organisations are accrediting workplace training programmes both to improve line manager skills sets and in an effort to raise educational levels.

Developmental relationships: coaching, mentoring and employee counselling

Fostering healthy developmental relationships in the workplace is critical to successful performance management. While little research has been conducted into the relationship between psychosocial support in the workplace and training effectiveness (one exception is Brinkerhoff and Montesino (1995) who found that social support increases training transfer), it has been assumed that the existence of constructive relationships and psychosocial support between managers and their direct reports is critical to effective performance. However, some research exists indicating that where employees feel supported by the organisation where they work, they are more likely to be emotionally attached to the organisation and have trust in their managers (Tan and Tan, 2000; Allen and Meyer, 1990; Wayne et al., 1997). Such findings underscore the social exchange view of commitment, whereby commitment respesents a dyadic concept contingent upon the level of engagement by both parties to the relationship (Shore and Wayne, 1993).

With the advent of boundaryless careers, forming developmental relationships is becoming increasingly important for individual career development. D'Abate et al. (2003) highlight the importance of development relationships to enhancing employee skills, improving socialisation within the organisation and in formulating career plans. Rock and Garavan define 'developmental relationships as either formal or informal relationships where the individual takes an active interest in and initiates actions to advance the development of another' (2006: 330). Central to successful developmental relationships are the three ideals of *assessment, challenge* and *support* required to help individuals grow and progress (McCauley and Douglas, 1998).

Mentoring provides a variety of benefits to employees at all levels of the organisation. It has long been perceived as a beneficial hierarchical relationship, where the mentee gains from the advice and guidance of a more experienced colleague. An examination of the literature identifies a myriad of benefits associated with well-structured mentoring processes. Research by Groves (2007) stresses both the psycho-social benefits (integration, motivation, acceptance, affiliation) and career facilitation benefits (career advocate, coach, challenging assignments, exposure) to mentoring interventions in organisations. Likewise, Higgins (2000) reports that having a mentor results in enhanced career development and advancement; speedier career progress; higher salary compensation and higher career satisfaction. In practice, most mentoring programmes are shifting from sponsorship mentoring (where the mentor holds a senior position and performs an advocacy role) to developmental mentoring (which emphasises mutuality of learning and self-direction) (Clutterbuck, 2008).

The field of coaching has experienced a strong revival in recent years. The CIPD annual survey report (2008) states that 71 per cent of UK organisations undertake coaching activities with employees: the main purpose of which is either general personal development or to remedy poor performance. Critically, coaching has been promoted as a tool allowing managers to adapt to change more rapidly and effectively (Jones et al., 2006). For his part, Bluckert (2005) outlines the role of a coach as one who creates enough space for the individual to take risks to learn, develop and change. Stern (2008) sees coaching as an integral component in the development of leader capabilities and equipping leaders for further challenges. Effective coaching programmes recognise the necessity of failure in the leadership growth process and help individuals overcome difficulties through the adoption of an experiential learning approach (Goffee and Jones, 2008).

Employee counselling is a growing field of research within HRD. In an era marked by downsizing and the end of paternalistic employment relationships, yet an era where employee engagement and increased devolved responsibility is commonplace, Lenaghan and Seirup (2007) insist that open and honest communication channels need to exist between employees and employers. They argue that counselling skills are important in rectifying work problems, particularly performance issues and that creating a warm welcoming environment is an important step in getting employees to engage with this concept. Likewise, Garvey (2004) sees a distinct therapeutic value in employee counselling where the agenda is owned by the individual and the emphasis is on individual development and growth.

The role of leadership in performance management

First class leaders select first class followers: Second class leaders select third class followers.

Much has been written about a supposed 'crisis in leadership' with the need for organisations to develop managers into leaders to achieve high performance. Both Groves (2007) and Rothwell (2002) identify shrinking mid-management layers depriving managers of critical on-the-job experiences, depleted resources for employee development and a global war on talent as creating shortfalls in crucial leadership positions. Such trends are forcing organisations to move beyond the short-term succession replacement agenda towards developing a leadership function, rather than developing individual leaders (Kur and Bunning, 2002). To this end, a growing trend relates to the increasing participation of managers in leadership development programmes to develop the leadership function (Groves, 2007).

Increasingly, organisations are recognising the importance of the leadership role played by line managers. As Rappe and Zwink (2007) report, the performance of line managers has an immediate effect on the organisation's bottom line and on employees. Research has shown that employees who feel supported in the workplace have been found to have higher levels of employee commitment (Wayne et al., 1997) and are more likely to have higher levels of performance (Eisenberger et al., 1990). In today's business climate, line managers are particularly expected to have competencies in the areas of communications, interpersonal and soft skills to fulfil the roles allocated through devolvement (Rappe and Zwink, 2007). Moreover, leadership is becoming a shared responsibility across the organisation and recognised as a 'dynamic, interactive influence process among individuals in groups for which the objective is to lead one another to the achievement of group or organisational goals or both' (Pearce and Conger, 2003: 1). In contrast to other leadership forms, shared leadership recognises the lateral influences on leadership as well as upward and downward influences (Bligh et al., 2006). It recognises the distributed nature of leadership and suggests that leadership is a pluralistic multivariate concept. For their part, Waldersee and Eagleson (2002) view leadership as a series of functions and characterise effective leadership as a balance between task-oriented and relations-oriented styles. This gives rise to the notion that leadership is not individually-centred but may exist across groups.

In line with this trend, the focus of much leadership development has shifted from individualised conceptions of leadership to contemporary relational approaches (Boaden, 2006). The mode for delivery for leadership development programmes has also changed. For his part, Mintzberg (2004) argues that there has traditionally been an overdependence on classroom-based teaching in leadership development programmes. Likewise Cohen and Tichy have stated that:

Most of what has been done in leadership development falls dramatically short. It has been too rote, too backward and too theoretical. It has rarely been tied to a business's immediate needs, nor has it prepared leaders for the challenges of the future. (1997: 97)

Critically, Leskiw and Singh (2007) identify a shift from traditional training (talk and chalk) approaches to programmes based on action learning principles. Likewise, Marcus (2004) signals a transition to customised, interactive learning programmes focused on real business issues combined with developmental relationships and supportive participant feedback. Typical items for discussion on such programmes are indicated by Doh (2003) who maintains that modern leadership development programmes need to focus on strategic and global issues, operations in decentralised environments, community perspectives, contingency planning and dealing with diversity.

More recent research indicates that the key distinction between average and superior performance, particularly at management level relates to emotional intelligence. It is estimated that emotional intelligence contributes to superior performance as much as 66 per cent for all jobs and 85 per cent for leadership positions (Kunnanatt, 2004; Goleman, 1995). Building upon the work of McClelland (1973) and Sternberg (1996), Goleman (1999) argues that superior performance demands emotional competence as well as technical competence. Likewise, he argues that emotional intelligence is more important to superior performance than a higher IQ. He identifies five dimensions of emotional intelligence, namely self-awareness, self-regulation, motivation, empathy and social skills. Emotionally intelligent managers are more socially skilled, thus exhibiting high levels of interpersonal effectiveness. Thus, they are equipped to show empathy, handle conflict effectively, build influential networks and manage stress.

In light of research findings indicating the desirability of emotional intelligence, much attention has focused on developing emotionally intelligent leaders. An empirical study by Groves et al. (2008) found that it is possible to enhance the emotional intelligence of individuals through deliberate training. Participants to the study partook in a leadership development programme focused on enhancing emotional intelligence and demonstrated higher capability in perceiving emotions, thinking with emotions, understanding emotions and regulating emotions when compared to a control group. A second study by Grant (2007) compared the impact of attendance at a long-term (13-weeks with weekly 2.5 hour workshops) versus short-term (2-day block intensive) coaching skills training intervention on the emotional intelligence levels of participants. He found that participation on the long-term programme led to increases in emotional intelligence, while participation in the short-term programme did not lead to changes in emotional intelligence. He concluded that longer-term interventions are needed to alter the underlying emotional intelligence levels of participants.

Conclusions

HRD performs an important role in improving employee performance. It examines the relationship between work structures, employee skills and strategic outlook in determining how overall effectiveness can be improved. It argues for performance improvements to be made employee-centred, such that adjustments to new systems and practices can be made seamlessly. Thus, HRD looks at making the organisational system more effective through making employee contribution more effective.

As the business environment has evolved, several key trends are distinguishable in how human resource development practices have adapted to support performance management initiatives. First, the advent of the knowledge age has shifted emphasis from the explicit to the tacit and focused attention on how HRD can more effectively transmit knowledge across functions and disciplines. Secondly, the need for strategic alignment and flexibility are viewed as core values underpinning HRD's role in performance management. HRD systems and practices must be adaptive to fit changing environmental circumstances – consequently, strategic HRD modelling has moved from the prescriptive to the descriptive. Third, in an era of devolvement, line managers are playing an ever-widening role in organisations. Their operational duties are increasingly matched to HR commitments and other devolved responsibilities. HRD professionals must recognise and bear responsibility for these changes and any impact on the quality of delivery. Failure to do so will invariably damage how HRD provision is perceived in the organisation and the importance attached to it.

The widespread acceptance of Ulrich's HR model has heralded significant changes in how HRD is internally aligned and structured. There is little doubt that the creation of an outward-looking proactive service, replacing a traditional administrative, subject-oriented function improves the credibility of HRD in the organisation. Through business partnering roles, HRD is aligning itself more closely with its client base and providing tailored services boosting the core capabilities of the organisation.

Fostering developmental relationships and developing future leaders remains vital to long-term success and sustainability. Recent years have seen a revival in coaching schemes and organisations are recognising the value of employee counselling as an important communication tool. There is also a realisation that leaders need to be developed throughout the organisation and that leadership responsibility does not solely lie with the CEO. Moreover, leadership research is progressively recognising the key role of emotional intelligence in nurturing closer bonds between employees and the organisation.

 Discussion questions

- Simmonds and Pedersen (2006) distinguish between the US performance outcomes paradigm and the UK learning and development paradigm. Is there a stronger role to be played by mentoring and coaching in the UK?

- Do line managers have the skills to operate effectively in devolved organisations?

- By devolving HRD issues to line managers, is the HRD function relinquishing control over core activities? Will this decision damage the reputation of the HRD function in the longer term?

- What key benefits arise to the employee from developmental relationships such as coaching and mentoring?

5 Human Resource Accounting

Peter Cleary

■ ■ Chapter objectives ■

The objectives of this chapter are to:

- understand the reasons for the under-representation of employee contribution in the knowledge economy;

- explore how the value of employee contribution can be accurately identified and measured;

- look at how employees play a role in long-term value creation in organisations;

- examine the unique characteristics of intangible assets and how they should be accounted for.

Introduction

While employees have always been important in the production of goods and the provision of services; land, financial capital and technology have traditionally been regarded as the primary engines of economic growth. However, with the recent emergence of the 'knowledge' economy, it has been suggested (Pilch, 2000) that human capital, i.e. employees, now represent firms' key assets. Indeed, it has even been argued that firms are increasingly differentiated on the basis of their ability to create, transfer, assemble, integrate, protect and exploit their knowledge assets (Teece, 2000).

The growing importance of employees and their knowledge is supported by amongst others, the former British Prime Minister, Gordon Brown, who stated in February 2000 that, 'those countries that can succeed will be those that can best unleash the potential of their people by drawing on the qualities of creativity, flexibility and adaptability, the work ethic and of course an open and outward looking approach to the world' (Pilch, 2000: 13).

However, it has been claimed that the increased importance of employees to organisational value creation has not been reciprocated from an accounting perspective, i.e. the reporting of firms' past and current financial performance is no longer sufficient for progressive and forward looking firms. Consequently, traditional accounting metrics are not necessarily the most effective means by which to evaluate the potential of firms whose worth is based on their employees' capabilities (Low, 2002). Instead, it has been suggested that firms should employ leading indicators to determine the state of their human resources (generally referred to as their human capital) (Fitz-enz, 2000). This form of accounting for employees has become known as 'human resource accounting', and the following section traces its development.

Human resource accounting

In 1995 the European Commission stated that firms should 'treat capital investment and investment in training on an equal basis', thereby allowing firms to enter some of their investments in training as assets on their balance sheet (Johanson, 1998: 1). Despite such calls for change, the human 'knowledge carrier' has traditionally been under-represented in conventional accounting, and where they are referred to, they have generally been regarded as a cost factor or as a resource needing to be 'utilised', 'depreciated', 'managed' or 'exploited'. The distinctive characteristics of human resources, i.e. they cannot be owned by a firm, can act on their own behalf, and have an internal production process called learning, has meant that an appropriate accounting treatment has yet to be developed despite over twenty years of attempts at doing so (Roberts, 2003; Sackmann et al., 1989).

The initiation of a concerted effort to account for employees began with the work of Hermanson in the mid-1960s. He coined the term 'Human Asset Accounting' to identify his attempts at incorporating employees into formal financial statements, especially the balance sheet (Roslender, 2000). The second phase of accounting for employees became known as 'Human Resource Accounting' (HRA) and was used for the first time by Brummet et al. (1968).

HRA was defined by the American Accounting Association (1996) as 'the process of identifying and measuring data about human resources and communicating this information to interested parties'. Essentially, HRA has three primary functions: (1) it provides numerical information about the cost and value of people as organisational resources, (2) it serves as a framework to facilitate decision-making, and (3) it motivates decision-makers to adopt a human resource perspective (Sackmann et al., 1989).

Flamholtz (1974) suggested that the impact of HRA on firms may be felt both internally and externally. Internally, HRA would establish a paradigm, based on the notion that employees are valuable resources and that any decisions impacting upon them should be based on an assessment of the cost and value involved: and secondly, it would provide information needed to manage human resources efficiently and effectively. Externally, HRA data would provide information to investors about the firm's human assets and thus help in valuing the firm (Scarpello and Theeke, 1989).

Most reviewers agree that during the first half of the 1970s HRA 'was one of the most researched subjects within accounting, consuming a vast amount of academic endeavour' (Roslender and Dyson, 1992: 311). However, by the end of the decade interest in the topic had declined from both the academic and corporate standpoints (Grojer and Johanson, 1998a). According to Flamholtz (1985: 2–3), one reason for this decline was the widely held erroneous belief suggesting that HRA was only concerned with treating people as financial objects; 'although preparing financial statements that included human resources was undoubtedly a part of HRA, it was not by far the most significant part'. However, because it was dramatic and innovative, 'putting people on the balance sheet' became its dominant image (Grojer and Johanson, 1998).

Parallel with developments in HRA, Cronbach and Glaser (1965) and Naylor and Shine (1965) developed models for estimating the financial utility of personnel selection and downsizing, using a concept named 'Utility Analysis' (UA). In an attempt at embracing both HRA and UA, Grojer and Johanson (1998a) advocated the concept of Human Resource Costing and Accounting (HRCA). However, during the course of the late 1980s and early 1990s, numerous academics commented on the perceived failure of HRCA. Scarpello and Theeke (1989) intimated that while it was an interesting concept, they found it hard to comprehend why there had not been a serious effort to develop valid and reliable measures, whereas Roslender and Dyson (1992) argued that HRCA failed to develop due to a lack of practical applications. Overall, it appears that the primary problem surrounding HRCA research in the 1990s seems to have been a failure to recruit new researchers rather than a lack of research problems (Grojer and Johanson, 1998a). As Cahill and Myers put it:

> **The major problem with human resource accounting was that it predominately involved descriptive studies of practical applications of techniques and was driven by normative prescriptions about the desirability of such action, without reference to or development of an explanatory theory. (2000: 14)**

At a workshop held in Brussels in 1998 by HRCA researchers and policy-makers, it was clear that after more than thirty years of debate, no consensus had been reached as to an appropriate means of reporting on human resources. This lack of accord may be partly due to the existence of multiple agendas amongst those expressing an interest in the topic, while it has also been suggested that interest in both the United Kingdom and Germany was low due to the dominance of financial accounting in these jurisdictions (Grojer and Johanson, 1998b). Additionally, the fact that the US Securities and Exchange Commission (SEC) declared that there is no evidence of an information interest in non-financial HRCA information from a capital viewpoint, diminished interest in the topic from a US perspective (Grojer and Johanson, 1998b).

Ultimately, until HRA advocates demonstrate a valid and generalisable means for measuring human resources in monetary terms, many feel compelled to recommend that researchers abandon further consideration of the possible benefits from the topic (Scarpello and Theeke, 1989). Therefore, it would appear that the proposition made by Rhode et al. stating that, 'the most apparent reason for the non-acceptance of HRA is an absence of demonstrated usefulness' (1976: 13) still holds true today. That said, the original rationale for initiating research on HRA remains as valid today, and probably much more so, than it was in the late 1960s. Despite the above, the following section examines the financial accounting and financial reporting response thus far to the increasing importance of human resources.

Financial accounting and financial reporting

Financial accounting has been repeatedly criticised in recent times for failing to keep pace with developments in the nature of economic activity. The primary criticism levelled at it in this regard concerns its attempt to measure the assets of the knowledge economy with accounting tools designed for the manufacturing economy (Pilch, 2000).

Claims that tangible assets should be measured and valued, while intangible assets (incorporating human resources) should not, is according to Lev (2000) equivalent to suggesting that 'things' are valuable, while 'ideas' are not.

The main problem here is that the unique characteristics of intangible assets do not fit within the traditional transaction based accounting system because; they are non-rival assets, their value can change without any transaction occurring, their benefits are uncertain and they are impossible to add up (Lev, 2000). The situation has degenerated to such an extent that many Chief Financial Officers are now questioning the ability of traditional accounting metrics to evaluate key elements of operating in the new economy (Anderson Consulting and Economist Intelligence Unit, 2000). To re-enforce this point, research conducted by PricewaterhouseCoopers found that less than 20 per cent of investors and analysts regard financial reports as particularly useful for evaluating the performance of knowledge based firms (Pilch, 2000). As Lev and Daum state, 'Traditional financial and management accounting is failing to support management adequately in today's environment: it is too narrow and too much focused on the past and present' (2003: 4).

A major factor contributing to this deficiency is the lack of a commonly accepted definition of intangible assets within the accounting community. However, based upon the numerous definitions that exist within the extant financial accounting rules and standards (see Table 5.1 for a review), it is possible to identify a number of common characteristics; intangible assets are usually defined as identifiable (separable) non-monetary sources of probable future economic benefits to an entity that lack physical substance, have been acquired or developed internally from identifiable costs, have a finite life, have market value apart from the entity and are owned or controlled by the firm as a result of past transactions or events (Canibano et al., 2000).

Table 5.1 Comparison of accounting standards for intangible assets

	FRS 10 **Goodwill and intangible assets**	**IAS 38** **Intangible assets**	**APB 17** **Intangible assets**
Definition of intangible assets	Non-financial fixed assets that do not have physical substance but are identifiable and controlled by the entity through custody or legal rights	An identifiable, non-monetary asset without physical substance held for use in the production or supply of goods or services, for rental to others or for administrative purposes	No definition
Classification of intangibles	A category: intangible assets having a similar nature, function or use in the business of the entity, e.g. licences, quotas, patents, copyrights, franchises and trademarks	Expending resources or incurring liabilities or the acquisition, development or enhancement of intangible resources such as scientific or technical knowledge, design and implementation of new processes or systems, licences, intellectual property, market knowledge and trademarks	Classified on several different bases: identifiability, manner of acquisition, expected period of benefit, separability from the entire enterprise

(Continued)

Table 5.1 (Continued)

	FRS 10 Goodwill and intangible assets	IAS 38 Intangible assets	APB 17 Intangible assets
Recognition	An internally developed intangible asset may be capitalised only if it has a readily ascertainable market value	An intangible asset should be recognised if: it is probable that the future economic benefits that are attributable to the asset will flow to the enterprise; the cost of the asset can be measured readily	An internally developed intangible asset should be recognised if it: (a) is specifically identifiable; (b) has a determinate life; (c) can be separated from the entity
Amortisation	Where intangible assets have useful economic lives they should be amortised on a systematic basis over those lives. Where intangible assets have indefinite useful economic lives, they should not be amortised	The depreciable amount of intangible assets should be allocated on a systematic basis over the best estimate of their useful lives	Intangible assets should be amortised by systematic charges to income periods over the estimated time to be benefited

Source: Brennan and Connell (2000: 208)

The most recent development in this area occurred with the introduction of International Accounting Standards (IAS) in 2005 for public firms operating in the European Union (EU). As a result of the measures introduced here, it has been claimed that policy-makers have finally begun to address the issue of accounting for human capital and thus should help to ensure that intangible assets will become more prominent for managers, controllers, auditors and investors which should have far reaching consequences for accounting and financial reporting (Lev and Daum, 2003).

However, at a broader level it also seems certain that based upon the requirements of IAS 38, much of what is commonly referred to as an intangible asset will not pass the stringent recognition test especially in relation to measurement. Furthermore, IAS 16 states that the revaluation of intangible assets is only allowed if a fair value can be determined by reference to an active market, which will invariably result in a limit to the financial reporting of human resources (Tayles et al., 2005b). Despite these limitations, the new standards will allow firms to disclose more human related information than was previously the case, which may lead to a further convergence of such disclosures in the future (Vergauwen and Van Alem, 2005).

Similarly, from a financial reporting perspective the Financial Accounting Standards Board (FASB) [1978: par. 34] has stated that firms should disclose information that is useful to a range of interested parties in making rational investment and credit decisions. Therefore, any event that is likely to affect a firm's current or future financial position should be published in its annual accounts (Canibano et al., 2000). However, a major consequence of the shift towards the knowledge economy is that it is becoming increasingly difficult for investors and other stakeholders to understand the value of companies, and the processes by which they create value (Pilch, 2000). As articulated by Dzinkowski:

> **Standard accounting models were designed for informing company manage-ment and stakeholders on stocks and flows of [financial] value. Most of these are quantifiable and subject to generally accepted accounting principles and practices (GAAP). In contrast, intellectual capital [incorporating human capital] is a relatively new and enigmatic concept, relating primarily to the intangible, highly mutable assets of the firm. As such, the current accounting model does not adequately capture their value nor represent them in a concise, meaningful format. (2000: 32–33).**

Even though financial statements were never devised to represent the market value of firms (Tollington, 2000) their usefulness to potential investors in this respect has diminished rapidly (Wallman, 1998). During the period from 1945 to 1990, book values and market values for all US companies were approximately equal. However, during the 1990s the average market-to-book ratio rapidly increased and is now greater than 3 for firms operating in traditional industries, while for technology and software stocks it can exceed 50 (Eustace, 2000). A study of more than 2,000 US manufacturing firms found that tangible assets accounted for just one-third of their stock market value in 1994, whereas a decade earlier this figure was closer to two-thirds (Pilch, 2000). As Malhotra points out, 'the more a company invests in its future, the less is its book value' (2000: 8).

In spite of these difficulties, there are potentially significant benefits for firms that understand and control the flow of relevant information, both tangible and intangible, to their key stakeholders. Basic finance theory suggests that the greater the investors' confidence in the accuracy of the information provided, the lower the returns they will demand for investing in that firm, and consequently the lower the cost of capital faced by the company (Thomas et al., 2002). Indeed, Pilch (2000) has reported that Research & Development (R&D) intensive firms face a higher cost of capital than less R&D intensive firms, due partly to the fact that the capital markets are less informed about their performance.

This issue is exacerbated by the fact that research now suggests that most of the privately disclosed information used by financial analysts in the fundamental analysis process relates to intangible assets (Holland, 2001; Mavrinac and Seisfeld, 1997; Coleman and Eccles, 1997). According to the results of a survey commissioned by Ernst & Young (1997), not only do institutional investors pay attention to non-financial indicators, but they also actively utilise such knowledge in making investment decisions. As outlined in their final report:

> **When non-financial factors were taken into account, earnings forecasts were more accurate, thus reducing the risk to investors. If a firm's non-financial data are strong, this could facilitate its ability to raise capital. The message is clear: non-financial factors can be used as leading indicators of future financial performance. (Ernst & Young, 1997: 7)**

As a result, an increasing number of firms are beginning to report information pertaining to their stock of intangible assets in their annual report, whilst ensuring that they do not disclose sensitive information which could potentially erode their competitive advantage (Marr and Gray, 2002; Bozzolan et al., 2006; Abeysekera,

2006). In a survey conducted by the Institute of Management and reported by Pilch (2000), 64 per cent of all US managers reported that their companies were actively experimenting with new ways of measuring, collecting and reporting non-financial data. However, this increased emphasis on non-financial information does not mean that financial accounting information has become irrelevant. Accounting for employees should supplement and not replace financial accounting, as value is created within firms through the interplay of both tangible and intangible assets (Bartram, 2000).

As regards the future direction for both financial accounting and financial reporting, the former Securities and Exchange Commission (SEC) Commissioner, Steve Wallman, has predicted that the disclosure of intangible asset related information will one day become the primary emphasis of a firm's annual report (Edvisson and Malone, 1997). Similarly, the American Institute of Certified Public Accountants has recommended that the US move towards a model of business reporting, as opposed to the narrower notion of financial reporting (Ashton, 2005).

To achieve this aim, the financial accounting challenge is to invent methods for managing investment in employees as well as a form of accounting measurement that can differentiate between those entities in which intangible assets are appreciating and those in which it is depreciating (International Federation of Accountants, 1998). However, it has been claimed that the current accounting standards for intangible assets (e.g. Financial Reporting Standard (FRS) 10 and IAS 38) have probably gone as far as possible in incorporating 'tradeable' forms of intangible assets in firms' conventional balance sheets (Tayles et al., 2005b). Therefore, much still remains to be done in this regard.

Having examined the financial accounting and financial reporting response to the increased importance attached to human resources, the following section considers the position in relation to management accounting.

Management accounting

The American Accounting Association (AAA) (1996) has defined management accounting as, 'the process of identifying, measuring and communicating economic information to permit informed judgements and decisions by the users of the information'. Whereas financial accounting predominantly focuses on the provision of information for external purposes, management accounting is primarily concerned with the provision of information for internal organisational use.

In unison with the changing informational requirements of firms, the role occupied by management accounting continues to develop and change. At the turn of the twentieth century, cost control was regarded as the most important aspect of managerial control, due primarily to the emergence of scientific management, which had stressed the need for managers to dictate to their employees how to perform tasks. Standard costing systems and variance analysis, which were developed in the 1920s, were used to control workers' behaviour, whilst management control systems were used to compare actual results with projections (Ittner and Larcker, 2001). Miller and O'Leary (1987) argued that the emergence of systems such as these served to highlight both the economic contribution of employees and the extent of their inefficiency.

By the mid-1960s, this focus had shifted towards the provision of information for managerial planning and control, epitomised by Anthony's (1965) management control framework. This was described as a means of ensuring that resources were obtained and utilised efficiently and effectively to achieve the firm's objectives (Ittner and Larcker, 2001; Andon et al., 2003).

Further evolution took place in the late 1980s with the advent of Strategic Management Accounting (SMA) within which management accounting assumed a strategic external orientation, i.e. the provision of information about a business and its competitors for use in developing and monitoring business strategy (Simmonds, 1981).

Over the course of the past two decades, developments in management accounting have provided more advanced techniques focused on issues such as a reduction of waste in business processes and a more strategic focus on the creation of firm value. However, recent research amongst both UK and US manufacturers has revealed relatively low usage rates for such systems (Bright et al., 1992; Szendi and Elmore, 1993; Drury et al., 1993; Burns and Yazdifar, 2001; Drury and Tayles, 1995).

Despite the enormous difficulties that it may entail, it is imperative that firms' management accounting systems are fundamentally transformed to facilitate them in reporting upon their stock of human capital (Kaplan and Norton, 2004; Sveiby, 1998; Edvinsson and Malone, 1997; Canibano et al., 1999; Skoog, 2002; Low and Kalafut, 2002). As Lev and Daum state:

> **Corporate reporting and internal management systems must provide a more holistic view that allows investors and managers to evaluate the performance of the total value creation system of the company. They must, therefore, integrate and deal much more than in the past with forward looking information and must adopt a more dynamic approach than traditional performance management concepts that are based on annual budgeting. (2003: 2, adapted)**

To this end, Tayles et al. (2002) cite the link between management accounting and intangible assets (including human resources) by arguing that for example, SMA can potentially provide a 'vital fulcrum' in leveraging a firm's intangible assets to achieve a competitive advantage. They posit the view that studies of the changing role of the management accountant reinforces a shift in the thinking about what constitutes a suitable role for management accounting in the twenty-first century (Tayles et al., 2005a).

Indeed, it has even been suggested that the new landscapes that accountants are being urged to colonise within the knowledge economy are in fact congenial to them. For example, Lynn (1999) claims that management accounting has a 'natural affinity' with human capital, and that the movement to manage intangible assets is fundamentally a management accounting issue. Similarly, Tayles et al. (2002) suggest that management accountants should be capable of assuming a leadership role in identifying where human capital resides within firms as well as the types of information that would be required to construct indicators to track its development. Supporting this argument, Booth (1998) has claimed that the measurement of human capital is actually unproblematic as it falls within conventional accounting skills, but that the real difficulty lies in the managerial processes of understanding human capital and using it to improve business performance.

Undoubtedly, management accountants have developed numerous tools to assist them in supplying relevant information for managerial decision-making. However, as human capital is intangible by nature, developing appropriate management accounting systems pertaining to this is not an easy task (Antola et al., 2005). This is emphasised by the fact that there is very little empirical evidence as to how management accounting handles human capital (Roslender and Fincham, 2001).

Although the majority of senior management appear to be aware of the importance of human capital to their firms' continued success and prosperity, it seems that they lack the appropriate management accounting systems required to provide relevant and timely information (Antola et al., 2005; Tayles et al., 2005a). The former Federal Reserve Board Chairman, Alan Greenspan, has criticised the accounting system for its inability to track investments in intangible assets and has warned of potential problems if the current situation remains (Stewart, 2001).

Of the research that has been performed, Roslender and Fincham (2004) in a UK based study found that a range of metrics had been developed to meet the emerging needs of managers, although such metrics were rarely informed by intangible asset considerations. These metrics were beginning to be incorporated into scorecard reporting frameworks, but were not designed for internal communication purposes. This study also found that reporting on intangible assets externally was not a major issue for firms, irrespective of any recognition of its contribution to sustained value creation.

In contrast, Sofian et al. (2004) found that firms high in intangible assets (i.e. those who derive their profits from innovations and knowledge-intensive services) report intangible assets internally, refer to intangible assets in their strategic decisions, capture intangible asset contribution in their performance measures, and invest mainly in intangible assets. Furthermore, the fact that many firms are now beginning to migrate to an indicator-based system of control through the use of, for example, the Balanced Scorecard, Intellectual Capital Accounts and the Intangible Assets Monitor would suggest that firms have finally begun to comprehend the benefits of utilising these forms of reporting.

The provision of financial information has, heretofore, been the main focus of the management accountant, but if the role is to add value and contribute proactively to organisational success in the future, management accountants need to take a more strategic focus, expand their view to a range of non-financial measures, and understand and demonstrate the links between improved knowledge management processes, organisational performance and intangible assets (Edwards et al., 2005). However, as with financial accounting and financial reporting, there is still much to be done as research conducted by Widener (2004) reported that firms still rely heavily on traditional financial measures even when intangible assets represent a significant portion of their asset base.

The future

Despite the difficulties that it will invariably bring, it is necessary for firms to account for their human capital as it is paramount to the long-term value creation process and therefore needs to be included within their accounts (Martin, 2004). Additionally, it also seems certain that from a human resource perspective, accounting for employees and their knowledge will always create challenges for those working in this area.

Unless the accountancy profession can respond positively to this challenge, it is likely to see its privileged position as a key management function under threat from other

Table 5.2 Theory at work – lessons from practice

Banking 365 and the Balanced Scorecard: The People Perspective (Ashton, 2003)

Dublin based Banking 365, a business unit of Bank of Ireland's Retail Division, is an example of an entity that migrated to the use of an indicator based performance management system. Specifically, they adopted the Balanced Scorecard at their inception as a direct banking operation in 1996.

On establishment, their vision was to create a world-class direct bank based on three strategic themes – customer satisfaction in selected markets, achieving low-cost delivery through self-service channels and operational efficiency, and sales growth. Underpinning these themes as enablers were the 'quality' of people in building a 'best-in-class' sales organisation, business process effectiveness and technology/IT systems.

Banking 365 regard their employees as a crucial lever for their strategy execution and consequently there was a clear focus on employee satisfaction from the outset (this was also one of the main reasons why they adopted the Balanced Scorecard as it explicitly recognises human capital as one of the main determinants of operational success). To this end, leveraging and developing people skills were divided into the following seven key elements:

- Recruitment
- Performance management
- A coaching environment
- Communication
- Training
- Motivation
- Management style

To ensure that employees understood the unit's strategy, a staff handbook was published detailing the business plan, e.g. sales targets and a customer satisfaction target of at least 90 per cent (which was subsequently achieved) and also outlining how Banking 365 was to succeed against each initiative. This communication mechanism supported other strategy awareness building mechanisms such as twice-yearly strategy updates for all staff and a monthly staff forum.

A recent Banking 365 staff survey confirmed that employees are indeed aligned to the firm's strategic goals and that they have been successful in keeping them satisfied:

- 81 per cent are satisfied working for Banking 365
- 87 per cent know what is expected of them
- 83 per cent feel they have sufficient authority to do their job well
- 83 per cent understand why the unit has to change
- 82 per cent are optimistic of future business success
- 90 per cent feel the business is committed to customer satisfaction.

Additionally, an initial finding from the scorecard's deployment led to the rethinking of the issue of staff retention within the group. Given the pressured nature of call centre work, a typical employee can operate effectively as an agent for approximately two years. However, when Banking 365 started to measure staff retention through the scorecard, it discovered that a high percentage of new recruits left within their first six months. This led to a change in the recruitment strategy, including the use of skills matching, psychometric testing and engaging employees on permanent contracts from the outset.

---

organisational groupings (Roslender, 2003; Guthrie, 2001). Indeed, research has already suggested that Information Technology (IT), finance and marketing departments have each begun to stake a claim as firms' primary information providers (Curran, 1998). As if to emphasise this point, Drury et al. (1993) found that the collection and reporting of non-financial data within firms rests, in many cases, outside the accounting function. If the private sector does not take the initiative to provide improved management and reporting models, then it seems certain that regulators will do it for them. Given these pressures, there has never been a better time for the accounting sector to begin the process of formulating a set of prescriptions for the future (Low, 2002).

- The knowledge economy has placed an increased importance on tacit knowledge. How can tacit knowledge be accurately valued?

- To date, HRD has not looked at accounting for employee contribution in any great depth. Why is this an important advance for the field?

- 'If you can't measure it, you can't manage it' – how can we ensure human resource accounting is not just mere speculation?

6 Creativity and HRD

Robin S. Grenier and David McGuire

■ ■ ■ **Chapter objectives** ■

The objectives of this chapter are to:

- consider the importance of creativity to the knowledge economy;

- identify the barriers inhibiting employee creativity in the workplace;

- explore the role of perspective, perception and positionality in the creativity process;

- examine how creativity is affected by the work environment and leadership support.

Introduction

In 1975, Steven Kerr wrote a seminal piece entitled 'On the folly of rewarding A, while hoping for B' examining the disconnect between expected organisational behaviour and rewarded organisational behaviour and identified a series of systems failures leading to individual underachievement and poor organisational outcomes. He demonstrated how many reward systems were compensating employees for substandard and poorly aligned performance leading to organisational stasis and showed how such systems were incapable of producing the discontinuous ground-breaking change so desired by their organisations. In today's fast-paced market-driven economy, creativity has been identified as a key driver of competitive advantage, enabling organisations to keep apace of changes in the external environment (Rajan and Martin, 2001). Creative ideas allow organisations to adjust to shifting market demand (Shalley et al., 2004) and significantly add to levels of innovation, effectiveness, and productivity in organisations (Amabile and Conti, 1999; Nonaka, 1991). As McLean (2005) points out, organisations depend upon employees feeding their creative ideas into the innovation pipeline to sustain growth and deliver upon rising customer expectations. Nonaka and Takeuchi (1995) define the 'knowledge creating company' as one whose sole business is continuous improvement through developing the intellectual capital of employees and creating new knowledge, products, processes and systems. Indeed, Matheson (2006) sees the emphasis on creativity as indicative of a broader movement among western nations away from the production of goods and services to the production of ideas and knowledge. In spite of its importance, levels of creativity in many organisations remain low. As Taggar (2002) points out, companies have tried numerous strategies to foster creativity, including restructuring work, selecting people on the basis of their attributes and behavioural training, finding to their cost that these strategies are often unsuccessful.

Why is creativity important and what is the role of HRD? Creativity underpins the innovation process and is central to the development of new products and services; to fostering a culture of continuous improvement and to enhancing and enabling core competencies within the organisation. To achieve these aims, HRD practitioners must understand the creative process and deploy interventions that promote creativity across the organisation. HRD practitioners must also have an appreciation of the importance of the work environment and leader support in enhancing or preventing creativity and must work to harness the unique insights flowing from an individual's background and experiences. With an acknowledgement of the role creativity plays in the innovation, success, and long-terms sustainability of organisations this chapter examines how creativity is recognised and fostered in the workplace through organisational and cultural strategies that encourage creative risk-taking amongst employees. The chapter is structured around three facets affecting the creative process: perception, perspective, and positionality.

Definitional issues

Creativity is defined as, 'coming up with fresh ideas for changing products, services, and processes so as to better achieve the organisation's goals' (Amabile et al., 2005: 367). Madjar (2005) maintains that definitions of creativity all include concepts of appropriateness and usefulness alongside notions of novelty and originality. Such views are echoed by Nickerson (1999) who argues that creativity must not only embrace novelty, but also a measure of utility, such as usefulness, appropriateness or social value. To this end, creativity needs to satisfy notions of commercial or cultural value and be built upon existing foundations and principles (Ward, 1995). In this regard, creativity is not a complete divergence from the past, but often takes the form of small incremental improvements that advance knowledge and understanding.

As a research topic, creativity has been under-represented in the fields of social and organisational psychology. Sternberg and Lubart (1999) identify six historical barriers to the study of creativity including its origins in a tradition of mysticism and spirituality; problems with the definition and criteria for creativity rendering it elusive and trivial; and the impression from commercial approaches to creativity that the field lacks a strong theoretical and psychological basis. To date, approaches to the study of creativity have been either cognitive, behavioural or personality-based. Cognitive approaches have explored the superstructure of the mind and considered how cognitive processes lead to the production of innovative ideas and processes (Gardner, 1993). Behavioural approaches have examined the role of both intrinsic and extrinsic motivation and how reward systems affect levels of employee creativity (Baer et al., 2003). Meanwhile, personality-based approaches have sought to identify individual traits which lead employees to be more creative in their work (Amabile, 1983; Barron and Harrington, 1981). More recent work has explored the social basis of creativity building upon the theories of social creativity (Watson, 2007), social capital and

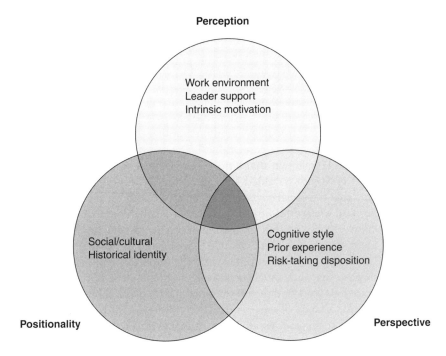

Figure 6.1 The Intersection of Perception, Perspective and Positionality

recognising the importance of communication and interaction in the creative process (Amabile, 1996; Perry-Smith, 2006).

A multi-factorial approach to examining creativity

Feldman (1999) recognises that approaches to creativity have been uni-dimensional and this tendency to isolate a single dimension of creativity has had the effect of distorting the research findings. Consequently, multi-factorial research designs will encourage a more weighted holistic approach to the study of creativity, its antecedents and effects. Research using conceptual models like the one presented in this chapter (see Figure 6.1), that emphasise the role of creativity in organisations, requires dynamic thinking utilising broad and complex processes of how individuals and organisations manage positionality, perspective and perceptions in order to strengthen organisation effectiveness.

Perception

Much like problem-solving, perception is based on data from rather inadequate information furnished by the senses resulting in a 'best guess' based on the visual stimuli, prior experience, and non-sensory information (Coren, 2003). There exists considerable research evidence demonstrating the power of perception in affecting organisational realities (Analoui and Karami, 2002; Parker-Gore, 1996). Perception affects how an employee makes sense of their work environment, the relationships with their supervisor and colleagues and their own level of self-efficacy and self-competence. Perception is socially constructed and influenced by the manner in which events are interpreted. Consequently, Power (1973) argues that to behave is to control perception and that we know nothing of our own behaviour but the feedback effects of our own outputs. In this subsection, we examine the effects of environmental conditions, supervisory support and intrinsic motivation on employee perception and creativity.

The work environment exerts a powerful influence on the creativity of employees. Scott and Bruce (1994) maintain that employees may attempt to be creative when they perceive that creativity is valued and supported by the organisation. Amabile et al. (1996) argue that the social environment can affect both the level and frequency of creative behaviour. Majaro (1988) maintains that a suitable creative environment needs to emphasise flexibility and group involvement; respect for diversity; open expression of ideas; the promotion of creative thinking and the setting of clear objectives. To this list, Shalley and Gilson (2004) add the importance of individual autonomy as they propose that individuals need to feel independent in the level of time they can devote to their work and the means by which the work should be completed. Emphasising the importance of environmental conditions, Csikszentmihalyi (1996) argues that it is easier to enhance creativity by changing the environmental conditions than by trying to get people to think more creatively. However, the reality as expressed by Amabile (1998) is that creativity is often undermined unintentionally in work environments that are established to maximise business imperatives of co-ordination, productivity and control. Likewise, McLean (2005) maintains that a culture that supports and encourages control will result in diminished creativity and innovation as control negatively affects levels of intrinsic motivation.

Leader support is a critical factor affecting an employee's self-confidence and their motivation to engage in creative behaviour. Amabile et al. (2004) argue that individuals are likely to experience both perceptual and affective reactions to leader behaviours. An individual's perception of the instrumental and socio-emotional support of their team leaders will affect their level of creativity (Oldham and Cummings, 1996; Scott and Bruce, 1994). Tierney and Farmer (2002) found that where supervisors supported an employee's self-confidence, this resulted in greater creative self-efficacy resulting in improved creative performance. Research by Andrews and Farris (1967) established that employees experienced higher levels of creativity when a more participative and engaging style was adopted by management. Similarly, a study by Zhou (2003) found that informational feedback to employees led to higher creativity than when feedback was delivered in a controlling or punitive manner. Finally, Jaussi and Dionne (2003) maintain that role modelling behaviour by supervisors is more likely to increase creative behaviour amongst followers – hence it is critical for supervisors to demonstrate creativity themselves and foster a climate which supports creativity.

While the literature on extrinsic motivation (i.e. monetary rewards and recognition) reveals a mixed picture regarding the effectiveness of such practices (Baer et al., 2003), research on intrinsic motivation shows a direct link to creativity (Amabile, 1996; Oldham and Cummings, 1996). It shows that intrinsically motivated individuals are more likely to be curious, take risks, cognitively flexible and experience positive emotions such as excitement and enthusiasm (Amabile et al., 1990; Deci and

Ryan, 1985; Utman, 1997; Zhou, 2003). Isen (1999) maintains that when individuals experience positive moods, they are likely to draw greater connections between divergent stimuli materials, use broader categories and identify more interrelatedness between stimuli. Similarly Amabile et al. (2005) maintain that creativity can be an agent for change where complex cognitive processes are influenced and shaped by, and simultaneously occur with emotional experience.

As this section points out, perception is critical to how employees relate to and with the work environment and peers, and as such is central in nurturing creativity in the workplace. The perception of the environment in which an employee works affects both motivation and the overall ability to generate creative and innovative ideas.

Perspective

Embracing multiple perspectives is critical to the creative process. Garavan et al. (2007) highlight the change of focus, composition and emphasis that occurs when individuals adopt a different perspective. They argue that perspectives empower innovative and creative thinking through opening the possibility of renewing and reinventing relationships between different factors and events. Similarly, Parker and Axtell (2001) argue that understanding frameworks different from your own and empathising with others is fundamental to collaborative working. They maintain that perspective-taking may involve a high degree of cognitive complexity and results in greater levels of empathy and positive attributions. Being open to new perspectives involves adopting an interpretivist epistemological viewpoint and can provide individuals with a rich way of envisioning new realities. Consequently, it follows that individuals do not passively interpret organisational practices, but seek to understand them by applying meanings, terms and concepts, derived from our stock of knowledge, language and the ongoing interpretation of others with whom we interact. It is this prior knowledge that acts as a basis for establishing a particular perspective and for testing new ideas, principles and arguments. An individual's prior experiences will influence what they work on, the approach to the work, the methods judged most adequate for this purpose, the outcomes and products considered most appropriate, and the framing and communication of those outcomes. Thus, opportunities within organisations for experiential learning can result in more creative and 'efficient' work requiring far less effort to isolate and solve problems and better preparation to handle complex problems (Bibby and Payne, 1996).

There is agreement that creativity requires a cognitive-perceptual style involving the ability to suspend judgement, collect and apply diverse material, the use of heuristics, and an ability to concentrate over long periods of time, in a setting where response options are open as long as possible (Shalley and Gilson, 2004; Amabile, 1998). Baer et al. (2003) examine Kirton's Adaption-Innovation theory and found that individuals with an adaptive cognitive style tend to operate within particular paradigms and procedures, while those with an innovative style are more likely to take risks and develop new approaches to solving problems. Familiarity with these characteristics and organisational supports to encourage adaptive and innovative styles is essential given the likelihood of strong external pressures of task completion in organisations.

Given these pressures, individuals are less likely to explore new pathways or suspend judgement and instead search for solutions that are adequate for the given task – resulting in increased productivity at the cost of creative, new solutions (Forbes and Domm, 2004).

Engaging in creative behaviour requires participates to take risks. Newall et al. (1979) suggest that creativity is an unconventional act which requires individuals to reject or modify previously accepted ideas. Tesluk et al. (1997) argue that an individual's level of creativity depends upon their predisposition towards risk and their willingness to contemplate and accept failure if it occurs. However, research indicates that individuals are more likely to prefer certain outcomes and engage in actions designed to limit their exposure to risk (Bazerman, 1994). Farmer et al. (2003) coin the term 'ego-investment' to delineate the level of risk an individual is prepared to commit to when being creative. They argue that the perceived risk in being creative goes beyond the loss of tangible rewards and entails a potential loss of self or a loss of sense of identity. Two factors that affect creativity in groups are social loafing and conformity. Thompson (2003) describes social loafing as the tendency of individuals not to work as hard in a group as they would alone. She argues that individuals will typically filter their contributions and only participate where they feel their comments are particularly valuable, potentially denying the group access to other useful information. In the case of conformity, she maintains that individuals will engage in bizarre behaviour to ensure their acceptance in the group and will be cautious about presenting ideas for fear of negative evaluation.

In summary, perspective emphasises the need for drawing from multiple viewpoints based on tacit knowledge and prior experience. By recognising the role of perspective in fostering creative processes, infusing experiential learning opportunities, and incorporating structures that allow for think time in the creative process organisations are better able to combat conformity and indolence, and encourage calculated risk taking.

Positionality

In order to understand and partake in the creative process, individuals need to acknowledge their own positionality. Maher and Tetreault (2001) define the notion of positionality as one where individuals do not possess fixed identities, but are located within shifting networks of relationships, which can be analysed and changed. These networks are based on cultures and subcultures and distinguished by internal variation (Aguilar, 1981). For his part, Takacs (2002) considers the notion of positionality as the multiple unique experiences that situate each of us in relation to each other. Positionality therefore encourages the identification of individual uniqueness as a reference point for differentiation from others. As Merriam et al. (2001) point out, if the perspective of the individual is limited by positionality then it is important to recognise that in order to understand another, one must first understand oneself. Helping employees to recognise their own positionality and subjectivity, and incorporating reflexivity encourages operation on multiple levels, thus promoting creativity in organisations (Etherington, 2004).

Acknowledging the historical, cultural and socially bounded nature of positionality requires an in-depth analysis of how social factors have affected our individual identity. Sheppard (2002) argues that positionality challenges the proposition that there is objective knowledge and sensitises individuals to the reality that their analysis is shaped by their social situatedness in terms of gender, race, class, sexuality and other axes of social difference. Similarly, McIntosh (1998) argues that in many instances, individuals need to acknowledge unearned advantage and conferred dominance in order to create better communication among groups and further higher levels of creativity. In an educational context, Fenwick (2007) maintains that the learner is not an object separable from the educator and consequently, the educator needs to acknowledge their own positionality through examining social identity markers as these will affect the creativity of learners.

Blake and Hanson (2005) contend that innovations are not simply products of place, but of the people embedded in particular places. By recognising the role of positionality in the creative process and encouraging employees to approach learning, work, and collaboration from different historical and societal positions, organisations can maintain an openness to diverse ideas leading to individual and organisational health (Weick, 1995). To do this requires individuals to acknowledge their own positionality, and organisations to understand their role in maintaining or challenging existing positions. Such considerations for the development of creativity have been explored by Robinson and Stern (1997), who consider five features that organisations can support in developing and sustaining creativity. The first is alignment. Here Robinson and Stern focus on the notion that creative ideas must be directed towards organisation goals in order for employees to recognise and respond positively to useful ideas. The second feature is self-initiated activity. This means that intrinsic motivation is necessary for employees to feel empowered to determine the problem they are interested in and feel capable to solve that problem. Unofficial activity is the third feature. Ideas need to be given a chance to develop and informal meetings provide a safe context for that incubation, until they are ready for judgemental resistance. Fourth, is serendipity-discoveries made through fortunate accident and the last feature is diverse stimuli. In this feature new settings or situations may offer new insight and motivate people to react differently or experiment.

Positionality can also serve as a lens for evaluating creativity. Shalley and Gilson (2004) recognise that an evaluation of creative work requires agreement from those considered knowledgeable within the field. In this regard, Egan (2005) advocates Amabile's (1996) consensual assessment technique as an appropriate method for accurately evaluating the level of creativity associated with a product, service, process or procedure. For their part, Elsbach and Kramer (2003) suggest that judging others' creativity is made easier by the existence of objective evidence. They posit that judgements about individual creativity can sometimes be rendered on the basis of tangible products, such as actual product designs, written reports or innovative programmes. Alternatively, they remark that an individual's creative potential may be inferred on the basis of their role status or reputation in the organisation. However, they conclude that there exists little agreement on universally accepted or empirically established standards for evaluating creativity and creative potential.

An examination of positionality brings to light the individual's place in developing creativity within the forces of the social institution, the cultural domain responsible for the transmittal of new ideas, and those responsible for bringing about change in the domain (Csikszentmihalyi, 1988). Reality is socially, culturally and historically constructed and underlines the importance of acknowledging one's own subjectivities and positions of power. Thus, it is only through acknowledging our own positionality that we can accurately evaluate and support creativity in the workplace.

Cultivating creativity is a difficult and complex process. While Perry-Smith (2006) identifies individual creativity in organisations as desirable, she recognises that it is often difficult to stimulate and may be stifled by a range of organisational practices, particularly during turbulent and uncertain times. Despite having some knowledge of the factors enabling creativity, limited research has been conducted to identify the organisational practices that inhibit creativity. Without a clear understanding of the practices that block creativity and the process by which this occurs, investment in initiatives designed to foster creativity may produce suboptimal results.

Future work is also needed to examine the social dimension of creativity. For too long, creativity has been viewed as a singular endeavour; an act of greatness or a spark of genius. In recent times, creativity in groups and teams is becoming increasingly important as work becomes internationalised to a greater degree and organisations place a stronger emphasis on communication, social capital and social networks. Creative work is contextualised (Mumford et al., 2002) and dependent on the capabilities, pressures, resources, and socio-technical system in which employees work (Csikszentmihalyi, 1999), as such an incorporation of social creativity (Watson, 2007) that includes the dimensions of perspective, perception, and positionality is key.

Empowering employees to be creative in the development and analysis of new ideas demands that HRD professionals create opportunities for employees to understand how they see themselves and help them engage in creative thinking and adopt multiple perspectives in their work. This can been achieved through the creation of participative safe environments (De Dreu and West, 2001), encouraging ongoing contact with those outside the organisation or in different areas of the organisation (Anacona and Caldwell, 1992; Dougherty and Hardy, 1996) while limiting the tendency of employees to choose to work with others similar to themselves (Tajfel, 1982). Moreover, HRD interventions need to embrace experiential learning and constructivist principles in order to create a learning environment supportive of creativity. Thompson (2003) argues that this may (initially) involve organisational support for seemingly purposeless and senseless things such as striving for quantity at the expense of quality; suggesting unrealistic ideas and creating space for individual thinking.

If, as researchers have suggested, some level of creativity is required in almost any job (Shalley et al., 2000; Unsworth, 2001), then creating the right environment for creativity is crucial. The degree of support will affect the value placed on creativity by employees. Supervisors and managers should receive training in how to appropriately support, encourage and manage risk-taking and creativity amongst employees. Top management support for creative endeavours will send a strong message to employees that the organisational culture welcomes, embraces and supports creativity. In addition, supervisors and managers should act as role models to employees in both encouraging and engaging in creative behaviours.

The concept of alignment will ensure consistency between actual behaviour and rewarded behaviour. A clear, transparent and accountable process for evaluating and rewarding creativity is required within organisations. Individuals need to be commended for taking appropriate risks, even where doing so occasionally leads to failure. Risk-taking is an important element in creativity and will ensure that an organisation remains innovative in its approach and direction and responsive to market changes. The use of extrinsic rewards needs to be carefully managed and matched by supervisory/managerial acknowledgement of employee efforts.

? Discussion questions

- Discuss the view that 'employees are paid for performance, not creativity'.

- Through processes and routines, organisations constrain creativity. How can routines be broken to encourage creativity, while important standards are maintained?

- Some research indicates the importance of employee diversity in fostering creativity. What challenges are posed by the objective of fostering creativity?

7 Adult Learning Theories

David McGuire

■ ■ **Chapter objectives** ■

The objectives of this chapter are to:

- identify the contributions made by cognitivism, behaviourism, social learning and critical learning approaches to understanding how employees learn;

- examine the principles associated with andragogy or adult learning;

- consider the importance of critical reflection in questioning taken-for-granted assumptions;

- look at the roles of individuals, educationalists and professional bodies in the learning process.

Introduction

Understanding how people learn is of crucial importance to furthering their development and potential. Without knowledge, comprehension and appreciation of the myriad of ways in which people learn, individual growth is blunted, organisational advancement stunted and community and society possibilities for advancement are diminished. As Gold and Smith (2003) argue, learning is the key factor for survival, sustainability and competitive advantage at the level of the individual, organisation and nation. Given the importance ascribed to learning, it is also worth noting that learning is not a singular process. Merriam (2001) has acknowledged, 'We have no single answer, no one theory or model of learning that explains all that we know about adult learners, the various contexts where learning takes place and the process of learning itself' (2001: 3). She argues that the knowledge base of learning comprises of a mosaic of theories, models, sets of principles and explanations.

In recent years, much attention has focused upon expanding conceptions of the learning process. Marsick and Watkins (1999) argue that there has been a shift away from a compartmentalised, almost assembly-line approach to learning towards a holistic integrated vision of learning connected to individual, organisational and societal development. Various forms of experiential learning, such as lifelong learning, workplace learning and self-directed learning are becoming increasingly prominent in the literature. Clarke (2005) argues that workplace learning is increasingly recognised as key to developing types of knowledge and skills important for operating effectively in modern organisations. Likewise, Smith (2000) point to the growing trend towards self-directed learning and the autonomous learner, indicating that greater responsibility is being placed on the individual for their own growth. Concomitantly, there has also been a recognition that learning is not purely an individual process, but also a social collaborative one (Slotte et al., 2004). The learning process has been transformed from a trainer/instructor led event to a learner-centred one.

Learning is often viewed as an overarching concept within which human resource development finds its place. Gold and Smith (2003) argue that the terms training, development, education and HRD seem to have been incorporated into the generic term learning. In agreement, Yang (2003) argues that learning is one of the key concepts in HRD and facilitating learning for individuals and organisations is one of the key roles for HRD professionals. Indicative of the importance of learning to HRD was a debate in the literature over whether the learning paradigm or performance paradigm was the dominant focus for HRD research and practice (Barrie and Pace, 1998; Kuchinke, 1998).

While the focus of this chapter deals with theories of learning, it is worth noting that learning does not occur solely in a formal setting. A great deal of learning takes place informally, unintentionally and incidentially (Eraut et al., 1998; Marsick and Watkins, 1990; Slotte et al., 2004). Indeed, a study by Marsick and Watkins (1990) showed that only 20 per cent of learning comes from formal structured training. Informal learning is defined as predominantly experimental and non-institutional, while incidental learning is regarded as unintentional, or a byproduct of a different activity (Conlon, 2004; Cseh et al., 1999). Watkins and Marsick (1994) maintain that informal and incidental learning are critical to organisational growth and effectiveness as it is through these forms of learning that learning flows readily from peer to peer, within and between teams, up and down the organisation, and between the organisation and the external environment.

The structure of this chapter draws upon Lee's (1996; Lee and Smith, 2004) schools of learning theory where she identifies cognitivism, behaviourism, and humanism as three key learning theories. She argues that cognitive learning can be equated with education and concentrates upon learning at the head level; behavioural learning can be equated with training and concentrates at the hands level and humanistic learning can be equated with development and concentrates at the heart level. To this structure, we add a fourth theory: Critical approaches to learning. While critical approaches do not describe mechanisms and processes by which people learn, they perform a valuable role in surfacing motives and the underpinning rationale for learning.

Cognitivist theories of learning

An emphasis on the processes involved in learning, rather than the products or outcomes of learning distinguishes cognitivism from other theories of learning. Both Harrison (2000) and Von Krogh et al. (1994) argue that traditional cognitivist approaches adopted a rationalist stance viewing cognition as the processing of information and the rule-manipulation of symbols. In agreement, Good and Brophy (1990) argue that cognitivists view learning as a reorganisation of the cognitive structure in which individuals store information.

In contrast to the reductionist stance of behaviourism, cognitive theories of learning embrace Gestalt principles, namely, that we experience the world in meaningful wholes. Blanton (1998) argues that our perception is broken up into organised wholes through our ability to organise data so that it makes sense. Aik and Tway (2003) argue that when an individual receives new information, it may attach itself to a pre-existing cognitive structure, change an existing structure or go into a new structure. This accumulation and organisation of experiences encourages new insights and facilitates break-through moments and the development of new knowledge and skills.

Cognitive processes represent an important mechanism by which individuals adapt to their environment. In order to deal with and process the large volume of information and arrive at meaningful decisions, individuals develop highly structured cognitive schemas. The association of various concepts through the creation of cognitive schema (or mental maps) has been long established as central to the functioning of individuals and society. Daniels et al. (1995) argue that schema act as simplifications, helping managers to overcome the limitations of short-term memory, when they search long-term memory for relevant information. Similarly, Sparrow (2000) maintains that cognitive schema serve as top-down or theory-driven aids, generated from experience and affecting a manager's ability to attend to, encode and make intelligent inferences from collected information.

Piaget (1952) differentiates two critically important dialetics in the learning process: assimilation and accommodation. This corresponds to the internal and external aspects of the learning process itself. As Piaget (1952) states:

> **The accord of thought with things and the accord of thought with itself express the dual functional invariant of adaption and organisation. These two aspects of thought are indissociable: it is by adapting to things that thought organises itself and it is by organising itself that it structures things. (1952: 7–8)**

In certain cases, an individual may reject new information where it does not fit with the existing structure or would cause substantial changes, which the individual is not willing to accept. Piaget's dialectic of assimilation and accommodation have been applied to areas of routine and non-routine problem-solving (Anderson, 1993; Billet, 1999; Shuell, 1990). In this context, it is argued that routine problem-solving reinforces and refines existing knowledge. Repetition of the activity serves to enhance understanding and embed knowledge more firmly within the individual's cognitive framework. In contrast, non-routine knowledge forces individuals to engage in the development of new knowledge or the extension of existing knowledge. Leont'ev (1981) describes the process of internalisation of new knowledge as not the transferral of an external activity to a pre-existing internal plane of consciousness, but the process by which the internal plane is transformed.

The cognitive preferences of individuals have important implications for the way in which individuals learn. Messick (1984) defines cognitive styles as 'consistent individual differences in preferred ways of organising and processing information and experience' (1984: 5). Evidence has emerged that cognitive styles will influence the choice of learning style and method (Hayes and Allinson, 1996). Consequently, Smith

(2005) advocates the use of instruments such as the Myers Briggs Type Indic. (MBTI) as a means of assessing the learning styles of individuals and adapting learnin, methods to suit these styles. Common dimensions measured by such instruments include sensing vs intuition and thinking vs feeling.

Critics of cognitivist approaches to learning have pointed to their inaccessibility and the difficulty in testing cognitive theories of learning. Wiltsher (2005) maintains that cognitivist theories of learning are biased towards learning that involves intentional rational thought. Robotham (2003) denounces the style approach to learning (i.e. fitting people into pre-ordinated learning categories). He argues that while this may allow a degree of programme tailoring, he maintains that dangers exist in encouraging the wholesale adoption of a particular learning style which may subsequently limit individual development.

Behaviourist theories of learning

The view that learning can best be understood through observable behaviour rather than private consciousness forms the basis for behaviourist theories of learning. Stewart (2002) argues that behaviourist theories of learning have two defining characteristics: the general rejection of the internal workings of the mind as an area of study and investigation and secondly, that human behaviour is the product of experience of and within physical and social environments.

As behaviourism is regularly defined in opposition to cognitivism, it is worth examining the objections behaviourists raise against the validity of cognitivism. Zuriff (1985) advances four key arguments against cognitivism:

- Cognitivism, with its focus on introspection is internally flawed and prone to error and distortion.

- Consciousness is private and subjective and consequently should be precluded from objective scientific examination on the basis that experiences are non-verifiable.

- Intersubjective agreement is not possible within a cognitive frame of reference. Therefore, communication and agreement on basic observations is not possible.

- Cognitivism is unreliable. The connection between a private event (introspection) and public verbal report of that event may not be always accurate.

The concept of association involving the connection between sense impressions called stimuli and activities or impulses to action called responses underpins research by Pavlov and Thorndike into how people learn. Howe (1980) maintains that the strength of the connection between the stimuli and response will be influenced by the degree of reward or punishment that results. Similarly, Skinner (1953) proposes that the degree of reinforcement through reward or punishment will influence recurrence of the behaviour.

The notion of conditioning is central to theories of behaviourism. Classical (Pavlovian) conditioning suggests that by virtue of our previous worldly experiences, we produce more accurate and efficient decision-making in those areas routinely experienced due to the associated nature of experience. It posits that much behaviour produces an instinctive response to the presence of a stimulus. Through a series of

...ents, Pavlov showed that dogs would respond to the stimulus of a bell ...anticipation of receiving food. A second form of conditioning known ...instrumental conditioning seeks to explain responses that are emitted ...ividual, rather than elicited as a consequence of a stimulus. In this ...ner recognises that some behaviour may not necessarily be caused by ...ulation, but by virtue of emission of a discriminated operant (Zuriff, ...ner (1953) states: 'The environment affects the organism in many ways which ... not conveniently classed as "stimuli" and even in the field of stimulation, only a small part of the forces acting upon the organism elicit responses in the invariable manner of reflex action' (1953: 9).

Modern approaches to behaviourism have increasingly recognised the contextual nature of behaviour and the difficulty in reducing behaviour to a simple stimulus – response equation. Social learning theory acknowledges that environmental factors play an important role in learning and behaviour.

Social learning theory

A prominent theory within behaviourism is social learning theory with its emphasis on the contextual nature of experience. Bandura (1977) argues that learning phenomena result from direct experience that can occur on a vicarious basis through observation of other people's behaviour and its consequences. Ormond (1999) identifies four core assumptions of social learning theory:

- Learning can occur without a change in behaviour.
- The consequences of behaviour play a role in learning.
- People learn by observing the behaviour of others and its consequences.
- Cognition plays an important role in learning.

The theory situates learning at the interaction nexus between the individual and the environment. However, as Gibson (2004) points out, social learning theory emphasises the cognitive processes involved in observation. Through observation, Bandura (1977) argues that individuals could visualise the consequences of actions and regulate their own behaviour.

Social learning theory (and socio-cognitive theory in its later form) addresses the behaviour of individuals in society from an agency perspective. The theory distinguishes three modes of agency: direct personal agency, proxy agency and collective agency as directing an individual's functioning and life circumstances. However, it acknowledges that in many spheres of life, individuals do not have control over the social conditions and institutional practices that affect their everyday lives (Bandura, 2002). In this respect, the theory proposes a socially mediated form of agency embracing notions of agency in individual and collective forms. Bandura (2002) also highlights the centrality and pervasiveness of personal efficacy beliefs as the core mechanism driving human agency. He advances two sets of expectations; expectations related to self-efficacy and expectations related to outcomes as the major cognitive forces guiding behaviour. In the former case, he argues that self-efficacy beliefs regulate human functioning through a series of cognitive, motivational, affective and decisional processes. He also points to the importance of collective efficacy ~~in~~ influencing the functioning of groups and the shaping of societal outcome~~s~~ latter case, the theory posits that individuals are more likely to undertake be~~haviour~~ they believe will result in valued outcomes than those that they do not see a~~s~~ favourable consequences.

Socialisation plays an important role in social learning theory by defining commonly acceptable social norms and boundaries. Brim and Wheeler (1966) view the function of socialisation as one of transforming the human raw material of society into good able citizens. In this regard, socialisation processes are loosely based around Cooley's theory of introspective mentalism (1909, 1922), which describes the process of how an individual is moulded, by the primary group of face-to-face associations in family, friends and neighbours to develop a social self.

Durkheim (1954) describes the influence of society on individual learning as follows:

> **The ways of action to which society is strongly enough attached to impose them upon its members are by that very fact marked by a distinctive sign, provocative of respect. Since they are elaborated in common, the rigour with which they have been thought of, by each particular mind is retained in all the other minds and reciprocally. The representations, which express them within each of us, have an intensity, which no purely private states of consciousness could ever attain; for they have the strength of the innumerable individual representations, which have served to form each of them. The very violence with which society reacts, by way of blame or material repression, against every attempted dissidence contributes to strengthening its empire by manifesting the common conviction through this burst of ardour. (1954: 236)**

In summary, social learning theory emphasises the reciprocal interaction of environment, behaviour and the person – with each other influencing and being influenced by the other (Gibson, 2004). As Lefrancois (1999) comments, social learning theory is both a behaviourist theory that assumes that a great deal of learning involves observation and imitation of models and a cognitive theory that recognises our ability to think, to symbolise and to figure out cause-and-effect relationships and to anticipate the outcomes of behaviour.

Humanist theories of learning

Humanistic approaches to learning trace their roots to the field of humanistic psychology and the work of Carl Rogers emphasising the importance of self-esteem, motivation and self-development (Addesso, 1996; Knowles, 1998; McGuire et al., 2004). Kramlinger and Huberty (1990) argue that the core assumption underpinning the humanistic approach is that learning occurs primarily through reflection on personal experience.

An appreciation of individualism and otherness is central to humanistic learning approaches. Humanist approaches to learning place the learner at the centre of all educational endeavours. Dewey (1916) maintains that the most important learning goals relate to the development of the individual and the development of citizenship. Lee and Smith (2004) argue that humanists stress perception, arguing that each individual creates their own version of reality, with the overall humanistic goal being one of support for the individual in their search for self-definition. Motivation therefore plays a critical role in driving individuals in their endeavours. McFadzean (2001) follows Maslow's writings in positing that individual self-actualisation is a driver of individual learning. Mele (2003) argues that self-actualisation can have two different meanings: developing personal idiosyncrasy, whatever that can be and developing the noblest potentialities of each human being.

Perhaps the greatest advocate of humanist approaches is Malcolm Knowles (1998) who developed principles for guiding and directing adult learning:

- Learning motivation: adults should know the rationale for learning something prior to instruction.

- Self-direction: adults are independent and are both responsible for their own decisions and capable of guiding their own learning.

- Role of experience: the experience of adults should be acknowledged and should form an integral part of the learning process.

- Preparedness to learn: adults will come to learning when they are ready to acquire new knowledge and skills.

- Learning focus: adults view learning as a vehicle to assist them in performing tasks and solving real-life situations.

Humanist approaches to learning have attracted certain criticisms. Purdy (1997) maintains that the individualist focus of humanist learning theories limits its ability to account for change and overemphasises the potency of individuals without due consideration for the effects of structure and collective action. Furthermore, he argues that humanist perspectives do not confront or challenge existing conditions, but help individuals adapt to the demands of the system. A similar argument is advanced by McGuire et al. (2004) who argue that the rhetoric of humanistic approaches, which espouses developmental ideals and focus on employee self-actualisation, is not matched by organisational actions of compressed career progression pathways, tight budgetary constraints and a market-driven economic philosophy.

A core component of humanism is the emphasis placed on experience in learning. McFadzean (2001) argues that humanist theories of learning are concerned with experiences and feelings, which lead to individual fulfilment and personal growth. Experiential learning theory explores the role that experience plays in shaping both action and reflection.

Experiential learning theory

Experiential learning concerns itself with the cognitive processing of experience involving in particular the elements of action, reflection and transfer. Experiential approaches are based on the premise that learning can be made more meaningful if it is grounded in the experience and context of the learner and that individuals learn more easily when engaged in active problem-solving (Holman, 2000). Similarly, Wilson and Beard (2003) argue that experience is the integrated process by which

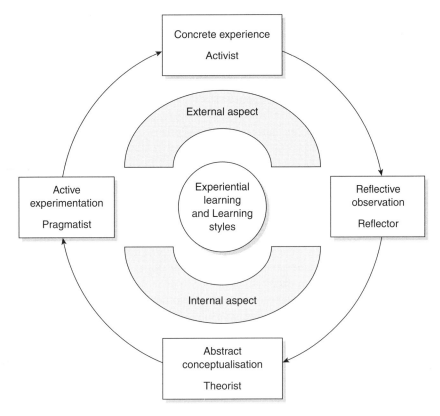

Figure 7.1   Experiential Learning and Learning Styles Model

action and thought are brought together. In this way, they argue that experience creates an organic whole of continuity, process and situation.

The experiential learning and learning styles model is presented in Figure 7.1. The experiential learning cycle involves four learning stages: concrete experience, reflective observation, abstract conceptualisation and active experimentation. Concrete experience involves the individual partaking in a new activity from which learning can occur. Reflective observation entails watching or observing others and/ or reflecting on one's own experiences of the activity. Abstract conceptualisation engages the individual in developing a theory to explain the observations and/or activity experienced. Finally, active experimentation involves the testing of such theories in a new situation. The model also acknowledges the important role played by different types of learning styles. Sadler-Smith et al. (2000) note that Honey and Mumford's learning styles questionnaire arose directly from Kolb's experiential learning cycle. The four learning styles identified are: Activist, Reflector, Theorist and Pragmatist. Activists are individuals who like to engage in new learning experiences and try things out. Reflectors enjoy examining situations from a variety of perspectives and observing and thinking about events. Theorists prefer problem-solving and developing concepts and frameworks within which to predict and explain events, while pragmatists are practical by nature and keen to try new theories or ideas.

Several criticisms have been levelled at experiential learning theory. Reynolds (1998) argues that it promotes an individualized perspective, neglecting the sometimes collectivist nature of learning. Wilson and Beard (2002) posit that by locating itself within the cognitive psychology tradition, experiential learning overlooks or mechanically explains and thus divorces people from the social, historical and cultural aspects of self, thinking and action. A third criticism by Thagard (1996) maintains that cognitive and experiential approaches neglect the role of emotion in human consciousness, reducing learning to a calculating, functional process.

Critical theory approaches to learning

Issues of power, domination and control underpin critical approaches to understanding the role of learning within organisations. Within a critical theory paradigm, learning is conceived as a subtle process for engendering commitment to existing systems of production and control. It recognises the existence of powerful interest groups and considers learning as an important socialisation mechanism for advocating specific values and ideals in furtherance of economic exploitation. Students are encouraged to subscribe to current ideas and thinking, while difference of views from the prevailing orthodoxy is discouraged and suppressed. As Poell and Van der Krogt (2003) point out, learning is relevant to the degree that it is related to the primary process of the organisation (i.e. the manufacturing of products or provision of services). Lahteenmaki et al. (2001) argue that learning is still frequently interpreted as a vehicle for manipulating employees and persuading them to achieve organisational aims which is a far from ideal conception of learning and its implementation in the workplace. The role of critical theory in advancing learning is therefore threefold:

- To challenge the centrality and necessity of the dominant role elites in defining reality and impeding emancipatory change (Alvesson and Wilmott, 1992).

- To render visible the ways in which social inequality reflects inclusive existing public spheres (Fraser, 1994).

- To promote approaches in which differences are resisted in the interests of developing more equal relations (Reynolds and Trehan, 2003).

In persuit of these objectives, critical reflection processes play a crucial role.

Critical reflection

An important aspect of critical approaches to learning is the individual's capacity to reflect upon both the learning content and process. While critical reflection is often considered soft and irrelevant to the results-oriented and bottom-line world of business (Marsick, 1988; Van Woerkom, 2004), Reynolds (1998) maintains that critical reflection is the cornerstone of emancipatory approaches to education encouraging students to confront the social and political forces, which provide the context of their work and question claims of 'common sense' or the 'way things should be'. Similarly, Giroux (1997) contends that critical reflection is essential in evaluating and understanding the epistemological underpinnings of so-called 'taken for granted' knowledge. Alvesson and Skoldberg (2000) argue that this involves the two processes of careful interpretation and inner reflection. In the first instance, they posit that careful interpretation calls for utmost awareness of the theoretical assumptions underpinning learning, the importance of language and the necessity of pre-learning.

Linstead et al. (2004) argue that theories provide a useful means of carefully interrogating ideas and worldviews in order to understand their impact and effect on others. Van Woerkom (2004) maintains that learning is often embedded in norms that also impact on an individual's identity, so that this identity may become submerged to some degree within a broader organisational or societal identity. Thinking outside the box can be a difficult endeavour as Douglas (1986) maintains that all the classifications that we have for thinking with are provided ready-made and consequently, for thinking about society, we have at hand the categories we use as members of society speaking to each other about ourselves.

An appreciation of the potency and pervasiveness of language is crucial to critical approaches to learning. Weick and Westley (1996) argue that language is the critical tool for reflection, both at the inter and intra-personal level. Weick and Westley (1996) state that discourses, particularly those situated within organisations are never politically neutral and are sediment with assymetrical power relations, reproducing structures in which there is differential access to valued and symbolic goods. Likewise, Habermas (1987) argues that communicative processes are undermined and distorted by structurally based inequities undermining opportunities for dialogue and learning.

The necessity for preunderstanding acknowledges the socially constructed nature of knowledge and learning. Social constructionism subscribes to the notion that knowledge and representations of reality are interactionally constructed, socially transmitted, historically sedimented, institutionally congealed and communicatively reproduced (Gunnarsson et al., 1997). It is oriented towards action and function and assumes that people use language to describe, explain or construct versions of the social world in which they live (Chimombo and Roseberry, 1998; Donnellon, 1986; Elliot, 1996; Gergen, 1985; Pettigrew, 1979; Pondy et al.,1983). It therefore follows that knowledge and learning cannot be easily separated from context and context, according to Henderson (2001) affects learning by constraining communication and inhibiting relationships for discourse. Likewise, Fenwick (2003) argues that an individual's learning is complex and multi-layered and linked closely with personal history and aspiration as well as organisational activities, vision and culture. Both Fenwick (2003) and Weick (1995) argue that professional development policies need to honour the diverse processes of individual's continuous sense-making within organisations.

Inner reflection involves directing attention towards the individual, exposing the effect of community and society as well as intellectual and cultural traditions. Alvesson and Deetz (1996) recognise that inner reflection allows an individual to identify if and how certain ways of organising, reasoning and representing the world constrains imagination, thought and decision-making. Van Woerkom (2004) maintains that learning is often embedded in norms that also impact on an individual's identity so that this identity may become submerged to some degree within a broader organisational and societal identity. Giroux (1997) recognises that culture is a terrain of competing knowledge and practice, where some sub-universes are culturally preferred over others. Similarly, Rusaw (2000) argues that individual domination is rooted in organisational and societal ideology, a set of systematic norms, beliefs, values and attitudes that people accept unquestioningly as guides to everyday thinking and behaviour.

In the following subsections, we examine the role of individuals, educationalists and professional bodies in learning from a critical theory perspective.

Role of individuals

As recipients and participants in the learning process, individuals are in a key position to question, challenge and critique the principles and assumptions underpinning learning. That many individuals do not engage in this process is testament to the existence of power and control mechanisms protecting and preventing awareness of dominant groups and hierarchies of knowledge. McIntosh (1988) argues that individuals who are members of the dominant group need to recognise their privileged position (of which they are meant to be oblivious) and realise that this unearned privilege has not been good for the individual's development as a human being and society's development as a whole. Understood as a matter of perpetual struggle between contending forces, hegemony, according to Rojek (2003) provides the means for controlling culturally or socially divergent groups within organisations. Brookfield (2003) argues that the concept of ideological hegemony suggests that ideas and actions of leaders gradually become internalised by followers as if they were their own and when in fact, they are constructed and transmitted by a powerful minority interest to protect the status quo.

The concept of hegemony provides an explanation for the lack of opportunity experienced by particular organisational and societal groups. Morrison (2009) is critical of the pervasiveness of the term 'equal opportunities' and how frequently organisations use this terms to create positive impressions of equality and good corporate citizenship. He argues that even the broadest definition often mistakenly conflates equality of access with equality of outcomes, ignores the complex social construction of education, its institutional arrangements, and the external influences upon both (Morrison, 2009).

Role of educationalists

The role of educationalists and course providers in the learning process is also subjected to scrutiny. While acknowledging that learning is ultimately the responsibility of the student, Dehler et al. (2001) argue that the task of the educator is to create a space in which learning can occur. Freire (1970) maintains that education is politically charged and either teaches the values of the dominant group or helps learners to reflect critically and take action to create a more equitable society. Similarly, Elliott (2003) argues that education, particularly management education has a utilitarian conception of education born of new right politics. She suggests that this is an ideological terrain whose contours encompass education as a socially valuable enterprise contributing to national economic prosperity as well as a consumer good obtained by individuals to further their careers. To this end, Giroux (1997) maintains that educational courses reproduce the values, social practices and skills needed for perpetuating the dominant social order. Horkheimer (1972) posits that the increasing centrality of economic forces and the diminishing resistance of cultural spheres is exerting control over individuals, societal norms and educational processes and outputs. In this regard, Dehler et al. (2001) maintain that textbooks treat knowledge as a storehouse of artefacts constituted as canon, where knowledge appears beyond the reach of critical interrogation.

Differences also appear in relation to the content of many of the courses provided. Commentators are pointing to an ever-increasing number of courses that are devoid of elements of critique. Grey and Mitev (1995) argue that students are resisting learning anything which they perceive as theoretical, impractical or irrelevant, preferring to learn specific techniques, which they see as useful, and mainstream management readily serves up a diet of such techniques. Both Linstead et al. (2004) and Salaman and Butler (1994) contend that many management schools have tended to propogate a view that managers value most practical techniques or methods that have direct or immediate application leading to a dumbing down of management theory to suit practitioners. Likewise, Elliott (2003) highlights the conflict between giving practitioners what they want, while simultaneously providing practitioners with what educationalists perceive that they need. Such conflicts result in what King (1995) sees as the dissonance between what students said they had gained from the educational programme and their performance back in the workplace. Dehler et al. (2001) argue that management education has become overly reductionistic and simplistic in holding to notions of management as a set of content areas to be learned. Likewise, Cavanagh (2004) acerbically views the role of modern management education as to fill the mind of the student, without altering it and to arm them with a portfolio of self-help theories and prescriptive management guides. This decline in standards affirms for Gibson (1986) the importance of critical theory approaches in arguing for constant vigilance towards attempts to pass off sectional viewpoints as universal, natural, classless and timeless ones.

Role of professional bodies

Adopting the role of gate-keepers, professional bodies embrace the language of standards and best practice to control entry to exclusive occupational clubs. This furthers the economic interests of the profession's members by ensuring a substantial premium is required to acquire the skills of the profession through training and education and to access those skills and services subsequently. Professional bodies promote homogeneity amongst its members. By requiring members to satisfy a number of preconditions, they effectively employ pre-selection procedures, engaging those who fit into the dominant culture of the profession. Sirotnik (1983) argues that the products of our created learning culture teaches dependence upon authority, linear thinking, social apathy and passive involvement. This promotes stasis among professions and a lack of impetus towards changing the status quo.

Critical reflection is an important skill in moving towards professional self-awareness and professional development. Fenwick (2003) argues that Schön's (1983) notion of the 'reflective practitioner' encompassing both critical reflection on action and reflection on uncertain, volatile and unpredictable situations continues to enjoy popular acclaim in professional development circles. Watkins (1989) ascribes to professional HRD bodies the task of assisting individuals and organisations in critically reflecting on what is oppressing them and how their organisations can free them to create new worlds and to design organisations not for control, but for adaptability. However Kipp et al. (2003) argue that critical reflection is problematic as it tends to be treated as an isolated skill, does not often take account of power issues and is often not warmly received by practitioners where it is resisted.

Beyer (2001) supports the adoption of normative value-laden approaches and argues that practitioners should be guided by 'the practice of possibility'. He argues that a sharper focus on values and ideals may reveal connections and purposes that are hidden or consciously submerged. In this way, Kipp et al. (2003) argues that practitioners may avoid having their work become nothing more than the dissemination of rhetoric.

The notion of critical discourse communities as a vehicle for emancipation has been advanced by several commentators (Kipp et al., 2003; O'Donnell et al., 2003). The mobilisation of members and an examination of the personal narratives of oppressed members may open potentially rewarding avenues for effecting individual and organisational change. Kondrat (1999) recognises that professional bodies are human constructions and have no existence apart from the human actions that constitute and reconstitute their form and substance. Consequently, critical discourse communities may engage the 'dialectic of enlightenment' (Horkheimer and Adorno, 1979) and liberate individuals from ideologically constrained ways of both thinking and acting (Bokeno, 2003). Table 7.1 summarises the key features associated with the four main schools of learning theory.

Conclusions

The range of learning theories presents a variety of perspectives through which learning can be examined. Cognitivist perspectives emphasise the psychological aspects of learning. Behaviourist perspectives give priority to the contextualised nature of individual action and the range of environmental factors influencing such action. Humanist perspectives seek to explain learning in terms of individual self-definition and self-actualisation, while critical perspectives draw attention to such conflicts and surface underlying assumptions in endeavouring to achieve emancipatory change.

Understanding individual learning is critical to the effective delivery of successful HRD practices. An appreciation of learning theories can lead to changes in the structure of learning interventions, the content of such interventions and how these are facilitated. Differences in learning theories reflect opposing axiological assumptions about human behaviour and also the conception of individuals as solitary or social beings.

Research on learning attests to the growing recognition of the individuality of learning processes. This uniqueness is explained by the perceptual nature of learning and a variety of social and environmental factors. Preserving individual distinctiveness and encouraging creativity ought to be the goal of learning events. However, the drive for standardisation and market forces often produce sub-optimal outcomes.

Table 7.1 Summary of learning theories

	Cognitivism	Behaviourism	Humanism	Critical theory
Objectives of theory	• To explore the central cognitive processes involved in learning • To examine how knowledge is acquired, stored, constructed and transferred • To develop more effective tools to assist the individual in storing and recalling knowledge • To facilitate an awareness of the perceptual nature of knowledge and the development of insight	• To establish processes of learning through the observation of behaviour • To examine the relationship between stimuli and responses and how these impact on learning • To identify the influence that environmental factors have on learning • To explore the effects of conditioning on the learning process	• To examine individual drivers of learning • To explore the influence of experience and reflection in driving action and behaviour • To identify the underlying principles of adult learning • To examine the learning of the individual as a whole person	• To challenge the centrality and necessity of the dominant role elites in defining reality and impeding emancipatory change • To render visible the ways in which social inequality reflects inclusive existing public spheres • To promote approaches in which differences are resisted in the interests of developing more equal relations
Core assumptions	• Operates according to Gestalt principles – experience as meaningful wholes • Adopts a rationalist stance rejecting the reductionism of behaviourism	• General rejection of the internal workings of the mind as an area of study • Human behaviour is the product of experience of and within physical and social environments.	• Individuals lie at the centre of learning and educational endeavours • Self-actualisation and self-definition is the goal of individual learners	• Asymmetry of power relations exists. Access to developmental opportunities controlled and restricted
Learning perspective	• Information should be structured to facilitate storage and mindmapping • Individual is active in learning process	• Responsibility for learning rests with the teacher. • Individual is passive in learning process	• Individuals have responsibility for their own learning in response to perceived needs. • Individual is active in learning process	• Individuals should engage in critical reflection • Individual is actively engaged in examining underlying motives
Locus of learning	• Head	• Behaviour	• Interaction with society	• Cognitive and behavioural awareness
Views of development	• Education	• Training	• Development	• Critical insight resulting in emancipatory change
Underpinning theories	• Schema theory • Mind-mapping	• Social learning theory • Reinforcement theory • Theory of connectionism	• Andragogy • Experiential learning	• Critical realist theory • Marxist theory
Leading theorists	Piaget, Kolb, Honey and Mumford	Pavlov, Skinner, Thorndike	Dewey, Rogers, Knowles	Freire, Habermas, Alvesson

Discussion questions

- With its internal psychological focus, cognitivism has little relevance for HRD practitioners in organising and developing learning interventions. Discuss.

- Behaviour is too random to be explained by learning. Discuss.

- Humanist approaches are naïve in underestimating the power of market forces on individual learning. Is this true?

- Which are the strongest environmental influences on learning?

- What changes could be introduced into the learning environment in order to redefine reality and introduce emancipatory change?

8 Workplace Learning and HRD

Ulla Thøgersen and Kenneth Mølbjerg Jørgensen

The objectives of this chapter are to:

- present the research field of workplace learning;

- describe a case of workplace learning and its implications for human resource development;

- describe some theories of learning, which have been very important in relation to workplace learning;

- discuss workplace learning in relation to human resource development.

Introduction

The aim of this chapter is to present the research field of workplace learning as a way of working with and conceptualising human resource development (HRD). The entry point is a case example from the research project 'Competence development in fringe areas' (Hviid et al., 2006). The project can illustrate some of the efforts within the field of workplace learning to understand and develop learning processes related to the workplace as both informal and planned learning activities. The overall aim of the particular project is to improve the interplay between general adult education and workplace learning to contribute to competence development, social cohesion and business development in Danish fringe areas. The project can demonstrate some of the challenges related to this interplay and also bring forth the need to conceptualise learning in and through work as something other than learning through education.

The chapter is organised as follows. Firstly, we describe a case example from the project 'Competence development in fringe areas' and we use the case to present some of the challenges related to workplace learning and especially the interplay between adult education and workplace learning. Secondly, we present some perspectives on the field of workplace learning by linking it to organisational learning and by investigating the concept of lifelong learning. In the last part of the chapter we will present different theoretical perspectives on informal learning and learning trough the practice of work. Included in this presentation are theories of informal learning

(Marsick and Watkins, 1990; Garrick, 1998); pragmatism (Dewey, 1916, 1991), tacit – explicit dimensions of knowledge combined with the distinction between knowing-that and knowing how (Ryle, 1949).

Theory at work – lessons from practice

The EU-funded development and research project 'Competence development in fringe areas' ran from August 2004 to December 2006 (Hviid et al. 2006). It had as its main aim to further general adult education to contribute to competence development, social cohesion and business development in Danish fringe areas (the counties of Viborg, Northern Jutland and Southern Jutland participated). The research in the project was carried out by a team of researchers from the Department of Learning, Education and Philosophy at Aalborg University. The research was based on seven diverse case studies in which a variety of methods were used: participant observation, qualitative interviews, document reading and questionnaire survey. The case studies are to a large extent characterised by an overall focus on the interplay between institutionalised adult education and workplace learning, namely investigating competence development based on the possibilities to link educational activities to the resources and opportunities for (informal) learning in the workplace.

The project mainly researches educational activities which have their setting within the Adult Education Centre (VUC – in the Danish abbreviation). The Adult Education Centre is oriented at general adult education which is preparatory, namely primary school and high school subjects needed to advance to further education. Hence the Centre has not been assigned to provide vocational competences as such, but preparatory courses related to specialist or general competences, e.g. in Danish, Mathematics and Languages. This orientation means that the Centre is mainly directed at the individual learner, and views education activities as a contribution to the life and education of the individual. The main educational model is school teaching, namely teaching of a specific subject to a group of students in a specific classroom at the school.

In the last few years, however, the Adult Education Centre has initiated activities under the headline 'Practice-related general adult education'. New activities include shorter programmes planned in co-operation with both public and private companies for a specific group of employees. The content and the course materials are geared towards the organisation's needs. The participants are often from the same organisation and the programmes are usually related to upskilling employees in relation to certain practice competencies. In some cases the programmes take place within the organisation (see also Hviid et al., 2006: 7f). The idea is that the Adult Education Centre can accommodate concurrent needs for both general competence development and specific competence development-related to work.

It can be noted as an absurdity that the development of practice competencies often seems to take place at a school away from the practice location. There are several examples of employees who go away for a course, return to work inspired, but fall back into the same routines without ever bringing the knowledge from the course back to the work context. This situation can hardly be talked about as development of practice competencies. Theories of knowledge and learning indicate that key practice competencies are acquired through informal and gradual learning on the job

(Lave and Wenger, 1991; Wenger, 1998; Schön, 1983). However, the interplay between education and workplace learning can prove valuable, for instance in upskilling employees with limited educational backgrounds, e.g. IT skills and reading skills as well as education generally can provide a place for reflecting on work practices based on the perspectives introduced in a course and on the dialogues it opens. This type of valuable interplay, however, is not a given result. The Adult Education Centre has initiated different activities intended to make the interplay fruitful; e.g. co-operation with the organisation in the planning process so the needs can be specified and course materials designed based on the work tasks and practices of the employees taking part in the course.

In the following section, we will introduce a case study from the project with the purpose of bringing focus to some of the challenges of practice-related general adult education. This in turn will lead us to discuss the field of workplace learning from different theoretical perspectives on learning.

Case study: The Metal Works Factory

The case description is based mainly on the research report of a particular case study written by Keller who was the main researcher in the particular study (Keller, 2005) and on an overview of the research project in general (Hviid et al., 2006). The context of the study is that all production workers (approximately 70) at a metal works factory attended a programme entitled 'Cooperation and communication' run by the Adult Education Centre. The majority of the workers are men; aged between 40 and 60 years and approximately two-thirds of the workers did not have any further education past primary school level. The organisation is in the process of outsourcing parts of production to the Ukraine and the Danish-based factory is to focus on delivering smaller aspects of the production process.

The programme was initiated by management when they learned that another local factory had benefited from attendance at such a programme. The programme facilitator prepared the content in co-operation with the organisation by holding interviews with management, the foreman and employees. The aim of the programme was to support processes in the organisation related to improved internal communication. Thus the programme looked at improving organisational practice rather than focusing on the content in isolation. The programme lasted 40 hours and took place over a period of five days: it started with attendance for two consecutive days, followed by an eight-week break and then attendance at the final three consecutive days. The programme took place at the local Adult Education Centre. Only one facilitator delivered the programme content and facilitator coverage of content was 80 per cent. The content was primarily tailored to the needs of production workers; however a special programme was designed to meet the needs of administrative workers and foremen. The workers were divided into groups of 8–9 persons from different departments in the factory.

Through observations and interviews, Keller investigated the learning processes related to worker participation on the programme. She was interested in the interrelation between three elements: (1) the co-operation between the organisation and the Adult Education Centre; (2) the formal learning situation related to the programme; (3) the informal learning situation related to the workplace (Keller, 2005: 33). In this section, we will focus on the interrelationship between the programme itself and workplace learning.

The programme was described as a success from both the perspectives of management and workers. Credit for the success of the programme was primarily attributed to the facilitator who managed to find a teaching style which fitted with the learning needs of participants in general. The content of the programme was related to different theoretical perspectives on communication and co-operation, e.g. transaction analysis and motivation theories. The facilitator, however, was described as being less interested in the theories from a scholastic perspective and more focused on the practical implications of theories and the use of the theories in relation to the everyday life of the participants. She encouraged the participants to provide examples from their daily life to understand the theories – and she encouraged the participants to enter into dialogue about their experiences and the theories. She was less interested in the right answers and the memorising of the theories than in the use of the theory to reflect on communication and co-operation in working life. A core aspect of her teaching style is the use of humour and dialogue. These factors were noted as important by the participants when they talked about the programme.

When asked about the outcomes of the programme, participants were more hesitant, especially in regard to its effect on daily work practices. One of the participants said: 'When you just get back from a programme, then it's all there with you, but then a month goes by and it's gone again. But it's like you can save some of it, if you are in a conflict with a colleague, then you can say "we were on a programme, what did we learn there?", that helps a little' (translated from Danish; Keller, 2005: 24f). Other interviews indicated that communication had slightly improved following the programme. Examples include that the CEO has improved the information flow from management to workers and that the workers in production have become quicker at helping each other. One informant also says that it is not so much the theories and tools that they use, but the programme has given him awareness about 'talking things through'. Another result of the programme has to do with the groupings of workers from different departments who attended the programme. Because of cross-departmental attendance, participants received a greater overview of the organisation as a whole in the sense that they now know more about the work of other departments. Keller notes, however, that it was generally difficult for the informants to evaluate the effect of the programme and find visible signs of improved communication (Keller, 2005: 25).

The case study can be used to pinpoint different challenges in relation to the interplay between adult education and workplace learning in regard to supporting the competence development of the employee as well as organisational development.

One challenge is the co-operation or partnership between the education institution and the organisation. In this case, the co-operation can be described as successful. The facilitator engaged in discussions with management to learn about the needs of the organisation and she used interviewing techniques to learn about the needs of programme participants. She seems aware of the different perspectives at play: employees and management. She used the information to develop and adjust the programme. However, some obstacles were encountered: e.g. obstacles of language; the education institution and the organisation use different concepts or vocabularies to talk about the same things or see things from their own perspectives – and are thus unable to understand the others' position. Participation in the design of the programme was also considered important as it related to ownership and motivation.

Another challenge is the targeted development of programme content and materials so that it meets the needs of a specific organisation. A core focus of practice-related adult education is that the programme materials are adapted to the work practice of participants. In the above case the facilitator discussed work-based practice by asking participants to give examples and participate in a dialogue about workplace issues. She also prepared and engaged in group discussions based on work practice. This can only be done if the facilitator researches the organisation and is aware of the organisation's characteristics and the work being done there. This also places a great emphasis on the facilitator's ability to move away from a curriculum-based teaching to re-thinking her materials from the point of view of work-based practice and organisation needs.

A third challenge is related to the follow-up of the programme; namely what happens at the workplace when the employees return from a programme. What are the possibilities for integrating the knowledge attained on the programme into daily work functions and routines? This was a key factor at play in the above case. The workers' experiences show that some positive outcomes have resulted – however, these are sometimes hard to pinpoint. This challenge can be named 'the gap-problem': the problem of maintaining and transforming educational knowledge in work contexts in order to develop practice competences. The problem can be described from two levels:

- Individual level: what are the opportunities and the obstacles facing the individual in carrying back the results of the learning process so that programme learning results in development of practice competences in working life?

- Organisational level: how can the organisation hold on to the learning of the individual and use this knowledge to develop the organisation?

These challenges indicate some research issues within the field of workplace learning. In the following sections of this chapter we will take a closer look at the field of workplace learning and present theoretical perspectives on learning in the workplace.

The research field on workplace learning

The research field of workplace learning is characterised by diverse theoretical and empirical perspectives on learning processes related to working life. The field has its roots in the area of adult education and theories of individual learning related to this area. It hereby distinguishes itself from the field of organisational learning which has its origins in management and organisational studies; however any clear line between the two fields can be hard to set (Elkjaer and Wahlgren, 2005). The difference can essentially be said to be a difference in perspective. Workplace learning takes its departure from an interest in the individual learning taking place at the workplace; for instance, research investigates how the workplace can be organised to provide the needed learning situations for the individual. Organisational learning mainly takes its departure from an organisational perspective and investigates how learning is involved and can be enhanced within the organisational system. However, both fields have as an effort to sustain the bonds between individuals and organisations in favour of enhancing the learning processes.

The concept of lifelong learning as the foundation for economic and societal development also plays an important role in relation to workplace learning. Seen from one perspective, lifelong learning is translated into lifelong education, namely that the adult worker participates in educational activities. However, from another perspective the concept can also attest to the fact that learning happens everywhere and all through life (Antonacopoulou et al., 2005; Jarvis, 1992). Jarvis argues in *Paradoxes of Learning* that:

> **learning is wider than education: education is only one social institution in which learning occurs, albeit the only one specifically directed toward it. ... But all the social institutions together cannot contain learning, since learning is fundamental to human being and to life itself. (Jarvis, 1992: 10)**

From this perspective the concept rebels against the patent of the educational system to claim 'learning' as its territory and it opens up the perspective that learning occurs in all spheres of life, including working life.

Over the past ten years the concept of lifelong learning has become an important guiding principle underpinning the knowledge society. The OECD, for instance, have published reports pointing to lifelong learning as an important answer to the challenges of globalisation, namely increased competition on world markets. OECD describes a need for employability and adaptability of the workforce related to the fast changing marked demands. Lifelong learning is seen to play a crucial role in relation to this need. The OECD report *Economics and Finance of Lifelong Learning* is introduced by the following passage:

> **Learning is an essential basis for progress in the 'knowledge society'; it is critical for economic growth and social welfare. ... [The report] aims to inspire future actions that ensure that lifelong learning serves as a sustainable and equitable strategy for human development. (OECD, 2001)**

The report points to learning as the decisive factor in improving competitiveness based on the premise that knowledge – which is seen to be the result of learning – is a valuable resource necessary to deal with global market conditions. The need for innovative and flexible workers, who can produce new ideas and products and adapt to sudden changes, is seen to be all-important. So is the need for reflective professionals, who not only use the knowledge they already have, but also know how to locate new information, improve their existing knowledge and readily adapt to changes in relation to job tasks. From these premises, the overall key of the report is that learning can and must contribute to the economic growth of the society by equipping the individual employee with the necessary competences to deal with innovation, flexibility and reflection.

These aims are essentially dealt with from within an economic instrumental framework, but can also be used to mark different perspectives on lifelong learning. In one perspective lifelong learning is a strategy for the economic good of society since learning is seen to be the key to creating and sharing knowledge and hence improving the innovative and competitive status of companies. The above report is an example of this perspective. From another perspective, lifelong learning is a strategy for the good of the individual. For instance, it can be linked to ideas such as 'education for all' and hence prove to be valuable in opening up equal access to knowledge. In this case learning could also have a liberating effect and equip individuals to participate actively and critically in society. The two perspectives do not have to collide. However, they do create room for possible tensions. We can envision situations in which individual learning interests are in unison with the need for employability of the workforce. The opposite situation, however, is also easily pictured: the individual becoming a working 'object' in the process of economic growth – learning being forced upon the individual and the result is stress and unhappy working lives. This reminds us of the necessity of a critical stance to taking learning only as a positive.

The OECD report testifies to a link between learning and adult life. It also examines the link between learning and working life in the sense that ongoing competence development related to work remains an important issue for organisations. From an educational perspective, this link means that education can no longer be viewed solely as what comes before work – something that qualifies you for a certain job function – but education is integrated into adult working life, e.g. continuing education based on further education programmes. In this sense, lifelong learning takes the form of lifelong education expressed by an interrelated and parallel movement of work and education in adulthood. However, Jarvis points out the concept of lifelong learning can also be used to emphasise that learning not only takes place in the context of educational institutions, but learning can be seen as a human condition in the sense that learning is an essential factor in the way we live in the world. We see this clearly in childhood. The child learns through its engagement with the world. She learns the materiality of things: things can be soft, hard, cold and warm. She learns to use cultural artefacts like a spoon or riding a bike. These learning processes display both learning as a spontaneous part of life taking place without us structuring the learning process and learning as a result of a more planned activity. Learning takes place in many situations throughout our lives, in different settings and in different forms. Not all learning (far from it) just happens by itself, but often learning is the result of a planned activity, e.g. the teaching of mathematics, reading a difficult theorist, learning how to use computer software or how to drive a car. From this perspective it becomes important how best to facilitate learning when we seek to learn something in particular. These reflections also bring attention to the workplace itself as a setting for different forms of learning.

It makes sense to distinguish between three settings for learning in relation to the adult learner: work, educational institutions and leisure time. Each of these settings works as a different context for the learning process; the context sets some conditions under which the learning takes place. If we focus on work, this context is not primarily oriented at learning, but at the work tasks at hand. Learning can be related to these tasks, often in a spontaneous way. And if learning is initiated formally in planned and structured learning situations, then these situations still must be looked at from within the work context and its particular logic: the task at hand needs to be accomplished either to make money (private organisations) or to provide a particular service to the citizen within a given budget (public organisations). This is different from the educational context which is primarily directed at learning. The work setting is also different from what we call leisure time in the sense that work takes place in the direction of some sort of management and within a formal organisation based on ongoing power relations and negotiations. The organisation holds particular interest and economic rationales are seen as essential to the existence of the organisation.

An important task for research in workplace learning is to study learning processes related to the work context. Questions asked within the research area are for example:

- How does the individual learn in and through work?

- How do education and work practices come together in learning processes related to work?

- How can we improve learning processes in relation to work settings?

Research in workplace learning is directed at both understanding and organising, implementing and facilitating learning processes in work practices. This can involve both education external to work and the integration of learning processes as an internal and natural part of the daily work. Also, the research often takes several perspectives into consideration related to questions of learning needs: who needs to learn what and for what reasons? It takes the perspective of the society by looking at tendencies within a society, e.g. descriptions of the knowledge society and lifelong learning, and (critically) discusses the need for learning in relation to these tendencies. It also looks to the particular organisation and to the competences the organisation requires from the employee. It takes the perspective of the individual, e.g. what are the employee's own desires for learning in order to create a good (working) life. And lastly, as a fourth dimension, it looks at the interplay between these three perspectives – and the possible tensions.

In the last part of this chapter we will present different theoretical perspectives on informal learning and learning through the practice of work.

Learning through the practice of work

When the researcher of workplace learning asks the question 'how does the individual learn in and through work?' she finds no theoretical consensus in the field regarding what learning is. Different theoretical platforms can be distinguished depending on their ontological perspective on learning: is learning a phenomenon existing in individual, interpersonal or contextual compositions, e.g. should we locate learning in cognitive processes, communication or organisational structures? From a pragmatic standpoint it would seem that all perspectives hold some truth as human living is a complex matter; in turning to only one perspective we risk overlooking this complexity. Learning is linked to the individual learner (someone is learning something) and learning processes are also intimately linked to the social context in which learning takes place. The individual learner is not alone in the world. Human existence is always a life with others and learning processes need to be located in the social context, namely in communication, culture and society. A key factor in learning theory is hence to describe human being and our presence in the world since learning theories are based on assumptions about the human subject, whether or not the theory explicitly argues for these assumptions.

The field of workplace learning is particularly known for bringing informal learning processes into focus, namely learning taking place spontaneously through work practices. This does not mean that the definition of informal learning is clear-cut. Garrick (1998) discusses the definitional complexities about informal learning and writes that different writings have surfaced over the years in relation to the phenomena of informal learning which in many ways carry different assumptions about the human subject. Inspired by Garrick (1998: 9) we can list the following entries to studies of informal learning:

- The pragmatist approach to learning (Dewey, 1916, 1991; Kolb, 1984; Schön, 1983).

- Learning from the social context (e.g. Lave and Wenger, 1991; Wenger, 1998).

- Tacit dimensions of knowledge (Polanyi, 1958, 1966).

- Enhancing informal and incidental learning (e.g. Marsick and Watkins, 1990).

Beginning with the last entry, we can look at Marsick and Watkins (1990) as an example of a theoretical and empirical study of informal learning at the workplace. Their overall aim is to contrast informal and incidental learning with more structured or formal forms of learning situations, e.g. workshops, seminars and training programmes in general. Incidental learning is defined as a byproduct of some other activity, for instance task accomplishment or interpersonal interaction. Hence, incidental learning is never planned or intentional. Examples given are learning from mistakes by trial–error experimentation and learning from interpersonal relations by internalising meaning construction about the actions of the other. Informal learning, on the other hand, can be both intentional and planned, but informal learning is non-institutional and predominantly experientially related to work activities. Examples are self-directed learning and help sought from mentors (Marsick and Watkins, 1990: 6ff). Further they write:

> **We are particularly interested in reaching people who work in human resource development because we believe that informal and incidental learning, which are difficult to organize and control, represent a neglected, but crucial area of their practice. (Marsick and Watkins, 1990: 3)**

The aim of Marsick and Watkins is to contribute to an understanding of workplace learning which human resource developers can use to enhance this type of learning.

Garrick criticises the distinction between informal and incidental learning and argues that it forms a false dichotomy (Garrick, 1998). He looks at the example of self-directed learning and writes that 'it seems unwarranted to separate "self-directed learning" from the beliefs and values that influence "incidental" learning' (Garrick 1998: 11). In other words: he questions the idea that you can separate the intentional and the non-intentional in arguing that informal learning is intentional and incidental learning is not. Rather he points to the need for a higher understanding of the complexity at stake in workplace learning. From this perspective he is also critical of the scope entailed in the work of Marsick and Watkins as he argues that they lack a critical stance to the human capital theory they imply when they seek to enhance or 'harness' the productive potentials of this learning process. He argues that this frames the concept of informal learning within a 'mercantilisation' of knowledge and an instrumental thinking which takes away focus from the situated ethics involved in the learning situations.

We believe that Garrick's point is important in a more general and critical discussion of the value of the workplace as defining the norms and standards for learning and education in society (see also discussion below on Dewey's pragmatism). This is also a discussion, which is absent in for example Lave and Wenger's (1991) and Wenger's (1998) very influential work on situated learning and communities-of-practice, which discusses how the social context influences learning. Their work has been critical in pointing to the informal learning processes that take place in everyday activities in workplaces and in other social groups. We will however not describe this theory now but will refer to the chapter on organisational learning and HRD. Instead we will look at two other theories, which have been important in linking work and learning: John Dewey's theory of learning known as pragmatism and Polanyi's theory of tacit knowing.

John Dewey's pragmatism

John Dewey has been an important influential source in linking work and learning as well as connecting learning and education to broader issues of democracy, ethics and emancipation. In this way, Dewey is quite distinct from many other learning theoreticians in anchoring his idea of learning to broader societal issues and to a broader philosophy. In Dewey's thinking there are three concepts, which we will deal with: *experience*, *thinking* and *problem orientation*.

Experience is a central concept in Dewey's thinking in being his ontological concept for knowledge. Experience concerns the reconstruction of meaning which is developed in interaction with the social circumstances in which the individual is situated. For Dewey experience is active living and doing in interaction or transaction with the world in such a way that the individual experiences the consequences of his action: 'When we experience something we act upon it, we do something with it; then we suffer or undergo the consequences' (Dewey, 1916: 139). However, there is also a passive element in experience so that one on hand experience is *trying* (the active side) and on the other hand experience is *undergoing* (the passive side). In this way experience is always interacting with the social world and it would be impossible to understand experience as disconnected from this social world.

Experience is as such culturally embedded and people are created through the relations in which they participate. In this way, Dewey understands learning and education in a broad sense as cultural education, because people have few skills when they are born:

> **Education, in its broadest sense, is the means of this social continuity of life. Every one of the constituent elements of a social group, in a modern city as in a savage tribe, is born immature, helpless, without language, beliefs, ideas, or social standards. (Dewey, 1916: 2)**

People are cultural products. Society exists in continuous process of transmission and transformation, whereby habits, language, beliefs, values are communicated: 'This transmission occurs by means of communication of habits of doing, thinking, feeling from the older to the younger' (1916: 3). Without communication, society could not sustain itself. He reminds us about the similarities between words like common, community and communication: 'Men live in a community in virtue of the things they have in common; and communication is the way in which they come to possess things in common' (1916: 4). Communication is in other words the source of both the individual's experiences and the sustainability of society and community.

Since communication is so important for experience, it is important to organise communication if we are to build the societies and communities that are desirable. It doesn't emerge by itself: 'Unless pains are taken to see that genuine and thorough transmission takes place, the most civilized group will relapse into barbarism and then into savagery' (1916: 3–4). The need for learning and education is therefore obvious for Dewey, and the purpose is to develop *thinking* as a tool to solve problems in society. Thinking however has to be organised around the matters of the world, that is around complex issues and *problems* and it is in this way that Dewey's pragmatism is relevant and has inspired workplace learning and work-based learning.

The idea that learning and education has to be centred around the problems of the world follows from his conception of experience. Dewey argues that experience implies two conclusions about education and learning. Firstly, experience is an active–passive process, which means that experience is not primarily cognitive. Secondly, the value of experience is in the perception of the relations, which leads to experience. And this means something in relation to education. Dewey argues that in the traditional school systems, we have separated mind and body where: 'The former is then thought to be purely intellectual and cognitive; the latter to be an irrelevant and intruding physical factor' (1916: 140). This is unfortunate because it breaks the intimate connection between activity and undergoing in experience. Dewey argues that it is impossible to conceive the bad results of this separation. It is also hard to exaggerate them.

Dewey mentions three consequences of the separation (1916: 142–144). Firstly, bodily activity is seen as a disturbing element. This means that teaching and learning is organised so that it suppresses and disciplines bodily activities, and instead focuses on the cognitive side. When this is unfortunate, it is because school produces an abnormal and artificial situation, where bodily activity is separated from experience. Bodily activity becomes a negative activity where the need to play is taken away from people.

Secondly, learning becomes mechanical, where the goal is to reproduce what the teacher says without really understanding what it means. This is a difference, which Ryle later refers to as the difference between knowing-that (theoretical and abstract knowledge) and knowing-how (knowing what to do in practice) (Ryle, 1949). Finally on the intellectual side, the separation of mind and body means that people learn to focus on things in themselves, without being able to see the relationships and circumstances, which these things are part of. Problem orientation is for Dewey the answer to avoid the separation of mind and body in education and learning. In other words, education, learning and HRD have to be organised around practical problems to obtain a creative oscillation between abstract theoretical thinking and the practical matters of the world.

According to another writer, Donald Schön, this integration of theory and practice is for example what takes place in professional practice. He argues that the practical world is not as simple as how most of the literature represents it. He agrees with Dewey that the practical world is characterised by complexity, uncertainty, contradictions and value conflicts (Schön, 1983). In the literature, professional practice has been presumed to be done according to the model of technical rationality. This model however presumes that the world is relatively stable and unequicoval and thereby calls for standardised solutions. According to Schön, professional practice is characterised by being anything but stable and unequivocal. Thereby his theory of professional practice becomes embodied in the reflective practitioner, who always uses theory to meet situational and shifting requirements and demands in a way consistent with how Dewey describes the relationship.

We may say that the reflective practitioner uses thinking in Dewey's understanding of the word. For Dewey thinking is man's tool for adapting to the environment. Thinking is a tool to solve the practical problems of the world. If thinking is valid/true depends on whether it is capable of solving the practical problems. According to

Dewey, thinking is where we put abstract concepts and models to work in relation to practical problems. Not all kinds of thinking or reflection are consistent with Dewey's notion of thinking. There is an element of reflection in any experience but there are different types of reflection. There is the type of reflection that is nothing more than trial and error learning of action and consequences until a rule-of-thumb has developed. This is habitual thinking in everyday life. But as Dewey notes: 'We see *that* a certain way of acting and a certain consequence are connected, but we do not see *how* they are' (Dewey, 1916: 145). That is, we observe a connection, but we don't understand the connection.

Thinking is for Dewey the form of reflection, where we try to understand the connection. It is a systematic and analytic approach to problem-solving based on inquiring into the problem in a deeper sense of the word. It is where 'the ground or basis for a belief is deliberately sought and its adequacy to support the belief examined' (Dewey, 1991: 2). It is in other words qualified thinking where talk and actions are justified. This is analogous to Ryle's distinction between knowing-that and knowing-how, where there is an integration between theoretical concepts and methods and the practical matters of the word. Thinking is present in intelligent practice, where we can justify our thoughts and actions. Thinking does not include habitual thinking, ideas by incident etc. It is more systematically explorative and therefore it is also strenuous and exhausting. It includes long periods of disturbances and insecurity: 'Reflective thinking, in short, means judgment suspended during further inquiry; and suspense is likely to be painful' (1991: 13).

Thinking is therefore not an instrument that people naturally possess. Most people are born with the potential, but this potential has to be stimulated and this is where education and learning comes in. It is also through education and learning that people develop themselves, but also society. Therefore education and learning is central for the accomplishment of the highest forms of society, which for Dewey is the democratic society. It is in other words through education that we create the foundation for democracy.

John Dewey's influence on learning, education and pedagogy in general has been enormous and his thoughts are – more than fifty years after his death – still important today in rethinking education and learning. For HRD and workplace learning, John Dewey's thoughts are relevant in providing an ontology and epistemology for integrating theory and practice, thus – apparently – bringing the workplace and learning together into an integrated unity. But as noted above, Dewey's thoughts have to be seen in relation to a whole philosophy integrating ethics, democracy, education, learning and the practical matters of the world. And in this respect, Dewey's philosophy is a philosophy of education of the individual by which the individual becomes capable of living and contributing to the democratic society. In using Dewey's theory on workplace learning and HRD there may be a conflict between the goals of education and learning in that the norms and standards for evaluating learning and education in relation to the development of the workplace or the development of society differs quite radically from each other.

Dewey's pragmatism has often been reduced to mean learning in practice through learning by doing. But this should not hide the fact that there are many more deep and rigorous thoughts about what education is and what purpose it serves in society. And therefore that learning by participating in ordinary activities is not at all learning in Dewey's sense of the word. We would argue that the purpose of education in Dewey's philosophy is very close to ideals of emancipation and the realisation of self through education. In this sense it diverges from workplace environments that through its norms, standards, routines actually dictate what learning is and what learning is not. Applying Dewey's philosophy of education in workplace environments may lead to a lot of confusion and the integration of theory and practice is not that straightforward after all. On the other hand this concern for the individual's education is also what could lead to more discontinuous and innovative learning in the workplace because here we need something that is different from the knowledge already present in the workplace.

We would argue that the focus on education – and not the workplace – is also common for other writers focusing on the integration of theory and practice. As noted, Schön's reflective practitioner (Schön, 1983) is in many ways the embodiment of Dewey's pragmatism. The reflective practitioner is also one, who handles the paradoxical, equivocal and conflicting matters of the world by applying scientific concepts and methods. She is integrating knowing-that into knowing-how (Ryle, 1949) thereby creating intelligent reflective practice. The focus on the integration between knowing-that and knowing-how is also the focus of another theory, which we will deal with now, namely the idea of tacit knowing. The theory of tacit knowing brings our attention to why we are not always capable of expressing what we know, despite that we actually know it, and brings our attention to bodily knowledge and the integration between mind and body, which Dewey was also looking at.

Tacit knowing

Polanyi's concept of tacit knowing has evoked considerable attention in recent years. Polanyi distinguishes between explicit dimensions of knowledge, which comprise formal systematic articulation of knowledge and tacit dimensions, which cannot be formally articulated. Polanyi's point is that the term 'tacit' is a distinctive characteristic of knowing and this is why he calls his famous 1966 book *The Tacit Dimension* (Polanyi, 1966). We cannot speak of explicit knowing (knowing-that) as a separate category of knowledge, because it relies on being tacitly understood and applied (knowing-how). As a consequence 'all knowledge is *either tacit or rooted in tacit knowledge*' (Polanyi, 1969b: 195). 'We can know more than we can tell' (1966: 1) does not only mean that we have knowledge that we cannot tell. It also means that in what we do say, there is also something unsaid, and which is needed in order to understand what is being said. Knowing to talk, understand and use language (e.g. Wittgenstein, 1983) is for example something that we need in order to communicate while words in themselves mean nothing and in themselves would be nothing more than meaningless grunts.

Polanyi uses the police method as an example. We can recognise a face among millions of people without being able to specify how we can recognise the face (1966: 4). But the police have invented methods for making it sayable; for example through a great collection of pictures of noses, ears, mouths etc. But this doesn't change the fact that before we had knowledge that we could not express. Furthermore, even if we have the tools by which we can communicate we cannot say how we combine the features (1966: 5). In other words, there is always a tacit dimension in what we do and say. Therefore the explicit and tacit need to be looked at as integrated. They are not distinct. They are rather dialectical categories of knowledge which are mutually dependent, mutually develop each other, yet are mutually exclusive (Hall, 1979).

Tacit knowing is thus knowledge, which we cannot explicate. It includes competencies like running, cycling, swimming, walking, driving a car, using tools and playing a lot of different games. It includes the embodied knowledge of surgeons, top athletes etc. This is knowing, which is tacit. *Explicit knowing* is knowing, which is rooted in tacit knowing. It is a formal systematic articulation of knowledge in language and writing. But it is knowledge which is rooted in tacit knowing because without it, we would not be able to use and understand language and writing.

When Polanyi speaks of tacit knowing, he speaks about the ability to recognise a face through integration of its particulars, without being able to identify these particulars. He looks at this integration in a certain way, namely as an active construction of experience made through the attempt to create knowledge. He thus shares Dewey's presumption that experience is active. This integration or framing of reality is for Polanyi the tacit power behind all knowledge.

> **However, I am looking at Gestalt, on the contrary, as the outcome of an active shaping of experience performed in the pursuit of knowledge. This shaping or integrating I hold to be the great and indispensable tacit power by which all knowledge is discovered and, once discovered is held to be true. (1966: 6)**

This integration is always both intellectual and practical. The Germans' 'wissen' and 'können' and Ryle's knowing-that and knowing-how (1966: 7). 'I shall always speak of "knowing," therefore to cover both practical and theoretical knowledge' (1966: 7). Intellectual and practical knowledge are thus fused in tacit knowing, and the highest forms of tacit knowing are expressed in scientific, technical, artistic or athletic genius. When Polanyi describes the dynamics in tacit knowing, he argues that tacit knowing is always characterised by from–to movements. It always contains two elements or two terms, where tacit knowing means going from one term to another. He uses different expressions here to describe this relationship. Sometimes, it is described as a relationship between the first term and the second term. He also speaks of the relationship between the proximal term and the distal terms or the relationship between subsidiary awareness and focal awareness.

However, he always speaks about tacit knowing as moving from one term to another and it is about the first term we have knowledge that we cannot tell. To take an example, Polanyi mentions an experiment in which a person was exposed to a number of meaningless spellings. After having been shown some of the spellings, the person was given an electric shock. After some time the person began to expect the electric shock by the sight of the shock-spellings. But he couldn't identify them. He had in other words a knowledge that he couldn't tell. In this example lies the basic structure of tacit knowing.

> **We know the electric shock, forming the second term, by attending to it, and hence the subject is *specifiably* known. But we know the shock-producing particulars only by relying on our awareness of them for attending to something else, namely the electric shock, and hence our knowledge of them remains *tacit*. (1966: 9–10)**

We move from something to something else: from the first term to the second term. In the face example, we move from the particulars of the face to the whole face without being able to specify the particulars. Practical skills have the same character. We need to combine muscular actions into practical skills without being able to specify the muscular actions. This relationship is referred to as the functional structure of tacit knowing by which we go from particulars to the whole and where 'we know the first term only by relying on our awareness of it for attending to the second' (1966: 10). But this integration also has consequences in terms of how we perceive and understand things. This is called the phenomenal aspect of tacit knowing. It consists in that the integration of the subsidiary into the focal means that both change their appearance. We only know the spellings through their meaning for us, the shock. In the face example we only know the ear through its participation in the whole. If we focus on the ear, it would be different. When we perceive persons for example we also understand the person in relation to the context in which the person is situated.

This means that in perceiving and understanding a given situation, we always rely on knowledge that we cannot tell. In understanding a situation as a teaching-situation we rely on the recognition of a number of contextual clues that we cannot tell. Polanyi argues that it is impossible to define all particulars in a given context. These are so innumerable that it is not possible to specify all of them. There is a second problem. Even if all of them could be specified, isolation from the others may change their appearance (Polanyi, 1969a: 124). Every time we concentrate our attention on one particular element in a context, our sense of its coherent existence is weakened and every time we move in the opposite direction, the particulars tend to be submerged in the whole. This leads to the point about particulars. They can be noticed in two different ways. We can be aware of them incomprehendingly, i.e. in themselves, or understandingly, in their participation in a comprehensive entity. In the first case we are aware of them *focally*, in the second we notice them *subsidiarily* in terms of their participation in the whole (Polanyi, 1969a: 128).

The relationship between explicit knowing and tacit knowing is related to the *semantic aspect of tacit knowing*. Tacit knowing can be possessed in itself, while explicit knowledge relies on being tacitly understood and applied. Words become transparent through tacit knowing in that we move or see through them to their meaning. We don't focus on the words in themselves. We focus on their meaning. The point is not that knowledge can be divided in a tacit part and an explicit part. The point is that knowledge is tacit. We cannot talk about explicit knowledge as a separate category of knowledge, because it relies on being tacitly understood and applied. In the same way explicit knowledge about HRD concepts, methods and tools relies on the tacit understanding and application of those concepts, methods and tools and thus how it is translated to concrete HRD – activities in workplaces and organisations.

In relation to our discussion on HRD and workplace learning, we would argue that Polanyi's theory of tacit knowing supplements Dewey's ideas of education in providing a much more comprehensive theory of experience and various aspects of experience (functional, phenomenal, semantic) and a more complete understanding of the interaction between individual and the social. Tacit knowing 'fuses the subsidiary awareness of the particulars belonging to our subject matter with the cultural background of our knowing' (Polanyi, 1969a: 134). In this sense, the borderlines between knower and known are dissolved. As such Polanyi's theory of knowing is similar to other authors, who have developed the notion 'distributed intelligence' (Brown and Duguid, 1996; Bruner, 1996). Bruner explains it in this fashion:

> **The gist of the idea is that it is a grave error to locate intelligence in a single head. It exists as well not only in your particular environment of books, dictionaries, and notes, but also in the heads and habits of the friends with whom you interact, even in what socially you have come to take as given. (Bruner, 1996: 154)**

Knowledge of what to think and act is not only located in a single head, it is also in the particular context and the habits of the friends with whom you interact. This includes tools, machines, information technology, weapons, pencils, paper, chairs, tables, books, notes, procedures, rituals, ceremonies, stories, bedrooms, kitchens etc. For example learning in workplaces happens in a context of clues from which people construct their interpretations and actions. In theoretical terms this notion of distributed intelligence has developed into, for example, communities-of-practice (see next chapter).

In relation to workplace learning and the relationship to HRD, the theory of tacit knowing could be applied as a way of understanding and improving the complex relationships between knowledge and learning that exist among people working together. The theory of tacit knowing thus combines formal and informal knowledge, individual and the social etc. But there are also problems in it. It is a very broad framework, which is very difficult to apply and use for more precise practical guidelines. This is, we think, because tacit knowing is an ontological concept just as experience is for Dewey. Secondly, it is interesting that Polanyi actually uses his theory of tacit knowing as a defence against the critiques of science, that there are certain types of knowledge that we cannot define or even tell as we have noted. For Polanyi is a scientist of a classical type and thus believes in Enlightenment, in the continuous accumulation of knowledge and in the ideas of scientific rationalism. So tacit knowing is not located within the linguistic turn in science, nor is it a critique of the value of science. Rather Polanyi's framework is very traditional in for example proclaiming a theory of the universe as a system filled with strata of realities, joined together meaningfully in pairs of higher and lower strata (1966: 35) including higher forms of life from lower forms of life.

> **We can see all levels of evolution at a glance in an individual human being. The most primitive form of life is represented by the growth of the typical human shape, through the progress of morphogenesis studied by embryology. Next we have the vegetative functioning of the organism, studied by physiology; and above it there is sentience, rising to perception and to a centrally controlled motoric activity, both of which still belong to the subject of physiology. We rise beyond this at the level of conscious behavior and intellectual action, studied by ethology and psychology; and uppermost, we meet with man's moral sense, guided by the firmament of his standards. (Polanyi, 1966: 36–37)**

Thus, Polanyi combines his ideas of tacit knowing, which in many ways resembles a theory of embedded and encultured knowing, with a notion of human being as a set of systems stacked up on top of each other to form a hierarchy (1966: 55). He also denotes it as evolution from lower being to higher beings and here scientific rationalism for Polanyi has been a major influence towards intellectual, moral and social progress (1966: 57). This reveals how Polanyi would think about education and learning as the driver of scientific rationalism leading to intellectual, moral and social progress.

Having presented some significant contributions to workplace learning and HRD, we will now conclude by discussing some of the critical issues in workplace learning that have been opened by the previous sections in this chapter.

Conclusions

We opened the chapter with a case study from a metal works factory. It does not go into the characteristics of informal learning in the workplace as such. However, the case illustrates the challenge of maintaining and transforming 'educational knowledge' in work contexts so that it can support or qualify problem-solving and know-how related to work practices. The above theoretical perspectives provide a framework for understanding the processes at stake in this transformation and the need for interaction between different forms of knowledge: explicit knowledge, representative knowledge or educational knowledge and implicit knowledge, tacit knowledge or practice-based knowledge.

The perspectives presented in this chapter all emphasise the value of education and learning as becoming embedded in practice. As such these perspectives argue for an integration of theory and practice. In practical terms however, workplace learning has often been understood as socialisation to practice where the purpose of learning has been narrowly understood as defined by the workplace. Most theories of workplace learning – except from situated learning and communities-of-practice – actually argue for a closer integration of theory and practice; not less theory and more practice, which sometimes underlie popular discussions on the subject matter and which is also sometimes a basis of misunderstanding when organisational and educational institutions work together.

Workplace learning thus seeks to organise learning and education in a new way but the question is, does this also change the purpose of education and learning? In theoretical terms, Dewey, Polanyi, Schön and Ryle would probably argue that the answer is no. In practical terms, the matter is probably a great deal more difficult to answer and probably lead to a lot confusions and misunderstandings. So this is one troubling aspect of workplace learning, which has to do with who defines the norms and standards of education and learning in workplace learning.

We take Gherardi and Nicolini's point of view and argue that there is difference between knowing-in-practice and knowing-a-practice (Gherardi and Nicolini, 2001). This is an argument for the value of education. Through education and learning, we free ourselves from the language of the workplace, but we do so in order to contribute to the language of the workplace. We are however not un-critical in relation to the contributions from the writers that we have dealt with in this chapter. While Polanyi in his formulations appears to be the most conservative and mechanistic here, his thoughts are also in many ways quite consistent with the overall progress and rationalistic thinking, which also dominates the other writers we have dealt with: Dewey, Schön and Ryle.

They are all advocates for the integration of knowing-that (scientific concepts, models, theory) into knowing-how. In other words, these writers see the value of education as a means of stimulating thinking or reflecting in action. But they also lack a critical stance towards their own language – that is theories, concepts and models – from which they act. In particular Ann Cunliffe and her colleagues have emphasised the differences in ontology here (Cunliffe, 2002, 2003). While the writers above are firmly rooted in the idea of scientific progress, the continuous accumulation of knowledge and the ideas of objective truth, Cunliffe and colleagues reject the notion of objective truth, and claims that theories, models and concepts are fundamentally part of scientific language with inherent truth and morality claims. Cunliffe and Jun

(Cunliffe and Jun, 2005) for example distinguish between reflection and reflexive, where they argue that reflection is linked to the idea of language as a mirror reality, while reflexive is linked to the idea of language as constructing reality. They distinguish between calculative thinking and meditative thinking, where the first is characterized by 'a "going toward" objects or willing something into truth by representing it as we think it is. This means an objective observer reflecting on a situation to understand what is really going on and to develop theories to explain that reality' (Cunliffe and Jun, 2005: s. 227). This differs from *mediative thinking* where the purpose is to question the basis of our actions: 'In particular, it means engaging in the reflexive act of questioning the basis of our thinking, surfacing the taken-for-granted rules underlying organisational decisions, and examining critically our own practices and ways of relating with others' (Cunliffe and Jun, 2005: s. 227).

Mediative thinking is reflexive thinking characterised as the attempt of avoiding being caught in 'definitive language and truth claims' (Cunliffe and Jun, 2005: s. 227). As such, Cunliffe and colleagues add a dimension, which is important in education and learning, if we are to maintain the idea of education as the source of intellectual, moral and social progress. We are somehow always caught by our language and one of the challenges is to question embedded truth and morality claims in language which guide how we perceive problems and solutions and how we perceive our relations with others. These questions are very deep and linked to our identity as individuals but also social identities expressed in questions of who we are as an organisation, what is our mission and so forth. Therefore Cunliffe and colleagues argue for reflexive thinking as a dimension in thinking that goes beyond reflective thinking and which becomes critical in a globalised capitalist system where things are changing rapidly.

 Discussion questions

- What can be done to integrate education and workplace learning in a way so that education is helpful in developing practical work competences?

- How can Dewey's concept of problem solving be helpful when organising and developing learning interventions at the workplace?

- Discuss the different types of knowledge presented in this chapter and discuss their relevance for HRD practitioners in organising workplace learning.

9 Organisational Learning and HRD

Kenneth Mølbjerg Jørgensen

██ ██ **Chapter objectives** ██

The objectives of this chapter are to:

- present the research field of organisational learning;

- describe a case of organisational learning as a means of conceptualising organisational learning;

- identity important contributions within the field of organisational learning;

- discuss organisational learning as a means of human resource development.

Introduction

As noted at the beginning of the book, HRD has evolved as a field of theory and practice with a tripartite agenda of human betterment, organisational enhancement and societal development. In this context the discourse on organisational learning (OL) has been very influential during the past 20 years. The theories, concepts and methods embraced by this concept are now widely applied as methods for organisational change and organisational development. In academic, consulting and management circles, OL is now widely established and used to solve organisational problems. The learning organisation (Senge, 1990) has undoubtedly been very successful in putting learning and organisation together on the agenda.

There is however no really solid evidence that OL has actually contributed significantly to the tripartite agenda of HRD noted above. In-depth case studies of the use of OL concepts and methods have shown a mix of very different results, which has something to do with the historical and geographical circumstances in which OL is used, the competencies and positions of the people using them and the identities of people, who are exposed to OL (Jørgensen, 2004; Dahl et al., 2005; Jørgensen and Rasmussen, 2005; Laursen and Rasmussen, 2007). In a project called Centre for Organisational Learning, which organised a number of different organisational learning projects in Danish companies and institutions, we focused on learning situations in organisations. We defined these as situations which were organised with the intention of facilitating the participants' learning, and which were thus organised with reference to a learning discourse. In this case, we didn't adopt the distinction between *learning* and *performance* but saw learning more broadly as changes in talk, actions and perceptions of self (Barrie and Pace, 1998). We concluded that these learning situations were affected by a multiplicity of forces and that learning as such could go in many different directions.

We see organisations as emerging on the grounds of a continuous and complex game of interactions, intentions, interests, and circumstances. OL is a discourse that intervenes in organisational life with the purpose of improving the way organisations work. But the discourse must itself be understood through how it works in practice. Thereby the theories, methods and concepts of OL acquire their meaning through how they are used in real-life practice. This implies that they gain their meaning in a complex interplay between different actors, interests and intentions. We understand organisations as a set of language games that continuously develop and evolve. But the discourse on OL is itself a language game that also continuously emerges and evolves. As such we cannot really define OL other than as a human practice which is continuously in a state of becoming.

The site of OL is where the language games that constitute organisational practices and the language games that constitute OL meet face to face. The scene of OL thus comprises potentially of a great variety of learning situations. It is in the interplay between these different ways of speaking and acting that learning may emerge, but as noted this is not decided from one place but from many different places. Firstly, we will describe a case of organisational learning, which we will use as the basis for discussing OL and to identify some of the characteristics of our approach to OL. Secondly, we conceptualise our approach to organisational learning as designed dialogues in organisations with the purpose of facilitating learning in such a way that improves the way organisations work. Thirdly, we describe some important theoretical contributions to the field of OL: Argyris' and Argyris and Schön's approach and the communities of practice approach (CoP).

Theory at work – lessons from practice

In this section, we will describe a case study from an OL project in a manufacturing organisation (Jørgensen, 2005), which we will use as an entry into discussing the field of OL.

Case study: OL in a manufacturing organisation

Eleven men met in a hotel in Jutland in Denmark on 16 March 2001. The theme for the meeting was a start-up seminar in an OL project in a manufacturing organisation. The participants were the following:

- Director A: Co-founder of the company
- Director B: Co-founder of the company
- Sales manager: employed since 1990

- Operations manager: employed since 2000

- Service manager: employed since 1983

- IT manager: employed since 1983

- Development manager: employed since 1999

- Production manager: employed since 2000

- Primary consultant

- Secondary consultant

- Researcher

The organisational circumstances in this company were characterised by an old conflict between two different groups: a group represented by the administrative-minded and sales-minded director B and the development-minded director A. Many development projects had been started to try to solve the conflicts and problems but without any success. Some of these projects had involved the primary consultant, who was an old acquaintance of director A.

The two directors and the two consultants had prior to the meeting signed a contract, which described the project's primary task, resource people, project description, concrete objectives, organisation, division of labour and roles. The six managers however heard about the project for the first time at this seminar. It was director B who welcomed everybody to the seminar. He looked back at a number of projects, which had never accomplished anything in the company. He emphasised that a solution to the company's problems had become more urgent because for the first time the company had a deficit. Director A joined him. He also looked back. He said that from its start-up the company had been dominated by an entrepreneurial spirit, which had gradually disappeared from the company. The purpose of the project was to create new norms, standards and routines in the company. He emphasised that the company had a strong management group (notes from meeting). The targets of the project were then presented.

> **The company wishes to work with organisational learning in regard to developing self-governing groups, delegation of responsibility and visible management. The work should be anchored in a management group with strategic responsibility. (contract for the company project)**

After that, the primary consultant presented the consultants' involvement in the project. He introduced the consultants' conceptions of their tasks. According to the consultants, their primary tasks were to visualise learning needs, to establish and evaluate consequences of intervention strategies and processes and to contribute in implementing desired changes (overhead presentation by the primary consultant, 16 March 2001). Then the secondary consultant presented some ideas about the project participants' role in the project. She used four concepts: *relation, construction,* the *psychodynamic* and the influence of the *unconscious* on human behaviour (notes from meeting). She described the role of the consultants as being on the edge of the system and as focused on the process. As such the consultants positioned themselves as process consultants.

The following point on the agenda was called 'Learning as a concept in the company'. It was a dialogue between all parties, which resulted in a number of proposals of what the company's problems were. It was a brainstorming session, which resulted in a number of arguments. This included issues such as:

- middle managers need to take more responsibility
- the need to listen to signals from the environment
- the need for better structures and systems
- the need for heightened motivation and a strong culture
- the need to make better decisions about products.

After this brainstorming session, the consultants presented the results of a questionnaire that all participants had completed prior to the meeting. This questionnaire was called a reflection instrument consisting of concepts that said a lot about the consultants' perceptions of what constituted a good organisation. This is an ideal organisation characterised by clear goals, clear action plans, clear communication, cohesive team structure, a high degree of openness and trust, clear perceptions of demands from the environment and demands in relation to implementation of new technology, consciousness about own competencies, systematic reflection, documentation etc. Apparently the ideal organisation has a logically systematic structure and is perfectly consistent from top to bottom! The schema was used to visualise and clarify problems in the organisation. It was part of *designed dialogues* where an attempt was made to visualise and clarify what the company's problems were on a deeper organisational level.

In designing these dialogues the consultants used what they referred to as a psychodynamic approach to OL. It provided them with a perspective from which they perceived problems and solutions. It underpinned the ways in which the consultants defined their own roles and engagement in the project. And it was an important reference point for considering the next moves in the project. In short, the psychodynamic approach gave the consultants a sense of meaning and direction. But the consultants were not alone in shaping the situation and the project. We will see how the consultants soon had to fight for their position in the project. The most interesting and dramatic situation at the first seminar was what happened towards the end of the seminar.

The discussion here centred on how to initiate the project. Several problems were revealed. The most interesting problem in this context was centred on the absence of clear goals in the organisation. In short the managers simply did not know what to do. It was therefore suggested that a strategy plan was drawn up for the company. It is interesting because the project was already put in jeopardy at this point. Therefore the primary consultant actually asked for clarification about what this meant for the project. As such the project and the consultants were already in a process of becoming marginalised. Two people were very active here. The first was the sales manager, who suggested that the two directors should formulate a strategy plan. The second was the operations manager who proposed two things: that the participants should bring with them three strategic points to the next meeting where the strategy plan would also be presented; and that the consultants should participate in that meeting but with a less significant role. It was an indication of what future roles and positions the consultants would later obtain in the project.

This became evident in the second meeting in the project where the strategy plan was presented. The consultants tried to organise the meeting by means of the concepts *relation* and *construction*. But these concepts only had a minor role. The most interesting aspect of this meeting was that the sales manager and the operations manager attacked the proposed strategy plan and established a different agenda for both the meeting and for the project. This happened quite early in the meeting. The problem with the strategy plan was that it was only a description of targets of turnover, main markets and market shares. The reactions towards these plans were very violent. The sales manager said that he wanted management – not numbers. He suggested that the strategy plan should be a lot more visionary with a description of 'how'. He said openly that he was really disappointed with the strategy plan.

After that there was quiet for a few moments before the operations manager called for a time-out. He said that he, as a new man in the company, maybe could see things from a different angle. He perceived the strategy plan as a tool that should define strategic goals. He found that the strategy plan mixed a lot of things. People had to distinguish between *what* they want with the company and *how* to get there. He used the distinctions strategic level, tactical level and operational level to emphasise that there was a difference. He reminded participants that he had asked them at the first meeting to bring with them three visions, which described what they wanted for the company. Therefore, the company needed a new plan that distinguished between what the goal of the company was and how to get there (notes from the meeting in March 2001).

So the situation was quite dramatic. The strategy plan proposed by manager A and manager B was rather unceremoniously floored. The atmosphere was tense for a few moments. However, the situation was relieved by manager A when he said that he found the operations manager's ideas very exciting and that his own draft was no match against that. This opened up a completely different dialogue. A new direction was created that apparently was accepted by the two managers. The meeting now developed into a brainstorm about visions and actions. By the end of the meeting, a number of visions and actions had been identified.

The meeting ended with a decision that another meeting needed to be held in order to finish writing down the visions. This should be done in collaboration between the operations manager and the sales manager. The project had taken another direction. But it turned out to be for a short period of time. After a couple of more meetings, the project was about something else. After a couple of months, the project broke down and was restructured with new participants and new goals. But the project never really became a powerful activity in the organisation. Further, the consultants were given a more peripheral role in the project; they couldn't control events, and their concepts and methods were not used at the two meetings. They had a role through their presence but it was a role defined by organisational interests and relations and it was not consistent with what they originally had in mind.

Their concepts and methods could not really find a substantive place in the project. They had been marginalised in the process and the project was no longer run according to their professional values. Instead it was the internal relations among the key organisational actors that controlled the content and structure of the project. After these events the project ran for a couple of months before it broke down completely.

We use this little story to identify our approach to OL, namely that OL is designed dialogues. Basically the story contains the events of two learning situations designed with the purpose of improving the way the organisation works through improving participants' learning. There are a number of actors involved, who have different positions in the company. And the project is situated in specific historical and geographical circumstances. There are two consultants, who try to organise the learning situations. The concepts and methods have their background in a specific approach to OL called the psycho-dynamic approach. The consultants legitimise their way of organising the learning situations with reference to this approach. So the multiplicity of the forces influencing and giving life to these situations are narratives and stories of people involved, their experiences and competencies as leaders, managers and consultants, the relationship between these actors, the company's history, the economic situation, age, gender etc. It is an example of an OL project that eventually failed despite there being openings in the second meeting that something new actually could happen – not because of the consultants' tools and methods but rather because some people, the operations manager and sales manager, tried to use the occasion for something else – according to their interests and intentions.

The case shows the multiplicity of forces inherent in learning situations and shows that these situations have a history and are situated in complex organisational circumstances. As noted by Jørgensen and Rasmussen (2005: 25) there are three different dimensions that are important in analysing learning in organisations:

- the dynamics within learning situations;
- the dynamics between learning situations;
- the dynamics between the organisation and learning situations.

Learning situations in organisations are thus social situations located in specific historical and geographical situations and evolve in a dynamic interplay between many different actors. We define OL as *designing dialogues* with the purpose of facilitating learning in such a way that improves the way organisations work. As such these dialogues should be constructed with reference to learning and improvement of the organisation to qualify as an OL project. Admittedly the definition is vague but we do not know how else to draw a borderline between what is and what is not OL. Further, the important idea here is non-essentialism. It follows that the interesting question is not really a question of definition; that is a 'what is' question. But rather how do these theories, concepts and methods work in relation to concrete organisational practices (Clegg, 1975; Silverman and Jones, 1976; Henriksen et al., 2004; Jørgensen, 2007). It follows that the learning that emerges from learning situations can go in many different directions. It can be more or less incremental or radical, it can be more or less legitimate or controversial etc.

This idea of designed dialogues derives from a *discursive position* where language becomes the centre of our attention. As such organisations are seen as emerging on the grounds of a continuous and complex game of interactions, intentions, interests, and circumstances (Jørgensen, 2007). Language is a distinctive feature of human activities (Gherardi and Nicolini, 2001: 50). Language games denote both the language and the actions into which language is woven (Wittgenstein, 1983: § 7).

This means that the concept also comprises 'tacit' ways of organising, where actors do not need to use words to co-ordinate and understand each other. Mimes, gestures, body language and actions are included in language games and as part of organising efforts. The ability to be an actor in an organisation is thus a question of the ability to participate in particular life forms and cultures (Wittgenstein, 1983: § 23). To participate requires much more than just speaking a language in a literal sense. To participate in organisations is to be able to use language to accomplish particular things along with other actors (Wittgenstein, 1983: §§ 10–14).

As noted in Chapter 11, language is inevitable if we wish to understand learning in organisations because language is the medium for the construction of experience. Thereby experience is in an ontological sense inter-subjective and dialogical. Multiple stories unfold and deconstruct spontaneously and responsively through the speaking of language. It is through language that we construct a sense of continuous self (narrative) and it is through language that these narratives and practices are shaken and disturbed and create new possibilities for learning. This happens through the simultaneous centripetal and centrifugal forces that according to Bakhtin intersect in any utterance (Bakhtin, 1981: 271–272). The potential for learning thus comes from the idea of human plurality as the basic condition of speech and action (Arendt, 1998: 175).

We were playing language games in the case of the OL project in the manufacturing company. Through our language, each of us inserted ourselves through our words and actions at the two seminars. We were actors in this world. We were actors in this world according to our experiences, training, education whereby we come to look at organisations, problems, solutions etc. in particular ways. The consultants acted according to their psycho-dynamic discourse and consulting experience in general. The directors and the managers participated through their experience, education and training, and I was also involved on the basis of my experience, education and training when I documented and evaluated the project. So the OL project was one example that the stories that follow from OL discourse are co-created and co-constructed, that they unfold dialogically and spontaneously in relationship with many different forces.

Designing dialogues with the purpose of improving organisational practices or language games are thus our basic understanding of OL. We believe that it opens up new ways of perceiving and working with OL and HRD. One of the implications is that academics, leaders and consultants etc. that work with OL and HRD may gain a more reflexive stance towards their own ways of thinking by more aware of the historical and contextual boundedness of their thinking and by exploring the multiple meaning of words (Cunliffe, 2002, 2003; Cunliffe and Jun, 2005). This follows from the idea that we are not in charge of language. It is the other way around (Michelfelder and Palmer, 1989: 2): 'Language is a social, not a private, fact' (Gherardi and Nicolini, 2001: 50). It means that the traditional binary separating monologue and dialogue is misleading because 'the term "monologue" cannot refer to the language of one person alone, for such a language would fail to communicate' (Gergen et al., 2004: 43). There is no such thing as a private language, because if it is private it cannot be used – and as such it doesn't constitute language. 'Thus monologue is better understood as an extended (or dominating) entry of a single voice into a dialogue; in this sense monologue is unevenly distributed dialogue' (Gergen et al., 2004: 43). As such, experience is always socially constructed and created in communication with people.

Further, what characterises language? According to Wittgenstein, language is characterised by being unfinished and unresolved. Language always develops and is therefore fundamentally incomplete. Language is like an ancient city: 'a maze of little streets and squares, of old and new houses, and of houses with additions from various periods; and this surrounded by a multitude of new boroughs with straight regular streets and uniform houses' (Wittgenstein, 1983: § 18). This relates to the fact that the meaning of words cannot be determined once and for all; they acquire their meaning through how they are used. And how many kinds of uses are there? There are countless different uses. And this multiplicity is not something that is given once and for all: 'new types of language, new language-games, as we may say, come into existence, and others become obsolete and get forgotten' (Wittgenstein, 1983: § 23).

Language acquires its meaning through relations and interactions with other people, symbols and artefacts in specific historical circumstances. It is always in a state of *becoming*: '[the] focus of our inquiries will become the spontaneously expressed, living, responsive, relational activities occurring out in the world between us for all to see' (Shotter, 2005: 114). In short, language and therefore organisations are fundamentally *open, polyphonic, equivocal, dialogical, unfinished* and it is fundamentally *unresolved*. This means that the development of organisations may go in many different directions. Further, since language is in charge of the human body and mind, human existence is also fragmented, heterogeneous and shaped dialogically; it may move in many different directions; it is fragmented and polyphonic and is basically an unfinished and unresolved project shaped and reshaped by past, present and future relations whereby interpretations of pasts, presents and futures are continuously reinterpreted and modified.

OL discourse

Designing dialogues with the purpose of improving the way organisations work is what OL is all about. These dialogues are designed with reference to the discourse of OL. From this point of view it is a fundamental misunderstanding to search for clarification and agreement of what OL is in terms of agreed concepts, methods and tools. As noted by Lee, this also characterises HRD as a discipline (Lee, 2001). Monica Lee thereby supports the claim here, that the problem posed by a number of other HRD scholars on lack of agreement and clarification (e.g. McGuire and Cseh, 2006) is no real problem at all. Viewed from a language game perspective the problem is not lack of agreement and clarification. Instead the problem is how we frame the problem in the first instance. Wittgenstein argues that it lies deeply in us to try to discover the essence of things – of OL for example. But the meaning of OL is not some secret essence waiting to be discovered but simply the way OL works in actual practice. In this case the meaning of OL is the way the theories, concepts and methods of OL discourse work in actual practice.

While the meaning of OL emerges in interplay between discourse and practice, the discourse of OL is itself a collection of practices. In other words the discourse of OL consists of sets of language games. These language games do not share some common characteristic that waits to be discovered. The reason why we include some theories, concepts and methods under the heading OL is because of what Wittgenstein calls *family resemblance* (1983: §§ 65–67), different languages look like and are related to each other just like sisters and brothers look alike and are related to each other but none the less are still very different from each other. In other words the theories, concepts and methods are related to each other in many different ways; for example sharing of language, sharing of interests, sharing of intentions, while they differ in other respects.

As such the discourse of OL should be viewed as socially constructed truth (Astley, 1985). This means that the discourse is characterised by continuous differentiation, development, destruction and reconstruction of concepts and methods. Theories are human constructs (O'Donnell, 2004; Jørgensen, 2006), manifested in linguistic practices produced by scientific communities. As such they cannot be separated from life, changing life forms, ways of being and various fields of inquiry (Pritchard et al., 2004). Therefore the discourse of OL consists of many different theories, concepts and methods. The purpose of a discussion of OL here is then not to try to identify the best way of doing OL. Instead it is to get to know OL. To get to know OL is to get to know the language of OL including the intentions, presumptions and ways of approaching OL, which are embedded in this language.

In the following section, I will introduce some important theoretical perspectives and paradigms within the field of OL. This includes two perspectives: (1) *the systems approach to OL* (Argyris and Schön, 1996), and (2) *situated learning and communities of practice* (Lave and Wenger, 1991; Wenger, 1998). These approaches, however, constitute only a fraction of the whole discourse of OL, which embraces a great number of different perspectives and theoreticians. Gherardi and Nicolini for example identify eleven different narratives of OL organised under five different sociological traditions (see Table 9.1).

Table 9.1 Narratives of OL according to five different sociological traditions

Sociological tradition	Narratives of organisational learning
The tradition of conflict	OL as the ideology of particular power groups OL as a policy of mobilising resources of power and conflict OL as an attempt to manage the tension between substantial and formal rationality
The rational-utilitarian tradition	OL as problem-driven search OL as the activation of an exchange network OL as an ecology of learning
The Durkheimian tradition	OL as a dependent variable OL as socialisation to a specific cultural codes
The microinteractionist tradition	OL as the transmission of knowledge within occupational communities OL as a label producing and produced by socially constructed reality
The postmodern tradition	OL as a discursive practice

I have chosen the two perspectives because they represent dominant ways of thinking about OL but also because they are based on different philosophical and sociological perspectives. However, the overall approach to OL adopted in this chapter is located within the postmodern tradition, where OL is seen as a discursive practice or as a language game. As such the systems approach and the CoP-approach constitute very different OL discourses that work through how OL consultants, OL academics, leaders, managers and HR people design learning situations. The idea that the meaning of these discourses depends on how they work in an interplay with other people opens up a critical discussion of how OL discourses are used as instruments in power struggles; that is it opens up questions of: who is speaking through OL?; who are subjected to OL?; what are the power/knowledge networks and structures embedded and embodied in OL discourse?; and who are marginalised by OL discourse? These are much needed critical questions and constitute an approach, which is inevitable in terms of developing any academic discourse like OL, HRD or intellectual capital for example (e.g. Jørgensen, 2006) because it creates this reflexive stance towards the discourse's ways of talking, acting and perceiving itself.

The postmodern approach thus operates with a more complex notion of power that is never located in one place but is located in a network of alliances, which is different from the simpler Marxist way of approaching power found in the tradition of conflict. The tradition of conflict directs attention 'to the structure of dominant and subordinate interest groups, to social conflict and to power systems. Its principal thesis is that society is based on conflict and that, in the absence of conflict, a process of domination prevails' (Gherardi and Nicolini, 2001: 36). The conflict is in other words perceived as the essence of society from which we cannot escape. The rational-utilitarian tradition is similar to the tradition in that it seeks to explain society; but it seeks to explain it 'in terms of people's rational motivations and the manner in which they rationally perform exchanges so that everything functions in the best possible way' (Gherardi and Nicolini, 2001: 38). Focus is directed towards the interaction and interdependence between markets and the behaviour of firms, where the organisation typically is treated as if it was an individual decision-maker (Cook and Yanow, 1993). In this way, we don't find it that relevant because we speak of HRD.

We will now describe the two approaches mentioned before. We will start out with a review of Argyris and Argyris and Schön's systemic approach to OL. This will be followed by a review of the communities-of-practice (CoP) approach to OL.

Review of Argyris and Argyris and Schön's systemic approach to OL

The systemic approach to OL represents a *technical understanding* of OL (Easterby-Smith and Araujo, 1999: 3). It is characterised by considering learning as one of the functions of the organisational system and draws on the theory of cybernetics (Gherardi and Nicolini, 2001: 40). One of the most well known authors within this tradition is Chris Argyris and his idea that learning is *correction of errors*. Argyris has in many books and articles developed this tradition within OL (Argyris, 1990, 1999; Argyris and Schön 1996). The basic idea is that learning is to correct errors. An error is a mismatch between an intention and the consequences of action (Argyris, 1999: xiii). Argyris' learning theory is thus based on a technical conception of feedback on the connections between intentions, actions and consequences. A mismatch will lead to an inquiry into these connections with the purpose of correcting the error.

The correction of error(s) may result in three different kinds of OL: *single-loop learning*, *double-loop learning* and *deutero-learning*. What characterises the theory is that it does not question technical rationality as the overall ideal. Therefore, interests, values and feeling are considered as irrational elements that lead to sub-optimisation and narrow-minded behaviour. They constitute typical organisational defenses (Argyris, 1990) that hamper rational and correct behaviour in organisations. Argyris' and Argyris and Schön's approach is designed to overcome such defences and correct the errors. As a consequence politics and interests are irrational elements that must be eliminated before learning can take place (Easterby-Smith and Araujo, 1999: 5). The basic distinction is thus between rational and irrational behaviour. Behind the theory is an assumption that there is one best way of correct behaviour for individuals and organisations. Much of the literature which relies on this understanding of OL is thus about overcoming organisational defences. Argyris call these *model I theories-in-use*. In order to create more effective learning, the change agent will introduce model II theories-in-use (Argyris, 1999: 56–57) with the intention of transforming the participants' espoused theories or values to action (theories-in-use; Argyris, 1999: 60).

Now we will turn to describe in more detail the important concepts of Argyris and Argyris and Schön's OL framework. As noted the correction of errors may result in three different ways of learning: single-loop learning, double-loop learning and deutero-learning. *Single-loop learning* is 'instrumental learning that changes strategies of action or assumptions underlying strategies in ways that leave the values of a theory of action unchanged' (Argyris and Schön, 1996: 20). Single-loop learning is correction of errors that take place in the organisation's normal way of performing. To take some examples, we can say that an organisation has systems that monitor the performance of the organisation. This includes information systems, budget systems, accounting systems, quality systems, production systems. These allow the participants to intervene in the organisation if it doesn't perform the way it was supposed to, thus correcting and modifying organisational behaviour without questioning the values upon which this behaviour is founded. For that reason, single-loop learning is not controversial but rather a normal case in organisations.

Double-loop learning is 'learning that results in a change in the values of theory-in-use, as well as in its strategies and assumptions' (Argyris and Schön, 1996: 21). Double-loop learning is thus a more profound way of learning. It may occur when single-loop correction of errors doesn't prevent the organisational error from reappearing again and again. In such situations learning of a more profound kind is needed. As such we may need a new approach to a problem and its solution. That is we change our values of our theories-in-use and gain a new perspective on the problematic situation. Since it is learning of a more profound type, double-loop learning is often controversial, very difficult and painful for the organisation's participants.

Both single-loop and double-loop learning rely on the process called *organisational inquiry* (Argyris and Schön, 1996: 11) triggered by the mismatch between expected results of action and the results actually achieved. Organisational inquiry takes place when individuals function as agents of an organisation according to its prevailing roles and rules. The distinction between individual and organisation is important for Argyris and Schön because it implies that we can begin to clarify what it means for organisations to learn. In fact the introductory chapter where they introduce their learning framework is called *What Is An Organisation That It May Learn?* In order for a group of people to be called an organisation, it must meet three conditions. It must:

- devise agreed-upon procedures for making decisions in the name of the collectivity;

- delegate to individuals the authority to act for the collectivity; and

- set boundaries between the collectivity and the rest of the world (Argyris and Schön, 1996: 8).

It is against this background that we can distinguish between organisational inquiry and individual inquiry. Organisational inquiry may result in OL when it yields a change in the design of the organisational practices (Argyris and Schön, 1996: 12). These practices include the environments for knowledge embraced by the organisations: the knowledge held by the individual members of the organisation but also in the organisation's files, policies, maps and physical objects. Further they include the embodiment of strategies for performing complex tasks. Organisational inquiry may lead to single-loop or double-loop learning but it may also result in a third form of learning, which is described as deutero-learning. This is 'learning how to learn' (Argyris and Schön, 1996: 29), which is described as a shift in the learning system of the organisation: 'An organisation's learning systems is made out of the structures that channel organisational inquiry and the behavioural world of the organisation, draped over these structures, that facilitates or inhibits organisational inquiry' (Argyris and Schön, 1996: 28). The structures of the learning system include channels of communication, information systems, the spatial environment, procedures and routines and systems of incentives. The behavioural world includes 'qualities, meaning and feelings that habitually condition patterns of interaction among individuals within the organisation in such a way as to affect organisational inquiry' (Argyris and Schön, 1996: 29). Together, the structural and behavioural features create the conditions for organisational inquiry, and they make it more or less likely that issues, dilemmas or sensitive assumptions will be addressed or avoided by the organisation. The OL system is thus a crucial condition for the type of inquiry that may take place in an organisation.

Argyris and Argyris and Schön thus provide a comprehensive model of OL, which has been widely used. Distinctions between single-loop, double-loop and deutero-learning have become world-famous through the work of Argyris and Schön. In relation to HRD the model is strictly a model for organisational development in the sense that individual learning is seen in relation to an organisational system. The systems approach is in other words about the development of organisations where the individual is seen strictly as a resource for achieving goals (Garavan et al., 2004) where there is little room for speaking about the expansion of individual skills and capabilities. The individual is part of the OL system; she has a role to play and has to obey the rules of the organisation. As such Argyris' and Argyris and Schön's framework reproduces a traditional tension in the OL literature, which has been conceptualised by using the metaphor of the *oxymoron* (Weick and Westley, 1996).

Accordingly OL is a concept that contradicts itself because learning is about the creation of difference while organising is about the creation of standards. In any case the relationship between the individual and the organisational level is a fundamental weakness in the model. The description of the relationship between the individual and organisation in the framework is very simple and it bypasses complex issues of identity, culture and relations of power that are very much part of this relationship and eventually will jeopardise how the framework may be used in practice. In practice the framework is often used to design learning situations in organisations which are outside of everyday organisational practice, and where change agents intervene in the processes in order to facilitate different kinds of inquiries into the organisation.

One example of an application of some of Argyris and Schön's ideas is the famous *Learning Organisation* (Senge, 1990). The learning organisation is first of all a management concept and is founded in systems theory. Its reference point is the modern hierarchical bureaucracy with a functional division of labour. This organisation leads to sub-optimisation and that people do not identify with the whole organisation. Instead the organisation becomes fragmented. The learning organisation is proposed as a solution to these problems by promoting systems thinking. The learning organisation consists of five disciplines:

- Personal mastery
- Mental models
- Shared vision
- Team learning
- Systems thinking

The fifth discipline is systems thinking. This is the most important discipline, and the new discipline, because it integrates the four other disciplines (Senge, 1990: 12–13). Senge is heavily inspired by Argyris and Schön. In the elaborations of the disciplines mental models and team learning, Senge draws explicitly on Argyris and Schön. But the simple concept of systems thinking advocated by Senge also bears some resemblance to the idea of overcoming organisational defenses by which individuals may gain a common shared organisational and strategic perspective thereby putting aside their own irrational and narrow-minded perspective of the world. In this way the systems approach is simple. However, this should not lead us to underestimate the power of actually organising inquiries in organisations thereby creating the conditions for learning in the organisation.

In summary, Argyris and Schön's ideas about OL have been very influential in working with organisational development. It has provided a lot of insights in how to construct and work with OL in practice. In relation to HRD however, the agenda of Argyris and Schön's work is somewhat narrow in focusing strictly on organisational development, not individual development, nor societal development. This does not mean that Argyris and Schön's model of learning does not imply learning at the individual level. But this learning is measured according to the adaptation of individuals' knowledge and skills to the organisational system of skills and competencies. Learning as a correction of error implies in other words an adaptation to the organisation's learning system. Learning implies that the individual aligns herself to the norms, standards and routines of the organisation. In the same way, organisations are treated as if they were individuals, in the sense that organisations learn when they adapt to the organisation's environment. The systemic approach relies in other words on biological metaphors where the individuals and organisations are seen as organic systems that are part of ecological systems (see also Morgan, 1986). This implies also that the systemic model of OL relies on a fairly narrow-minded world-view where there is no real discussion of for example of whose norms, standards or routines. The presumption seems to be that these can be objectively and unambiguously defined. Organisational double-loop learning is seen as a change in the values behind action.

To be effective, this kind of learning should lead to deutero-learning, where the learning becomes embedded in the norms, standards and routines of the organisation. In this way the systemic model reproduces a traditional view of organisations as stable systems disrupted by dynamic periods whereby organisations move from disequilibrium (error) to a new equilibrium (adaptation). In other words, the learning model is *reactive*.

On a more practical level, the model of learning is a cognitive model, where learning implies changing the mental models of the organisation members. The tools for learning are thus learning situations where organisation members are given time and space for reconsidering their speech and actions with the purpose of realigning their speech and actions with the OL systems or both realigning speech and actions and the OL at one and the same time. These learning spaces are typically organised outside of the everyday realm of speech and actions and the facilitator, typically a leader or a consultant, acts as a process consultant, who intervenes in the process with the purpose of moving the members from model I – theories in use to model II – theories in use. This way of organising learning situations reveals their rational basis, but it is also a rather narrow way of organising learning because it does not imply working with the everyday settings from which speech and actions emerge.

Having discussed Argyris and Schön's systemic approach to OL, we will now present the CoP approach to OL, which has a very different philosophical and sociological tradition.

Communities-of-practice and HRD

Communities-of-practice (CoP) is based on social learning theory. The focus is on how people construct meaning when they interact in working life with each other, with technologies and with tasks (Easterby-Smith and Araujo, 1999: 4). The basic starting point is in other words that learning emerges from social interactions. This understanding is inspired from anthropologists like Geertz for example (Geertz, 1973), who view knowledge (interpretations, perspectives, values and feelings) as embedded in the way in which people communicate. Therefore knowledge is not something that is private. Rather it is public in the sense that people use publicly accessible symbolic tools (myths, concepts, stories, narratives, rituals, traditions, procedures) for communicating, collaborating and interacting with others.

Cook and Yanow's study of how OL is linked to organisational culture (Cook and Yanow, 1993) is one example. They argue that no matter if OL takes place in relation to playing basketball for the Boston Celtics or in relation to flute production (Cook and Yanow, 1993: 437–439, 443–448), it always goes in interaction with other people, technologies and circumstances. The media for acquiring, sustaining and changing meaning are the symbols that people use in order to communicate. Another important example of social learning theory is situated learning (Lave and Wenger, 1991) and communities-of-practice (Brown and Duguid, 1996, 2001; Wenger, 1998).

Wenger offers a comprehensive theory of social learning. Learning is seen as situated in a concrete historical context, where participants are offered learning possibilities from the social community. Learning is seen as embedded in the active negotiation of meaning that takes place among participants in relation to tools, systems, procedures, techniques, concepts, ways of talking and doing things, stories, narratives etc. These symbolic tools are called reifications that along with modes of participation constitute the memory of the community (Wenger, 1998: 52–63).

Learning emerges in the relations between participation and reification and is linked to all aspects of social life captured in the four basic concepts of the CoP-model: *meaning, practice, community* and *identity* (Wenger, 1998: 5). Reality is seen as socially constructed and the basic distinction is not between rational or irrational behaviour but of understanding or misunderstanding of the social rules in the community. Wenger's theory provides a broad framework for intelligent action. He, however, does not provide any methods and techniques for OL. He offers a language or conceptual framework, which may be used to talk about learning, and which may be used to describe, analyse, understand and assess the attempts to create learning in organisations. In the opening chapter of *CoP*, Wenger states the purpose as follows:

> **Yet in our experience, learning is an integral part of our everyday lives. It is part of our participation in our communities and organisations. The problem is not that we do not know this, but rather that we do not have very systematic ways of talking about this familiar experience. Even though the topic of this book covers mostly things that everybody knows in some ways, having a systematic vocabulary to talk about it does make a difference. An adequate vocabulary is important because the concepts we use to make sense of the world direct both our perception and our actions. We pay attention to what we expect to see, we hear what we can place in our understanding, and we act according to our world views. (Wenger, 1998: 8)**

The strength of Wenger's contribution is clearly this language on learning, which is linked to the organisation's and the participants' social life. This language provides the opportunity to talk about the organisation's culture, the identities of the participants and its relations of power. CoP has made a significant contribution to HRD in understanding the interplay between HRD concepts, methods and tools and the specific culture in which these are applied. McGuire and colleagues for example argue that 'there is a critical lack of theoretical rigor and research related to the impact of cultural issues in the field of HRD' (McGuire et al., 2002: 25). They argue that culture is a highly complex, intangible and elusive concept (McGuire et al., 2002: 25, 36). We would suggest however, that HRD concepts and methods can be applied in a range of very different cultures. What matters is *how* HRD is practised. For that we need a language in order to understand practice and to work intelligently with practice. CoP contributes to HRD research and practice by offering a conceptual framework for understanding community and culture. Thereby it creates a foundation for more intelligent HRD practice. HRD is a set of language games that comprise concepts, methods and techniques for developing human resources on different dimensions of practice; i.e. individual, organisational and community. We need however an understanding of the cultures, traditions and conventions in which they are applied, to create a more reasonable HRD practice, which is concerned and adapted to the matters of the world.

The problem is however that CoP is a general learning theory offering many points of entry for researchers, academics and practitioners. We have only a broad framework for understanding learning in organisations at our disposal, and further we are given no concrete guidelines for designing dialogues in organisations. As such, the CoP approach has been subjected to a considerable critique. For example, Storberg-Walker criticises the multiple works on CoP for not developing an applied theory of CoP that researchers can test, apply and adapt (Storberg-Walker, 2008). We would rather put it differently because we feel that this critique is framed from a different understanding of what theory is, than social learning theory. From our viewpoint we feel that the problem in CoP is a lack of normative guidelines for designing learning in organisations. CoP as well as social learning theory in general allows you to describe, analyse and understand learning but it doesn't provide a lot in terms of how we can critically evaluate learning and the conceptions of truth and justice on which learning and change in organisations rest. These conceptions of truth and justice are embedded in the norms, standards and routines in the organisations and are thus tacitly accepted by the CoP approach as the right governors of what is appropriate talk and action (e.g. Jørgensen, 2007: 39–41).

The very broad framework also means that it is quite difficult to get a good grasp of things. There are lots of concepts that are connected to each other and link with each other to a considerable degree. As such CoP may also be used in relation to many different problems. Ardichvili (2008) discusses CoP as an approach in which we can talk about knowledge sharing in a different way from the traditional knowledge management way (Nonaka and Takeuchi, 1995; Ray and Clegg, 2005) of knowledge sharing. He identifies motivators and barriers for the continuous constitution and reconstitution of virtual CoPs that stem from 'interactions among community members, community members and members of the larger institutional environment and community members and numerous tools that constitute the community's "repertoire"' (Ardichvili, 2008: 549). From a CoP perspective, knowledge sharing would imply continuous mutual engagements, the establishment of a joint enterprise, where members align their talk and actions and the development of a shared repertoire through which members can communicate with each other.

Jørgensen and Keller (2008) choose identity as their entry point to CoP and thus to OL and HRD. They suggest that learning and HRD is about negotiating identities in organisations and communities. They suggest that this idea has a development potential that dissolves the dualism between the individual and organisational level currently present in the HRD literature. The implications are that we may create a new framework for understanding HRD where the focus is on the mutual development of the individual and the organisation. According to CoP, identity is closely linked to practice; in fact these are two sides of the same coin (Brown and Duguid, 2001). Jørgensen and Keller argue that this means that learning, development and identification is closely linked to cultures and communities. Identity implies an interest in the identification processes of individuals within social networks. When individuals participate in negotiation of meaning, they also negotiate their identities. These identification processes make negotiation processes meaningful to them.

As such focus is not strictly on the individual level at the expense of the organisational level. One tension in the HRD literature between the individual and organisational level is addressed here (Garavan et al., 2004). Garavan and his colleagues argue that approached from an individual level perspective HRD is concerned with the expansion of individual skills and capabilities, while HRD approached from an organisational level perspective is about the development of organisations, which implies that the individual is perceived as a resource for achieving goals (Garavan et al., 2004: 419–421). Weick and Westley (1996) have used the metaphor of the *oxymoron* to describe a similar tension in the OL literature. OL contradicts itself because learning is about the creation of difference, while organising is about the creation of standards. Jørgensen and Keller argue that identity is one way of overcoming these tensions in that identity dissolves the distinction between the two levels. Working with identity is to work with the individual and the collective at one and the same time; they constitute each other. It does not make much sense to talk about individual identities because individuals identify themselves by means of something and with something out there – in the collective or in the culture. Individuals use socially produced and accessible symbols and resources to construct their identities (Geertz, 1973; Bruner, 1996). These publicly accessible symbols are considered as *identity capital* (Pullen, 2005). When people use these resources they construct the culture but they also construct themselves.

This relationship between the individual and the social is one of the basic ideas of social learning theory; namely that individuals learn by gaining access to culturally specific forms of *participation* (living in the world, membership, acting, interacting, mutuality etc.) and *reification* (forms, points of focus, documents, monuments, instruments, projection etc.) (Wenger, 1998: 55–63). Learning is learning to participate according to the norms, traditions and conventions of this culture. Learning is moving from being a legitimate peripheral participator (Lave and Wenger, 1991) to becoming a member of a community, group or organisation. The individual practices, however, within this community are different. Individuals have different positions and they contribute differently to the community. In this way the individual and the social are mutually constitutive. Learning is always dependent on individuals, who talk and act but it cannot be accomplished without the cultural toolbox embedded in forms of participation and reification and without which it would be impossible – or at least meaningless – to talk and act.

Identity is important here. Identity is the individual's construction of a trajectory that connects past, present and future. Identification is to give temporal significance to the activities within which people are engaged:

a community of practice is a field of possible trajectories and thus the proposal of an identity. It is a history of possible pasts and of possible futures, which are all there for participants, not only to witness, hear about, and contemplate, but to engage with. (Wenger, 1998: 156)

By the process of engagement, learners gain access to practice and thus to possible pasts, and possible futures. To engage with CoP is thus to gain insight into learning histories that interpret the past and point in different directions in the future. This is what Wenger calls a trajectory. This construction of trajectory depends on access to forms of participation and reifications that may organise and (re)direct individuals' experiences. Learning and development in other words are the results of interactions between individuals' experience and practice. Imagination is an important dimension in identity construction and it can make a major difference for our experience of identity and potential learning inherent in our activities.

But as noted, there are also weaknesses in Wenger's notion of identity. For example, even if Wenger introduces the idea that identity is temporal (Wenger, 1998: 154), he doesn't offer a very convincing account of how to work with this temporality. This is because, Wenger relies solely on CoP – and thus the informal learning processes that take place through participation in practice – in creating learning. He relies in other words on culture for the creation of learning. There are no normative guidelines for critically evaluating CoP. We believe that this reveals that Wenger is quite uncritical about relations of power inherent in the ways communities work and CoP is for that reason not really concerned with the education and learning of the individual. Wenger works with a notion of power, but this is not a very critical notion of power. Despite obvious similarities in terms of emphasising actors (participation) and language (shared repertoires), this makes Wenger's approach distinct from the postmodern approach and other critical approaches to OL. Instead, Wenger legitimises relations of power.

To summarise, CoP has made a significant contribution in understanding the interplay between HRD and culture and thus for understanding complex issues of knowledge sharing, collaboration, and identity in other ways than usually seen in the literature. There are however no concrete normative guidelines for working with learning in practice. Wenger and social learning theory only provide us with very broad categories which may be used for understanding but not really for critical evaluation. In terms of critically evaluating Wenger's approach to HRD and learning, we would say that it is only *pre-reflexive practice* (Gherardi and Nicolini, 2001: 47–51). However, in a world of flexibility, change, innovation etc. we need to explore practice by means of reflection and reflexivity. Many people know how to partici-pate in practice, but they cannot talk sense about this practice. In order to participate intelligently – and not blindly – people need to be able to talk sense of the practices they participate in (Ryle, 1949; Dewey, 1991); that is to be intelligent practitioners (Schön, 1983; see also previous chapter on workplace learning). In terms of creating such learning situations Argyris and Schön's systems approach to learning has a lot more to say about how to design dialogues and for creating different kinds of reflec-tion and reflexivity. Their approach is however quite insensitive to identity, culture and community, which is one of the reasons that systems approaches to OL and HRD often fail. They have no room for actors with irrational feelings and senses, who have their intentions and own interests.

Conclusions

OL has made an important contribution in providing a framework for linking organ-isational development with learning. But there is still no really solid evidence that OL has actually contributed widely to HRD in terms of human betterment, organisa-tional enhancement and societal development. In the case study presented in this chapter, the result was a failure. The same goes for a number of the other companies involved in the same programme. In this project we observed a lot of difficulties in linking OL discourse to the individual and corporate identities and life forms in organisations (e.g. Jørgensen, 2004). Looking back we may conclude that we found out that an organisation is a very complex, fuzzy, equivocal and multidimensional configuration to work with. This makes it hard to work with OL. It makes it even harder when we have to maintain involvement and engagement through a longer period of time. In this respect the focus on the organisational level or dimension is problematic, because in order to be successful we have to make the OL activities into somebody's activities both at the top, middle and bottom of the organisation. We may say that we have to transform the OL project into an individual learning project and here we believe that the theories of workplace learning become relevant again. In any case the focus on the organisational level is a problem in OL literature because at the bottom-line – no matter if we conceive of the individual as governed by cognitive rationality or as a social being – it is the individual that learns, and we have to focus on individuals even if we want them to learn something that is organisationally relevant. Here we have to find ways that balance the actors' intentions with the organisation's intentions and here we find identity fruitful as a way of working with HRD and learning. We will deal with this issue in relation to organisational development in Chapter 10 and especially in Chapter 11.

 Discussion questions

- Discuss how to design dialogues that can facilitate improvement of organisational practices. Take into consideration the three dimensions of learning situations.

- Discuss how language, power and organisational learning relate to each other.

- Discuss the different perspectives on organisational learning presented and discuss their relevance for HRD practitioners in organising organisational learning.

10 Organisational Development and HRD

Lars Bo Henriksen, Dorte Sveistrup and
Hanne T. Andersen

■ ■ **Chapter objectives** ■

The objectives of this chapter are to:

- present the research field of organisation culture;

- describe a case of organisation culture as a means of conceptualising organisational change;

- identify important ways of describing and understanding organisational change and organisation culture;

- discuss organisation culture and human resource development.

Introduction

It is common knowledge that organisations are different and the ways things work in different organisations are not always the same. This insight has led organisation scholars to use the concept of 'organisation culture'. Organisation culture, however, is one of those fuzzy management concepts that have been misused on so many occasions, in management fads, in dubious management training schemes and in less valid management research, that it has almost lost its meaning. Organisation culture seems to be able to mean anything and everything and therefore nothing in a research context. In this chapter we present some perspectives on the workings of the organisation culture concept in the context of a case study of organisational change and human resource development (HRD).

It is said that the consequences of organisational changes such as mergers and acquisitions are first realised by the people involved when names, signs and titles are changed (Cartwright and Cooper, 1992). If so, the difficulties of organisational changes cannot be reduced to a technical or structural matter. It is something much more complicated – something that involves cultures, identities and world-views. The people in TAX (the company on which the case study is based following a merger) knew that. Even if the merger dates back a year the very unpleasant experience of the merger still haunted many and the merger was to some a key reference point from which all new initiatives were evaluated. The management of TAX did not understand that. 'We are through and done with that' said one manager. The employees, on the other hand, had seen numerous initiatives since the merger that changed their work conditions and the way their work was organised and they still blamed the merger for everything.

In this chapter we will take a closer look at organisational changes and human resource development (HRD) from an organisational culture point of view. We will argue that the cultural perspective is capable of analysing some of the problems that organisations like TAX face and also that a cultural perspective provides useful insights to HRD practitioners on how to do something about it.

Organisation culture – background

Organisation culture was not always in fashion. Once management was about mimicking the large American conglomerate; all business was big business, so the story goes, and all other businesses should grow big as soon as possible producing mass products for mass markets (see e.g. Chandler, 1962). Then in the early 1970s, the era of the first oil-crises, people in the west discovered that Japanese manufacturers were rather good at making cars, motorcycles, radios and all other sorts of consumer goods. In fact the Japanese were so good that they out-competed many western companies. The Japanese threat, as it was called, was explained by noting differences in national culture. The Japanese culture was much more suited for industrial production as the Japanese workers were much more inclined to follow rules and orders; consequently, he/she was much more efficient and effective in manufacturing processes. Later it turned out that the Japanese success owed as much to skills in production planning and engineering design as to national culture, but the idea of the importance of cultural differences was introduced and turned out to be a robust and long-lived explanation of almost anything and everything in and around organisations (Morgan, 1986: 111–141; Jaffee, 2001: 165–176).

With the introduction of national culture as an explanatory force, the next step towards organisation culture was not far away. In their search for excellence, Peters and Waterman (1982) found that successful companies possessed certain characteristics that together would become known as organisation culture. These characteristics were presented in buzzwords such as 'A basis for action, close to the customer, autonomy and entrepreneurship, productivity through people, hands-on, value-driven, stick to the knitting, simple form, lean staff, simultaneous loose-tight properties' and so on (Peters and Waterman, 1982). As is readily apparent, most of the buzzwords and underlying ideas emphasised agility, speed and most important, value creation through skilled and able employees. The idea of culture as an important aspect of organisations now entered a wide variety of studies, programmes and books and 'organisation culture' became a household term in any debate related to organisations, HRD and management.

Organisation culture defined

On 24 August 2007, the CEO of Scandinavian airline SAS Mats Jansson, announced in a press release that SAS needed a new organisation culture. Setting aside this rather strange way of addressing SAS employees – through a press release – this shows that by now managers and employees have become so familiar with the concept of organisation culture that it can be used in a press release. It also shows that the CEO has some kind of notion that organisation culture is something that can be changed and that it can be changed for the better. The clear message in the press release was that without a change of organisation culture SAS would not be able to face the challenges of the future.

Organisation culture is often described as a set of social processes, images, symbols and rituals (Morgan, 1986: 123), as shared meanings, beliefs, values and assumptions (Jaffee, 2001: 165) or, in a simpler way, as basic assumptions, espoused values and artefacts (Schein, 1992). Such definitions attempt to get hold of or grasp something that is supposed to be part of or characterise a specific organisation in order to make us wiser about the workings of that organisation. The intention is, in the first place, to give us a better understanding of the organisation. A type of understanding that goes beyond colourful brochures, mission statements and annual reports – the forms of company information that never tell the whole story about an organisation. Therefore, we need information about the people in the organisation; what they think, what they believe in, what expectations they have and so on. If we could find ways of retrieving that kind of richer information, we could also diagnose problems and ultimately find some remedies to solve them. When Mats Jansson wanted to change the organisation culture of SAS he wanted to increase profits and secure the long-term survival of the company and he wanted to do that through changing belief systems, values etc. in the company. This was not about investing in new technologies, launching new marketing campaigns or whatever. It was about making employees think differently. This is no easy task. Attempts to change organisation cultures could be seen negatively as attempts to perform some kind of social engineering where management intervenes in such dangerous areas as employee identities and their world-views. It could also be interpreted positively, as attempts to take employees and their world-views seriously into consideration. That is, an attempt where management actually try to understand the employees and assist them in developing their perceptions of their work – thereby changing the organisation culture. Which interpretation we favour depends on the perspective in question and the actual events of the real change and development programme; it is inherently empirical and contextual.

As with any other approach in the social sciences, organisation culture is divided into several conflicting paradigms, each claiming to be able to describe, analyse and understand the phenomenon. These paradigms possess certain characteristics and consequently make them more or less able to aid our understanding of organisations and organisation culture. This could be the functionalist approaches where culture is seen as one aspect of the organisation (Schulz, 1990; Smircich, 1983). From this perspective, organisation culture resides alongside the organisation's technology, economy, administrative systems, skill base etc. Culture then becomes something that an organisation possesses and organisation culture is something that can be altered in the same way as technology, administrative systems etc. It also makes culture into something measurable in the sense that cultures are either weak or strong or they can be measured as effective or in-effective. This can, in some instances, be helpful in understanding organisation culture, but when it comes to guiding organisational changes, and developments in organisation culture the objectifying element of the functional approaches will often result in them falling short in attempts to alter employees' world-views and guide people in the process. The reifying aspect of the functional approaches makes it unable to fully understand employees – organisation culture is not a thing and cannot be treated as such – the measurements can only, at best, show us something but cannot provide us with the means to *do* something in order to change and develop an organisation culture.

As an alternative to the functional approach symbolic approaches are also available. A symbolic approach will treat organisation culture as a metaphor for the belief systems, world-views, and realities that bind the organisation together. In this sense an organisation *is* a culture, an organisation is not first and foremost an economic unity as in the functionalist approach, but is a social setting like any other social setting – families, clubs, unions – that can be understood through the people involved (Schulz, 1990; Nørreklit, 1983; Henriksen, 1992). Thereby culture is not a thing but a metaphor. The methods used to understand organisation culture from a symbolic approach could be participation, observation and other means to see and understand. But, when it comes to altering organisation culture the symbolic approaches also lack the means of doing so. The symbolic approach has often – rightly – been accused of emphasising consensus and the unifying aspects of organisation culture, having a somewhat romantic conception of organisation culture. The inherent romanticism would consequently neglect key issues related to conflict and power (Jørgensen, 2007).

A narrative/theory of reality approach to organisation culture

In recent years narrative approaches (Boje, 2001; Czarniawska, 2005; Polkinghorne, 1988) and actors approaches (Henriksen et al., 2004; Jørgensen, 2007) have tried to further develop the symbolic approach to organisation culture, so it would become capable of countering the inherent reification of the functionalist approaches and the inherent romanticism of the symbolic approaches. By introducing direct participation and power analysis it is possible to not only describe and understand, but most critically, to aid management and employees in their quest for changes. A narrative approach could take its point of departure in the fact that people in organisations tell stories about their work, about the management, and about themselves. Through these stories it is possible to learn about the organisation and the people in the organisation; about the way they see the world, the way they think and what they expect. With a conceptualising method and a theory of reality (Henriksen et al., 2004) the narratives can be turned into an understanding of the organisation culture; this understanding should aid management and employees in understanding their organisation and thereby enabling them to engage themselves in change projects. The theory of reality (see Figure 10.1 and Table 10.1) takes its point of departure in the idea that every organisation member possesses a world-view, a reality – that is, a certain way of seeing, interpreting and understanding the world in terms of facts, logic, values and communication.

This reality will have an idea of what is in the world – an idea of what would count as facts. The reality will also have expectations for the future, this is a logic that tells people what they can expect to happen if they do this or say that. All members of an organisation will possess values that guide their actions. Values are ideas about what the world should be like – what is right and what is wrong – and values are what makes it possible for the organisational member to act, the values tell them what they

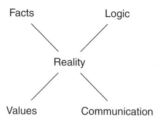

Figure 10.1 Reality as facts, logic, values and communication

Source: Henriksen et al. (2004: 19)

Table 10.1 Theory of reality

Facts are material realities, artefacts, historical facts, what is, what is said, what has been said, what people do and what people have done. Fact is a condition for reality. Actors need facts about the world. Without facts actors would experience only illusions. Facts are, however, not simple and uncomplicated. Facts, and what should be counted as a fact, are not necessarily initially clear to actors. What should count as fact are negotiated with other actors or handed down by tradition.

Logic can be material, formal, social or subjective. Logic cannot exist in an objective manner. It can only work through human beings. Facts are transformed to possibilities through logic. In order to create a future with a changed organisation the actors need logic to show them future possibilities. Possibilities are needed if the actors wish to, or need to, create a different future.

Values comprise what is valued. Values describe wishes, ambitions, and interests. Values give meaning to reality. Without values reality would be rather cold and numb. Actors need values so that they can choose between different possibilities. Values, therefore, are a vital element in actors' realities.

Communication is access to social realities. Without communication there would only be individual realities. Realities are socially constructed through communication. The only way that researchers and fellow actors can gain access to realities is through the way that they are communicated. Language, therefore, is vital for the creation of social life and for communication between actors.

Source: Henriksen et al. (2004: 12)

like and dislike and guide them on what they would like to change. This is why the organisational members are called 'actors' in the theory of reality. Together facts, logics and values constitute the actors' realities, and these realities are communicated through language. Through the actors' actions and interactions the elements of facts, logic, values and communication are integrated into the actors' realities. Fortunately, most often actors in organisations share realities and this is why we can use the term organisation culture, because together these shared realities constitute a culture.

Through the conceptualising method consultants – observants – try to disclose and understand the realities of the actors. This is done though dialogues with the actors. In the conceptualising method the idea of a dialogue takes a precise and specific meaning. The idea is that the observant and the actors in a joint talk – a dialogue – gradually work out the meaning of the word they use, in order to prevent misunderstandings. As in the case of TAX, when the observants wanted to know about the merger they requested the actors to tell what *they* meant by merger. The consultants did not take their point of departure in a textbook definition of a merger, but in the actual events as experienced and perceived by the actors. This is a point where the conceptualising method distinguishes itself from many other approaches, but also what makes it possible to diagnose the real problems of an organisation – through dialogue with the people involved (Henriksen et al., 2004: 24). How all this would work in real life is illustrated in the TAX case story about changes, HRD and organisation culture.

Organisation culture – the story of TAX

The people in TAX had seen numerous change initiatives, rationalisations, downsizing schemes, lean projects, evaluations and first and foremost mergers and restructuring programmes. They were confused, bewildered, and the overall employee mood could only be described as rather low. They could not see the effects of one initiative before the next one was introduced and most initiatives and programmes were cost/budget cutting exercises to the core. So, through the different management initiatives the people in TAX had learned that most changes are changes for the worse – things will possibly not get any better – changes will most likely end up in confusion, dismay and conflict. Unsurprisingly, the people at TAX had learned that it is best to avoid management initiatives and changes in general. Together with the changes and mergers it was announced that within four years the staff payroll would be cut by one-third. This led some of the most skillful employees to leave the place and those that remained were in a very insecure situation. The merger, more than any other, haunted the employees. Most of them met new managers and new colleagues, and even if most said that the new colleagues were very nice people, it turned out that a new unified culture was not in place and this caused a lot of insecurity. On top of that, the new IT systems did not arrive as promised – 'next year maybe'. The training courses that were supposed to facilitate the new work modes were delayed; and the new phone system did not work either.

In all, this was a rather unfortunate situation, even if the employees, when asked, could see possibilities and future improvements due to the merger and the proposed changes, they seemed not quite convinced. Management, on the other hand, was not really aware of all this, they wanted projects that could unify the organisation after the merger and thereby increase productivity and reach the performance targets. Therefore the management launched the New Ideas Project and they also called in external help from two consultants. The basic idea behind the New Ideas Project was to have employees use their skills and insight to improve the work of TAX. If people in TAX could see or visualise new possibilities or new ways of improving their work, they should involve others in their ideas and help each other to do something about it. It was also hoped that the new project would help establish a unified organisation culture that most thought was badly needed after the merger.

The reception of this project among the employees was rather half-hearted. Some saw it as just another one of those management shenanigans that they had already experienced too many of. Others saw it as a fine opportunity to get away from daily routines and others again, did not mind at all, but no one seemed very enthusiastic about it.

Because of their initial talks with management and employees the consultants were very well aware of the diverging realities. The talks – dialogues – with employees led the consultants to realise that something was not working as intended in TAX.

They knew that management and employees did not see the same situation – the same reality. Their realities would only marginally be able to work together to reach the desired goals. A major challenge for the consultants was therefore to work on the different realities and make it possible for managers and employees to work together.

Normally TAX people would engage themselves in discussions about their work, that is, they would come up with new ideas that would improve their work, their work modes and their working environment in general. From an organisation culture point of view we could say that continuous improvement was part of the organisation culture and this was the case through the engagement and interest the employees showed in their jobs and their work. But, unfortunately, this is not the case any more. People seemed disinterested; they kept quiet, kept things to themselves and did not discuss and improve. The consultants saw New Ideas as an opportunity that would bring back the employees' engagement in their work and also make it possible for the management to realise and understand the real problems within the organisation.

The consultants' first encounter

At the first meeting between the consultants and the management the consultants presented their method, which consisted of interviews – dialogues – with management and employees, workshops and some seminars. The management presented their ideas and after an intense and constructive discussion it was agreed how to move forward with the project. The consultants, however, were eager to stress that the project was about creating an ideas culture not concrete ideas – the management should not expect the consultants to come up with new ideas. This was also agreed at this meeting and the consultants were assigned to the task.

The consultants' first move was to host two workshops where they confronted two very specific problems; first to counter the resistance from some employees. Many saw projects like New Ideas as a complete waste of time and as something that would only disturb the work that people should do anyway – a nuisance. The consultants called this cynicism and they wanted to confront this head on. The second problem was the merger. It was quite obvious that without a proper elaboration of the experiences of the merger no new project would get anywhere. This had all become quite clear in the initial talks with TAX employees.

The first workshop was quite successful. The consultants and the employees discussed projects, cynicism and what to do about it. Most of the time was dedicated to discussing 'irrelevant projects' and how the New Ideas could avoid ending like the other projects that most often just petered out. It was agreed that if the New Ideas Project should stand any chance of success it should be solidly anchored in the departments and in the individual work groups. A successful project, it was concluded, was a project that made a positive difference in daily work routines.

The second workshop concerned the merger. Each employee was asked to tell a 'merger story', positive or negative. The idea was to bring forth stories about the merger as these stories would reveal the employees' construction of the events of the merger. The idea was to see what kind of role the merger still played in the employees' conception of TAX. This second workshop was also rather successful, as the employees liked the idea about merger stories.

Using the theory of reality as a diagnostic tool, it became clear that the realities of the employees did not help them very much in the new TAX world. The employees saw thorough and patient work as good work, but now speed and the collection of points were to be valued. This, of course, affected the employees' conception of what would count as facts ('good work' or points) and what would count as logics (thorough/patient work or fast work). When communication changed as well – from discussion in the work groups, to a kind of top-down commanding – it is no wonder that the employees were confused and something needed to be done.

After the workshops the consultants had another meeting with TAX management. At this meeting the consultants presented the results of the workshops. They told about the merger stories and the wish for anchoring the project in the departments and the work groups. This made the consultants come up with two very specific choices for the management to make. Either the management could ignore the merger stories and thereby ensure that cynicism remained the centrepiece of the future organisation culture. Or, they could take the stories seriously and thereby secure the support of the employees for the project. The choice was rather obvious and in addition the consultants outlined a programme for the rest of the project. This programme would be a human resource development (HRD) programme, that – if successful – would ease the tensions resulting from the merger, reintroduce engagement initiatives and consequently create a unified organisation culture. The programme included a four point scheme. First, the management should listen and take seriously the stories that the employees told. Even if management considered the stories 'not true', they should listen, as the stories show what and how the employees think about their work and their workplace. Second the annual employee development talks should be used in a much more conscious and targeted way, so both employees and the management will find them useful and worthwhile. They should be dialogues. Third, the management should use and involve the workgroups and the project group, like the project group established in connection to the New Ideas Project, to manage changes, development and new initiatives. Finally, the management should make visible to the employees that their ideas are taken seriously and that they do make a difference. They should make sure that experiences and new ideas are exchanged between departments and work groups.

These first rounds of encounters were evaluated by the management and by the employees and the evaluations were mainly positive. The employees liked the talks and they especially liked the idea of merger stories. There were still some reservations, though, concerning the whole idea of having projects of this kind; would it have any impact at all or would it end up like all the other projects? The management on the other hand, also liked the idea of merger stories as it made them see the reasons for some of the resistance they felt from employees. The management, however, also had its reservations. This concerned the role of the department managers, as the management, through the project came to realise that the role of the department managers was never really defined and many department managers were only reluctantly participating in joint projects, minding only the business of their own department.

The New Ideas Project and its future were discussed between the management and the consultants at a meeting. One of the main topics was the evaluation of the project. During the meeting new information that would change the whole perspective of the New Ideas Project was provided. First, a new division of work was announced. As part of the merger the employees had been introduced to individual evaluation or performance appraisal and (brownie) point schemes. This had meant an individualisation of work which had turned out to be counter-productive to the overall organisational goals. The individual employee was much more concerned with collecting points from small and easy tasks, than engaging themselves in larger and much more complicated cases. This has meant a decrease in turnover and earnings – even if each individual employee had reached their target points. Instead the work would be organised in project groups and individual evaluations would be abolished. The management did not like this idea; they feared that people would not work as hard as previously when they were not individually evaluated. The second piece of information concerned a re-launch of the ideas bank. Previously there had been a database that was supposed to collect and store good ideas, but it did not work as intended – it was more or less ignored by the employees. But now, as a further development of the New Ideas Project and as a consequence of the changes in the division of work, it was to be re-launched.

As a consequence of these changes the New Ideas Project was to be closed down. There would no longer be any use for it. This came as a big surprise to the consultants, but the management saw it in a quite different manner. They saw New Ideas as a very useful project that made them realise some of their problems and gave them a plan for future work. First of all they now had a story about the merger they could work on. The merger stories made them realise that there were things in the past that still mattered and would have to be taken into consideration in future decision-making. They had also realised that they needed to solve the problem of middle management. The role of the department managers would have to be negotiated and explicated. Finally the management saw, as a consequence of the New Ideas Project, that there were employees in all departments who understood the importance of New Ideas. That is, in the future there should be no problems in distributing new ideas to the departments as there would be no problems in getting new ideas and storing them.

Real problems in TAX

As noted above, this all came as a big surprise to the consultants. It was a lot of changes in just one go and it would end the New Ideas Project in the middle of the process – and only confirm that changes are frequent and lead nowhere, and that such projects will always just peter out. The consultants were of course glad to see their plan put into action. But the overall draft of the proposed changes would cause a lot of concern. First, replacing the New Ideas Project with a database that once had proven useless seemed not a very promising move. And to end the New Ideas Project without giving proper feedback to the employees seemed not too promising either. It was doubtful if any of the changes would stand a chance in the real world of TAX, taking into consideration the turbulent past and the world-views of the employees. This made the consultants think and make the following analysis that they later presented to the management. The analysis was concerned with the paradox that became obvious to them during their work with TAX.

First of all there is the cynicism towards participating in projects and towards changes in general. The management wanted engagement and initiatives from the employees, but with the frequent change of plans and the numerous projects petering out, this simply increased cynicism and prevented the kind of engagement that was the main goal in the first place. As long as the employees would get no feedback and see no results from the projects – see no real changes in their work conditions – they will continue to see such projects as a complete waste of time, only preventing them from doing their work. And they will be just as hostile towards changes as long as the experiences from the merger are still setting the stage for future change initiatives; engagement will be absent. With the New Ideas Project this will only get worse as the cynicism will live on. One example is the very important role of the department managers. The management had started talks with the department managers in order to clarify their role in the organisation. This was a direct result of the New Ideas Project, but the management never informed anybody about this and the employees could therefore not see the effect of the project and the cynicism could live on.

Consultants' second encounter

As a kind of conclusion to the project the consultants presented the analysis to the management. These conclusions could also stand as general lessons for most HRD projects and organisation culture studies.

The first important aspect of successful human resource development projects is ownership, that is, who is responsible for the project. Who owns the project and who is responsible for the practical arrangements and who will take action? This could also be termed negatively: who is to blame when things go wrong? In the case of TAX it was not quite clear who was responsible for the project. The obvious choice would have been the management, but it was not quite clear what role the department managers and the consultants would play. In the beginning the department managers were almost forgotten, and were given no role in the project, even if the employees stressed the importance of the project being solidly placed in the departments. During the work with the New Ideas Project it became clear that the role of the department managers had never been thoroughly discussed at all. This had to be done and the project only made that clear. Also the role of the consultants seemed to be unclear. The management was told right from the start that the consultants would host seminars, conduct interviews and participate in meetings. The goal was to aid the development of a new organisation culture. The project was about assisting in developing new work modes that would increase the number of new ideas. Despite this being made perfectly clear from the beginning, the management later started to ask the consultants for new ideas, showing that the role of the consultant was not made clear enough at the beginning. This could only cause confusion.

The conceptualising method prescribes dialogue as the remedy to avoid confusion, but in this case it seemed that only in the beginning of the project was this dialogue successful. This also relates to the consultants' second point in the analysis.

The goals of the project have to be made clear. Did the management want to engage themselves and their organisation into a long-term development project or were they eager to see results – eager to have a quick fix? At the beginning of the project the management indicated that they were ready for a long-term project and they signalled that they were ready, and had the patience it would take, to wait for the results. But later on they seemed very eager to see some fast and visible results from the project, such as when they asked the consultants for new ideas. There is a general lesson in this as well. Changes in organisations and changes in organisation cultures are not possible through a quick fix. On the contrary they take a lot of patience and a lot of hard work and first and foremost all parties involved need to be – actually – involved. In this case, the management forgot to involve the department managers and it turned out to be crucial for the success of the project. This also points to the consultants' third point in the analysis, the question about engagement. As with any other human endeavour the chance of success is most likely if people are involved and interested in the case. The consultants recognised the employees' attitude of cynicism and they immediately saw that they had to do something about it. This cynicism was a cumulative result of past events. New Ideas was just one project in a series of projects and as all previous projects had more or less failed, the employees asked why this one should be a success? The consultants confronted the problem head on and had the employees tell their stories about the rather traumatic merger. By taking the merger stories seriously it was in fact possible to take the employees seriously and show them that somebody listened and cared about them and their stories and consequently their world-views. The cynicism was a major problem and would be to any HRD project dealing with organisation culture. In order to confront the cynicism the merger stories played a vital role. The consultants pointed to the fact, as a fourth point in their analysis, that the stories were very important and that management and employees should be very aware of the stories told. Especially the fact that the stories told in public by the management were very different from the stories told off record. In TAX this was definitely the case and a fact that the employees had a completely different conception of TAX to management. When the management, at the beginning of the project, listened to the merger stories they were in fact on to something. They had a chance to get access to the employees' own stories and thereby learn about the world-views of the employees. But later in the project they seemed to have stopped listening and thereby they ensured that the cynicism could live on. The management had some good intentions with the project, but they seemed to have changed their ideas concerning the project along the way and when they wanted to replace the New Ideas Project, as a larger HRD project, with a simple database, then they finally gave up confronting the cynicism and relinquished the opportunity of changing the organisation culture within TAX.

Conclusions

The story about the New Ideas Project in TAX is a story about organisation culture, human resource development and narratives. It is also about management and the organisation of work and the very difficult task it is to change people's world-views. The consultants' fifth and final point in their analysis concerned time and resources. Did the management really realise what they had started? Did they end the project so abruptly because they realised that this would be a very difficult and maybe painful process to end the cynicism and create a new ideas culture? Maybe, and therefore the project that on the surface seems to have failed, could turn out to be a huge success, if only the management would realise the kind of time and resources that would be necessary in order to change things – and use that insight for the next project. The work with the New Ideas Project made clear that in order to do something about the problems that the management and the employees face they need to do something about the organisation culture. New technology alone would not have solved the problems and new organisation structures would not have done much either. New technologies were introduced – new IT and phone systems – but did not work as intended. New organisation structures were frequently introduced and did not change anything. Both technologies and structures are important, but without a change in the realities of the employees and the management – in what we here termed culture – the changes would not have any impact at all. Without a thorough discussion of previous events, especially the merger, the proposed changes did not stand a chance of being successful. This is why culture matters.

From the analysis of the problems in TAX, the consultants concluded that in order to reach the goals of a successful change project, or any other HRD project for that matter, there are certain conditions that the actors – management as well as employees – need to take seriously. First, time and resources are necessary. This should come as no surprise, as this would count for most projects – quick fixes are hardly a way to secure a lasting success of any project. They also found that engagement, ownership and the ability to listen to what actually was said were important elements of the project. This should hardly come as a surprise either, but through the analysis guided by the theory of reality it became clear that the realities of the management and the employees were so diverse that, under any circumstances, it would be difficult to handle a change project. The ideas of what should count as facts were different. The management was eager to reach the performance targets and therefore saw points and the fulfilment of performance targets as facts, while the employees through previous training and experience saw 'good work' as important. The logic of the management emphasised fast work and that was not in accordance with the employees' idea of thorough and patient work. In the same vein the values were different and in all it could be said that no quick fix could ever bridge the gap between such diverse realities, let alone make them work successfully on the same HRD project. That would take time and a lot of effort to create new realities that could work together on a successful project.

From a theoretical point of view there are lessons to be learned as well. It is clear from the case that in order to understand what is going on in TAX, it is necessary for the consultants (observants) to engage themselves in the organisation. A thorough analysis is one that is able to understand the problems the management and the employees face and also find ways to do something about them. The dialogues, the conceptualising method and the theory of reality helped the consultants realise that. They did not start out with a predefined HRD programme, but through their analyses they gradually worked out the real problems in TAX and in accordance with these analyses they were able to propose actions and new language games (e.g. the merger stories) that were able to aid the actors in their work. This insight also shows that students of organisations, consultants and anyone else concerned with HRD and change processes should be cautious when selecting a cultural perspective. It would certainly matter what type of perspective is preferred in order to develop the organisation and to develop its human resources. Not all perspectives will be able to bridge the gap between realities – but the conceptualising method has the theoretical and methodological strength to address and identify such realities. This is the key step in any HRD project related to changing an organisation culture.

Discussion questions

- Discuss how organisational culture and organisational change relate to each other.

- Discuss the difficulties faced by actors involved in organisational development, e.g. what are the obstacles for changes and how could organisational culture influence the change processes?

- Discuss how to facilitate organisational change. Take into consideration the realities of the actors involved. For example, why do managers and employees see things differently even if they are part of the same organisational culture?

- Discuss what can be done by HRD practitioners. Can they, for example, change the organisational culture in order to facilitate change?

11 Identity and HRD

Kenneth Mølbjerg Jørgensen and
Lars Bo Henriksen

■ ■ Chapter objectives ■

The objectives of this chapter are to:

- clarify why identity is important in relation to human resource development;

- develop the notion of identity by reference to the theory of reality described in the previous chapter on HRD and organisational development;

- describe the relations between the theory of reality, narrative and living story;

- draw the implications in relation to managing HRD and organisational change in general.

> **There is little reason to expect one's loyalty to a group or an organisation to be reciprocated. It is unwise ('irrational') to proffer such loyalty on credit when it is unlikely to be repaid. (Bauman, 2004: 30)**

Introduction

In the previous chapter we saw that human resource development (HRD) was closely linked to the identities of the employees and to the stories they tell. Through the stories it was possible to get to know about the actors and it was possible to help them understand and possibly change their organisations. In this chapter we will elaborate on this through a discussion of identity in relation to HRD. The previous chapter concluded that any HRD project needs time and resources and furthermore needs engagement, ownership and the ability to listen, if a project is to succeed.

In other words, successful HRD activities rely on the mutuality of interests between the actors involved in the organisation. We will use the concept of identity as an entry point into a discussion of how we may create a development, which balances actors' intentions and interests with the development of shared interests and intentions – e.g. cultures and communities or collective identity.

We hope to contribute to an understanding and dissolution of inherent dualisms and contradictions currently in the HRD literature (e.g. Weick and Westley, 1996; Garavan et al., 2004). Here it is often argued that theories, concepts and methods work on different levels, with conflicting intentions. Many of these conflicts are as much a result of the ways in which organisations have been constructed in the past than as a result of 'natural' conflicts of interests. In modernity, organisations were built in which the purpose was to efface and marginalise the human face in favour of instrumental and objective rationality. The bureaucracy was the organisational expression of modernity (Weber, 1971). But this meant that modernity was accompanied by alienation, exploitation, stress etc., because of an ever-increasing search for effectiveness and rationalisation of work processes.

As a consequence of modern management concepts and instruments, we have lost the stories of ordinary people in favour of linear and rationalised narratives of management (e.g. Boje and Durant, 2006; Jørgensen and Boje, 2009). The case of TAX was one example that we need to listen to those stories in order to create and design for more appropriate HRD programmes.

We have organised the chapter as follows. First we describe our model of inter-subjective experience. Next, we describe the concept of living story. Living story is a description of integration and disintegration and thus contains centripetal and centrifugal forces of language within it. Third, we discuss the implications in relation to HRD, where we discuss the possibilities of HRD as a tool for the mutual constitution of individuals and organisations.

Social construction of reality

We build our approach on the theory of reality presented in the previous chapter but we elaborate on the model in this chapter, where we construct it as a holistic model of actors' inter-subjective experience (Henriksen et al., 2004). This is a contrast to the more simple models of management and HRD, which often are based solely on logic and facts, but tend to forget values and communication. Thus, they forget what makes an actor an actor. Hannah Arendt notes for example on the meaning of language and communication:

> **Speechless action would no longer be action because there would no longer be an actor, and the actor, the doer of deeds, is possible only if he is at the same time the speaker of words. The action he begins is humanly disclosed by the word, and though his deeds can be perceived in its brute physical appearance without verbal accompaniment, it becomes relevant only through the spoken word in which he identified himself as the actor, announcing what he does, has done, and intends to do. (Arendt, 1998: 178–179)**

In the elaboration of the theory of reality in this chapter, we focus on experience as inter-subjective experience and communication thus becomes the focus point of our interest. The reason is that it is through communication that actors and communities are mutually constituted. We will take our starting point in Wittgenstein's concept language games (Wittgenstein, 1983), which for us describes inter-subjective and multi-layered experience.

This involves not only the spoken or written word but involves feelings, senses, body language and actions. Language or language games are polyphonic and plural (Bakhtin, 1981; Arendt, 1998) and this means that experiences are also multi-layered, fragmented and plural. This is evident in employees' and managements' different experiences of the same situation and also evident on a personal level, like when employees find themselves in a conflict between their critique of management and their loyalty to the organisation and to their colleagues.

We follow Bakhtin and argue that experience is constituted through the dynamic interplay of two simultaneous forces: the centripetal forces of language which is what brings order to language. We refer to these forces of language as the narrative forces by which individuals construct themselves as meaningful individuals in the world. Narrating is the process by which individuals integrate past, present and future (Ricoeur, 1984; Cunliffe et al., 2004).

We describe the narrative forces of language as a process of integration, because this process is what makes the everyday experiences meaningful for the actors. These forces seek to overcome heteroglossia – the condition that the word uttered in that place and that time will have a different meaning than under other conditions (Bakhtin, 1981: 263, 428). The centripetal forces seek to unite and bring order but they operate in the midst of heteroglossia (1981: 271–272) – that is in 'a language' that is stratified into a multiplicity of languages; languages of social groups, professional languages, generic languages, languages of generations etc.

Heteroglossia is what ensures the dynamics and development of language. There are always centrifugal forces that ensure processes of decentralisation and disunification alongside the verbal-ideological centralisation and unification (Bakhtin, 1981: 272). The centrifugal forces of language arise from the fact that words are equivocal with a multiplicity of potential meanings; and from that being is always social and thus dialogical – influenced by a multiplicity of different force relations that destabilises and shakes being.

The centrifugal forces will thus reveal that the sense of being is an illusion – that what is actually the case is that we are always in a state of becoming. This implies that our organisations are also always in a state of becoming. And it also goes for the human construct HRD (Lee, 2001). As an example, the managers and employees in TAX are continuously reconstructing themselves and the organisation through their interactions, interpretations and negotiations.

The construction of narratives and organisation are the results of centripetal forces, which bring order to life. But at the same time language is equivocal and multiple and exposes being to disturbances and differences that destabilises and shakes being. Different groups in TAX had for example different languages and interpreted things differently and this was the source of continuous challenges to the rational management concepts that had been put to work in TAX. In the end, it called for a different approach to change where the actors and joint conceptualisation became the centre of analysis – a method which however was also challenged by other languages.

This notion of language and of the centripetal and centrifugal forces of language can be related to our model of reality construction. As noted, the model proposes that actors construct their realities by integrating four dimensions: facts, logic, values and communication. The idea in the model is to visualise some important dimensions of reality construction that go in daily life through our participation in language games (Wittgenstein, 1983).

The basic ontological position is that reality becomes socially or inter-subjectively constructed by playing language games (Jørgensen, 2007). Language games or communication are thus central in understanding both organisations but also individuals. They are mutually constituted by playing language games. This means that the other dimensions – facts, logic and values – are integrated in communication. They do not refer to distinct dimensions but are merged in the speaking and co-speaking of language – in communication with others. The dimensions are described below.

Facts (world) comprise forces in time that interact with human experience. Arendt notes for example, that action and speech are always concerned with the matters of the world 'out of which arise their specific, objective worldly interests' (Arendt, 1998: 182). She distinguishes between a physical worldly in-between, which consists of the worlds of things and the worlds of physics and a subjective in-between, which consists of deeds and words and owes its origin to men's acting and speaking.

This subjective in-between is not tangible but despite this, this in-between is no less real. She calls this reality the web of human relationships (Arendt, 1998: 182–183). We will refer to the first in-between as *objective time* and the second in-between as *objectified time*. The relationship between objective time, objectified time and human time may be more or less intimate, but this does not mean that these forces can be reduced to the same.

Objective and objectified time exist as a fact and condition for human existence and it is expressed in words, concepts, artefacts, rituals, symbols etc. (Henriksen et al., 2004: 19–20; see also the previous chapter). As such there is a distinction between what we may call world (time) and reality (human time). The world is what it is. Reality is our sense of, our knowledge of and our feelings for this world (Henriksen et al., 2004: 17).

Reality is what works for us. The relationship between time and human time is mediated by language where the use of language is governed by tacit rules such as norms, traditions, conventions etc. (Wittgenstein, 1983; Shotter, 2005). We use language as a toolbox for constructing realities. It implies that using language and playing language games is an active process of constructing reality. Language is in other words not an objective mirror of reality.

We play language games according to the contextual rules-of-the-game in a particular culture. These rules are often tacit and have the character of norm, tradition, convention, use, etc. They are historically created ways of talking and acting that have been learned and internalised through upbringing, education and participation in the cultural life of particular families, organisations, communities and other social groups.

Communication is thus central in talking about reality as socially constructed. It would be impossible to talk about culture, community, society or history without communication (Dewey, 1916; Geertz, 1973). Communication or dialogue is thus a matter of life and death for an organisation (Gergen et al., 2004). Playing language games is important for human existence. We may say that the world is reduced to reality through the process of playing language games in the sense that construction of reality is an identification process that seeks to reduce different events into the same.

It creates 'sameness' in the sense of constructing similarities between events – not in seeing them as the same. As such construction of reality is to construct a familiar world for the actors. We draw here on the notion of family resemblance, which is Wittgenstein's solution to the question of how we are capable of using the rules of the game in new situations.

We are capable of using language in new situations. But this is not because situations are the same but because they look like other situations. Instead of situations being the same there are networks of similarities that overlap and criss-cross each other (Wittgenstein, 1983: § 67). In dealing with everyday situations, actors draw on how they have learned to use language in similar situations – thereby constructing reality. They use the past to construct the present. Through family resemblance, situations are constructed as relatively similar.

But family resemblance is not only recognition but is a construction. It is a projection from the individual to the world. Therefore construction is also a matter of identification. Even if world and reality are different from each other, reality construction actually constitutes the actors' endless efforts to reduce the world to something that is familiar to them – that is creating sameness between world and reality. Reality construction is in this way an identification process, which is essential for our very existence.

Identification is a way of making reality manageable through an active process of construction, whereby meaning is projected from the body to the world in a way where the meaning is projected away from us (Polanyi, 1958, 1966). As such reality is a projection where the projection is the result of a learning process. Knowledge goes from the body to the world and we depend on the body in our actions and understandings.

We know the body from what it does in the world. Hall describes it as follows: 'Insofar as I act, I am not conscious of myself but from myself' (Hall, 1979: 276). Hall also uses the description 'participating in' to denote the active process by which we create reality. 'On this epistemology, I am not a detached, impersonal observer in knowing, but on the contrary, I pour myself into things' (Hall, 1979: 275).

In co-constructing reality, two other dimensions are integrated. The first dimension is logic, which denotes the process that transforms facts to possibilities. It is through logical processes that facts are transformed into future possibilities and choices. We may speak about different kinds of logic that are embedded in playing language games: material, formal, social or subjective. A material logic describes rules, procedures and guidelines embedded in material technologies or systems like accounting systems, budget systems, quality systems, production systems, etc.

Formal logic comprises the kinds of logic that can be found in mathematics and scientific theories. Subjective logic comprises individuals' learned way of creating possibilities from particular situations: this includes the use of methods, systematic ways of thinking etc. This kind of logic may have been internalised through upbringing, experience or formal education. Social logic comprises socially produced conditions for transforming facts into possibilities; e.g. division of labour, location in time and space, en-cultured ways of thinking and acting.

If our speech and actions were only controlled by logical processes our reality would be completely instrumental and lifeless. But this is of course not the case. By doing something, we don't just do something in a lifeless way. Activities mean something for us. That is, temporal significance is attached to situations. We create temporal significance through our values. Values comprise what is important and valuable for us. Values determine what we like and dislike.

Values create meaning in life and they constitute our point of direction in life. It is through values that we assess possibilities as serious, inspiring, threatening, reprehensible or unimportant. Actions are thus symbolic (Geertz, 1973) and linked to the temporality of our existence. Through our values we extend ourselves in time, because values are embedded in how we experience the past, present and imagined futures and how we construct continuity between past, present and future.

Identity as living storytelling

Facts, logic and values are merged in communication. But we have not yet described the forces of integration – and of disintegration. We will use the concept living storytelling to capture these forces. We are inspired by Derrida who argues that story has no borderlines. It is at once larger and smaller than itself. It is entangled in a play with other stories, is part of the other, makes the other part of itself etc. and it remains utterly different from what Derrida calls its homonym, narrative (Derrida, 2004: 82).

Stories occur in the moment and they go on in unpredictable directions. Stories are living because they are becoming and are shaping our individual and communal identities and imagined futures. Stories are never finished, not necessarily whole, and are still alive in the here and now. Boje notes (2001: 18) that stories float in a soup of bits and pieces of story fragments. They are never alone but live and breathe in a web of other stories and self-deconstruct with each telling.

We use living storytelling to emphasise that construction of reality has been influenced and is influenced by a multiplicity of force relations. Construction of reality takes place in specific historical and geographical conditions that include political and ethical dimensions, material conditions etc. Words and actions are where people's realities are communicated in time and space. They are always constructed by people, who are part of the world and interact with the world. These interactions influence both the world and people's realities.

In other words, when people construct their realities they are under the influence of both objective time and objectified time. Living storytelling is the construction of human time in this respect. There is a continuous, dynamic and dialectical interplay between time and human time in the sense that both depend on each other and influence each other – yet time and human time are mutually exclusive forces, which can never fully comprehend or embrace each other.

To use living storytelling to denote human time is unlike Ricoeur, who suggests that 'time becomes human to the extent that it is articulated through a narrative mode, and narrative attains its full meaning when it becomes a condition of human existence' (Ricoeur, 1984: 52). Ricoeur uses the word narrative for human time. In distinguishing between story and narrative we are inspired by Derrida, who argues that story and narrative are homonyms as we noted before. Story and narrative appear to be the same but are quite different from each other. The expression 'homonym' however reveals that they are often taken to mean the same – also in the literature.

Ricoeur's conception of narrative is linked to a hermeneutical theory of the construction of experience as a mimetic circle (Ricoeur, 1984: 71–76; Cunliffe et al., 2004: 270–271). He explores the relations between time and narrative through what he calls three moments of mimesis. What brings these moments together is the power of configuration, which is the result of the intermediary position between the two operations, which Ricoeur calls mimesis1 (pre-understanding) and mimesis3 (after-understanding), and which constitutes the two sides of mimesis2 (plot and understanding).

Ricoeur thus conceptualises the relations between time and narrative by showing the mediating role that emplotment has between the moment of practical experience, which goes before emplotment, and the moment of refiguration that follows it. He argues that we are following 'the destiny of a prefigured time that becomes a refigured time through the mediation of a configured time' (Ricoeur, 1984: 54).

According to Ricoeur, human time is historical: there is a before and an after with intimate relations between them. Bruner notes that narrative segments time 'by the unfolding of crucial events – at least into beginnings, middles and ends' (Bruner, 1996: 136). The argument for narrative is that through narrative we place ourselves in time and create coherence, continuity and order through an integration of past, present and future (e.g. Clandinin and Connelly, 2000).

Identity is intentional and transforms diverse events or incidents into a meaningful whole. It draws together heterogeneous factors such as 'agents, goals, means, interactions, circumstances, unexpected results' (Ricoeur, 1984: 65; Chappell et al., 2003: 45). Narrative thus represents form – a construction of order or contingency from many different forces. Czarniawska (1997: 11) argues that narrative is based on a notion of narrative rationality, where narrative replaces conventional models of formal rationality (Czarniawska, 1997: 22).

As noted we, however, prefer the term storytelling or living storytelling. With this concept, we emphasise that the construction of human experience is always inter-subjective and plural, ambiguous, open-ended, emergent and often progresses in unpredictable ways. Living storytelling opens up for an understanding of the complexity of human living, the fragmented character of being and how it is continuously responsive to the activities in which people and other people participate. With its emphasis on unity, coherence, rationality, narrative only covers one side of the story of human experience.

With the concept of story we wish to maintain the openness of human experience and avoid narrative closure. As noted, Jacques Derrida makes a sharp distinction between narrative and story. He believes that narrative is linked to the idea of rational progress, objective truth and subsequently it portrays time as a linear process. Derrida speaks for example of narrative as a demand for truth, which implies the perception that the phenomena have beginnings, middles and ends, borders and boundaries.

He argues that the demand for narrative is to tell exactly what happened (Derrida, 2004: 72) and further that it demands and is capable of organising a narrative sequence and telling the truth (2004: 81). By this token he argues that narrative is 'a violent instrument of torture' (2004: 78), which imprisons lives in a linear rationality that excludes other voices. In the literature there are several stories of implementation of management concepts, which have been fairly monological and through implementation have excluded the stories of other people.

Management programmes like lean management, new public management, total quality management, learning organisation or even HRD are often based on linear rationality and a fairly monological voice, which serves particular groups in the organisation (i.e. managers) but excludes others. By taking command and becoming the norms and standards of speech and actions, these management programmes becomes a violent instrument of torture directed against the life-worlds of other people.

It may seem that this conception of narrative as a violent instrument of torture is too simple and negative. We may however use Derrida's critique of narrative to highlight the troubling aspect of narrative, which is that it provides a kind of more or less systematic and structured meta-perspective on human experience in the sense that it integrates past, present and future and thus creates unity and continuity across time and space – or in other words creates unity across the multiple situations, which constitute human life.

This is quite evident in the management programmes mentioned above, which often are presented as time-less truth that in the most rigorous modern fashion denies past experiences of the employees any place in the construction of the future of the organisation. Narrative as such only covers the centripetal forces of language and is as such incapable of capturing the dynamics of life.

The dynamics of life arises from the continuous interaction with a multiplicity of forces by which narrative is also shaken, disturbed, disrupted and perhaps even dissolved. These are the centrifugal forces of language. The centrifugal forces of language emerge from social interactions and are as such the sources of learning which might be more or less continuous or discontinuous. Arendt (1998: 184) uses the term stories as the kind of results of these interactions.

Stories here are thus the results of the interactions, which go on in everyday life through language games and as such it is more emergent, spontaneous, responsive to local circumstances, plural and polyphonic. Experience as living story is thus a description of multi-layered and fragmented experience that may develop and evolve in many different directions. Narrative order in which we step out of situations and creates integration between past, present and future is a very important part of being but it is not the whole story. It rationalises our life story, which is however much more complex, multi-layered and paradoxical.

As such there is a continuous tension between how we story and re-story our lives from each moment to the next, and how we narrate these stories into a continuity and order. Both are acts of interpretation as we see them, but there are different layers of interpretations. In ordinary everyday conversations (language games), for example, a continuous storytelling process occurs in which participants make sense of the situation in which they are a part (e.g. Silverman and Jones, 1976; Boje, 1991), but this doesn't necessarily imply that such situations are well-plotted and can be explained by reference to a single principle.

The same conversation may simultaneously contain elements of sexism, feminism, identity, power, competence, globalisation, local tradition, rationality and a multiplicity of other potential elements. This doesn't make them into bad stories or less understood stories – at least not for the people involved in the continuous storytelling because what is important is that these people understand each other. Similarly we might tell other people what happened in particular situations but without giving specific explanations about what the story is all about.

According to Wittgenstein (e.g. Wittgenstein, 1983: §§ 71–75) these examples illustrate what being part of particular language games means for instance. Namely that we are able to communicate and understand each other because we have learned to use language in particular ways and without having to explicate particular explanations of what words, concepts, models, descriptions mean. The stories that evolve from participating in language games are constructed and deconstructed in the moment and evolve into other interpretations and stories, still other interpretations and stories etc.

We may say with Boje that the actors are always chasing the story, which is in some sense never-ending (e.g. Boje, 2001); on the other hand it always involves new beginnings, because to act means taking an initiative, to begin and to set things into motion (Arendt, 1998: 177).

Narrative order and story disorder are thus countervailing forces that exist side by side, and which ensures the continuous development of world and reality. By emphasising living storytelling, we intend to maintain that reality becomes socially constructed through ongoing interactions between actors, technologies and circumstances. Living storytelling implies continuous evolvement and change of realities. Narrative order is an abstraction and illusion but none the less an important illusion in creating order and direction in our lives.

But the problem of narrative is that it displaces and overlooks discontinuity, fragmentation and ambiguity. In other words, narrative closure is where we become seduced by the narrative and forgets and overlooks that difference, the other voices and complex interactions inherent in creating social realities.

Living storytelling and HRD

The concept of living storytelling is an expression of the idea that identity is dialogical and can be used to discuss the relationship between the individual and the organisation (workplace, culture, community, etc.) and how HRD may interfere with this relationship. Identity as living storytelling expresses the idea of the mutual constitution of the individual and the organisation. It does not make sense to speak of one without the other.

As such living storytelling seeks to capture the dynamics that Dewey spoke of in biological metaphors as the interaction and later the transaction between organism (individual) and environment (organisation) (e.g. Dewey, 1916). Dewey was before the linguistic turn in social sciences and used another language to capture the dynamics between the individual and the organisation. Yet his learning philosophy known as pragmatism is interesting in that Dewey emphasised that we needed to dissolve inherent dualisms in the way we think about learning and development; e.g. individual/ organisational, mind/body, theory/practice etc.

As such individual learning and changes in identity are inherently bound up with questions of power, ethics, culture, community etc. and the other way around. And this close relationship is perhaps also one of the reasons why we have begun to take an interest in bringing learning and practice closer together. We take the ideas of workplace learning, organisational learning and culture as examples of trying to re-think education and learning. We have dealt with these issues in the three other chapters. Here we will concentrate more broadly on issues of identity and how we may understand HRD in relation to identity. Bauman (2004) suggests the following about identity:

> **The idea of 'identity' was born out of a crisis of belonging and out of the effort it triggered to bridge the gap between the 'ought' and the 'is' and to lift reality to the standards set by the idea – to remake reality in the likeness of the idea. (Bauman, 2004: 20)**

Bauman believes that the concept of identity is usually tacit and taken-for-granted. We do not usually reflect too much about who we are. In everyday situations identity works tacitly in merging the individual and the social (see next section). When this merger is relatively unproblematic it is a sign that our language works and where our narratives of who we are, are relatively unchallenged by daily encounters with other forces.

When our language does not work, it is an indication that the relationship between the individual and the social is problematic. It may happen in periods of rapid change; technological, social, economic or others. Or it may happen as a consequence of internal organisational changes; managerial, structural, cultural or others. Or it may happen due to some combination of these factors.

It is perhaps because present-day organisational life is characterised by relatively rapid changes that the contemporary interest in identity has emerged in learning and educational research (Lave and Wenger, 1991; Wenger, 1998; Chappell et al., 2003; Sfard and Prusak, 2005) and in organisational research (Czarniawska, 1997; Ainsworth and Hardy, 2004). 'You tend to notice things and put them into the focus of your scrutiny and contemplation only when they vanish, go bust, start to behave oddly or otherwise let you down' (Bauman, 2004: 17).

In other words, it is suggested that the interest in identity stems from increased tensions between individual identities and the development in our organisations, communities and cultures; tensions which are due to increased changes, which may cause our language and our narratives of selves to be eroded. In other words, we become incompetent members of society because the rules of the language games – that is the norms and standards of the social world in which we work and live – change.

These rules are the very guidelines for individuals when they construct their identity in the organisation. They constitute the criteria for competence and incompetence: what it is one should strive for when one wants to become a member of the group, the organisation or the community. Through its language games the organisation communicates certain logics and values of talking and acting.

These logics and values are expressed in narratives, stories, in organisational role models, in punishment and rewards, distribution of resources, organisation of career patterns, distribution of authority etc. Hence, the rules of language games within organisations are practices of surveillance (Hardy and Clegg, 1996; Clegg, 1989) in the sense that these rules govern talk and actions towards conformity and normalisation.

HRD, including organisational learning, workplace learning and organisational development in a broader sense, has emerged among others as a reaction to these rapid changes in society. In this way, we may see HRD as a continuous effort to bridge the gap or sustain the bonds between individuals, organisations and the contexts in which these organisations occur: to ensure that there is what we may call a shared understanding between the individual, collective and contextual dimensions of any social and organisational practice.

HRD understood as a language game (Jørgensen and Keller, 2008) carried by actors such as consultants, managers, researchers, and HR people, must be understood through how it works in order to create and sustain the bonds between these three dimensions. In this respect the model of reality construction is useful for identifying the challenges that confront HRD. We use it as a model of inter-subjective experience and in this respect it underlines the need for shared understanding.

It does so by claiming that reality construction always must be integrated with the matters of the world (the factual dimension). We cannot sustain constructions, which are not concerned with the matters of the world or are inconsistent with this model. Our constructions of reality would be illusions and dream worlds and the consequences may be dramatic.

In organisations, such examples would include failed strategies but also failed management programmes because of misunderstandings of how employee realities look like. A deep understanding of the world and of the dynamics of the world is almost always the best foundation for intelligent business and organisational solutions. A failed integration is in other words a symptom of misunderstanding and lack of shared understanding.

In this context, HRD is concerned with developing logic, which generates valid possibilities of how to act in the world. This includes the ability to use social structures (social logic), the ability to use techniques, methods and concepts that are learned and internalised (subjective logic), and the ability to use systems and technologies (formal and material logic). The logic used in any work function in an organisation is based on complex systems of logics working together to create possibilities in the world.

Individuals' logic must conform to the organisational rules-of-the-game in order to be recognised as valid knowledge. This illustrates complex and classic issues in learning and education literature: how to integrate education and practice and how to use learning and education for transforming practice. Further, organisations are created by complex games, which include power struggles that lead to the construction of certain possibilities rather than others.

Professionals read the world differently and see different possibilities. Certain types of knowledge are legitimate in some organisations while they don't count in other organisations. These differences are manifested in different strategies, different routines, and different practices. Different voices are heard under different organisational configurations and traditions. Some are included, some are excluded.

And sometimes the appropriate diversity for acting appropriately in complex multi-voiced contexts is hampered by the organisation's efforts to create consistency and integration in its actions. It is a continuous challenge to create the right balance between diversity and integration and create room for listening to multiple voices and at the same time being able to act and make decisions.

The creation of different possibilities and the choice among possibilities rely on the actors' values. It is through values that certain possibilities and choices become meaningful or non-meaningful to them. Through values we attach temporal significance to the possibilities that we see. We may be able to identify ourselves with them or we may feel alienated. What is important is that the energy and motivation comes from values.

This energy and motivation may be positive but it may also be negative and lead to alienation, lack of motivation and the organisation will lose energy. Once again we may say that the condition of success of an HRD programme relies on joint storytelling or joint conceptualisation so that a shared identity may emerge. If there is no joint conceptualisation, there is no reason that employees will identify with changes like the ones in TAX. It is not their project. It is the managers' project.

The mutuality of interests of individuals and organisations can only be accomplished through joint conceptualisation in which we may say that organisational issues are transformed to be individual issues also – by creating ownership and engagement through involvement.

Conclusions

Organisational changes and HRD programmes need to be aligned with living stories in the organisation. At the outset, this was certainly not the case, when the consultants entered TAX in the previous chapter. Here, the employees had been exposed to numerous change programmes, performance measurement systems etc., which on one hand created a distance between work and values.

These programmes were consistent with the violent narrative in proclaiming a linear logic that was removed both from the professional values of the employees but also was dysfunctional in terms of the organisation's overall mission. The violent narrative embedded in the change programmes and systems excluded and marginalised the actors in such a way that it sought to reduce actors to instrumental behaviour. Therefore they couldn't influence the process and take part in the necessary integration process.

They did not understand – or they refused to accept – the new logic guiding their work, the interpretation of facts and the construction of new facts. The distance in how the objective and objectified forces of time was constructed by different actors revealed a lack of shared understanding and consequently also a lack of a joint enterprise and alignment to common goals. In this sense the violent narrative represents a case of failed integration and consequently also of a failed HRD programme.

The actors' identities were questioned, they were not taken seriously and the result was frustration, lack of interests, lack of energy and also lack of integration in terms of fulfilling TAX's role in relation to society. As such we need to create a joint conceptualisation in organisations when we want to change our organisations in order to create integration on all dimensions: integration with objective and objectified forces in time, integration between logic and values and subsequently a language that works.

The development of human resources and the development of efficient and valuable structures rely on joint storytelling in which the living stories can evolve and create the basis for appropriate identification of who we are as an organisation, and what role we play in larger society.

 Discussion questions

- Discuss the notion of identity and how we can create shared identity in an organisation.

- How can the theory of reality be helpful in understanding identity and what dimensions are important in creating sustainable identities?

- Discuss the implication of identity in relation to managing HRD.

12 Futures and Strategic Learning – Strategy Narrative and Storytelling

Kenneth Mølbjerg Jørgensen

■ ■ Chapter objectives ■

The objectives of this chapter are to:

- reflect upon the challenges that future strategic initiatives pose for HRD;

- elaborate how narrative and storytelling relates to strategy and learning;

- describe storytelling methods for strategic HRD.

The limits of my language are the limits of my world. (Ludwig Wittgenstein)

Introduction

We have been concerned with how HRD has been linked to various kinds of learning, development and change in organisations in previous chapters. We have argued that identity is intimately linked with HRD. We are now moving towards another aspect of HRD, which is linked to the alignment of organisational activities with the organisation's institutional framework. Thus we discuss how HRD is linked to the strategic development of organisations.

Strategy is usually referred to as the alignment of resources within the organisation and the organisational environment (Klausen, 2003; Johnson et al., 2009). This distinction between organisation and environment is not used here, because it implicitly presumes a relatively clear boundary between what the organisation is and what the organisation is not.

The organisation is instead conceived as a network of language games; a concept presented in the chapter on organisational learning and HRD. The fundamental question is then not what the organisation is and what it is not. The important question is instead how the organisation *works* (Henriksen et al., 2004; Jørgensen, 2006, 2007). The work of organisations integrates a potentially great number of actors including leaders, employees, customers, citizens, suppliers, trade unions etc., who participate in the language games from their particular positions and with their particular intentions.

Through language and through playing language games reality is constructed. Hannah Arendt refers to this process as co-constructive storytelling because reality is constructed in interaction with others (Arendt, 1998: 178–179). Organisations are storytelling organisations (Boje, 1991). Boje argues that storytelling is the preferred sense-making currency of human relationships. He argues that in organisations, people engage in dynamic interpretations and reinterpretations of storylines through which organisational and institutional artefacts, words, concepts, past stories, strategies and other symbols are given meaning.

As noted in the chapter on identity and HRD, individual and collective identities are created through these storytelling processes. Language comprises the linguistic resources for storytelling and thus identity construction. Through language games actors story what the organisation is about in interaction with other actors. Embedded in this network of language games are norms and standards for speaking and acting.

The organisation is embedded in institutional structures in which specific norms, standards for what the organisation could and should do are framed. Such institutional structures include norms and expectations to the organisation's products and services but also legal and juridical regulations and informal norms and standards for what is considered legitimate and non-legitimate. At the same time, these norms and standards are continuously challenged and contradicted by numerous forces and changes.

As such organisations are continuously constructed, reconstructed, modified and changed through a dialectical interplay between storytelling and resistant forces that challenge these stories. From this point of view organisational action becomes through a process of collective storytelling whereby the organisation's resources are concerted and translated. Strategy and strategy formation is concerned with the alignment of these resources with the institutional framework in which the organisation is embedded. It includes considerations about relations with customers, suppliers, managers, employees, trade unions, banks, public authorities, natural environment and so forth. Through these relationships the stories of the organisation are created.

The premises of the chapter are the following: First the strategic challenges of an organisation are not as simple as they have often been presented in the strategy literature. In classic strategy textbooks, the strategic goal is often simply stated as profit maximisation. The strategic process is sketched as a top management planned and directed process of making rational decisions according to the strategic goal and to align production, marketing, sales, finance and human resource management according to the strategic goals.

Instead, a more complex picture of strategy formation is used where collective storytelling has to meet plural, inconsistent and contradictory demands and goals. This image is further complicated by continuous changes in opportunities, preferences, technologies, environments and resources; among others due to globalisation. The circumstances under which strategy is framed is *liquid* to use a term from Bauman (2004). Under such circumstances strategy formation is best understood as what Mintzberg et al. (1998) call an *emergent* process.

This leads to the second point which is how we conceive *strategic capability*. A common definition of strategic capability is that it comprises 'the resources and competences of an organisation needed for it to survive and prosper' (Johnson et al., 2009: 95). The term 'resources' is thus used for the organisation's potential.

Johnson et al. (2009) distinguish between *physical resources* (machines, buildings, production capacity etc.), *financial resources* (capital, cash, debtors, creditors and suppliers of money), *intellectual capital* (patents, brands, business systems, customer databases etc.) and *human resources* (mix, skills and knowledge of employees and other people in the organisation's network).

Resources, however, only becomes living, when they are being used and applied. This is where they use the term competences, which comprise 'the skills and abilities by which resources are used deployed effectively through an organisation's activities and processes' (Johnson et al., 2009: 96). Such competences among others comprise leadership and management, collaboration between actors, their ability to adapt, innovative capability, relations with customers and suppliers, and the experience and learning about what works and what does not work.

Central to the concept of strategic capability are *unique resources* and *core competences*, which are capabilities for competitive advantage. Unique resources are resources that critically underpin competitive advantage and that others cannot imitate or obtain. As noted by Johnson et al. it is however more likely that an organisation achieves competitive advantage because it has distinctive *core competences* (Prahalad and Hamel, 1990). These are the skills and abilities by which resources are deployed through an organisation's activities and processes such as to achieve competitive advantage.

Since organisations are subjected to continuous changes and thus that strategy formation is emergent, core competences are not a static quality of organisations. To continuously develop and revise core competences is increasingly important. Further there is increasing pressure to develop new core competences. This includes using resources in another way, combining them differently, finding new resources and to create new relationships and processes.

HRD is critically important in this process of revising, modifying and creating core competences. It is through human agency alone that core competences are constructed and created. Buildings, machines, systems, technologies, capital or intellectual are nothing in themselves. They have to be used for the creation of value and this requires human agency. HRD is thus critically important for strategy formation. And it has become even more important due to continuous changes, which provide new opportunities, challenges and threats to organisations.

This is a challenge on several dimensions as noted in the previous chapter on identity construction, where we argued that HRD could be seen as a continuous effort to bridge the gap or sustain the bonds between individuals, the organisation and the context or institutional framework in which the organisation exists. This is collective storytelling, which seeks to ensure:

1   That the actors in the organisation get the possibility of constructing their own identities in the organisation, so that each actor can obtain a meaningful position in the organisation.

2   That it becomes possible to talk about the organisation as an actor, that is as an organisation, which is an organisation in the sense that actors are to a certain degree at least committed to a shared goal, and in which a legitimate formal and informal structure is obtained that supports this goal. This also means that there is an integration between the individual and the organisation in the sense that it makes sense to talk of a shared identity.

3   That the identities constructed and thus the collective storytelling creates satisfactory and legitimate actions in relation to the institutional framework in which the organisation is embedded.

To work with HRD from these premises and in the light of the organisation's strategic challenges includes working with learning in a way which challenges inherent assumptions and prejudices in organisations. Strategic HRD for the future involves exploring language and our narrative understandings of cause–effect linkages; e.g. it involves a much more reflexive approach to HRD.

The chapter is then organised in the following way: Firstly, it explores the relations between narrative, strategy and learning. Secondly, it examines the links between strategy, storytelling and learning. Thirdly, it presents a case from management education, which seeks to combine reflective and reflexive learning. Finally the chapter looks at and discusses three different examples of working with reflexivity in organisations: genealogy, deconstruction and carnivalesque storytelling.

Narrative, strategy and learning

To highlight the importance of reflexivity in relation to strategy, we may compare it with a popular concept in the management literature, namely *narrative*. The traditional conception of strategy is that it is a narrative. It implies a conception of time as a linear and causal relationship between past, present and future (Jørgensen and Boje, 2009).

As such, it is not incidental to compare strategy with narrative. Firstly, strategy contains a narrative of where to go in the future in terms of goals and means. This includes questions like where the organisation wants to go and by what means (organisational, technological and human resource developmental etc.) it wants to achieve these goals. As such strategy implicitly contains imagined causal relationships between actions and consequences. These can be either learning from the past in the sense of how the organisation and individuals interpret what has happened in the past and what consequences it has had; for example what works and what does not work etc.

It can also be imagined relationships in the sense of interpretations of what the organisation stands for and interpretations of the linkages between present actions and future consequences. As such the notion of core competence defined above describes the organisation's learning of what works and what does not work, who we are and who we are not, where our strengths and weaknesses lie. Fundamentally this comes down to interpretations of past actions and consequences, which are projected into the future.

This leads to the second point, that it is neither incidental to use narrative in relation to learning. Argyris and Schön's work, Dewey's work and Weick's work on learning – as well as many, many others – are centred on how we interpret the relationship between actions and their consequences, how this learning stems from past events and how we project them into the future. As such, narrative is based on a notion of narrative rationality to use an expression from Czarniawska (1997: 22), where narrative replaces conventional models of formal rationality.

Finally, this also explains why the organisation's identity is closely linked to strategy, because narrative has been described as a basic condition of human existence. As noted in the chapter on identity and HRD, Ricoeur has argued that time becomes human time to the extent that it is articulated in a narrative mode, and that narrative attains its full meaning when it becomes a condition of human existence (Ricoeur, 1984: 52).

Ricoeur explores the relations between time and narrative through a three-fold circle of mimesis, where emplotment ties the three moments of pre-understanding,

understanding and after-understanding together. Time is historical with a before and after and it is through narrative that we place ourselves in time and create coherence, continuity and order through an integration of past, present and future.

This relationship between narrative and learning is emphasised clearly by Clandinin and Connelly. They follow Dewey and argue that one criterion of experience is continuity in the sense that experience grows out of other experiences and lead to other experiences: 'Wherever one positions oneself in that continuum – the imagined now, some imagined past, or some imagined future – each point has a past experiential base and leads to an experiential future' (Clandinin and Connelly, 2000: 2).

In sum, strategy and learning is linked directly to narrative. We may imagine strategy as the organisation's 'human time' by which it seeks to place itself in relation to a complex world and create coherence, continuity and order through interpretations of the relations between past, present and future. As noted by Boje, most work on strategy has the character of strategy narrative. He argues that strategy narrative has a logo and five sentences: motto, plot, mission, vision and founding narrative (Boje, 2008: 100).

Logo: the symbol of the organisation.

Motto: The moral sentence that binds logo to the sentences that follow (Nike: 'Just Do It', IBM: ('Think' etc.)

Plot: The sentence stating the sequence of events that will get the organisation from mission to vision. For example, Nike's plot:

- Deepening the relationship with customers
- Delivering superior, innovative products to the marketplace
- Making our supply chain a competitive advantage, through operational discipline and excellence; and
- Accelerating growth through focused execution.

Mission: The sentence that answers the questions: 'Who are our customers?', 'Why do we exist?'

Vision: The sentence that answers the question: 'Where are we going?'

Founding narrative: The sentence that answers the question: 'Where did we come from?' (Boje, 2008: 100–101)

In relation to learning, strategy narrative is consistent with reflective learning or reflective practice, which we dealt with in Chapter 8 on workplace learning. As noted, this concept was developed by Donald Schön (1983), who developed it as a description of how professionals think in action. He draws on theoretical contributions from Wittgenstein, Polanyi and Dewey. According to Schön, professional action is characterised as intelligent or reflective action. This means that actions are qualified with reference to theoretical, formal or scientific knowledge. There is a difference whether one acts by rule of thumb or from habit or whether one is capable of arguing why she acts the way she does. Reflective action is characterised as the latter.

As such the reflective practitioner acts according to particular narratives, in the case of professionals these narratives have the character of theory, formal or scientific knowledge. But we may replace these narratives with strategy, where actions are qualified with reference to strategy narratives and make the same kinds of conclusions. In this sense, the relation between two forms of knowledge, *knowing-that* and *knowing-how* (Ryle, 1949) may be applied here. Knowing-that is applied here as knowledge of logo, motto, plot, mission, vision and founding narrative and knowing-how as knowledge of how to execute this in practice.

The purpose of Ryle's work is on one side to move attention towards what takes place in practice. On the other side, Ryle's work is by no means a rejection of abstract and theoretical knowledge. But this knowledge has to be assessed in relation to what takes place in practice:

> **Both in describing the minds of others and in prescribing for them, they are wielding with greater and less efficiency concepts for mental powers and operations. They have learned how to apply in concrete situations such mental-conduct epithets as 'careful', 'stupid', 'logical', 'unobservant', 'ingenious', 'vain', 'methodical', 'credulous', 'witty', 'selfcontrolled' and a thousand others. It is however, one thing to know how to apply such concepts, quite another to know how to correlate them with one another and with concepts of other sorts. Many people can talk sense with concepts but cannot talk sense about them; they know by practice how to operate with concepts but cannot talk sense about them; they know by practice how to operate with concepts, anyhow inside familiar fields, but they cannot state the logical regulations governing their use. (Ryle, 1949: s. 7)**

The ideal for Ryle is the intelligent or reflective action; in other words that you know what you are doing. Routinised and unreflected action is not considered part of this. Gustavsson argues that thought has to be part of the whole process. This includes that knowledge is considered a skill. But skill implies that an argument can be carried through about what has been accomplished. To do something from routine or habit, is not enough to say that we know something. Knowledge is to know what to do and why it is done. Action is done with an intention in mind (Gustavsson, 2001: 102–103).

Knowledge is possessed when actions can be qualified. Similarly John Dewey argues that thinking is the human instrument for solving complex problems. Thinking is something else than reflection. He argues that there is an element of reflection in any action. Dewey however, distinguishes between two kinds of reflection. Some types of reflection are nothing more than trial and error learning where feedback follows action until a rule-of-thumb has been accomplished, that if we do that, this will happen. Such types of reflection are widespread and when they have been socialised into social practice, it is something done from sheer habit.

But as noted by Dewey: 'We see that a certain way of acting and a certain consequence are connected, but we don't see how they are' (1916: 145). Thinking is the kind of reflection, where we try to understand these connections. Thinking is systematic, explorative and analytical in its approach to practical problems: 'the ground or a basis for a belief is deliberately sought and its adequacy to support the belief examined' (Dewey, 1991: 13).

Obviously all strategy narratives cannot live up to the standards proposed by Dewey as a proper discourse governing the use of actions in organisations. Many types of learning leading to strategy narratives may actually have the character of simple trial and error, where feedback has followed actions until a rule-of-thumb has been accomplished. We may actually assume that strategy narrative as a result of a systematic learning process in organisations is the exception rather than the rule.

However, the basic point remains that strategy narrative is similar to formal theoretical knowledge in the sense that they presume a logical cause–effect relationship; e.g. 'if we deepen the relationship with customers we will do better overall' etc. Further, strategies and especially strategy narratives stem from the scientific discourses of management thus to some extent claiming scientific validity and reliability of the knowledge embedded in strategy. In this sense, the discourses of science and strategy are not separate.

Finally, strategy narrative works as an ideal of how to think strategy and is broadly established in different management education programmes. Narrative also works as an ideal of learning as mentioned above. This is clearly evident in Dewey's work. He argues that the source of learning is the experience of a problem defined as the experience of a new bothersome and doubtful situation. The function of reflection is:

> **to bring about a new situation in which the difficulty is resolved, the confusion cleared away, the trouble smoothed out, the question it puts answered. Any particular process of thinking naturally comes to its close when the situation before the mind is settled, decided, orderly, clear, for then there is nothing to call out reflection until a new bothersome or doubtful situation arises. (Dewey, 1933: 100)**

Further, he argues that 'inquiry is the controlled or directed transformation of an indeterminate situation into one that is so determinate in its constituent distinctions and relations as to convert the elements of the original situation into a unified whole' (Dewey, 1991: 108). The object of learning in Dewey's work is thus narrative in terms of creating certainty, coherence, unity, and identifying cause–effect linkages between action and consequences.

But even if narrative works as an ideal of learning and strategy narrative as an ideal of strategy, we might question this narrative notion and ask the question if this kind of strategic learning will work in the future. In any case, I suggest that this narrative learning is only one side of it and that we need a more complex notion of strategy and learning in order to meet future challenges of continuous change and an ever-increasing complexity in the organisation's institutional framework.

The problems of strategy narrative are threefold: firstly, there is the problem that strategy narrative implicitly presumes a simplistic view of the relationship between actions and consequences. Strategy narrative is a reduction of complexity into a simple linear relationship of past, present and future. In this sense, strategy narrative works with a representation of time, which Morson calls foreshadowing. He argues that foreshadowing 'robs the present of its presentness by lifting the veil on a predetermined future' (Morson, 1994: 117). In foreshadowing the sequence of events is already given as the specific outcome of a linear sequence of events or in other words as part of what Boje calls a BME (beginning, middle, end) narrative (Boje and Durant, 2006).

Robbing the presentness of the present implies here to rely on simple explanations, myths, prejudice, habit without allowing for a deeper interrogation into the multiple possible directions to take. In other words, strategy narrative as a result of learning also inherits non-learning and non-interrogation. In a world which is increasingly liquid and complex, this kind of approach is hardly appropriate. If it stands alone, it soon becomes past.

Secondly, there is the problem that strategy narrative is relatively monovocal instead of polyvocal. In relation to the characteristics of language as complex and multi-voiced, strategy narrative often represents only a few dominant voices in the organisation. Narrative strategies are usually written by one expert or a dominant coalition of stakeholders (Boje, 2008: 99). Strategy narrative in other words only represents the voice of a particular dominant group of people.

When I have argued that strategy as such can be seen as the organisation's 'human time' by which it seeks to place itself in relation to a complex world, it is important to note that this is mostly a dominant coalition's human time, not a human time that represents all stakeholders within the network of relations that constitute the organisation. Organisations comprise all kinds of voices; e.g. dominant, oppressed, anonymous and marginalised voices.

This implies that strategy narrative represents only a fragment of the organisation. Further, it implies that strategy narratives are inconsistent and may even be opposed to the identities of many of the organisation's stakeholders, who subsequently lack both ownership and motivation for supporting the strategy.

This relates to the third problem of strategy narrative, namely that narratives tend to be relatively narcissistic and self-preserving. This is a problem of any language and it can be stated as a problem of being caught up in 'definitive language and truth claims' (Cunliffe and Jun, 2005: 227) as noted also in Chapter 8.

Language is interwoven with identity, and this means that we tend to stick to and defend our narratives – otherwise we couldn't believe in ourselves and what we do. If these definitive language and truth claims are challenged, we subsequently often take it very personally. As a consequence of this, we stick to myths, prejudices and our pre-understandings (mimesis1) determine our after-understandings in a way in which we may reproduce old definitions of problems and old conceptions of solutions instead of rethinking the organisation. Subsequently the old arguments and the old conflicts are also reproduced.

In a world which is increasingly liquid this is obviously not the solution in terms of learning to face the challenges of tomorrow. In such a world we need to work with another dimension of learning, one that is capable of questioning and rethinking our narratives and language. Next, we describe such an approach, which takes its starting point in what I refer to as a storytelling approach consistent with the concept of living story that we discussed in Chapter 11 on identity and HRD. This approach is more consistent with reflexive practice.

Storytelling, strategy and narrative

An alternative to strategy narrative is to take a storytelling approach to strategy formation. A storytelling approach emphasises living story instead of narrative as the basic starting point. As noted in the identity chapter, story is living because they are becoming and are shaping our individual and communal identities and imagined futures. They are never finished, not necessarily whole, and are still alive in the here and now.

Living story implies that construction of reality has been influenced and is influenced by a multiplicity of force relations. Constructions of reality take place in specific historical and geographical conditions that include political and ethical dimensions, material conditions etc. Storytelling is in other words plural and polyphonic. We emphasise with storytelling that construction of human experience is always inter-subjective and plural, ambiguous, open-ended, emergent, continuously evolving and it progresses in unpredictable ways.

Table 12.1 Characteristics of narrative and storytelling

Narrative	Storytelling
Monologic	Dialogic/plural
Linear	Fragmentary
Closed	Open
Retrospective	Emergent
Rational	Irrational
Unambiguous	Ambiguous
Objective or subjective	Inter-subjective

The differences between narrative and storytelling are summarized in Table 12.1.

A storytelling approach to strategy implies seeing organisations as results of complex chains of interactions, negotiations and struggles between many different actors, groups, departments, other organisations, institutions etc. What characterises organisations is not unity but multiplicity. They are inter-subjectively constructed, and they progress in unpredictable and irrational ways. Organisations are continuously constructed, reconstructed, modified and changed through interactions between actors by which the organisation's resources are concerted and translated into some degree of alignment with the organisation's institutional framework.

Implications in terms of learning and HRD are that storytelling thus emphasises ante-narrative rather than narrative. Boje defines ante-narrative as non-linear, incoherent, collective, unplotted and prenarrative speculation, at best a proper narrative can be constituted (Boje, 2001, 2008). Story is before – 'ante' – narrative. To emphasise story instead of narrative means to uphold the unfinished character of interpretations. It is thus an attempt to free stories from the linear beginning, middle and end.

In this connection, storytelling implies working with a notion of open time, which Morson calls sideshadowing as different from foreshadowing mentioned above. Sideshadowing is defined as a way of understanding and working with multiple possibilities (Morson, 1994: 117). Sideshadowing seeks to restore presentness to the present in acknowledging multiple possible futures. It conveys the sense that actual events might not have happened; that there are always alternatives and other possibilities: 'instead of casting a foreshadow from the future, it casts a shadow from the side, that is from the other possibilities' (Morson, 1994: 118).

The notions of *reflexive practice*, which I believe becomes a crucial dimension of HRD practice in the future, are caught in the notions of sideshadowing and ante-narrative in being directed towards suspending our interpretations of beginnings, middles and ends and in working with multiple pasts, multiple presents and multiple futures. Where narratives are taken for granted in reflective practice, they are always questioned and disturbed in reflexive practice.

The difference between reflective and reflexive thus mirrors a fundamental difference in ontology and thus meaning of the two terms. Ann Cunliffe and colleagues have emphasised the difference (Cunliffe, 2002, 2003; Cunliffe and Jun, 2005). They argue that the concept of reflection is linked to the idea of mirroring reality in an objective way. They refer to Schön here, who described – as noted before – how professionals linked theoretical ideas to the conception of problems and solutions in practice and where there was a continuous play between these conceptions and reality (Cunliffe and Jun, 2005: 226).

This process involves a continuous reflective conversation between the practitioner and the situation in order to improve the solution. This is a process where new methods, new hypotheses and new theories are continuously developed. But this is not a reflexive process because an ontological conception of theory and concepts as an objective mirror of reality is maintained. Schön, Dewey and Ryle stick to this conception of reality, which is mirrored in their language, where they use concepts like hypotheses test, inquiry, data etc. This implies the presumption that the truth is out there waiting to be discovered. It is the task of science to discover it and to put it into play in regard to practical problems.

If this presumption of reality is abandoned in favour of the presumption that reality is socially constructed through storytelling and playing language games the basis is created for understanding reflexivity and the reflexive practitioner as one who continually questions her own narratives and language and tries to see other possible futures. The reflexive practitioner questions the language she uses in conceiving problems, solutions, ends, means and relevance etc.

As noted in Chapter 8 on workplace learning, Cunliffe and Jun make a distinction between 'reflection' and 'reflexivity' by referring to Heidegger's distinction between *calculative thinking* and *mediative thinking*. The former is characteristic of an objective observer reflecting on a situation to understand what is really going on and to develop theories to explain that reality. Mediative thinking is different in seeking to question the foundation of our thinking and to be open for other possibilities.

Reflexive thinking involves that we begin to question our concepts, notions and model – that is our language. The attempt is to avoid being caught in definitive language and truth claims as noted before. We are prisoners of our language. The challenge is thus to try to become more aware of the presumptions and prejudices embedded in language; for example how our language conditions the way we conceive reality including problems, solutions and relationships with others. These are deep questions which relate to our identity and stories of selves and others. Reflexivity is therefore also difficult and painful.

In addition to questioning, reflexivity implies the recognition of otherness as opposed to the narcissistic and conservative language of strategy narrative. Strategy storytelling is directed towards listening to and understanding other voices, because it is from such interactions that people may learn something new about reality and themselves; by trying to recognise, listening to and appreciate others' voices.

Walter Benjamin has argued that the 'storyteller is the figure in which the righteous man encounters himself' (Benjamin, 1999). Storytelling is in this way a more ethical or democratic approach to leadership and strategy formation at the same time as it has a big potential for learning by systematically listening to other voices. Boje has argued that strategies need to be more polyphonic in embracing many different voices.

He defines polyphonic strategy story as one 'written, visualized or orally told by all the stakeholders to an organization' (Boje, 2008: 99). The argument is thus that story-telling and reflexivity is intimately linked with the notion of shared identity or shared language that bridges the gap and sustains the bonds between individuals, the organisation and the institutional framework in which the organisation exists.

The balance between these dimensions is of course impossible to achieve. There are inconsistencies, paradoxes and direct conflicts of interests among the many different actors in organisations. This is because people's logics, values and contexts are so different from each other. These differences between them stem from professional background, experience, position, work assignments, personality, age, gender, religion, race etc.

But this doesn't mean that we cannot work with these differences and taking them into account when a process merges into a strategy. Further, to argue that shared identity is impossible to achieve doesn't mean that we cannot work with making strategies more plurivocal thus creating more ownership and motivation for the chosen strategies.

This leads to some remarks about the storytelling approach to strategy formation. As Jørgensen and Boje have argued in a recent paper on business ethics, intentions are not to destroy narrative. Intentions are to create a more democratic relationship between the narrative and storytelling and to re-situate the previous hegemonic relationship between the two terms, where narrative was emphasised and where we forgot storytelling (Jørgensen and Boje, 2010). This will stiffen strategy and it will ultimately only be the strategy of the few. But we also need to create narrative order because otherwise we would not have an organisation.

The storytelling approach adds a critical dimension to strategic thinking in creating the foundations for more innovative, dynamic and flexible strategy work in organisations. But it does not replace other dimensions. The effectiveness of storytelling relies on being in a dynamic interplay with other dimensions of learning including strategic learning.

Next I will move onto one example from management education, where intentions are to combine, among others, reflective and reflexive practice. We then move to a short description of different methods for creating reflexive practice and create new possible futures. I concentrate on three methods: *Genealogy, deconstruction* and *carnivalesque storytelling.*

Theory at work – lessons from practice

A case from management education may illuminate how to work with reflective and reflexive practice. The case is a new Master's programme that is being offered by a consortium that consists of Copenhagen University, Copenhagen Business School and Aalborg University. The programme is directed towards experienced employees that hold a relevant bachelor degree. It is a supplementary training programme, where participants study part-time for a period of two years in all. Further it is a flexible programme, where participants have to put modules together themselves to form a coherent whole.

It is directed towards current and future leaders in the public sector. The purpose of the programme is to develop the competencies of public leaders so that they become able to conduct professional leadership in a politically managed, public context. Intentions are to strengthen the public leader's competence to reflect and to develop own leadership practice.

As such the goal is that public leaders become more reflective in the sense that they become able to apply theory in order to act and to argue for these actions systematically. The second goal is however, that leaders become able to reflect upon and develop own leadership practice. While the first relates to *reflective practice*, the second relates to *reflexive practice*.

This new way of thinking about education is linked to the idea that increasingly education as well as HRD is not solely a question about qualifying people for a particular job. Rather, the world has become so complex and fluid that it has become necessary that leaders and other employees gain the competencies in rethinking and reconfiguring organisational practices including their own practices.

This ability to question and reflect upon one's own leadership practices is referred to as reflexive competencies and personal development competencies in the Master's programme, which combines purposes of obtaining more traditional competencies with new reflexive competencies. In more detail, the Master's programme operates with the following set of competencies.

- Contextual knowledge: knowledge of values and conditions for leadership of and in public organisations and political fields.

- Theoretical competencies: knowledge of theories and their application. Capabilities in observing and documenting own leadership practice.

- Reflexive competencies: capabilities in reflecting upon own points of observation and interpretations of possibilities for action, the context for leadership and leadership practice.

- Practical leadership competencies: capabilities in (1) identifying development needs and possibilities for action, (2) transforming visions and strategies to actions, and (3) in balancing demands for efficiency, quality, implementation and daily operations.

- Personal development competence: consciousness of own competencies, preferences, values, actions and context.

Even if I have discussed and emphasised reflective practice and reflexive practice above, it is important to realise that all the competencies are closely linked and to some degree at least are mutually constitutive. Contextual and theoretical knowledge, for example, are necessary competencies in describing and understanding one's own leadership practices.

Both types of competencies comprise a language by which it becomes possible to understand and frame leadership practice and where leaders can improve. This means that the new types do not replace other types of competencies. The emphasis on reflective and reflexive practices is instead symbolic of a still more complex view of competencies and the recognition of new important dimensions of competencies.

It is to establish a proper combination and interplay of these competencies, which is important because otherwise an HRD strategy would be seriously amputated and incapable of facing the complex demands that many organisations experience today. The challenge can in other words be stated as creating a dynamic interplay between narrative order and story disorder and thus to avoid that our narratives, including strategy narratives stiffen and die.

The emphasis on reflective competencies implies that contextual and theoretical knowledge need to be translated into practical leadership competencies. In other words, there needs to be an integration of theory and practice, in the sense that leadership actions become theoretically grounded and reflected. The reflective practitioner practices intelligent practice – she knows what to do and why this is so. For this reason, the Master's programme consistently uses a problem-oriented pedagogy throughout all its modules in order that theoretical knowledge becomes integrated with the participants' practical problems.

In contrast reflexive competencies are characterised by the ability of reflection upon own language and conceptual framework. Reflexive practice is directed towards own ways of understanding and framing the world, its problems and its solutions. The programme thus systematically trains participants in distancing themselves, observing and reflecting on own practice and what conditions this practice. We use various techniques for that.

In one instance, I used *deconstruction* (see later) in order that participants gained a more critical stance towards their own ways of framing problems and solutions in their texts. Here the intention was to train participants to see their text as a political text in which their own presumptions and prejudices played a big part. Through this kind of feedback, intentions were to pave the way for alternative ways of perceiving and understanding problems and solutions.

Other techniques and methods that we are going to use in the programme are different types of dialogues such as Team Reflection, coaching, appreciative inquiry and other types of methods for playing with language in order to obtain alternative understandings. The purpose of establishing reflexive practices in the programme is not however only to obtain a more critical stance towards own leadership practice. It is also to refigure it, or to re-narrate it so to speak, but in a way in which it is more professional but also grounded within the relationships that constitute the organisation.

In the Master's programme, this is trained in different ways. Participants, for example, have to put their own study programme together from a mix of modules and argue for this in relation to their own professional development. Further, participants have to carry through a leadership development programme by practising on their own practice. Here reflexive practices are used continuously to challenge participants' presumptions and understandings of situations in order that these participants become more aware of own leadership practice and the relationships that condition it.

Storytelling methods for strategic HRD

The three storytelling methods that I describe here do not in any way cover all methods that are or claim to be reflexive. I have selected them here, because of their common characteristics in trying to play with language, breaking up the linear relationships of narrative and create new and alternative understandings and possible futures. To be applied in a storytelling strategy process, we need to keep in mind the ontological characteristics of storytelling as being inter-subjective, dialogical and plural.

This point leads to the more normative view of creating a strategy process that is plurivocal and seeks to give voice to all the stakeholders in order to create a powerful strategy. This aspect of creating a strategy process in not dealt with further in this chapter. I will instead concentrate on describing methods for opening up for alternative voices in the dialogical processes leading to strategy formation.

Further, I see the storytelling methods described here as fundamental methods, which can be applied in many different learning situations and in combination with more 'practical' learning methods or models, which are well-known from the literature. This includes methods and models like portfolio, supervision, therapy, coaching, appreciative inquiry etc. A number of such methods and models have already been described in this book.

The point is that these methods and models may be used to create both reflective and reflexive learning situations depending on the specific organisation of the learning situations in which they are applied. The key storytelling competence is still to learn to be able to read and listen to alternative voices and interpretations and avoid that dialogues become fixed by relations of power that govern what can be and what cannot be said in strategy process. The methods described below have been selected in that spirit.

Genealogy

The notion of genealogy comes from Foucault's application of Nietzschean genealogy in relation to power analysis (Foucault, 1984; Jørgensen, 2002, 2007). When genealogy is applied here, the idea is to see strategy as emerging in specific historical and geographical circumstances, where the emergent strategy is one of many different possibilities.

It is applied here because genealogy questions the legitimacy of strategy in terms of focusing on marginalised and forgotten voices. Thus it often reveals that strategy is the voice of only a dominant coalition of the organisation's stakeholders. Further, it reveals that strategy is an accident; a result of a completely irrational and non-linear process, which could have ended up differently. In this way it opens up history and is consistent with sideshadowing.

The practice of genealogical analysis is thus a special kind of historical analysis where Foucault seeks to construct an alternative memory that is different, more nuanced and varied than the memory embedded in present day narratives and language. Narratives that tend to represent the strategic process as only pointing in one necessary direction and as more rational than it was. The point is that present-day narratives and language act as a smokescreen that seeks to legitimise particular outcomes and thus represent the course of events in a particular way.

By writing a genealogy of a strategic process through exploring the sequence and characteristics of events that led up to the strategy, the idea is to obtain a different understanding of the past that will point in different directions in the future. As such genealogy is reflexive in breaking up linear relations of beginning, middle and end by confronting them with brute history.

When applied in organisations genealogy and power analysis is conducted with the purpose of revaluating the values on which organisations, institutions, phenomena or events are founded. This kind of analysis seeks to make us more conscious of where conceptions of truth and justice, which are embedded and implicit in strategic language and actions, come from.

Genealogy is systematically suspicious of any statement and any narrative because it looks at such actions as framed by relations of power at work in everyday organisational life. Genealogy is open for worst cases to occur including cases of violence, tyranny, corruption, nepotism etc. Genealogy does never presume that a strategy process is polite, civilised, noble, pragmatic or reasonable. Actors in them might as well be evil, immoral, obnoxious, selfish and capable of doing whatever it takes to promote their own intentions or interests.

The problem is that multi-layered, complex and plural history is often represented in simple linear narratives. In these narratives, we lose the actors, the complex struggles and sophisticated plays by which a strategy was born. Genealogy seeks to reconstruct historical development by bringing attention to whom, where and when in a way which is aligned with marginalised voices. In Boje's words, intentions are to figure out whodunit: Who wrote the strategy, a board, a dominant coalition etc.? (Boje, 2008: 102–103). Who were marginalised and left out? In other words, who is speaking and from where does she get her authority to speak.

Genealogical analysis of a strategy should make it possible to follow from where strategy came, how it progressed, developed and changed through interactions and negotiations among actors in different positions and with different intentions. Genealogical analysis thus scrutinises concrete historical events in terms of actors (and their interrelationships), chronology and context thus exposing dominant accounts of history to mockery and laughter.

It is relevant for the analysis of strategy formation in the sense that it seeks to dig in behind the scenes and visualise the complex political network of relationships at work in regard to major strategic decisions and events. Genealogical analysis thus tells a more varied and complex story of why particular decisions were made and imple- mented and why the legitimacy of these events was represented the way it was.

My study of organisational change in a bank (Jørgensen, 2007) is one example where the emergence of a particular strategic management decision was explored in order to create an alternative memory of these actions and events that diverge from official and dominant narratives and accounts of the present. The story questions these narratives and accounts by revealing among others how controversial relation- ships among actors and past failures of managing change influenced the decision. Relationships and failures that were however not part of the organisation's legitimate vocabulary and memory.

Deconstruction

Deconstruction is related to genealogy, or we may put it differently, genealogy is one way of deconstructing a 'text'. Still there are also differences in the sense that decon- struction reads words and actions through the relations they have to that outside of it. Thus deconstruction tends to emphasise spatial context and its relations to the text, while genealogy tends to be more focused on the context of history and time. Deconstruction was developed by the French philosopher Jacques Derrida, whose primary focus was to question dominant narratives in western discourses through a deconstructive reading of the text.

Derrida suggested that there is nothing outside of the text, which basically means that there is no essential referent or transcendental signified and where text means something much broader than the pages of a book and includes the politics and ethics of action, material conditions, architectures, institutions and technologies (Derrida, 1997: 158; Boje, 2001: 22). In short, strategy, strategic actions, technologies, structures and architec- tures that support strategy are texts that can be subjected to deconstruction.

Deconstruction emphasises the inter-subjectivity, complexity and pluralism of texts. Texts such as strategies are living and can evolve in multiple directions. Any beginning, middle and end of a text then represent an illusion of closure and misun- derstands the co-livingness of story that always deconstruct a strategy for instance. Deconstruction happens or it takes place in the sense that a strategy as an example of text is always exceeded by its relation to that which is outside it. Deconstruction thus takes place (Jones, 2007: 520).

To read a strategy for example, implies perceiving it as a political text in which is embedded hegemonic relationships. Typical hegemonic relationships in strategy are for example that leader voices are hegemonic of employee voices, that profit is hegemonic of ethics, that rationalisation is hegemonic of learning etc. Embedded in strategy formation may be a variety of hegemonic relationships which implies that some perceptions of what constitutes good leadership practice or good strategic practice dominate over others. We may also see organisational texts as a place where strategic discourse is hegemonic of other competing discourses of where the organisation should go.

A deconstructive reading implies the reversal of such hierarchical relationships and privileging the weak term over the other hegemonic one (Culler, 2003). The deconstructive move is in the first place to overturn the hierarchy and to reorganise the textual field for establishing the ground for a new balance of views between the two (Boje, 2001; Derrida, 2002; Jørgensen and Boje, 2010).

When applied here in relation to strategy, intentions are to perform a critical reading of an organisation's strategy by focusing on who is talking, who is oppressed, who is marginalised and who is completely left out and secondly aligning themselves with the marginalised and oppressed. Deconstruction implies recognising otherness and it is systematically suspicious of any truth and morality claim. Such claims would be deemed as the judgements of the self-righteous ones, as narcissistic and it would be subjected to scrupulous critique.

In this way, deconstruction is an effective means of constructing a reflexive distance to the voices embedded in strategy formation including own voices. Its usage is unlimited in that it can be applied to any text, to any strategic document or action, to any narrative of what constitutes good strategic and narrative practice. But again the intention is not to efface narrative or strategy narrative from the face of the earth. Intentions are to create a balance of views and a more democratic relationship between narrative and storytelling voices (Jørgensen and Boje, 2010) in order that narratives do not stiffen and petrify.

Carnivalesque storytelling

Carnivalesque storytelling is the last storytelling method dealt with here. And it is not really a method, or an established approach but rather an umbrella concept which emphasises the reorganisation of language and alternative modes of expression as ways of bringing forward alternative voices to established ones. The notion carnivalesque storytelling is inspired by Bakhtin's notion of carnival (Bakhtin, 1994).

It relies on a distinction between two very different forms of language. Firstly, there is official and orthodox language. This language is characterised as dogmatic, monolithic and authoritarian. In organisations it would characterise the organisation's official language controlled by dogmatic expectations, roles, norms and standards. Such communicational practices are often the symbolic manifestations of particular disciplinary practices of power (Foucault, 1979) that govern appropriate talk and actions in terms of governing expectations, roles, routines in different spheres of societies and organisations.

Secondly, there is the carnival type of language; the people's unofficial language. This language relieves the burden of hierarchical positions, ranks, roles, expectations in communication. We use carnival as a metaphor of what Bakhtin calls the people's second life characterised by the suspense of established truth and conceptions and organised on the basis of laughter (Bakhtin, 1994: 198). In organisations, carnival language would expose the gay relativity of established truth and conceptions. These established truth and conceptions in organisations are linked to the image of spectacle in that they are linked to a presumed way of living guided by a particular mask and raison d'être.

The teachers of the purpose of existence – to use a phrase from Nietzsche (1974) – are not priests or moralists – but leaders, managers, investors, stockholders, brokers etc. who are all part of a globalised capitalist world, which is considered a modern spectacle – an image of presumed happiness and smiling people – that distracts people from 'recovering the full range of their human powers through creative practice' (Boje et al., 2003). Spectacle implies a form of social life where individuals passively consume commodity spectacles and service without active or direct participation and involvement.

As argued previously, organisational communication is dominated by orthodox conservative language that freezes the dynamics of the organisations and captures in an insubstantial form of living. We may be inspired by Bakhtin's metaphor of carnival laughter to denote particular instances in organisations in which established ranks and hierarchies are suspended and where more liberating and innovative language may emerge. I refer to this kind of language as carnivalesque storytelling.

I use it to denote three instances of listening and recognising alternative voices. I call the first *reorganising space*, the second *alternative modes of expression* and the third for *listening to people's second life in organisations*.

Reorganisation of space is inspired by Bakhtin's carnival or feast. For Bakhtin the marketplace and the carnival were places which allowed for new innovative language to emerge and in which it was allowed to subject the establishment to parody, mockery and laughter. I am not saying that organisations should organise a carnival, a feast or a parody or something else for that matter. I use carnival as a metaphor for establishing a new and different space and thus allow for alternative stories to emerge.

This kind of 'feast' should be very different, spontaneous and continuously evolving. It is completely different from the official feast that asserts all that was 'stable, unchanging, perennial: the existing religious, political, and moral values, norms and prohibitions. It was the triumph of a truth already established' (Bakhtin, 1994: 199). Carnivalesque spaces in organisations would thus involve for example playing with constructing different spaces but also reorganising these spaces by playing with roles and norms, new words, new techniques and by inviting untraditional people with untraditional talents to the scene.

This leads to the second point that I call alternative modes of expression. Derrida has argued that writing seems to favour exploitation rather than enlightenment of mankind (Derrida, 1997: 101). I use it here because the modern organisation, e.g. the bureaucracy, has been dominated by writing (Weber, 1971) and thus by a particular rational language. We meet strategic language through textbooks and journal articles and it is the ways leaders and managers are taught to speak.

Management is here no different from the development in other parts of society. A development, that Benjamin mourned because he argued that the art of storytelling was coming to an end and was being gradually replaced by information (Benjamin, 1999). The result is a cold, causal, flat, stylised and stiffened language, where the attempt is to take out all subjectivity, art, poetry, spirit etc. 'Every morning brings us the news from the globe, and yet we are poor in noteworthy stories. This is because no event any longer comes to us without already being shot through with explanation' (Benjamin, 1999: 89). According to Benjamin, this is the modern way of communicating, which has been embedded in modern management language and strategic language. As such strategic language is restrictive.

Carnivalesque storytelling would open up other modes of expressions in terms of bringing more dynamics to language: this includes art, music, jokes, jargon, theatre, poetry, body language, sport etc. But more importantly it also brings attention to ordinary skills, expressions and language of crafts men, technicians, IT specialists, professionals, who develop their own language as part of their work and profession.

The key point is not that this necessarily replaces writing and strategy narrative. The key point is that allowing for alternative expressions might help in reorganising language and creating new relationships between people by gaining new understandings of who other people are and what they stand for. Meeting people through ordinary formal information channels in organisations is restrictive of what can take place, which means that roles, positions and talk are fixed. Breaking up relationships and reconfiguring them into new relationships may involve the reorganisation of space and by allowing for alternative modes of expression.

The final point is called listening to the people's second life in organisation. As mentioned above, we may distinguish between the organisation's official language and the organisation's unofficial language created by people's second life. When entering into an organisation as a change agent, who do we listen to?

Often, we listen to the organisation's official language and narratives. We read strategy documents, founding narratives and we talk to official representatives. It is harder to gain access to the unofficial language or underground language in the organisation. The language, jokes, humour, jargon, and phrases used in conjunction with daily work and collaboration with colleagues, in smoking rooms, canteens, informal meetings etc.

But it is probably here that we have the potential of really getting to know the organisation if we learn to listen to these voices. In the critique of modern society, Benjamin says at one point that the realm of narrative has been removed from the realm of everyday speech (Benjamin, 1999: 86) as a result of the secular productive forces of history.

Applied here it can be used to indicate the danger of strategy narrative being removed from living day-to-day interaction and oral storytelling. As mentioned previously, it is probably the case that strategy narratives only represent a fragment of voices and as such is inconsistent with the identities of its members. Learning to listen to underground voices is an attempt to avoid that strategy and living day-to-day storytelling evolve in separate directions.

 **Discussion questions**

- Why is HRD important in relation to future strategic challenges in organisations?

- What is the relationship between narrative, storytelling and learning?

- How can we create a more dynamic interplay between strategy narrative and storytelling in organisations?

- Try to identify a strategy in an organisation and expose it to genealogical analysis and/or deconstruction. What story emerges from that?

13 Leadership Development
David McGuire

------ ■ ■ **Chapter objectives** ■ ------

The objectives of this chapter are to:

- examine the four key streams of leadership (trait, behavioural, contingency/situational and transformational);

- explore the developmental implications flowing from leadership theories;

- consider the criticisms levelled at leadership theories.

------ **Introduction** ------

Are leaders born or are they made? Such has been the starting point for much discussion about leadership theory and the potential for developing effective leaders. While leadership theories often accurately describe key characteristics of the leadership experience, the ensuing explanation of leadership development interventions is often generic and only rarely connected to a particular leadership theory. To add to the confusion, leadership development is often conflated and confused with management development (Mabey and Finch-Lees, 2008: 33; Sadler-Smith, 2006: 280) necessitating a clear demarcation of boundaries and clarity regarding the purposes and outcomes of leadership development.

Despite early concerns about progress in the field of leadership development, some advances have been made in recent years. As early as 2000, Lynham noted that:

> There exists a deficiency of real scholarly knowledge about leadership development. The majority of research in the field of leadership development has focused on the what of leadership, rather than the how of leadership development resulting in a lack of knowledge and empirical evidence regarding the subject of leadership development. (121)

Further criticisms of leadership theories come from Zaccaro and Klimoski (2001) who argue that leadership theories are largely context-free and do not pay sufficient attention to structural contingencies that can affect and moderate leadership conduct. For his part, Avolio (2007) maintains that leadership theories overlook the role and support of followers and he advocates a more integrated approach to developing leadership theories.

This chapter seeks to provide an integrated framework for linking leadership theories with specific developmental interventions. It provides a synopsis of four prominent leadership theories (trait, behavioural, contingency, transformational) and examines the developmental potential emanating from such leadership theories, identifying specific developmental interventions associated with those theories. The chapter concludes with a discussion of how an integrated framework linking leadership theories and developmental interventions aids our understanding of how we approach and think about leadership development.

An integrated framework for linking leadership theories and developmental interventions

The search for a single leadership theory that is applicable across all contexts and can be used to identify potential leaders has assumed considerable attention in the leadership literature. As different theories investigate various elements of the leadership experience, it is instructive to look across all theories to explore how leaders can be developed most effectively. The rationale for examining leadership development from a holistic perspective is advanced by Olivares et al. who state:

> **Leadership development, as a type of human development, takes place over time; it is incremental in nature, it is accretive; and it is the result of complex reciprocal interactions between the leader, others, and the social environment. Hence, effective leadership development realizes that leaders develop and function within a social context; and, although individual-based leader development is necessary for leadership, it is not sufficient. Leadership requires that individual development is integrated and understood in the context of others, social systems, and organisational strategies, missions, and goals. (2007: 79)**

To this end, the integrated framework aims to present a cross-cutting analysis of the key features of mainstream leadership theories and the developmental implications that flow from them.

Trait leadership

Trait leadership views the possession of particular inherent qualities enabling an individual to distinguish themselves in a leadership role (Pierce and Newstrom, 2008: 65). It advances the view that leaders are made and that leadership research can usefully identify key leadership characteristics such that individuals possessing key traits can be promoted to leadership positions within organisations. The key thrust of trait leadership research has therefore been to identify the qualities of effective leaders and produce inventories and questionnaires that test for levels of innate traits within individuals. To this end, trait leadership to some degree has reflected leadership trends more generally. Allio (2005) is critical of the modern inclusion of traits such as humility, credibility and modesty as little more than evidence of a current backlash against charismatic leadership advocates. In agreement,

Fiedler (1996) maintains that there is an overemphasis on traits and leaders who have abilities, skills and resources that are useful to the organisation will be selected and accepted as leaders.

One of the earliest theories of trait leadership is that of 'great man theory' (James, 1880; Bernard, 1926). It advocated that leaders would naturally rise to leadership positions possessing all the necessary skills and traits to make them effective in their role. According to Bass (1990), the great man was believed to be unique and have features that would differentiate him for others. An added dimension to the theory suggested that the progeny of 'great men' would also become effective leaders. Great man theory was common in the 1930s and 1940s with Mostovicz et al. (2009) maintaining that through describing and cataloguing the traits of effective leaders, others could learn about and emulate such traits, making their leadership efforts more effective. However, research evidence on great man theory yielded inconclusive results (Stodgill, 1948) with the added criticism that the theory was elitist, discriminatory towards women, promoted nepotism and lacked attention to situational factors.

Much of the focus on trait approach to leadership examines the big five personality traits which includes extroversion, neuroticism, agreeableness, conscientiousness and openness (Costa and McCrae, 1992; Goldberg, 1990). Briefly defined, extraversion looks at an individual's outward orientation, sociability and level of assertiveness. Neuroticism explores an individual's levels of anxiety, tension, stress and levels of negative emotions. Openness examines an individual's outlook and perspective, the broadness of their interests, adventure-seeking nature and level of imagination and creativity. Agreeableness looks at an individual's sense of altruism, level of friendship and easy disposition. Finally conscientiousness considers an individual's commitment to a task, their level of self-discipline and sense of duty. Research studies which have examined the relationship between these five factors and leadership effectiveness have found mainly contradictory results. Judge and Bono (2000) identified agreeableness as the strongest predictor of transformational leadership – a finding contradicted by Ployhart et al. (2001) who found that agreeableness was not predictive of transformational leadership. In the latter case, the authors uncovered a strong correlation between openness and transformational leadership. The clear difference in findings between Judge and Bono (2000) and Ployhart et al. (2001) may be accounted for by the difference in organisational settings – Judge and Bono conducted their study in an organisational context, whereas the Ployhart et al. study was carried out in a military context. A later study by Lim and Ployhart (2004) discovered that both openness to new experiences and agreeableness were not positively related to transformational leadership but found a positive relationship for extraversion and transformational leadership. This finding for the importance of the trait of extraversion was supported in Leung and Bozionelos (2004) who highlighted that extraversion was positively linked to prototypical notions of effective leaders.

A more recent application of trait leadership has been the contribution of Daniel Goleman in the area of emotional intelligence. In their book on Primal Leadership, Goleman et al. (2004) found that emotional intelligence was linked to superior business performance. Goleman defined emotional intelligence as 'The capacity for understanding our own feelings and those of others, for motivating others and ourselves whilst using leadership, empathy and integrity' (1999: 82) and identify four characteristics of emotional intelligence as self-awareness, self-management, social awareness and relationship management. One of the key findings of Goleman's work (Goleman, 1995) is that emotional intelligence was found to be twice as importance as intelligence in producing effective leaders. For their part, Sosik and Megerian (1999) found that managers with high levels of self-awareness were considered to be more effective leaders than those who were not self-aware. An empirical study by Dulewitz and Higgs (2004) proved that the emotional intelligence components of self-awareness, sensitivity and influence can be successfully developed through training interventions, while conscientiousness and intuitiveness were less amenable to training.

There is evidence to suggest that many traits linked to superior leadership performance can be successfully developed. Allio (2005) maintains that there is a strong need to design experiments that establish a causal relationship between training initiatives and improvements in leadership and such evidence is beginning to emerge. There is considerable consensus among leadership experts (Doh, 2003) that certain leadership traits (but not all) can be acquired and developed through leadership development programmes. There is also agreement that some leadership skills can be more easily acquired and that some individuals will acquire leadership skills more quickly than others. Doh (2003) argues that leadership programmes should adopt a holistic approach and include mentoring, coaching, and trial-and-error experiences to help individuals acquire particular traits and skills.

Behavioural leadership

Arising out of the criticisms levelled at trait leadership, researchers began to turn their focus to looking at the behaviours displayed by leaders. Behavioural leadership research focuses on the actions taken by leaders and believes that leadership is a set of behaviours that can be learned and perfected. As such, leadership is viewed as an observable process with leaders using different leadership styles to bring about desired results in given situations (Jacques et al., 2008). As Ehigie and Akpan (2004) point out, discussion on behavioural leadership styles is often presented as on a continuum and in this section, we will examine three dimensions: relation-oriented versus task-oriented (Likert, 1961); autocratic versus democratic versus laissez-faire (Lippitt, 1969) and transactional versus transformational (Bass, 1985).

Democratic versus autocratic versus laissez-faire

This leadership style dimension originated from studies carried out at the University of Iowa in the 1930s. According to Kustin and Jones (1995), an autocratic leadership style is characterised by high levels of managerial direction and low levels of employee involvement. This style is very directive and results-focused and typified by one-way communication, centralised power and an expectation of obedience and loyalty on behalf of employees. In contrast, Kustin and Jones (1995) explain that a democratic leadership style embraces a more supportive form of leadership with higher levels of employee input, autonomy, involvement and self-direction. Finally, a laissez-faire style describes a situation where the leader allows the followers to make the decisions. The leader takes little action to influence the group and generally allows the group total freedom in relation to its activities.

Relation-oriented versus task-oriented

The University of Iowa studies were followed by a series of studies conducted at Ohio State University which examined leadership style in terms of initiating structure and

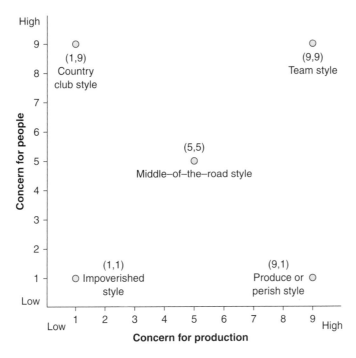

Figure 13.1 Blake and Mouton managerial grid

consideration (Stogdill, 1974). Initiating structure explores the extent to which a leader organises and defines employee roles and work and structures the roles of the leader and team members, whereas consideration examines the leader's commitment to building trust, respect and rapport with employees and listening to their ideas and opinions (Robbins et al., 1997). The Ohio State University studies were followed by leadership research carried out at the University of Michigan which classified leaders as being production-oriented or employee-oriented. Leaders who were production-oriented focused on the technical aspects of work, emphasising high performance levels and output, whereas employee-oriented leaders looked to identify and fulfil employee welfare needs in the workplace and developing interpersonal relations. The Ohio and Michigan studies were popularised with the publication of the Blake and Mouton (1964) Managerial Grid (see Figure 13.1), which identified five leadership styles along two axes labelled concern for production and concern for people. The authors argued that the most effective leadership style was the 9.9 team style (i.e. managers who exhibited both a high concern for production and a high concern for people).

Transactional/transformational

With the transactional/transformational dimension, Bass (1985) focused on the exchanges that take place between leader and followers. Transactional leadership was characterised as a form of leadership where the follower was motivated by the rewards provided by the leader in fulfilment of particular tasks or activities. Cardona (2000) describes transactional leadership as a zero-sum where the form of exchange is either economic or social. In contrast, transformational leaders succeed in moving followers beyond a zero-sum scenario in getting them to transcend their

own self-interests and bring about significant change for the benefit of the organisation or society as a whole. Further details on transformational leadership can be found
in a later section of this chapter.

Since the early 1980s, behavioural leadership research has increasingly focused on the
possession of so-called behavioural competencies. As defined by Boyatzis (1982), a
competency is 'an underlying characteristic of a person, which results in effective
and/or superior performance in a job'. In essence, Boyatzis began by identifying the
key characteristics of effective performance and leadership and positioning such
competencies on a scale between threshold level and superior performance level.
Competencies are thus increasingly used by organisations for a variety of purposes: as
performance standards and norms; as developmental tools to further employee skills;
as measures from which to award bonuses and incentives; to identify candidates in
the succession planning process and to assess key qualities during the recruitment
process. In the UK, a competency-based approach is used by many national certifica-
tion bodies and forms the basis for the national vocational qualifications (NVQ) and
Scottish vocational qualifications (SVQ) systems.
  In terms of research studies, authors have attempted to define leadership competencies in a variety of situations and contexts. For example, Mussig (2003) focuses on
isolating the characteristics of values-driven leadership in an increasingly value-driven
world. He identifies honesty, sustainability, commitment and understanding/supportive
as key emotional and relationship competencies required for this form of leadership.
McKenna (1998) examines cross-cultural understandings of leadership and the
components of leadership. He found that leadership cannot be singularly defined but
varies according to the national and cultural context. Finally, Boak and Coolican
(2001) highlight six competencies (acting strategically; influencing and inspiring
others; taking action; developing a high performance team; making decisions; evaluating and learning) as critical to effective retail leadership.
  In summary, the core thrust of behavioural leadership revolves around the belief
that leadership can be taught and that research can usefully identify the key components of successful leadership. Thus, many organisations have invested considerable
resources in developing competency frameworks for leadership development and
succession planning purposes in order to identify and increase the effectiveness of
leaders across their organisations. Competency-based development programmes are
now widespread throughout most organisations and are being used to frame and
underpin many HR initiatives and practices.

Situational leadership

Situational leadership emphasises the importance of flexibility of leadership approach
and situational awareness when a leader is faced with a particular problem or circum-
stance. It highlights the reality that leaders need to be adaptable in formulating
leadership responses and analyse subordinates, task, organisation and environment
that is facing them. This section will analyse the three most common theories that
fall within the category of situational leadership, namely contingency leadership;
path–goal theory and situational leadership.
  Contingency leadership is one of the earliest theories that falls under the category of
situational leadership and arises primarily from the work of Fiedler (1964, 1967).

Fiedler's original framework (1964) looked at building an understanding of the factors which determine how a leader's personality attributes affect group performance. Adapting the behavioural leadership dimensions of 'task-orientation' and 'relationship-orientation', Fiedler set out to analyse a leader's motivational disposition through the development of the least preferred co-worker scale. The instructions to the least preferred co-worker scale asks respondents:

> **Think of the one person in your life, with whom you could work least well. This individual may or may not be the person you dislike most. It must be the one person with whom you had the most difficulty getting the job done, the one single individual with whom you would least want to work – a boss, a subordinate or a peer. Describe the person as he or she appears to you by rating them along the following dimensions. (Fiedler, 1964, 1967)**

Respondents are then provided with dichotomous sets of dimensions such as 'pleasant–unpleasant', 'boring–interesting', 'nasty–nice' and 'open–closed'. From such ratings, a determination can be made about whether a leader is more task-oriented or relationship-oriented. Through his research, Fiedler (1967, 1971) found that task-oriented leaders were more effective when situations were classified as favourable or unfavourable; whereas relationship-oriented leadership were more effective in moderately favourable environments.

However, to determine the degree of favourability of a particular environment, Fiedler (1964) identified three situational components, namely: leader–member relations; task structure and positional control. Leader–member relations looks at the strength of the relationship bond between the leader and followers and the degree of mutual trust and respect that exists. Task structure examines the nature of the work carried out in terms of clarity and ambiguity (Fiedler, 1964). Finally, positional control is a measure of the leader's ability to influence subordinates (Miller et al., 2004). Once the degree of favourability of a particular environment is established, leaders will be clearer on whether a task-oriented or relationship-oriented leadership style is required.

Northouse (2010) identifies a number of weaknesses with contingency theory. First, he argues that the theory does not adequately explain what organisations should do when there is a mismatch between the leader and workplace situation. Second, he identifies a problem with the face validity of the least preferred co-worker scale and argues that it is cumbersome to use in real-world contexts as it requires three separate instruments to test each of the components of the theory. Finally, he suggests that there are problems in relation to the selection of the 'least preferred co-worker' in that respondents are not instructed in how this person should be selected and may confuse 'least preferred co-worker' with 'least liked co-worker'.

Path–goal theory arises out of the research conducted by Robert House in the 1970s. House (1971) viewed one of the primary roles of leadership as enhancing the psychological states of employees such that key outcomes could became realisable and attainable and brought satisfaction to employees. House and Mitchell (1974: 84) advance two key propositions for their theory, namely:

1   Leader behaviour is acceptable and satisfying insofar as subordinates see such behaviour as an immediate source of satisfaction or instrumental to a future satisfaction.

2 Leader behaviour is motivational (increases effort) to the extent that (a) such behaviour makes employee satisfaction contingent upon effective performance by employees and (b) leaders support employees through coaching, guidance and support in order to enable employees to achieve effective performance.

In essence, House identifies an important function of the leader as one of removing obstacles and barriers facing employees and preventing them from achieving effective performance. House (1996) argues that leaders should complement the environment they are working in and make linkages for employees between employee effort and goal attainment and reward. He identifies four types of leader behaviour (directive path–goal clarifying leader behaviour; supportive leader behaviour; participative leader behaviour and achievement leader behaviour) arising out of the 'task-focused' and 'consideration-focused' dimensions of the University of Ohio and Michigan studies. As such, House argues that leaders control the resources that employees value and need to adopt leader behaviours that make employees respond appropriately to the needs of the organisation.

Situational leadership was developed by Hersey and Blanchard (1969) to recognise that effective leadership depends upon the adoption of an appropriate leadership style and on the development level of employees working for the leader. Four particular leadership styles (telling, selling, participating and delegating) were identified which could be used depending upon the maturity level of employees (Lussier and Achua, 2009). The four leadership styles identified were also broadly based upon the 'task-focused' and 'consideration-focused' dimensions found in the University of Ohio and Michigan studies. A telling leadership style was one characterised by high levels of task-focus with low emphasis on relationship-building and takes the form of the leader issuing instructions for followers. A selling leadership style is one that is high on both task-focus and relationship development. It centres on meeting employee needs as well as task completion and does this through regular communication and feedback as well as coaching, employee involvement and employee recognition. A participating leadership style gives emphasis to supporting employees with less focus on task-related elements. It underlines the importance of team behaviours, co-operation and joint decision-making. The final leadership style labelled delegating is low on both task and relationship components and involves the leader handing over decision-making responsibility to employees. It is indicative of a laissez-faire approach to management.

The second aspect to situational leadership looks at the development level of employees and how ready followers are to respond to the instructions of the leader. Hershey and Blanchard (1988) assesses follower readiness along two dimensions: Ability (job readiness) and Willingness (psychological readiness). They argue that where followers show a high level of self-efficacy, then leaders should adopt a participating or delegating style. However, where employees have a low development level, leaders need to adopt a more directive (i.e. telling or selling) style.

In conclusion, the three theories that fall within the situational leadership paradigm broadly constitute a development of early research on behavioural leadership. They recognise the importance of flexibility in leader approaches to problem-solving and advocate a thorough analysis of environmental factors in advance of adopting a particular leadership style. The development of leaders under the situational leadership paradigm generally involves training leaders to recognise, understand and diagnose the organisational environment; making them more aware of the bonds that exist between leaders and followers and helping leaders assess their own level of control over resources and authority. It also focuses more clearly on leader style, highlighting a clear correlation between leader style, follower responsiveness and overall leadership effectiveness.

Transformational leadership

Transformational leadership refers to the ability of the leader to inspire followers to transcend their own interests and work towards the benefit of all (Nadler and Tushman, 1990). Some of the core tenets of transformational leadership revolve around the ability of the leader to inspire and bring about significant change; articulation of a clear vision; the strong relationship between the leader and followers and the awareness and fulfilment of follower needs and values. There are four recognised characteristics of transformational leadership (labelled the four I's), namely: idealised influence; inspirational motivation; intellectual stimulation and individualised consideration (Burns, 1978; Posner and Kouzes, 1988; Bass, 1990; Keegan and Den Hartog, 2004).

Idealised influence looks at the ability of the leader to act as a role model to his/her followers and inspire them through the example of his/her practice and example. Abu-Tineh et al. (2008) maintain that to set an appropriate standard, transformational leaders need to have a personal philosophy; engage with a set of principles about how people should be treated and ensure consistency between the values they set and the actions they pursue. Both House (1977) and Bass (1987) insist that modelling behaviour has a powerful effect on followers and inspires followers more forcibly towards achieving the vision set out by the leader. As such, modelling behaviour brings with it a stronger level of allegiance and higher bonds of trust between leaders and followers (Coad and Berry, 1998). Through modelling behaviour, leaders communicate important values, a shared sense of purpose, self-sacrifice, persistence and determination, setting them apart and thus winning them the admiration and support of followers (Gillespie and Mann, 2004).

Inspirational motivation involves the ability of the leader to articulate a clear vision of the future that is inclusive, attractive and attainable to followers. Through presenting a compelling vision of the future, leaders engage in a developmental journey with followers, helping them build the skills and resources necessary to realise the vision and connecting with the innermost needs of followers. Kouzes and Posner (1995, 2002) argue that transformational leaders generate much excitement and enthusiasm amongst followers towards the vision through the skilful use of metaphors, imagery, empathy, positive reinforcement and praise. Through the articulation of the vision, the leader must show an awareness of the process and likely road that will need to be travelled towards achieving the desired endpoint. Owen (1999) regards visioning as a critical function of leadership and sees it as the awakening and aligning of the spirit towards achieving a common shared goal.

Intellectual stimulation explores the leader's powers of creativity and critical reasoning and his/her ability to question old ways of doing things as well as his/her capacity to formulate new strategies and action plans. The transformational leader must be knowledgeable and be able to project their ideas in a convincing and persuasive manner. Javidan and Waldman (2003) argue that the transformational leader needs to be able to connect the overall vision to the follower's own situation and that the overall vision and message must be solid enough to withstand criticism for vested interests. In this way, the transformational leader needs to help followers overcome individual and collective obstacles to progress. Abu-Tineh et al. (2008) argue that the transformational leader must be willing to learn from their mistakes; test out new ideas; take risks and be prepared to admit their failings. As Sarros and Santora (2001) point out, the notion of intellectual stimulation involves the leader working through problems in an open egalitarian manner embracing the highest standards of honesty and integrity, yet challenging followers to find and achieve the optimum solutions.

Individualised consideration looks at the close bonds that are formed between the leader and followers and how such relationships are critical in bringing about change. Bass and Avolio (1994) describe individualised consideration as including time spent teaching and coaching others; identification and development of follower strengths and being attentive to follower concerns. This characteristic of transformational leadership recognises that followers need encouragement, motivation and reassurance to achieve the high standards expected of them. In so doing, leaders need to recognise and praise achievement as well as showing tolerance and understanding for mistakes if they occur (Kouzes and Posner, 1995, 2002). Forging a close relationship between leader and follower is critical in realising significant change and helps to elevate followers towards realising their potential.

Developing transformational leaders is not a simple task. While Doh (2003) argues that presentation skills and public speaking are skills that can be taught, there are elements of the leadership process (and particularly the connection/nexus) between leaders and followers that remain something of a 'black box' and mystery to research-ers and academics alike. An exploration of transformational leadership practices by Abu-Tineh et al. (2008) indicated that training leaders to develop and communicate a shared vision energises followers and creates a greater sense of meaning and purpose. They argue that the creation of a shared vision creates a bridge between the present and the future fostering long-term commitment to organisational effectiveness. A second study by Gill et al. (2010) found a strong positive relationship between trans-formational leadership and employee empowerment resulting from the increased level of trust between leader and employee leading the latter to take greater owner-ship of organisational problems. Finally, a study by Garcia-Morales et al. (2008) identified a positive relationship between transformational leadership and the two variables of organisational innovation and organisational performance. They found that the shared cultures and open supportive structures created by transformational leaders encourages employees to engage creatively with their work and stimulate higher levels of organisational learning. Table 13.1 summarises the key features of the four main leadership theories.

Conclusions

Leadership is a composite of multiple aspects and experiences. Consequently, a single leadership theory can never fully capture the entirety of the leadership concept, but can facilitate a greater understanding of various facets of leadership. While research has been produced for more than 100 years looking at the character-istics of effective leadership, it appears on the surface that the concept remains as elusive as ever. Indeed, it is arguable that the leadership 'pill' (to use Blanchard and

Table 13.1 Key features of leadership theories

	Trait theories of leadership	Behavioural theories of leadership	Situational theories of leadership	Transformational theories of leadership
Underpinning philosophy	The possession of particular inherent qualities enabling an individual to distinguish themselves in a leadership role	The actions and behaviours of leadership will determine their overall effectiveness. Certain leadership actions are likely to lead to more effective outcomes	The leadership style to be adopted is determined by the level of situational control, the relationship with followers and level of positional power	The ability of the leader to inspire followers to transcend their own interests and work towards the benefit of all
Key characteristics	• A large number of different traits have been identified by various authors • The big five personality traits include: neuroticism; extraversion; openness to experience; agreeableness and conscientiousness	• Within the Ohio Studies: Consideration and Structure • Within the Blake and Mouton Studies: Concern for People and Concern for Production	Under Contingency theory, there are two key factors (From Fiedler): • A leader's task or relationship motivational orientation • A leader's situational control (examined in relation to leader–member relations; task structure and positional control)	The four key characteristics of transformational leadership are: • Inspirational motivation • Intellectual stimulation • Individual consideration • Idealised influence
Key contributors	Stogdill (1948, 1974); Mann (1959); Bass (1990); Kirkpatrick and Locke (1991); Judge et al. (2002); Goleman et al. (2004)	Fleishman et al. (1955); Tannenbaum and Schmidt (1958); Blake and Mouton (1964); Blake and McCanse (1991)	Fiedler (1967); House (1971); Hershey and Blanchard (1988)	Bass and Avolio (1994); Tichy and Devanna (1990)
Relationship with followers	Often assumes a close relationship due to possession of particular leadership traits	Advocates that the best leaders are concerned with both people and tasks. Encourages greater standards-based employee participation	The state of the relationship with followers will determine the appropriate leadership action to be taken	Relies upon a close inspirational relationship between the leader and followers
Developmental rationale	Leader will become more effective if specific traits are more fully developed	Through training and learning, leaders will be able to determine the appropriate leadership actions to be taken.	Leaders are trained to assess the environmental context and adopt appropriate actions which fits with the specific context	Leaders are training to respond effectively to followers needs and connect with them on a deep individual level

(Continued)

Table 13.1 (Continued)

	Trait theories of leadership	Behavioural theories of leadership	Situational theories of leadership	Transformational theories of leadership
Developmental interventions	• Use of trait based inventories to establish degrees of possession of particular traits • Trait-based specific training programmes (such as EI training interventions)	• Self-analysis inventories followed typically by communications and team-building activities • Competency-based development activities (may include empowering, coaching and motivational approaches)	• Self-analysis inventories to determine degree of task or relationship orientation • Environmental analysis inventories to establish degree of situational control	• Follower analysis inventories • Developing of coaching, mentoring and communication skills with followers • Improvement of leaders listening skills • Counselling and feedback sessions to increase leader effectiveness
Criticisms of theory	• Some difficulties exist in specifically defining particular traits • Most trait theories lack specific weightings for particular traits • Most trait theories view traits as universal, regardless of context	• Behavioural theories seek universal understanding of leadership without taking into account context-specific factors • Assumes that the leader will demonstrate the same set of behaviours across all subordinates	• Requires leaders to have a malleable style and to adopt their leadership approach according to the particular situation • Lack of empirical support for contingency approaches	• Many transformational theories seek leaders in a 'hero' mode, which can sometimes lead to abuse of power • Encourages followers to go beyond their self-interests and pursue outcomes contrary to their best interests

Muchnick's (2005) term) will always retain a secret ingredient that will remain elusive to research.

That said, significant progress has been made in relation to various stands of leadership and towards making leaders more effective. Trait-based leadership research has usefully identified various qualities necessary for effective leadership. Indeed, research on emotional intelligence continues to emphasise and prove the importance of emotional intelligence in the make-up of leaders. Research on behavioural leadership has arguably led to the development and adoption of competency frameworks which are used across organisations to frame HR practices and leadership development programmes. Contingency and situational leadership research has made us more aware of the need for leaders to act flexibly according to the circumstances facing them. Finally, transformational leadership has taught us a lot about the bonds that tie leaders and followers and how such relationships can be strengthened and developed.

In conclusion, developing leaders is a complex process and remains something of an art. However, as the research base continues to grow, we can refine this art and improve the effectiveness of our leaders. Good practice leadership development programmes acknowledge the multi-faceted nature of leadership and the need to draw across all four strands of leadership theory to produce well-rounded and effective interventions.

 Discussion questions

- Aside from emotional intelligence, how has trait theory contributed to our knowledge of how we develop effective leaders?

- 'The best predictor of future performance is past performance.' Discuss the view that an effective leader can only be identified through his/her previous actions.

- Does transformational leadership place too much emphasis on oratory and charisma?

14 Diversity and HRD

David McGuire

The objectives of this chapter are to:

- explore why HRD has largely neglected diversity issues to date and why diversity should play an important role in HRD;

- investigate the benefits of diversity training in organisations;

- consider the barriers faced by minority groups in the workplace and how these can be overcome;

- examine ways in which organisations can embrace diversity in the workplace.

Introduction

Modern workplaces have become a melting pot of diversity – with employees of different genders, ages, races, abilities, sexual orientations and religious outlooks. In this context, there is an increasing awareness on behalf of organisations of the need to understand, accommodate, value and leverage such difference and in doing so realise important competitive advantages. In a globalised market, organisations are seeking to connect with consumers' beliefs and cultural norms and are engaging employees who can bring knowledge of these important attributes to the table. Indeed, organisations have learned the high costs associated with an insufficient understanding of local customs and values and are also realising that regional and national markets are not homogeneous entities, but are comprised of groups of consumers with particular traits. More generally, the benefits of valuing workplace diversity have been articulated by Cox and Blake (1991) as enhanced creativity and problem-solving; reduced employee turnover; more successful marketing campaigns to underrepresented societal groups; greater flexibility to adapt to changing market conditions and an increased level of productivity.

With such advantages, why then are some organisations resistant to the notion of diversity? Research has indicated that diversity resistance often takes three forms: the cost argument; the political correctness argument and the cultural preservation argument. In relation to cost, some critics claim that the costs of workplace diversity outweigh the benefits and that diversity advocates engage in 'distant cheerleading', praising workplace diversity at a distance without having to deal with practical concerns on a daily basis (Dick and Cassell, 2002). The political correctness argument sees workplace diversity with its attendant diversity training programmes as a form of political correctness which will invariably lead to needless nervousness and caution on behalf of members of the majority group. Such commentators hold the view that diversity training is a perverse form of 'reprogramming' designed to intimidate and blame members of the majority group for historical segregation (Stewart et al., 2008; Holladay and Quinones, 2008). Finally, proponents of the cultural preservation argument seek to preserve a homogeneous monoculture whereby diversity is ignored and treated as a non-issue. In such environments, new employees are forced to assimilate pre-existing norms and values and cultural challenge is not permitted (Sippola, 2007; Andresen, 2007).

In the field of HRD, diversity concepts have faced a considerable degree of resistance. Bierema (2009) notes that diversity is rarely discussed in HRD textbooks, research and academic programmes. With its foundations in democratic values (Hatcher, 2006), it can be argued however that HRD has an important role to play in examining the ethical and social impact of organisational policies and practices and liberating organisations from the dominance of privileged interests. However, such progress will be difficult to achieve. As McGuire et al. (2005) point out, humanistic ideals in organisations are often overlooked by an instrumental focus on increasing shareholder returns, profit and market share. Consequently, diversity advocates must present a strong case for making diversity a cornerstone of organisational policy and convince organisational decision-makers that a diversity and equality agenda is complementary to organisational goals, rather than contrary to them.

This chapter explores the need for diversity training in the workplace and looks at the benefits and criticisms that have been levelled at it. It then examines the challenges and obstacles faced by employees because of their gender, race or sexuality and outlines HRD interventions that can be deployed to improve openness to diversity in the workplace. Finally, a series of conclusions are drawn in advancing HRD's role in promoting diversity in the workplace.

Diversity training

As a response to legislative requirements and increasing levels of diversity, many organisations have instigated diversity training programmes as a means of dispelling myths regarding diversity, identifying appropriate behaviours and making managers more aware of their responsibilities towards different groups in the workplace. The social goals of diversity training programmes are usually to significantly reduce the incidence of prejudice, bullying and harassment in the workplace and to foster a positive working environment for all employees. To this end, diversity training has become popular as a means of protecting organisations both against a damaged public reputation and against the actions of errant misguided employees and managers.

Through the use of didactic (lectures, videos, persuasion and education) and interactive (discussions, role playing, simulations, case studies) approaches (Pendry et al., 2007), diversity training often seeks to identify individual feelings about diversity, distribute information about legal requirements and organisational policies and outlines the personal impact of discrimination experiences (Hite and McDonald, 2006). For this part, Anand and Winters (2008) argue that diversity is increasingly being positioned as a competency in organisations as it often leads to a more open diverse environment leading to higher levels of creativity and divergent thinking.

Safeguarding employee identity is a core objective of diversity training and diversity initiatives in organisations. As Losert (2008) points out, the increase in working hours experienced across westernised countries has led to difficulties in maintaining a healthy work/life balance leading to a strong need to be able to assert one's own true identity in the workplace. Through diversity training, employees can therefore positively affirm their own distinctiveness secure in the knowledge that this distinctiveness will be respected by the organisation. There is increasing awareness that in many cases, identity is indeed socially constructed leading to the acceptability of certain behaviours affecting the culture, symbols and ethos of the organisation itself. This emphasises the importance of embedding values of openness and respect for difference across the organisation.

Several pitfalls have been identified in conducting diversity training programmes. Sanchez and Medkik (2004) argue that focusing on awareness-level training only (where knowledge and insights are provided) without behavioural coaching and diversity skill development poorly equips employees and managers in resolving differences in the workplace. Hite and McDonald (2006) highlight problems associated with poorly devised training which is often of too-short duration, ignores the role of power in diversity issues and is a one-off event rather than a sustained systemic process. They also point to inadequacies of diversity training evaluation, where participant reactions become the predominant focus, rather than organisational culture change.

In summary, diversity training has the potential to have a transformative effect on organisational behaviour and culture, provided it is designed correctly and is strategically linked to an organisational commitment to valuing diversity. Where diversity training is postured on blaming members of the dominant group for discrimination and workplace/societal divisions, it is likely to trigger defensive responses, making individuals resistant to change (Lindsay, 1994; Karp and Sutton, 1993). Furthermore, in cases where diversity training involves overly sensitive material and highly personalised experiences, individuals may become uncomfortable and react unfavourably to the training provided.

Gender and the workplace

The participation of women in the workplace and management positions is not new. As Miles (1988) points out, in pre-industrial times, women balanced household chores alongside aspects of agricultural work such as diary, milking, butter and cheese-making. Despite long-term participation in the labour market, inequalities still exist with male working age employment in the UK (79.6 per cent) surpassing female working age employment (69.1 per cent) (Office for National Statistics, 2009). Pay disparities across the gender divide still persist in the UK with men currently earning 12.8 per cent more than women (Office for National Statistics, 2008). Consequently, it is worth examining why such structural inequalities still exist in an era defined by employment law regulations and a strong focus on equal opportunities.

Removing the barriers to full female participation in the workplace and creating a level playing field across both genders requires both an understanding of the obstacles inhibiting full involvement and the development of comprehensive HRD solutions to address issues of inequity and discrimination. O'Neil and Bilimoria (2005) identify three critical factors distinguishing men's and women's careers, leading to differences in workplace experiences. First, they argue that women are differentially tasked with child-rearing and household responsibilities and this has a much greater impact on women's careers than men's. They posit that women's developmental and promotional opportunities are moulded by family responsibilities and this influences career continuity and advancement in the workplace. Second, O'Neil and Bilimoria maintain that women's careers have a distinct relational emphasis which is markedly different from men's. Indeed, Ackah and Heaton (2004) establish that the burden of finding a sustainable system of coping with household and family responsibilities is a key factor explaining why women's careers have not fitted within a traditional upward advancement model with its assumption of a stay-at-home spouse. For this reason, women's careers are marked by periods away from the workplace and are more fragmented and discontinuous than men's careers. Third, O'Neil and Bilimoria found that women's under-representation at higher organisational levels constrains their progress and career advancement. The lack of identifiable role models, the persistence of a dominant masculine culture and continued stereotyping and gendered role behaviours has fostered an environment where a minority female presence at board level is accepted.

Coined by journalists Carol Hymowitz and Timothy Schellhardt in a 1986 *Wall Street Journal* article, the metaphor of the 'glass ceiling' describe both the obstacles to women's career advancement and the scarcity of women in top leadership positions. Described as 'a transparent, but real barrier based on discriminatory attitudes or organisational bias, that impedes or prevents qualified individuals (including but not limited to women) from advancing into management positions' (Gibelman, 2000: 251), the glass ceiling hinders succession planning and development initiatives as well as impeding organisational creativity. Van Vianen and Fischer (2002) identity a masculine organisational culture as leading to the persistence of the glass ceiling. They argue that masculine cultures consist of hidden assumptions, norms and practices that promote communication practices, images of leadership, organisational values and definitions of success which promote the masculine over the feminine.

Since the glass ceiling came to light, three other concepts have emerged that have attempted to explain the difficulties that women have experienced in accessing top leadership positions. The concept of 'glass escalator' was developed by Christine Williams (1992) to explain the steady acceleration of men through the organisational ranks. She maintains that men are sometimes faced with invisible pressures to move up the career ladder in particular professions. She alludes to a set of gender privileges that men possess which more easily places them on an upward trajectory. The concept of 'glass cliff' was introduced by Michelle Ryan and Alexander Haslam (2004) to explore a phenomenon whereby women's suitability for promotion rises when the chances of failure increases. In their research, Ryan and Haslam (2007) found that because women were more likely to be appointed to top management positions during crisis periods, the risks to their leadership increase and they are more likely to encounter rising levels of conflict and higher stress levels leading to greater exposure to criticism. Finally, the term 'Lucite ceiling' appears to have been coined by Diana Henriques (1991) in an article written in the *New York Times*. In the article,

Henriques describes a transparent glass ceiling made from solid unbreakable Lucite to depict the double-marginalisation experienced by women from minority ethnic backgrounds. She argues that minority ethnic women are even more unlikely than (majority) white women to achieve senior management positions and face even greater obstacles and levels of inequality.

More recently, the re-emergence of the 'Queen Bee' concept has been used to describe the lack of support for women in senior management from other women. Mavin (2008) employs the concept to examine the lack of female solidarity caused by some women's opposition to changes in traditional sex roles. She acknowledges the sexist nature of the term and argues that many women in senior management positions will choose to work with men and separate themselves from other women in the organisation, thus withdrawing opportunities for career advancements and looking after her own self-interests. Rather than being a role model for other women, Mavin argues that queen bee managers are fiercely competitive and aggressive engaging in fortress-keeping and information-withholding behaviour to realise her career ambitions. In summary, she characterises the queen bee as an individual senior women who accepts and understands organisational power bases and sacrifices her femininity to achieve career success.

Several HRD interventions have been shown to help women overcome gender barriers in the workplace. One such intervention is mentoring. According to Kram (1985), mentoring performs two important roles. Firstly, it provides individuals with valuable career support in the form of sponsorship, increased exposure and visibility and coaching sessions. Second, mentoring performs a psycho-social role whereby individuals benefit from friendship, advice, guidance and feedback. Ehrich (2008) maintains that the mentoring process allows women to build levels of self-confidence, learn new leadership skills and construct powerful networks across the organisation and beyond. In addition, Monserrat et al. (2009) maintain that effective mentoring programmes can help prevent career mistakes, increase levels of job satisfaction and produce higher levels of affective and continuance commitment in the organisation.

Networking is an equally important HRD intervention in women's career development. As the glass/lucite ceiling and queen bee concepts often resist access to networking, this can result in their under-representation at senior levels of organisations. Tonge (2008) asserts that social networks can provide access to important information and to further relationships with other connected individuals as well as providing important support and encouragement in an individual's career development. She argues that networking is essential to success in any professional career and that the primary advantage derived by women from networking is that of social support. For their part, Donelan et al. (2009) suggest that social networks may help women overcome feelings of isolation and insecurity and enable greater access to role models.

Race and the workplace

Racial barriers still persist in the workplace. While Sir Trevor Phillips, chairman of the UK Equality and Human Rights Commission (2009) reports on research that racial prejudice in the UK has markedly declined, he points out that sharp inequalities persist. He argues that educational success is strongly linked to race and racial disadvantage in itself is often associated with socio-economic disadvantage. In this way, individuals from an ethnic minority background may enter the workplace at a disadvantage to the majority white community. Research supporting such linkages can be found in the UK Race to the Top report (published by Business in the Community, 2009) which points out that just 5.6 per cent of ethnic minority individuals reach senior management positions, despite these groups representing over 10 per cent of the UK population. Similar racial inequalities persist in the US. Research indicates that pay differentials based around pay still exist with black men still paid less than white men (Rodgers, 2006). Weeks et al. (2007) argue that notwithstanding the fact that the US represents a melting pot of diversities, blacks tend to fall into lower socio-economic groupings than whites and it is often difficult to distinguish judgments made on racial or socio-economic grounds.

Much of the difficulties encountered by ethnic minorities in the workplace can be traced back to the concept of privilege. McIntosh describes privilege as 'an invisible container of unearned benefits that operates in such a way as to maintain its invisibility, to keep its beneficiaries ignorant of its presence, and to preserve its existence' (1993: 31). By its nature, privilege works to retain its invisibility as by acknowledging privilege, whites must recognise that race as well as hard work contributed to their achievements (McIntosh, 2002). Consequently, the experience of organisations and the workplace is not uniform for all employees. As Grimes (2001) points out, the power of the privileged races can set limits on what activities can be performed and who can perform them. She maintains that knowledge is political and involves a context and a situation such that objective knowledge mostly coincides with the viewpoint of the majority dominant group and the viewpoint of minority groups is marginalised.

According to Barrett et al. (2004), individuals from a minority racial background must overcome a range of institutional and personal challenges to achieve career success. Such challenges exist to protect the privileged position of the dominant majority and serve to limit and exclude access to career opportunities and development to minority employees. Barrett et al. describe institutional challenges as 'structural and environmental barriers such as limited access to vocational guidance and assessment, tracking into "appropriate" jobs and discrimination in hiring, promotions and transfers' (2004: 86). They go on to describe personal challenges as pertaining to specific individual problems or issues and provide examples such as low self-confidence, limited career exploration, greater career indecision and an unwillingness to play the political game.

The experience of exclusion and isolation is particularly common for individuals from a minority racial background. Minority racial employees are more prone to stereotyping as a result of lower numerical representation and having to adapt to a majority culture that is inhospitable and alien to them (Browne and Misra, 2003). In relation to culture, Hite (1996, 2007) describes the inescapability and pervasiveness of institutional racism as requiring minority racial employees to develop reserves of resilience, inner strength, confidence and impeccable skills. Faifua (2008) notes increasing moves towards worker mobilisation through trade unions and workplace groups. He argues that this often arises out of the need to combat a sense of isolation; a drive to reassert identity and promote unity in the workplace and an attempt to open new opportunities for individuals and groups. This attempt to re-establish community seeks to bring minority employees together under a banner of common aspirations and reassert democratic ideals at the heart of the workplace.

Alongside networking and worker mobilisation, mentoring also plays an important role in widening opportunities for employees from a minority racial background. A key discussion in the research literature examines whether the mentor to a minority racial employee should come from a white background or minority racial background. Barrett et al. (2004) advocate being mentored by a white male as they tend to have stronger networks and more influence. However, they acknowledge that having someone from the same racial background brings with it more candid communication due to commonalities of experience. While covering many of the same points as Barrett et al. (2004), a different conclusion is reached by Thomas (2001) in relation to mentoring minority racial employees. Thomas (2001) argues that having a mentor of the same racial background leads to closer, fuller, developmental relationships. He argues that having a mentor from a minority background is particularly important in an individual's early career where the minority racial employee may need to build confidence, credibility and competence. However, Thomas et al. (2007) caution that regardless of racial background, mentors need to have the necessary competencies to effectively mentor individuals and training may often be required to develop mentor skills to an appropriate level.

Sexuality and the workplace

Openly expressing one's sexuality in the workplace is still fraught with difficulty. Ward and Winstanley argue that 'sexuality is an under-researched area of diversity in work organisations as well as being one of the most difficult to research' (2005: 447). Alongside this fact, there is an acknowledged lack of robust statistical data on the proportion of the UK population who self-identify as lesbian, gay, bisexual or transgendered (LGBT) (Colgan et al., 2007). Kirby (2006) maintains that the workplace sometimes represents a hostile environment for LGBT individuals and a place where they may be likely to face discrimination. She argues that such discrimination often results from fear, stereotyping and misunderstanding, indicating that there exists a need to educate workplace managers and supervisors on sexuality in the workplace alongside greater research on the topic.

LGBT people often face a range of discriminatory practices and behaviours in the workplace. Gedro et al. (2004) argues that such practices and behaviours can include being passed over for raises or promotions; having to take on additional responsibilities; being subjected to verbal harassment or property damage and loss of respect from colleagues and co-workers. Likewise, Kirby (2006) argues that individuals who disclose their sexual orientation (other than the majority heterosexual orientation) in the workplace are more likely to encounter negative attitudes and receive fewer promotions. This often leads to LGBT people closeting their sexuality or alternatively, taking on the persona of a heterosexual while at work.

The suppression of sexuality (and identity) while at work has significant consequences for LGBT people in the workplace. In a forthcoming article, Gedro (2010) argues that lesbians face dual pressures emanating from their gender and sexuality. She posits that lesbians also encounter pressures related to gender expression. She explains that gender expression relates to how an individual portrays his/her gender identity to others through behaviours, dress, hairstyles, voice and other body characteristics. As such, lesbians are often expected to follow traditional female-role norms, yet gender expression does not correlate neatly with sexual orientation. Consequently, the dominance of heterosexual norms often forces LGBT people to act and behave unnaturally in the workplace.

The decision to 'come out of the closet' or disclose one's sexuality in the workplace is a major decision for LGBT people. Research by Schmidt and Nilsson (2006) identifies that the early stages of sexual identity development for LGBT people can be characterised by homonegativity, identity confusion, inner turmoil and feelings of personal alienation. Consequently, it may take some time for individuals to reach a fully integrated gay identity. Nam Cam Trau and Hartel (2004) argue that the decision to come out is often made through balancing identity issues with the priority placed on careers and relationships. Gedro et al. (2004) identifies several stages in a process of coming out. First, LGBT people often learn about pre-screening, which involves trying to ascertain what the response of a boss or supervisor will be once their sexuality becomes known. In so doing, an assessment is made on the degree of homosexual tolerance on the basis of music, art, belief, movies etc. Second, upon deciding that it may be safe to reveal one's sexuality, individuals carefully select the timing and communication method by which to disclose their sexuality. Third, LGBT people may engage in a process of educating others about the challenges and issues they face and advocating changing policies and procedures to be more open and respectful of people of all sexual orientations.

Human Resource Development has an important role to play in supporting LGBT people in the workplace. HRD professionals need to ensure that organisational policies are open and inclusive and work with managers and supervisors to make them aware of workplace issues affecting LGBT people. In relation to organisational practices, Barbosa and Cabral-Cardosa (2007) note that selection decisions tend to favour familiar applicants in order to avoid the uncertainty associated with the 'unknown' – consequently, this may disadvantage applicants having a sexual orientation different from the majority. Barbosa and Cabral-Cardosa (2007) also emphasise the importance of developing an open tolerant organisational culture as prescribing a particular dress code and look may reflect the outlook of the dominant majority. Bairstow and Skinner (2007) argue that discriminatory practices may exist in reward practices with some benefits only available to heterosexual couples such as unequal pensions, health care provision, access to bereavement leave, company car use and access to other corporate services.

Conclusions

To date, the field of HRD has devoted only limited attention to diversity issues in the workplace. A study of four years of AHRD proceedings by Bierema and Cseh (2003) concluded that gender and race issues were considerably under-represented in HRD research and much HRD research neglects diversity issues. To treat organisations as singular entities devoid of diversity is to ignore the richness of employee backgrounds and experiences. If organisations are to prioritise creativity and innovation, then it is imperative that unique perspectives are valued and appreciated. Thus, it is critical that organisational barriers faced by diverse groups are identified and addressed.

A 'cradle to grave' review of organisational practices needs to be adopted to ensure that such practices meet the needs of both the dominant group and diverse group.

The direct and indirect effects of organisational practices need to be considered as such practices can often affect the culture that exists within the organisation. Enabling employees to live their identity within the organisation without fear of harassment or reprisal will lead to employees with higher levels of job satisfaction and job commitment. Thus attention needs to be devoted to integrating diversity within an organisation's structural, political and cultural framework.

HRD interventions can be usefully deployed towards embedding diversity as a core objective of the organisation. Mentoring and networking activities will allow minority individuals to forge important relationships and help them develop and advance their own careers. Such interventions can boost an individual's level of self-confidence and can assist individuals to link up with important role models. Diversity and awareness training can make supervisors and managers more aware of the challenges facing diverse employees and help them support employees facing instances of workplace discrimination.

 Discussion questions

- Why do organisations resist diversity? How can HRD adopt a more proactive role?

- How can the HRD function support minority employees in the workplace?

- What is the business case for embracing diversity in the workplace?

15 International HRD
David McGuire

■ ■ Chapter objectives ■

The objectives of this chapter are to:

- investigate the effect of culture on the character of HRD;

- examine the cultural boundedness of HRD theory and practice;

- present a framework looking at the internationalisation process for organisations;

- identify the HRD opportunities that arise through the internationalisation process.

Introduction

The notion of international human resource development, is a relatively new development within the maturing field of HRD (Woodall et al., 2002; Evarts, 1998). In cost-competitive markets, the standardisation of HRD practices across overseas operations has the potential for producing significant financial and human capital savings, improving productivity and streamlining operational procedures (Lunnan et al., 2002). In addition, the increasing use and application of e-learning and computer-based training has resulted in the delivery of HRD solutions that are timely, current and immediately accessible worldwide (Russell et al., 2003; Lytras et al., 2002). However, in spite of technological advances fuelling standardisation of HRD offerings and increasing structural configurations across global organisations, individual behaviour within these organisations continues to manifest nationally culturally-based dissimilarities (Adler et al., 1986). Furthermore, an outcome of globalisation has been the identification of 'uneven' patterns of economic and social development, making more visible the disparities that exist in education and skill levels (Metcalfe and Rees, 2005). Consequently, HRD has a dual role to play; firstly in developing economic and social well-being and secondly as a means of leveraging value from human capital (Woodall, 2005).

The lack of emphasis on international HRD stems directly from the origins and early development of the field. Both Jankowicz (1999) and Weinberger (1998) argue that academic research in HRD is primarily western and uni-cultural in orientation and strongly influenced by the perspectives of US scholars. Indeed, several calls have been made in the literature for academics to move beyond foundational issues, such as defining the boundaries and scope of HRD towards demonstrating the true value of HRD to the organisation's bottom line and its applicability in different cultural contexts (McGuire and Cseh, 2006; Ruona et al., 2003). Metcalfe and Rees (2005) argue that current international HRD scholarship that is genuinely international in design and focus remains sparse and fragmented. For their part, Littrell et al. (2006) identify the lack of a unifying theoretical framework as a key factor inhibiting cross-cultural and international HRD endeavours. They advocate the need for greater empirical research to establish the efficacy of current theoretical frameworks. However, Ardichvili and Kuchinke articulate the importance of exercising care in international HRD research in the following terms:

> **Our ability to conduct international HRD research that produces useful results depends not so much on our choice of methodologies, but on our ability to incorporate in our investigation culture as a major influencing factor and to account for culture's influence on phenomena under investigation. And to do this, we need a better understanding of our own and others' centrally conditioned perspectives and assumptions. (2002: 161–162)**

As we move towards a view of HRD that is strategically linked to long-term organisational objectives (Garavan et al., 2004) and recognise HRD professionals as 'learning architects' (Harrison and Kessels, 2004: 90), the challenge for HRD is to construct viable international HRD frameworks and demonstrate the capacity of HRD to add value to the organisation across different cultures. As Wang and McLean (2007) argue, the discipline of HRD needs to develop to accommodate the extensive amount of cross-national work being done by trans-national corporations, trans-national non-government organisations and trans-national political entities. In response to the call for greater research into the field of international HRD, this chapter presents a framework describing four phases of internationalisation and outlining the HRD priorities that exist under each phase. It is envisaged that this framework will provide a mechanism for discussing and understanding cross-cultural and international HRD approaches by organisations.

Constructing an international HRD framework

Cross-cultural issues in HRD have to date focused almost exclusively on the training of individuals without consideration of the larger issue of the applicability and transferability of actual HRD practices across national boundaries (Bartlett et al., 2002; Wexley and Latham, 2002: 310). The importance of developing a strong research stream in this area is clear. Cultural differences and national contexts have important implications for our thinking about HRD (Marquardt, 1999; Marquardt and Engel, 1993). Weiss (1996), for example, argues that effective communication with culturally diverse individuals and groups requires an understanding of both cultural assumptions and differences. In a review of the state of HRD internationally, McLean and McLean (2001) argue that cultural and value systems, the nature of the economy, government and legislative influences, educational system influences and the role of professional organisations represent under-researched dimensions of HRD.

Within the broader management literature, much attention has been devoted to the training provided to expatriates and those persuing short-term overseas assignments as well as the long-standing convergence/divergence debate on management practices (McGuire et al., 2002; Forster, 2000; Leiba-O'Sullivan, 1999). Advocates of a culture-free thesis include Edwards and Ferner (2002), who identify a 'country of origin' effect as one of the major influences on HRM practices in multinational companies. Similarly, Noble (1997) signals that institutional isomorphic tendencies may be at work amongst nation-states in the adoption of training policies. In contrast, both McGaughey and DeCieri (1999) and Huo and Von Glinow (1995) hold strongly to the view that the form and content of functional specialisation that develops with growth will vary according to culture. Such dichotomies ignore the reality that multinationals will decide upon their overseas approach, taking into account factors such as strategic importance of the subsidiary, degree of experience in international management and long-term objectives. In addition, several studies have pointed to the natural progression of companies from country of origin practices to host country practices over time as companies become more experienced and comfortable with the host country environment (Jackson, 2002: 57, Walker, 2001: 72). Arvidsson (1997) points to the notion of certainty as being highly influential in determining an organisation's internationalisation strategy. He argues that in cases of high uncertainty regarding an overseas market, the organisation will adopt a gradual internationalisation approach, making incremental investments over time. Such views acknowledge the accepted reality that the internationalisation process is a multi-stage evolving process and characterising the organisation's approach as fitting the convergence or divergence thesis may only reflect the organisation's approach at one particular point in time. While Nadkarni and Perez (2007) refer to several studies showing that firms new to internationalisation, start with low commitment activities and gradually increase their commitments to international markets, their own research challenges their findings and shows many firms are not adverse to making high international commitments from the offset and that domestic resources and competitive action propensity affect early international commitments.

Iles and Yolles (2003) identify international HRD alliances as an increasingly popular resource-efficient means of securing knowledge transfer and diffusion across national boundaries. They argue that alliances may provide organisations with rapid market entry and access to academic and technological resources in the host country. They maintain that alliances offer significant opportunities for organisational learning, particularly in relation to the transfer of culturally embedded knowledge; provided issues of control, trust and conflict are properly managed.

Acknowledging the complexity of the internationalisation process, the framework in Table 15.1 examines the provision of international HRD under four separate stages of the internationalisation process. The framework builds upon Adler and Ghadar (1990) typology which identifies the four internationalisation phases as multi-domestic, international, multinational and transnational. The multi-domestic strategy refers to a country-by-country configuration with each national operation having complete autonomy. Walton (1999) describes this structure as a decentralised federation and posits that this structure ensures the organisation is responsive to social, cultural and political issues. The international strategy is often viewed as an organisation's first major step in overseas expansion. It sees the organisation retaining a large measure of control over the subsidiary through the use of expatriate assignments and retention of key decision-making by headquarters. The multinational strategy has as its principal objectives price

Table 15.1 International HRD framework

	Multi-domestic	International	Multinational	Transnational
Structural issues				
Type of structure envisaged	Organisation in each country will be influenced by cultural, social and political factors. Structure will be unique to host country	Overseas subsidiary is largely developed and controlled by home country management to support overseas objectives	A standardised structure exists across international markets. It makes use of centralised hub and distribution outlets	No overriding organisational dimensions. Equal power held by each of the subsidiaries within the group
Nature of structural relationship	Organisation in each country is completely independent, with no linkages to organisation in other countries	Overseas subsidiary is dependent on home country management to provide strategic direction, but decides on mechanisms for local implementation	Overseas subsidiary is integrated within a global system with other subsidiaries in order to increase productivity and effectiveness	Subsidiary may be organised by division or country and integrated through normative control
Level of strategic input	Strategy is determined at national level taking into account local factors	Overseas subsidiary has little, if any strategic input. Strategic objectives will be determined by home country management	Strategy is determined on a global basis with input from all subsidiaries	All subsidiaries have an equally important role in strategy formulation
Autonomy	Organisation in each country is completely independent and free to determine policy and strategy	A dependency relationship exists between subsidiary and home organisation; however, some discretion is given to the subsidiary in the method of implementation	Overseas subsidiary has very limited autonomy due to standardised products and processes	Subsidiaries are highly autonomous and successful practices are disseminated to other subsidiaries within the organisation
Technology	Level of technology is dependent on standards and general practices of a particular country	Modern technology provides the mechanism for maintaining control of overseas subsidiaries and providing the strategic direction required	Technology is an integral component in a system designed to satisfy price competitiveness and customer satisfaction	Technology is used to promote learning and knowledge transfer for the benefit of the group as a whole
Competitive advantage	Determined by local factors and will vary considerably according to the country	Competitive advantage of home country organisation and overseas subsidiary will be determined by home country management	Competitive advantage in one country is significantly influenced by its position in other countries	Competitive advantage can be derived in many different countries and regions simultaneously

Table 15.1 (Continued)

	Multi-domestic	International	Multinational	Transnational
Cultural issues				
Value of cultural experience	No emphasis placed on cultural experience. Nationals of the particular country are mostly employed	Overseas subsidiary will recruit from the host-country for lower level managerial functions	Due to standardisation and global integration, culture becomes a less important variable	Culture is regarded as very important in ensuring customer needs are identified and satisfied
Benchmarking/ evaluation	Measurement against particular country standards with no reference to international standards	Performance of overseas subsidiary will be evaluated and benchmarked against home country standards	Subsidiary performance is measured over time and across regions	Widespread use of evaluation and benchmarking across a large number of dimensions
Adaption of HRD provision to local norms and values	HRD will be closely matched to accord with local norms and values	Overseas subsidiary will seek to adapt to local cultural norms	A standardised HRD model is used with room for local cultural customisation	HRD is adapted to local norms and customs. Cultural sensitivity is a critical issue
Long-term orientation	Due to its independence, the organisation is free to determine long or short-term objectives	Very much a 'wait and see' approach adopted. Use of long-term expatriates to provide continuity and ensure subsidiary is on a secure financial footing	Competitive advantage of organisation in one country is significantly influenced by its position in other countries	Long-term orientation is very much prevalent. Subsidiaries are focused on future development
HRD issues				
HRD priorities	HRD priorities will be determined through analysis of individual and organisational needs and with reference to skill standards	HRD priorities will be determined by home country management exclusively	HRD will be derived from global strategy and relative performance of overseas subsidiary	HRD priorities will be determined locally. Experiential learning and knowledge management are key organisational issues
Competency/skill development	Emphasis on skill development to respond to local organisational needs	Skill development will respond to strategic needs identified by host country management	Overseas subsidiary will follow global competency model of organisation and skill gaps will be identified on a regional basis	Customer satisfaction, global mindset, strategic capabilities, learning on the fly and thinking outside the box are critical competencies

(Continued)

Table 15.1 (Continued)

	Multi-domestic	International	Multinational	Transnational
Responsibility for HRD activities	Local management will take responsibility for HRD Activities	While local facilitators may be involved in HRD delivery, home country management will assume overall responsibility	Each subsidiary is responsible for HRD activities in conjunction with overall strategy of home country management	Subsidiary has complete responsibility for its own HRD activities
Team development	Teams will be comprised entirely of nationals of the particular country and objectives will be local	Teams will be comprised of host country nationals, but objectives will be determined by home country management	Regional teams with some inter-liaison to establish best practice models	Multifunctional teams, multinational teams are adopted to exploit organisational synergies
Cost of HRD provision	HRD will be funded completely from organisation profits	HRD will be funded from profits of overseas subsidiaries. Resources will also be provided by home country management	Cost of HRD will be borne by the particular subsidiary	HRD is regarded as critical to organisational development. Cost of HRD provision is regarded as an investment
Key actors in the HRD process	Local management are key decision makers	Home country managers are key decision makers	Home country management are interested in strategic issues and devolve operational issues to subsidiary	Local subsidiaries are key decision makers
HRD Outcomes	HRD will help organisation to achieve locally set goals	HRD provides home country management with means for upskilling overseas employees to home country standards	HRD will allow organisation to meet price competitiveness and product standardisation objectives through formation of regional teams and global competency frameworks	HRD contributes to the enhancement of individual, organisation and society at large. Push to make learning more transferable across organisation
Career development	Individuals develop within the local organisation in a stepwise hierarchical manner	Individual develops within the local organisation. Some possibilities exist for expatriate assignment, especially if individual is a member of home country management	Career development opportunities exist within the company. High probability of working on regional teams. Expatriate assignment is likely for management	Large number of career development options. Possibilities exist for vertical and horizontal career development, as well as international assignment. High degree of internal career mobility exists
Status of the Individual	'Colleague' working for local company servicing locally identified market needs	'Employee' working for overseas firm adopting an expansionist international agenda	'Member of global team' servicing regional market through the provision of standardised quality products	'Partner of global, locally-sensitive team' servicing local market through the provision of customised quality products

Source: Adapted from Adler and Ghadar (1990)

competitiveness and product standardisation and consequently adopts a centralised approach to maximise organisational efficiencies. It establishes regional hubs for product dissemination and utilises modern technologies for intensive communications (Walton, 1999). The transnational strategy involves complete adaption to local markets of global products. It emphasises cultural diversity and advocates concepts of knowledge management and experiential learning (Jackson, 2002: 47).

The multi-domestic organisation

The multi-domestic organisation is characterised by a local approach to business and employee issues. Each subsidiary is treated as a distinct autonomous entity and possess a high degree of flexibility enabling it to respond quickly to changing market conditions and national requirements. Adler and Ghadar (1990) characterise this approach as indicative of a product orientation.

Structural issues

Firms operating within a multi-domestic structure are equipped to respond flexibly and quickly to changing local conditions. Consequently, the firm is highly exposed to local cultural, political and economic factors. Berggren (1996) describes the principal advantage of a multi-domestic approach as one of being local world-wide, allowing for increased decentralisation, local accountability and increased transparency. He argues that such approaches enable organisations to claim they have 'many home countries' and sensitises managers to local cultural standards. In agreement, Allred and Steensma (2005) maintain that an organisation operating a multi-domestic approach to internationalisation tends to cater to the specific needs of the local customer and tailors their product offerings to the different countries they serve. In this regard, Ghoshal and Nohria (1993) characterise the multi-domestic approach as having weak forces for global integration and strong forces for local responsiveness. Allred and Steensma (2005) argue that a multi-domestic approach leads to a localised value chain where a 'let a thousand flowers bloom' orientation may lead to greater innovation and success.

Cultural issues

A multi-domestic approach embraces local values and customs and operates according to nationally recognised rules and procedures. Experience in other cultures is not valued as firms adopting this strategy emphasise local knowledge and standards. By adopting a multi-domestic approach, organisations avoid the reality that many firms face in that failure in overseas business settings most frequently results from an inability to understand and adapt to 'host country' ways of thinking (Ferraro, 1990; Tung, 1981; Hays, 1974). However, deferring to local values and norms does not necessarily result in an asynchronous culture. Peterson (1997) argues that cultural frames that affect business are multidimensional in that employees are shaped by not only national-societal values, but also organisational affiliation and occupational alliances.

An examination of HRD issues highlights a country-specific approach to HRD. Firms operating multi-domestic approaches compete in independent domestic markets and consequently this requires an indigenous workforce that understands and is responsive to local market conditions (Adler, 1994). This suggests that there may be considerable geographic differentiation of HRD practices and activities. Connelly et al. (2007) describe the role of HRD under a multi-domestic approach as one of developing managers and employees in sensing and exploiting local opportunities using region-specific and non-transferable knowledge. Social networks perform an important role in providing access to tacit knowledge and attuning product and service offerings to local norms and standards. For these reason, Belis-Bergouignan et al. (2000) argue that under a multi-domestic approach, subsidiaries are not deemed to possess any specific set of competences, especially in terms of technology and know-how, which could be transferred to the centre. Consequently, he maintains a one-way relationship of domination subsists, and there is no reciprocity between the areas in which the company's subsidiaries are located.

The international organisation

The international organisation adopts a market orientation and is characterised by a drive for increased growth, efficiency and market penetration (Adler and Ghadar, 1990). The international organisation operates under a headquarters and multiple subsidiary model with a high level of centralised control.

Structural issues

Operating a number of subsidaries allows an organisation to have a presence in a number of international markets and gain from cost benefits derived through standardised learning and development programmes and the harmonisation of organisational processes and procedures. Connelly et al. (2007) argue that the international firm creates value by the transfer and leveraging of core competencies and resources from headquarters to the subsidiary. They argue that some degree of local customisation is permitted; but that this is often limited in scope. Likewise, Bartlett and Ghoshal (1998: 50) identify the dependence of the subsidiary on the parent as a key aspect of an international firm and highlight the high level of control retained by headquarters through sophisticated management systems and specialist staff. Bartlett et al. (2004) maintain that with an internationalisation strategy, products are developed for the home market and only subsequently sold abroad. They maintain that in the early stages of internationalisation, many managers tend to view the overseas subsidiary as a distant outpost whose role is to support the domestic parent company through contributing incremental sales and upholding the company's revenue stream.

Cultural issues

In examining the reasons why firms seek to internationalise their operations, Bartlett and Ghoshal (1998: 98) identify the search for new markets, resources and cheap labour as key factors motivating overseas and international expansion. However, Armagan and Ferreira (2005) argue that the political culture of the firm's home country will exercise a strong effect on the firm's internationalisation strategy. For this reason, it is arguable that international organisations will recruit lower level managers who they can mould to fit with the dominant home country ethos and standards. None the less the subsidiary is likely to adapt to local cultural norms and is likely to hire long-term expatriates who are familiar with and capable of negotiating both cultures.

HRD issues

Due to the emphasis on centralised control by headquarters, the overseas subsidiary will have limited autonomy in relation to HRD matters. Responsibility for HRD matters will normally be devolved for operational matters but most strategic decisions will be taken by management in the home country. Hakanson (1990) identifies the key reasons for the strengthening of central control on subsidiary operations as stagnating global demand; increasing competitive pressure to boost efficiency and the need for specialisation. While HRD may be cited as important to growth prospects, HRD is likely to be funded by subsidiary profits with resources being managed by home country management. Opportunities are likely to exist for overseas placements and expatriate assignments but subsidiary operations are likely to be regarded as secondary and individuals will see their development as primarily within the home country organisation.

The multinational organisation

The multinational organisation has a significant presence in overseas environments and leverages opportunities from different geographical markets. For his part, Dunning (1993) defines the multinational organisation as one which engages in foreign direct investment and owns or controls value-adding activities in more than one country. Overseas subsidiaries possess a high degree of flexibility and are sensitive and responsive to changes in local conditions.

Structural issues

There are many variables which can affect the structure adopted by the multinational organisation. Miroshnik (2002) maintain that a multinational organisation is a complex organisational form which usually has fully autonomous units operating in a number of countries which possess a great deal of independence to address local issues such as consumer preferences, political pressures and economic trends. The nature of the structural relationship between headquarters and the subsidiary organisation has received attention in the literature. Malnight (2001) argues that internally differentiated structures are associated with a strategic shift in the focus of organisations to outside a company's home market. He argues that the benefits of a multinational framework result not only from the strength of dispersed units, but also from the nature and management of linkages between them. More recent contributions view the multinational as a network of affiliates capable of sustaining knowledge and information flows through a series of common systems (McGraw, 2004).

One of the criticisms of the multinational form of overseas management is the lack of co-ordination and control exercised by head office. Chang and Taylor (1999) emphasise this point and maintain that as multinationals expand their operations, the level of uncertainty associated with overseas investment will increase and complex issues of organisational control will need to be addressed to ensure that different parts of the organisation are contributing to the overall goals.

Cultural issues

Negotiating common cultural meanings is a difficult challenge for multinational organisations. Garabaldi de Hilal (2006) maintains that the complexity of multinational organisations increases the probability that their culture tends to differentiation and that different systems of meanings, or sub-cultures can greatly affect the operations of those organisations. For this reason, multinational organisations will often advocate standardised processes and systems with some room for local cultural customisation. Subsidiary performance is likely to be measured over time and across regions. Some research indicates that the multinational country of origin may exert considerable influence on organisational strategy. McGuire et al. (2002) argue that while cultural characteristics may shape managerial attitudes, beliefs and values, it is the nationality of subsidiary ownership that is a strong determinant of corporate strategy. Hennart and Larimo (1998) suggest that multinational companies based in countries where the dominant cultural traits are high power distance and low uncertainty avoidance may have an inherent preference for full ownership of their foreign subsidiary and consequently may be more likely to assimilate parent and subsidiary cultures.

HRD issues

The responsibility for HRD issues is a contentious one with a lack of consensus in the literature. On the one hand, de Pablos (2004) argues that human resource management systems are likely to be transferred to the overseas affiliate for two reasons: firstly, multinational organisations will seek to reduce their level of uncertainty when operating internationally by using the nearest management practices that have worked in the country of origin and secondly, if the management system of the country of origin offers a distinctive advantage, then this advantage may be duplicated when transferred to the overseas affiliate. However, there exists evidence from empirical studies of local autonomy in relation to HRD practices. In examining the impact of global and local influences on HRD practice, Collings (2003) found that the subsidiary possessed considerable autonomy in relation to HRD content issues while headquarters were concerned with budgetary issues. This supports earlier research by Tregaskis (1998) who revealed considerable support for local national context as a determinant of HRD practice over the country of origin of the multinational.

The transnational organisation

The transnational organisation has been recognised as the highest form of business internationalisation. However, despite achieving much coverage in textbooks, it remains relatively rare in practice. Rugman (2005) argues that of the world's largest 500 multinationals, only a handful – nine – operate a truly global or transnational strategy. Iles and Hayers (1997) define transnational organisations as ones which successfully transcend cultural, geographic and managerial barriers in achieving organisational effectiveness. By working beyond borders, transnational organisations hope to achieve a global presence and harvest regional and geographic synergies.

Structural issues

Transnational organisations are structured to provide autonomy and flexibility to subsidiaries to allow them to respond to local opportunities. Coakes (2006) maintains that transnational organisations are pluri-located, integrated communities that focus on a network of competencies across the world. The potency of transnational organisations lies in the speed by which subsidiaries in the network can react to changing market conditions. Bartlett et al. (2004) maintain that transnational organisations recognise the demands to be responsive to local market and political needs and the pressures to develop global-scale competitive efficiency and consequently can react well to political and economic volatility. The dispersed, yet specialised nature of resources and activities of subsidiaries requires intensive co-ordination and shared decision-making. In identifying the three goals of transnational organisations as the achievement of global efficiencies of scale/standardisation; flexibility to local conditions/differentiation and worldwide learning or global diffusion of innovation, Bartlett et al. (2004) recognise that transnational organisations fluctuate between a centralised and decentralised organisational structure.

Cultural issues

Transnational organisations operate in multi-cultural environments, but seek to move beyond cultural boundaries in their business activities. Iles and Hayers (1997) argue that developing and managing the transnational organisation requires individuals to move beyond the embeddedness of organisational systems, processes and cultures towards thinking, leading and acting from a global perspective. They point to the existence of three separate cultures within transnational organisations (national culture, corporate culture and professional culture) and that cultural differences need to be recognised, valued and used to the organisation's advantage. MacLean (2006) maintains that it is the flows of communication, information and knowledge that are a critical component of the competitive capabilities possessed by transnational corporations and ensuring that these flows are not distorted, diverted or blocked is essential to the development and maintenance of core competencies.

HRD issues

The management and coordination of HR activities across the transnational organisation is decidedly complex and involves balancing a series of competing priorities (geographic, business and functional). Kidger (2002) argues that the transnational organisation requires geographic managers who are accountable for local responsiveness; business managers who are responsible for global efficiency and integration and functional managers who are accountable for knowledge transfer and learning. Operating within such a dynamic structure requires a flexible approach to HR issues. Engle et al. (2001) argue that traditional, structurally embedded job based HR processes are inadequate to address the complexity created by the need to balance an in-depth local understanding with the co-ordination of global capabilities and resources required by transnational organisations. Consequently, Choy (2007) argues that within transnational organisations there is a strong need for HR structures that are culturally responsive in order to enhance interactions among staff from different cultures and nationalities. Likewise, Stedham and Engle (1999) argue that international HRM and HRD systems can act as repositories and levers to support cultural change through first changing individual attitudes and mindsets, then interpersonal relationships and processes and finally formal structures and responsibilities.

Conclusions

The framework established by this chapter clearly confirms that an organisation's international HRD approach is contingent on the stage that the organisation has reached in the internationalisation process. It indicates that the more international experience an organisation attains, the greater the devolvement of control to management of the overseas subsidiary. In later stages of the internationalisation process, overseas subsidiaries are empowered to provide greater strategic input and stronger linkages are forged between subsidiaries. This is particularly significant in the area of HRD as the further an organisation progresses in the internationalisation process, the greater the flexibility of the subsidiary to determine and respond to locally identified needs through targeted HRD interventions. In such cases, the subsidiary is also able to draw upon the experiences and best practices of other subsidiaries and may be involved in multinational teams focused on organisational development.

The type of structure adopted by the organisation during the internationalisation process will affect the product and service delivery as well as degree of autonomy exercised by the subsidiary. Such matters are often dictated by the overall objectives decided upon for the subsidiary. For the multi-domestic and international organisation, the overseas subsidiary is an off-shoot of the main organisation and exists on a dependency basis. Multinational and transnational organisations exercise greater levels of independence and relations with headquarters are dictated by a need to maximise operational efficiencies.

The chapter identifies opportunities for particular groups depending on the stage of internationalisation reached by the organisation. For instance, an international organisation typically seeks continuity and stability, characteristics which can be met by long-term expatriates. Likewise, individuals with high mobility and language skills will be valued by transnational organisations as they are adaptable to change and can be located in various geographic environments. Consequently, internationalisation provides openings to individuals who are not geographically restricted and who enjoy working in a diverse cultural environment.

Finally, responsibility for HRD activities operates on a continuum from full owner-ship by headquarters to complete devolvement to the subsidiary organisation. The framework shows that the decentralisation of HRD takes place on a gradual strategic basis until the subsidiary achieves full autonomy. Complete ownership of HRD activities allows the subsidiary to achieve a greater level of customisation in line with the ideal of local responsiveness. However, in such instances, it is likely that subsidiar-ies will be provided with templates for provision of interventions in order to maximise organisational efficiency.

 ? Discussion questions

- What are the key obstacles faced by the HRD function in 'exporting' HRD programmes to overseas subsidiaries?

- Should organisations be seeking to impose a singular culture across all global business units?

- What types of cost-efficiencies can be derived from cross-cultural standardisation?

- What key facets should an internationalisation strategy possess?

16 Reflections on HRD

David McGuire

■ ■ **Chapter objectives** ■

The objectives of this chapter are to:

- reflect upon the changing state of HRD;

- identify six grand HRD narratives;

- present a vision for the future of HRD.

Introduction

HRD lives in a constant state of becoming. It lives in the boundaries and interfaces of organisations, questioning assumptions, proposing alternatives and making organisations more relevant to the environments in which they operate. Through a broad interdisciplinary base, HRD embraces the concept of development and moves the field beyond a narrow training focus, giving it a strategic remit and a commission to advance innovative structures and models for organising and engaging employees in a more effective manner. In so doing, HRD becomes not only change-ready, but a change leader moving organisations towards dynamic, proactive, sustainable solutions and giving organisations an appetite for continuous learning and transformation.

At the individual level, HRD works with the individual to develop their potential, bringing meaning and satisfaction to work. It equips employees with the knowledge and skills necessary to adequately fulfil job tasks, but should also make employees future-ready in preparing them for challenges that lie ahead. Career planning and development should be essential elements in the employee's continuing formation and should represent the nexus by which individuals and organisations prepare their common futures. In this way, HRD should foster greater self-esteem and motivation amongst individuals and should contribute to a higher quality of working life and sense of accomplishment.

At the organisational level, HRD is linked to the overarching objectives of innovation, efficiency and effectiveness. Firstly, HRD is a critical approach to preparing organisations for tomorrow's challenges. Through creating a trained, flexible, adaptable workforce, organisations can meet and lead environmental change. Second, HRD can deliver real and substantial improvements to organisational systems. The knowledge economy demands more integrative, cross-functional approaches that draw upon unique competency sets and leverage tacit understandings (or the knowledge that exists between and behind individuals). Third, in today's competitive age, HRD encourages a spirit of entrepreneurialism and innovation across all employee groups. Employees are encouraged to be autonomous and work smarter – indeed, it is arguable that the dual concepts of devolvement and empowerment serve to heighten pressure particularly amongst middle and senior managers for more innovative strategic solutions. Finally, with the pervasive, all-consuming nature of technology, HRD has a distinct role in ensuring fit-for-purpose, ease of user-interface and client customisation.

At the societal level, HRD is associated with the vocational and economic agendas. HRD is tasked with developing appropriate structures for delivering knowledge and skills training to individuals and communities. HRD is linked to the investment agenda whereby the economic vitality and potential of regions is determined by labour quality and infrastructure provision. A key concern at this level is the alignment of industrial development policy with educational resources and community-based support. As Porter (1990) indicates, the competitive advantage of regions and attractiveness of regions to inward investment often depends upon specialist investment in education and training.

In this final chapter, we examine the six grand HRD narratives identified in this book. Each narrative emphasises particular approaches to HRD, reflecting specific assumptions about the task of HRD and how it will add value. Through examining these narratives, we hope to arrive at a more fuller understanding of human resource development. Finally, we offer a vision for the future of human resource development with some suggestions for advancing the field.

Six grand HRD narratives

As an interdisciplinary field, one of the great merits associated with HRD is that it offers space for competing paradigms and alternate views on how individuals, organisations and society can be developed more effectively. Throughout this book, we have attempted to present a series of ideas, concepts, theories and practices on how HRD can be deployed more effectively. Such discussions have as much as possible avoided prescriptive recipes as we have tried to engage the reader in a deeper, research-based, critical understanding of the assumptions underpinning particular approaches.

In this section, we attempt to summarise the key overarching narratives informing the text. In so doing, we hope to persuade the reader of the diversity of thought characteristic of the field and that such diversity is not all-limiting but rather enriches both theory and practice in the field.

The definitional narrative: These chapters seek to educate readers on the origins of the field, purpose of the field, key stakeholders in the field; conflicting agendas being pursued and reflections on the future of the field. They examine how HRD has been shaped by a variety of influences and they articulate the key values informing HRD theory and practice. Such chapters are important for clearly setting the foundations for any discussion of HRD as they bring readers to a closer understanding of how HRD distinguishes itself from other interventions and how HRD has addressed some of the criticisms levelled at it.

The training narrative: While HRD has evolved to embrace strategic initiatives, it retains its traditional roots to the fields of training and evaluation. In these chapters, we seek not only to rehearse conventional training theories, but rather attempt to bring forth new perspectives on training and alternative approaches to evaluation. Training and evaluation continue to constitute core 'bread and butter' activities within HRD and retain great importance in the toolkits of HRD practitioners. Thus, the training narrative will remain an important voice in the future of HRD.

The performance narrative: Developing high performing employees has long been a key goal of HRD practitioners. These chapters examine how organisational structures have evolved and changed to better deliver sustainable high performance. They examine how HRD professionals are engaging with employees across the organisation through developmental interventions designed to foster higher levels of commitment and performance. These chapters also examine how the value of human resources are measured and reported in the financial statements of the organisation. The issue of employee creativity traverses the performance and learning narratives as creativity can be linked to openness to learning and experiential, but employee creativity can generate high performance in organisations.

The learning narrative: Understanding individual and organisational learning is an essential requirement for the HRD professional. Learning constitutes the underpinning mechanism through which individuals contribute to the organisation. Learning lies at the core of education, training and development processes. In relation to organisational learning, the contributions of Senge and Argyris and Schön show us how learning can be incorporated into complex organisational systems, such that learning can become incorporated into the organisational culture transforming both systems and modes of behaviour.

The identity narrative: This chapter examined how identity is created through a socially constructed process. Consequently, an individual's identity can be shaped through interaction with the organisation and its processes. Within this paradigm, individuals may live in tension with organisational norms, values, policies and practices. Identity may therefore become shaped by reward and punishment, resource distributions and career development patterns.

The international HRD narrative: The chapter examines the role of HRD in multidomestic, international, multinational and transnational firms. It examines how HRD is shaped by national cultures and explores the degrees to which HRD programmes can be standardised across cultures. It looks at the changes that occur in HRD structures as firms continue to expand their international operations and the effect on overall control exercised over the HRD function.

The six grand HRD narratives are illustrated in Figure 16.1.

A vision of HRD

HRD is not new. While some may argue that HRD is a maturing field (Evarts, 1998) or reaching adolescence (Lee and Stead, 1998), the reality is that HRD in a holistic

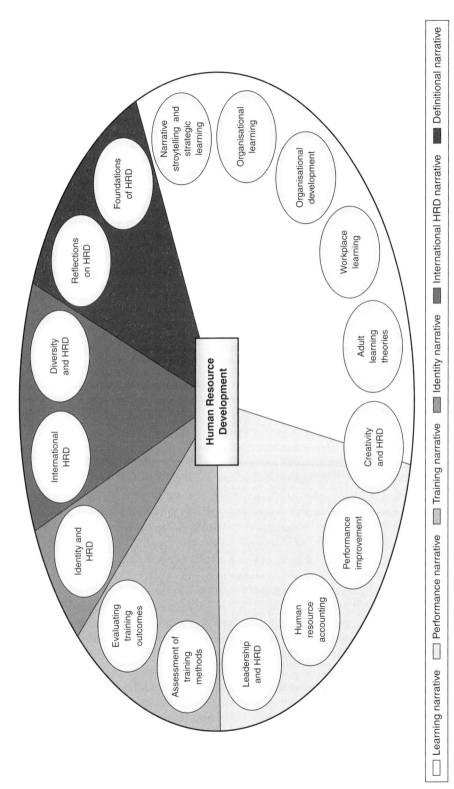

Figure 16.1 Six grand HRD narratives

Legend:
Learning narrative
Performance narrative
Training narrative
Identity narrative
International HRD narrative
Definitional narrative

Human Resource Development

Foundations of HRD
Reflections on HRD
Narrative storytelling and strategic learning
Organisational learning
Organisational development
Workplace learning
Adult learning theories
Creativity and HRD
Performance improvement
Human resource accounting
Leadership and HRD
Assessment of training methods
Evaluating training outcomes
Identity and HRD
International HRD
Diversity and HRD

form has been with us for a very long time. The seeds of HRD were sown long before Harbison and Myers (1964) formally defined the concept of human resource development. For generations, progressive organisations and managers have realised the importance of developing their people. They understood that upskilling, engaging with and motivating employees were crucial tasks in building a successful profitable organisation and satisfied committed workforce. They recognised the reality and necessity of building mutuality between the interests of employees and those of the organisation. In such matters, HRD is not new. So, what is new?

Each year, much is written about HRD with claims of original insights and revolutionary thinking. New models are presented to supplant previously accepted paradigms and to fit changing organisational and societal contexts. Researchers compete to develop better and more advanced solutions to age-old problems. In many cases, the problems haven't changed, but the remedies have become much more effective. And in other cases, the problems haven't changed and only small incremental improvements have occurred.

So, with all of this new thinking and the greater volume and dissemination of ideas, which theories and practices should be followed? Which applications are universal and which are context specific? How do we distinguish the effective from the ineffective? The answer to these questions lies in the relativity of the HRD concept. The fact that agreement cannot still be reached on a consensual definition of HRD some 40 years after its original formulation points to an evolving, shifting field in tune with the transitions of organisations and society. It acknowledges that there can be no one true HRD, but multiple variants of HRD fitting particular contexts and situations. The universal becomes local and adjusted to fit particular factors and circumstances. Effectiveness depends upon best fit and close alignment of HRD solutions with problem characteristics.

In short, there is a need to develop the evidence base for HRD. To be truly innovative and effective, HRD solutions must work well. Innovation rarely occurs in a vacuum. Notwithstanding some exceptional cases, innovation builds upon existing contexts and problems, but frames solutions in a ground-breaking and creative way. In some cases, innovation occurs through reclaiming lost insights and revisiting long forgotten research studies. In this regard, new perspectives often involve presenting old wine in new bottles. They entail communicating old accepted truths in a manner that connects with modern realities and contexts. This may require employing new technology and tools to deliver practical applications more efficiently and with greater effectiveness.

So, where is the value in repackaging old theories and concepts? Like management, HRD is an art as well as a science. Just as there is no single best artistic masterpiece, HRD recognises the value of Tayloristic 'one best way' approaches, but strongly acknowledges their limitations. The myriad of circumstances and contexts that exist at organisational and societal levels demands a plethora of tools that are timely and appropriate to contemporary realities. The development of new approaches needs to be an ongoing iterative process. In so being, it needs to be attuned to the changing economic, social, political and environmental realities facing organisations and society.

New perspectives on HRD challenges stasis and fosters a progressive dynamism about the HRD concept, its value and purpose. They promote diversity of thought and generate conflict through forcing HRD practitioners to move beyond their narrow comfort zones towards critical reflexivity and deeper thinking about HRD's purpose and functions (Garavan et al., 2007). The moving shifting character of HRD has recently been identified by Sambrook (2008: 218) when she discusses HRD stretch – the development of multiple collaborative relationships pulling the field along horizontal and vertical dimensions.

To my mind, relationships lie at the core of HRD. Through HRD, individuals become more connected to each other, to their work, to their organisations, to communities and to society. That HRD creates multiple relationships means that it must reconcile conflicting needs and agendas. In this regard, the HRD discipline and profession are formed around a tension in values (McGuire et al., 2007). Viewing HRD through a multi-perspectival lens allows greater appreciation and understanding of individual interests, motivations and priorities. As Torraco (2004) points out, acknowledging different perspectives creates flux, where differences may initially appear wider than they are in reality. However, it is only through exposing difference and questioning assumptions that HRD can truly progress and remain relevant as a field of study.

 Discussion questions

- What global factors are affecting the field of HRD? How are they affecting the field?

- Six grand narratives are identified in this chapter. Which narratives are under-represented in the literature? Why is this the case?

- What suggestions do you have for the future development of the field of HRD?

References

Abeysekera, I. (2006) The Project of Intellectual Capital Disclosure: Researching the Research. *Journal of Intellectual Capital*, 7(1), 61–77.

Abu-Tineh, A.M., Khasawneh, S.A. and Al-Omari, A.A. (2008) Kouzes and Posner's Transformational Leadership Model in Practice: The Case of Jordanian Schools. *Leadership and Organization Development Journal*, 29(8), 648–660.

Ackah, C. and Heaton, N. (2004) The Reality of 'New' Careers for Men and for Women. *Journal of European Industrial Training*, 28(2/3/4), 141–158.

Addesso, P.J. (1996) *Management would be Easy – If it Weren't for the People.* New York: AMACOM.

Adler, N.J. (1994) Competitive Frontiers: Women Managing Across Borders. *Journal of Management Development*, 13(2), 24–41.

Adler, N.J. and Ghadar, E. (1990) Strategic Human Resource Management: A Global Perspective. In R. Pieper (ed.), *Human Resource Management in International Comparison*. Berlin: de Gruyter.

Adler, N.J., Doktor, R. and Redding, G. (1986) From the Atlantic to the Pacific Century: Cross-Cultural Management Reviewed. *Journal of Management*, 12(2), 295–318.

Aguilar, J.L. (1981) Insider Research: An Ethnography of a Debate. In D.A. Messerschmidt (ed.), *Anthropologists at Home in North America* (pp. 15–26). Cambridge: Cambridge University Press.

Aik, C. and Tway, D.C. (2003) Cognitivism, Constructivism and Work Performance. *Academic Exchange*, 7(3), 274–278.

Ainsworth, S. and Hardy, C. (2004) Discourse and Identities. In D. Grant, C. Hardy, C. Oswick and L. Putnam (eds), *The Sage Handbook of Organizational Discourse*. London: Sage Publications.

Alagaraja, M. and Dooley, L.M. (2003) Origins and Historical Influences on Human Resource Development: A Global Perspective. *Human Resource Development Review*, 2(1), 82–96.

Allen, N.J. and Meyer, I.P. (1990) The Measurement and Antecedents of Affective, Continuance, and Normative Commitment to the Organization. *Journal of Occupational Psychology*, 91, 1–18.

Allio, R.J. (2005) Leadership Development: Teaching Versus Learning. *Management Decision*, 43(7/8), 1071–1077.

Allred, B.B. and Steensma, H.K. (2005) The influence of industry and home country characteristics on firms' pursuit of innovation. *Management International Review*, 45(4), 383–412.

Alvesson, M. and Deetz, S. (1996) Critical Theory and Postmodernism Approaches to Organizational Studies. In S.R. Clegg, C. Hardy and W.R. Nord (eds), *Handbook of Organization Studies* (pp. 191–217). London: Sage.

Alvesson, M. and Skoldberg, K. (2000) *Reflexive Methodology*. London: Sage.

Alvesson, M. and Wilmott, H. (1992) Critical Theory and Management Studies: An Introduction. In M. Alvesson and H. Wilmott (eds), *Critical Management Studies* (pp. 1–20) London: Sage.

Amabile, T.M. (1983) *The Social Psychology of Creativity*. New York: Springer-Verlag.

Amabile, T.M. (1996) *Creativity in Context*. Boulder, CO: Westview Press.

Amabile, T.M. (1998) How to Kill Creativity. *Harvard Business Review*, 77–87.

Amabile, T.M. and Conti, R. (1999) Changes in the World Environment for Creativity During Downsizing. *Academy of Management Journal*, 42(6), 630–640.

Amabile, T.M., Barsade, S.G., Mueller, J.S. and Staw, B.M. (2005) Affect and Creativity at Work. *Administrative Science Quarterly*, 50(3), 367–403.

Amabile, T.M., Conti, R., Coon, H., Lazenby, J. and Herron, M. (1996) Assessing the Work Environment for Creativity. *Academy of Management Journal*, 39(5), 1154–1185.

Amabile, T.M., Goldfarb, P. and Brackfield, S.C. (1990) Social Influences on Creativity: Evaluation, Coaction and Surveillance. *Creativity Research Journal*, 2, 231–253.

Amabile, T.M., Schatzel, E.A., Moneta, G.B. and Kramer, S.J. (2004) Leader Behaviors and the Work Environment for Creativity: Perceived Leader Support. *The Leadership Quarterly*, 15, 5–32.

American Accounting Association (1996) http://aaahq.org/index.cfm

Anacona, D.G. and Caldwell, D.F. (1992) Demography and Design: Predictors of New Product Team Performance. *Organization Science*, 3(3), 321–341.

Analoui, F. and Karami, A. (2002) How Chief Executives' Perception of the Environment Impacts on Company Performance. *Journal of Management Development*, 21(4), 290–305.

Anand, R. and Winters, M.F. (2008) A Retrospective View of Corporate Diversity Training from 1964 to Present. *Academy of Management Learning and Education*, 7(3), 356–372.

Anderson, B. (1999) Industrial Benchmarking for Competitive Advantage. *Human Systems Management*, 18(3/4), 287–296.

Anderson, J.R. (1993) Problem Solving and Learning. *American Psychologist*, 48(1), 35–44.

Anderson, J.R. (2000) *Cognitive Psychology and its Implications*. New York: Worth Publishers.

Anderson, V. (2007) *The Value of Learning: From Return on Investment to Return on Expectations*. London: CIPD.

Anderson Consulting and Economist Intelligence Unit (2000) eCommerce and the CFO: A framework for finance in the new economy. http://accenture.tekgroup.com/article_display.cfm?article_id=3606

Andon, P., Baxter, J. and Fong, C.W. (2003) Management Accounting Inscriptions and the Post-Industrial Experience of Organizational Control. In A. Bhimani (ed.), *Management Accounting in the Digital Economy*. New York: Oxford University Press.

Andresen, M. (2007) Diversity Learning, Knowledge Diversity and Inclusion: Theory and Practice as Exemplified by Corporate Universities. *Equal Opportunities International*, 26(8), 743–760.

Andrews, F.M. and Farris, G.F. (1967) *Supervisory Practices and Innovation of Scientific Teams*. Paper presented at the Proceedings of the American Psychological Association.

Anthony, N. (1965) *Management Control Systems*. 3rd Edition. Boston: Harvard Business School.

Antola, J., Kujansivu, P. and Lonnqvist, A. (2005) *Management Accounting for Intellectual Capital*. Paper presented at the 77th Manufacturing Accounting Research Conference, Tampere, Finland.

Antonacopoulou, E., Jarvis, P., Andersen, V., Elkjaer, B. and Høyrup, S. (eds) (2005) *Learning, Working and Living. Mapping the Terrain of Working Life Learning*. New York: Palgrave Macmillan.

Ardichvili, A. (2008) Learning and Knowledge Sharing in Virtual Communities of Practice: Motivators, Barriers and Enablers. *Advances in Developing Human Resources,* 10(4), 541–554.

Ardichvili, A. and Kuchinke, K.P. (2002) The Concept of Culture in International and Comparative HRD Research: Methodological Problems and Possible Solutions. *Human Resource Development Review*, 1(2), 145–166.

Arendt, H. (1998) *The Human Condition*. Chicago: The University of Chicago Press.

Argyris, C. (1990) *Overcoming Organizational Defenses – Facilitating Organizational Learning*. Boston: Allyn and Bacon.

Argyris, C. (1999) *On Organizational Learning*. Malden, MA: Blackwell Business.

Argyris, C. and Schön, D.A. (1996) *Organizational Learning II – Theory, Method and Practice*. Reading, MA: Addison-Wesley.

Armagan, S. and Ferreira, M.P. (2005) The Impact of Political Culture on Firms' Choice of Exploitation-Exploration: Internationalization Strategy. *International Journal of Cross Cultural Management*, 5(3), 275–292.

Armstrong, M. (1999) *A Handbook of Human Resource Management Practice*. London: Kogan Page.

Arvidsson, N. (1997) Internationalisation of Service Firms: Strategic Considerations. In G. Chryssochoidis, C. Millar and J. Clegg (eds), *Internationalisation Strategies*. London: Macmillan.

Ashton, C. (2003) Case Study: Banking 365 in *Building a Strategic Balanced Scorecard – A Best Practice Framework*, Business Intelligence. http://www.business-intelligence. co.uk/reports/strat_bsc/default.asp

Ashton, R.H. (2005) Intellectual Capital and Value Creation: A Review. *Journal of Accounting Literature*, 24, 53–134.

Astley, W.G. (1985) Administrative Science as Socially Constructed Truth. *Administrative Science Quarterly*, 30(4), 497–513.

Atkinson, H. (2006) Strategy Implementation: A Role for the Balanced Scorecard?, *Management Decision*, 44(10), 144–160.

Avolio, B.J. (2007) Promoting more Integrative Strategies for Leadership Theory-Building. *American Psychologist*, 62(1), 25–33.

Baer, M., Oldham, G.R. and Cummings, A. (2003) Rewarding Creativity: When does it really matter? *The Leadership Quarterly*, 14, 569–586.

Bairstow, S. and Skinner, H. (2007) Internal Marketing and the Enactment of Sexual Identity. *Equal Opportunities International*, 26(7), 653–664.

Bakhtin, M.M. (1981) *Dialogic Imagination – Four Essays*. Austin: University of Texas Press.

Bakhtin, M.M. (1994) Folk Humour and Carnival Laughter. In P. Morris (ed.), *The Bakhtin Reader – Selected Writings of Bakhtin, Medvedev, Voloshinov* (pp. 194–206). London: Edward Arnold.

Baldwin, T.T. and Ford, J.K. (1988) Transfer of Training: A Review and Directions for Future Research. *Personnel Review*, 26(3), 201–213.

Bandura, A. (1977) *Social Learning Theory*. Englewood Cliffs, NJ: Prentice Hall.

Bandura, A. (2002) Social Cognitive Theory in Cultural Context. *Applied Psychology: An International Review*, 51, 269–290.

Barbosa, I. and Cabral-Cardoso, C. (2007) Managing Diversity in Academic Organisations: A Challenge to Organisational Culture. *Women in Management Review*, 22(4), 274–288.

Barratt, I.C., Cervero, R.M. and Johnson-Bailey, J. (2004) The Career Development of Black Human Resource Developers in the United States. *Human Resource Development International*, 7(1), 85–100.

Barrie, J. and Pace, R.W. (1998) Learning for Organizational Effectiveness: Philosophy of Education and Human Resource Development. *Human Resource Development Quarterly*, 9(1), 39–54.

Barron, F. and Harrington, D.M. (1981) Creativity, Intelligence and Personality. *Annual Review of Psychology*, 32, 439–476.

Bartlett, C.A. and Ghoshal, S. (1998) *Managing Across Borders: The Transnational Solution*, 2nd edn. Boston, MA: Harvard Business School Press.

Bartlett, C.A., Ghoshal, S. and Birkinshaw, J. (2004) *Transnational Management: Text, Cases and Readings in Cross-Border Management*. Boston, MA: McGraw-Hill.

Bartlett, K.R., Lawler, J.J., Bae, J., Chen, S. and Wan, D. (2002) Differences in International Human Resource Development Among Indigenous Firms and Multinational Affiliates in East and Southeast Asia. *Human Resource Development Quarterly*, 13(4), 383–405.

Bartram, P. (2000) Capital Plan. *Financial Management*, December, 10.

Bass, B.M. (1985) *Leadership and Performance Beyond Expectations*. New York: Free Press.

Bass, B.M. (1987) *Leadership and Performance Beyond Expectations*. New York: Free Press.

Bass, B.M. (1990) *Bass and Stogdill's Handbook of Leadership*, 3rd edn. New York: Free Press.

Bass, B.M. and Avolio, B.J. (1994) *Improving Organizational Effectiveness Through Transformational Leadership*. London: Sage.

Bass, B.M., Avolio, B.J. and Goodheim, L. (1987) Biography and the Assessment of Transformational Leadership at the World-Class Level. *Journal of Management*, 13(1), 7–19.

Bassi, L.J and Van Buren, M.E. (1999) The 1999 ASTD State of the Industry Report. *Training and Development*, 53(1).

Bauman, Z. (2004) *Identity – Conversations with Benedetto Vecchi*. Oxford: Polity Press.

Baumard, P. (1999) *Tacit Knowledge in Organisations*. London, Sage.

Bazerman, M.H. (1994) *Judgment in Decision-Making*. New York: Wiley.

Beattie, R.S. (2006) Line Managers and Workplace Learning: Learning from the Voluntary Sector. *Human Resource Development International*, 9(1), 99–119.

Beaver, G. and Hutchings, K. (2004) The Big Business of Strategic Human Resource Management in Small Business. In J. Stewart and G. Beaver (eds), *HRD in Small Organizations: Research and Practice*. London: Routledge.

Bednar, A.K. and Cunningham, D. (1991) *Theory into Practice: How do we link? Instructional Technology: Past, Present and Future*. G. Anglin. Englewood, CO, Libraries Unlimited: 88–101.

Belis-Bergouignan, M.C., Bordenave, G. and Lung, Y. (2000) Global Strategies in the Automobile Industry. *Regional Studies*, 34(1), 41–54.

Benjamin, A. (1994) Affordable Restructured Education: A Solution through Information Technology. *RSA Journal* (May), 45–49.

Benjamin, W. (1999) The Storyteller – Reflections on the Work of Nikolai Leskov. In H. Arendt (ed.), *Illuminations* (pp. 83–107). London: Pimlico.

Berge, Z. and Verneil, M. (2002) The Increasing Scope of Training and Development Competency. *Benchmarking*, 9(1), 43–61.

Bergenhenegouwen, G.J. (1990) The Management and Effectiveness of Corporate Training Programmes. *British Journal of Educational Technology*, 21(3), 196–202.

Berggren, C. (1996) Building a Truly Global Organisation? ABB and the Problems of Integrating a Multi-Domestic Enterprise. *Journal of Management*, 12(2), 123–137.

Bernard, L.L. (1926) *An Introduction to Social Psychology*, New York: Holt.

Beyer, L.E. (2001) The Value of Critical Perspectives in Teacher Education. *Journal of Teacher Education*, 52(2), 151–163.

Bhutta, K.S. and Huq, F. (1999) Benchmarking – Best Practices: An Integrated Approach. *Benchmarking: An International Journal*, 6(3), 254–268.

Bibby, P.A. and Payne, S.J. (1996) Instruction and Practice in Learning to Use a Device. *Cognitive Science*, 20, 539–578.

Bierema, L.L. (1997) Development of the Individual Leads to a More Productive Workplace. In R. Rowden (ed.), *Workplace Learning: Debating Five Critical Questions of Theory and Practice*. San Francisco: Jossey-Bass.

Bierema, L.L. (2009) Critiquing Human Resource Development's Dominant Masculine Rationality and Evaluating its Impact. *Human Resource Development Review*, 8(1), 68–96.

Bierema, L.L., & Cseh, M. (2003) Evaluating AHRD research using a feminist research framework. *Human Resource Development Quarterly*, 14(1), 5–26.

Biggs, J. (2003) *Teaching for Quality Learning at University*. London: Open University Press and Society for Research into Higher Education.

Billet, S. (1999) Guided Learning at Work. In D. Boud and J. Garrick (eds), *Understanding Learning at Work*. London: Routledge.

Bing, J.W., Kehrhahn, M.T. and Short, D.C. (2003) Challenges to the Field of Human Resource Development. *Advances in Developing Human Resources*, 5(3), 342–351.

Blake, M.K. and Hanson, S. (2005) Rethinking Innovation: Context and Gender. *Environment and Planning*, 37(4), 681–701.

Blake, R.R. (1995, March) Memories of HRD. *Training and Development*, 49, 22–28.

Blake, R.R. and McCanse, A.A. (1991) *Leadership Dilemmas: Grid Solutions*, Houston: Gulf Publishing Co.

Blake, R.R. and Mouton, J.S. (1964) *The Managerial Grid: The Key to Leadership Excellence*. Houston: Gulf Publishing Co.

Blanchard, K.H. and Muchnick, M. (2005) *The Leadership Pill*. New York: Pocket Books.

Blanton, B.B. (1998) The Application of the Cognitive Learning Theory to Instructional Design. *International Journal of Instructional Media*, 25(2), 171–177.

Bligh, M.C., Pearce, C.L. and Kohles, J.C. (2006) The Importance of Self and Shared Leadership in Team Based Knowledge Work: A Meso Level Model of Leadership Dynamics. *Journal of Managerial Psychology*, 21(4), 296–318.

Bluckert, P. (2005) Critical Factors in Executive Coaching – The Coaching Relationship. *Industrial and Commercial Training*, 37(7), 336–340.

Boaden, R.J. (2006). Leadership development; does it make a difference? *Leadership & Organization Development Journal*, 27(1), 5-27.

Boak, G. and Coolican, D. (2001) Competencies for Retail Leadership: Accurate, Acceptable, Affordable. *Leadership and Organisational Development Journal*, 22(5), 212–220.

Boje, D.M. (1991) The Storytelling Organization: A Study of Story Performance in an Office-Supply Firm. *Administrative Science Quarterly*, 36(1), 106–126.

Boje, D.M. (2001) *Narrative Methods for Organizational and Communication Research*. London: Sage Publications.

Boje, D.M. (2008) *Storytelling Organization*. London: Sage.

Boje, D.M. and Durant, R.A. (2006) Free Stories! *Tamara Journal for Critical Organization Inquiry*, 5(3), 19–37.

Boje, D.M., Luhmann, J.T. and Cunliffe, A. (2003) A Dialectic Perspective on the Organization Theatre Metaphor. *American Communication Journal*, 6(2).

Bokeno, R.M. (2003) Introduction: Appraisals of Organisational Learning as Emancipatory Change. *Journal of Organizational Change Management*, 16(3), 603–618.

Booth, R. (1998) The Measurement of Intellectual Capital. *Management Accounting*, 76(10), 26–28.

Boud, D. and Garrick, J. (1999) *Understanding Learning At Work*, London: Routledge.

Boyatzis, R.E. (1982) *The Competent Manager: A Guide for Effective Management*. New York: Wiley.

Boyatzis, R.E. and Kolb, D.N. (1995) From Learning Styles to Learning Skills: The Executive Skills Profile. *Journal of Managerial Psychology*, 10(5), 24–27.

Bozzolan, S., O'Regan, P. and Ricceri, F. (2006) Intellectual Capital Disclosure (ICD) – A Comparison of Italy and the UK. *Journal of Human Resource Costing and Accounting*, 10(2), 92–113.

Bramming, P. (2004) *The One and the Many: Contemplating Conceptions of Individual and Organisation in Relation to Human Resource Practices*. Fifth European Conference on Human Resource Development Theory and Practice, University of Limerick.

Brennan, N. and Connell, B. (2000) Intellectual Capital: Current Issues and Policy Implications. *Journal of Intellectual Capital*, 1(3), 206–240.

Bright, J., Davies, R.E., Downes, C.A. and Sweeting, R.C. (1992) The Deployment of Costing Techniques and Practices: a UK Study. *Management Accounting Research*, 3(2), 201–211.

Brim, O.G. and Wheeler, S. (1966) *Socialisation after Childhood: Two Essays*. New York: Wiley.

Brinkerhoff, R.O. (2006) Increasing Impact of Training Investments: An Evaluation Strategy for Building Organisational Learning Capability. *Industrial and Commercial Training*, 38(6), 302–307.

Brinkerhoff, R.O. and Montesino, M. (1995) Partnerships for Transfer of Training: Lessons from a Corporate Study. *Human Resource Development Quarterly*, 6, 263–274.

Brookfield, S.D. (2003) *The Concept of Critically Reflective Practice*. San Francisco: Jossey-Bass.

Brown, J.S. and Duguid, P. (1996) Organizational Learning and Communities-of-Practice – Towards a Unified View of Working, Learning and Innovation. In M.D. Cohen and L.S. Sproull (eds), *Organizational Learning*. London: Sage Publications.

Brown, J.S. and Duguid, P. (2001) Knowledge and Organization: A Social Practice Perspective. *Organization Science*, 2, 198–213.

Brown, T.C. and McCracken, M. (2004) *The Relationship between Managerial Barriers to Learning and Transfer of Training: Preliminary Results*. Fifth European Conference on Human Resource Development Theory and Practice, University of Limerick.

Brown, T.C. and Morrissey, L. (2004) The Effectiveness of Verbal Self-guidance as a Transfer of Training. *Innovations in Education and Teaching International*, 42, 255–271.

Browne, I. and Misra, J. (2003) The Intersection of Gender and Race in the Labor Market. *Annual Review of Sociology*, 29, 487–513.

Bruce, R.W. (1933) Conditions of Transfer of Training. *Journal of Experiential Psychology*, 6, 343–361.

Brummet, R.L., Flamholtz, E.G. and Pyle, W.C. (1968) Human Resource Measurement – a Challenge for Accountants. *The Accounting Review*, 43(2), 217–224.

Bruner, J. (1996) *The Culture of Education*. Cambridge, MA:Harvard University Press.

Bryans, P. and Smith, R. (2000) Beyond Training: Reconceptualising Learning at Work. *Journal of Workplace Learning*, 12(6), 228–235.

Burns, J. and Yazdifar, H. (2001) Trick or Treat. *Financial Management*, March, 33–35.

Burns, J.M. (1978) *Leadership*. New York: Harper and Row.

Burrow, J. and Berardinelli, P. (2003) Systematic Performance Improvement – Refining the Space Between Learning and Results. *Journal of Workplace Learning*, 15(1), 6–14.

Business in the Community (2009) *2009 Benchmarking Report: Transparency at the Heart of Diversity*. London: Business in the Community.

Cahill, D. and Myers, P.J. (2000) *Intellectual Capital and Accounting Concepts: Unresolved Issues in Human Resource Accounting*. Paper presented at the British Accounting Association's Annual Conference, Manchester, England.

Caldwell, R. and Storey, J. (2007) The HR Function: Integration or Fragmentation? In J. Storey (ed.), *Human Resource Management: A Critical Text*. London: Thomson Learning.

Callahan, J. and Dunne De Davila, T. (2004) An Impressionistic Framework for Theorizing about Human Resource Development. *Human Resource Development Review*, 3(1), 75–95.

Callahan, J.L. (2007) Gazing into the Crystal Ball: Critical HRD as a Future of Research in the Field. *Human Resource Development International*, 10(1), 77–82.

Callahan, J. and Dunne De Davila, T. (2004) An Impressionistic Framework for Theorizing about Human Resource Development. *Human Resource Development Review*, 3(1), 75–95.

Campbell, C.P. (1994) A Primer on Determining the Cost Effectiveness of Training – Part 1. *Industrial and Commercial Training*, 26(11), 32–38.

Campbell, C.P (1998) Training Course/Program Evaluation: Principles and Practice. *Journal of European Industrial Training*, 22 (8), 323–344.

Canibano, L., Garcia-Ayouso, M. and Sanchez, M.P. (1999) The Value Relevance and Managerial Implications of Intangibles: a Literature Review. In J.E. Grojer and H. Stolowy (eds), *Classification of Intangibles*. Jouy-en-Josas, France: Groupe HEC.

Canibano, L., Garcia-Ayouso, M. and Sanchez, P. (2000) Accounting for Intangibles: A Literature Review. *Journal of Accounting Literature*, 19, 102–130.

Cappelli, P. and Singh, H. (1992) Integrating Strategic Human Resources and Strategic Management. In D. Lewin, O. Mitchell and P. Shewer (eds), *Research Frontiers in Industrial Relations and Human Resources*. Industrial Relations Association, Madison University of Wisconsin.

Cardona, P. (2000) Transcendental Leadership. *Leadership and Organisational Development Journal*, 21(4), 201–207.

Carter, S.D. (2002) Matching Training Methods and Factors of Cognitive Ability: A Means to Improve Training Outcomes. *Human Resource Development Quarterly*, 13(1), 71–87.

Cartwright, S. and Cooper, C.L. (1992) *Mergers and Acquisitions: The Human Factor*. Oxford: Butterworth-Heinemann.

Cavanagh, J.M. (2004) Head Games: Introducing Tomorrow's Business Elites to Institutionalised Inequality. In C. Grey and E. Antonacopoulou (eds), *Essential Readings in Management Learning*. London: Sage.

Chakravarthy, B.S. (1985) Measuring Strategic Performance. *Strategic Management Journal*, 437–457.

Chalofsky, N. (1992) A Unifying Definition for the Human Resource Development Profession. *Human Resource Development Quarterly*, 3(2), 175–182.

Chalofsky, N. (2004) *Human and Organization Studies: The Discipline of HRD*. Paper presented at the Academy of Human Resource Development Conference, Austin, Texas.

Chalofsky, N. and Lincoln, C. (1983) *Up the HRD Ladder*. Reading, MA: Addison-Wesley.

Chandler, A.D. (1962) *Strategy and Structure: Chapters in the History of the Industrial Enterprise*. Boston: Harvard University Press.

Chang, E. and Taylor, M.S. (1999) Control in Multinational Corporations (MNCs): The Case of Korean Manufacturing Subsidiaries. *Journal of Management*, 25(4), 541–553.

Chang, L.C. (2007) The NHS Performance Assessment Framework as a Balanced Scorecard Approach: Limitations and Implications. *International Journal of Public Sector Management*, 20(2), 101–117.

Chappell, C., Rhodes, C., Solomon, N., Tennant, M. and Yates, L. (2003) *Reconstructing the Lifelong Learner – Pedagogy and Identity in Individual, Organizational and Social Change*. London: Routledge Falmer.

Chartered Institute of Personnel and Development (CIPD) (2007a) *The Changing HR Function: Survey Report*. London: CIPD.

Chartered Institute of Personnel and Development (CIPD) (2007b) *The Value of Learning: A New Model of Value and Evaluation*. London: CIPD.

Cheng, E.W.L. and Ho, D.C.K. (2001) A Review of Transfer of Training Studies in the Past Decade. *Personnel Review*, 30(1), 102–118.

Childs, M. (2005) Beyond Training: New Firefighters and Critical Reflection. *Disaster Prevention and Management*, 14(4), 558–566.

Chimombo, M.P. and Roseberry, R.L. (1998) *The Power of Discourse*. New Jersey: Erlbaum.

Cho, D.Y. and Kwon, D.B. (2005) Self-directed Learning Readiness as an Antecedent of Organisational Commitment: A Korean Study. *International Journal of Training and Development*, 9(2), 140–152.

Choy, W.K.W. (2007) Globalisation and Workforce Diversity: HRM Implications for Multinational Corporations in Singapore. *Singapore Management Review*, 29(2), 1–20.

Clandinin, D.J. and Connelly F.M. (2000) *Narrative Inquiry – Experience and Story in Qualitative Research*. San Francisco: Jossey-Bass.

Clark, C.S. and Dobbins, G.H. (1993) Exploratory Field Study of Training Motivation: Influence of Involvement, Credibility and Transfer Climate. *Group and Organisation Management*, 18(3), 292–307.

Clark, R.E. and Blake, S.B. (1997) Designing Training for Novel Problem Solving Transfer. In R.D. Tennyson, F. Schott, N. Seel and S. Dijkstra (eds), *Instructional Design: International Perspectives*. Mahwah, NJ: Lawrence Erlbaum.

Clarke, N. (2005) Workplace Learning Environment and its Relationship with Learning Outcomes in Healthcare Organisations. *Human Resource Development International*, 8(2), 185–206.

Clegg, S.R. (1975) *Power, Rule and Domination*. London: Routledge and Kegan Paul.

Clegg, S.R. (1989) *Framework of Power*. London: Sage.

Clutterbuck, D. (2008) What's Happening in Coaching and Mentoring? And What is the Difference between Them, *Development and Learning in Organizations*, 22(4), 8–10.

Coad, F.C. and Berry, A.J. (1998) Transformational Leadership and Learning Organization. *Leadership and Organization Development Journal*, 19(3), 164–172.

Coakes, E. (2006) Storing and Sharing Knowledge: Supporting the Management of Knowledge Made Explicit in Transnational Organisations. *The Learning Organisation*, 13(6), 579–593.

Cohen, E. and Tichy, N. (1997) How Leaders Develop Leaders. *Training and Development*, 51(5), 58–73.

Coleman, I. and Eccles, R. (1997) *Pursuing Value: Reporting Gaps in the United Kingdom*. Report submitted to PricewaterhouseCoopers. http://store.barometersurveys.com/docs/PWC_Pursuing_Value_UK.pdf

Colgan, F., Creegan, C., McKearney, A. and Wright, T. (2007) Equality and Diversity Policies and Practices at Work: Lesbian, Gay and Bisexual Workers. *Equal Opportunities International*, 26(6), 590–609.

Collings, D.G. (2003) HRD and Labour Market Practices in a US Multinational Subsidiary: The Impact of Global and Local Influences. *Journal of European Industrial Training*, 27(2/3/4), 188–200.

Collins, D. (2002) Performance-Level Evaluation Methods Used in Management Development Studies from 1986 to 2000. *Human Resource Development Review*, 1(1), 91–110.

Communications, B. (2001) How Frequently will you Use these Training Delivery Methods this Year? *Training*, 38(1), 118.

Competitiveness (1996) *Creating the Entreprise Centre of Europe*. London: DTI Publications, HMSO.

Conlon, T.J. (2004) A Review of Informal Learning Literature: Theory and Implications for Practice in Developing Global Professional Competence. *Journal of European Industrial Training*, 28(2/3/4), 283–295.

Connelly, B., Hitt, M.A., DeNisi, A.S. and Ireland, R.D. (2007) Expatriates and Corporate-level International Strategy: Governing with the Knowledge Contract. *Management Decision*, 45(3), 564–581.

Cook, S.D.N. and Yanow, D. (1993) Culture and Organizational Learning. *Journal of Management Inquiry*, 2, 373–390.

Cooley, C.H. (1909) *Social Organisation: A Study of the Larger Mind*. New York: Charles Scribner's Sons.

Cooley, C.H. (1922) *Human Nature and the Social Order*. New York: Charles Scribner's Sons.

Coren, S. (2003) Sensation and Perception. In D.K. Freedheim, W.F. Velicer, J.A. Schinka and R.M. Lerner (eds), *Handbook of Psychology* (Vol. 1, *History of Psychology*). Hoboken, NJ: Wiley and Sons.

Costa, P.T. and McCrae, R.R. (1992) *Revised NEO Personality Inventory (NEO-PI-R) and NEO Five-Factor Inventory (NEO-FFI) Manual.* Odessa, FL: Psychological Assessment Resources.

Cox, T.H. and Blake, S. (1991) Managing Cultural Diversity: Implications for Organisational Competitiveness. *Academy of Management Executive*, 5(3), 45–57.

Crabb, S. (2008) Spending Time with a Master. In CIPD (ed.), *CIPD Recipe for Success.* London: CIPD.

Craig, R. (1976) *Training and Development Handbook* (2nd edn). New York: McGraw-Hill.

Cronbach, L.J. and Glaser, G.C. (1965) *Psychological Tests and Personnel Decisions* (2nd edn). Urbana, IL: University of Illinois Press.

Cseh, M., Watkins, K. and Marsick, V. (1999) *Reconceptualising Marsick and Watkins Model of Informal and Incidental Learning in the Workplace.* Paper presented at the Proceedings of the Academy of Human Resource Development Conference, Baton Rouge, LA.

Csikszentmihalyi, M. (1988) Society, Culture and Person: A Systems View of Creativity. In R.J. Sternberg (ed.), *The Nature of Creativity* (pp. 325–339). Cambridge: Cambridge University Press.

Csikszentmihalyi, M. (1996) *Creativity: Flow and the Psychology of Discovery and Invention.* New York: Harper Collins.

Csikszentmihalyi, M. (1999) Implications of a System Perspective for the Study of Creativity. In R.J. Sternberg (ed.), *Handbook of Creativity* (pp. 313–328). Cambridge: Cambridge University Press.

Culler, J. (2003) Deconstruction. In J. Culler (ed.), *Critical Concepts in Literary and Cultural Studies* (pp. 52–71). London: Routledge.

Cunliffe, A.L. (2002) Reflexive Dialogical Practice in Management Learning. *Management Learning*, 33(1), 35–61.

Cunliffe, A.L. (2003) Reflexive Inquiry in Organizational Research: Questions and Possibilities. *Human Relations*, 56(8), 983–1003.

Cunliffe, A.L. and Jun, J.S. (2005) The Need for Reflexivity in Public Administration. *Administration and Society*, 37(2), 225–242.

Cunliffe, A.L., Luhmann, J.T. and Boje, D. (2004) Narrative Temporality: Implications for Organizational Research. *Organization Studies*, 25(2), 261–286.

Cunningham, I. and Hyman, J. (1995) Transforming the HR Vision into Reality: The Role of Line Managers and Supervisors in Implementing Change. *Employee Relations*, 17(8), 5–20.

Curran, P. (1998) Turning Information into Knowledge for Competitive Advantage. *Management Accounting*, 76(4), 26–27.

Czarniawska, B. (1997) *Narrating the Organization – Dramas of Institutional Identity.* Chicago: The University of Chicago Press.

Czarniawska, B. (2005) *Narratives in Social Science Research: Introducing Qualitative Methods.* London: Sage.

D'Abate, C.P., Eddy, E.R. and Tannenbaum, S.I. (2003) What's in a Name: A Literature-Based Approach to Understanding Mentoring, Coaching and Other Constructs that Describe Developmental Interactions. *Human Resource Development Review*, 2(4), 360–385.

Dahl, P.N., Jørgensen, K.M., Laursen, E., Rasmussen, J.G. and Rasmussen, P. (2005) *Organisatorisk læring – Resultater fra forskningen i Center for Organisatorisk Læring.* Aalborg: Aalborg Universitetsforlag.

Daniels, K., De Chernatony, L. and Johnson, G. (1995) Validating a Method of Mapping Managers Mental Models of Competitive Industry Structures. *Human Relations*, 48(8), 975–991.

Davies, A.J. and Kochhar, A.K. (1999) Why British Companies Don't Do Effective Benchmarking. *Integrated Manufacturing Systems*, 10(1), 26-32.

DeBusk, G.K., Brown, R.M. and Killough, L.N. (2003) Components and Relative Weights in Utilisation of Dashboard Measurement Systems like the Balanced Scorecard. *British Accounting Review*, 35, 215–231.

Deci, E.L. and Ryan, R.M. (1985) *Intrinsic Motivation and Self-Determination in Human Behavior*. New York: Plenum.

De Dreu, C.K.W. and West, M.A. (2001) Minority Dissent and Team Innovation: The Importance of Participation in Decision Making. *Journal of Applied Psychology*, 86(6), 1191–1201.

de Pablos, P.O. (2004) The importance of relational capital in service industry: the case of the Spanish banking sector. *International Journal of Learning and Intellectual Capital*, 1(4), 431–40.

Dehler, G.E., Welsh, A. and Lewis, M.W. (2001) Critical Pedagogy in the 'New Paradigm'. *Management Learning*, 32(4), 493–511.

Delpachitra, S. and Beal, D. (2002) Process Benchmarking: An Application to Lending Products. *Benchmarking: An International Journal*, 9(4), 409–420.

Densten, I.L. and Gray, J.H. (2001) Leadership Development and Reflection: What is the Connection? *International Journal of Educational Management*, 15(3), 119–124.

Derrida, J. (1997) *Of Grammatology*. Baltimore, MD: Johns Hopkins University Press.

Derrida, J. (2002) *Positions*. New York: Continuum.

Derrida, J. (2004) *Living On. Deconstruction and Criticism* (pp. 62–142). London: Continuum.

Dewey, J. (1916) *Democracy and Education. An Introduction to the Philosophy of Education*. New York: Free Press.

Dewey, J. (1933) *How We Think*. Boston: D.C. Heath.

Dewey, J. (1938) *Experience and Education*. New York: Collier Books.

Dewey, J. (1991) *How We Think*. New York: Prometheus Books.

Dick, P. and Cassell, C. (2002) Barriers to Managing Diversity in the UK Constabulary: The Role of Discourse. *Journal of Management Studies*, 39(7), 953–976.

Dick, W. and Carey, L. (2001) *The Systematic Design of Instruction*. New York: Addison-Wesley.

Dilworth, L. (2003) Searching for the Future of HRD. *Advances in Developing Human Resources*, 5(3), 241–244.

Dionne, P. (1996) The Evaluation of Training Activities: A Complex Issue Involving Different Stakes. *Human Resource Development Quarterly*, 7(3), 279–299.

Doh, J. (2003) Can Leadership be Taught? Perspectives from Management Educators. *Academy of Management Learning and Education*, 2(1), 54–67.

Donelan, H., Herman, C., Kear, K. and Kirkup, G. (2009) Patterns of Online Networking for Women's Career Development. *Gender in Management: An International Journal*, 24(2), 92–111.

Donnellon, A. (1986) Language and Communication within Organisations: Building Cognition and Behaviour. In H.P. Sims and D.A. Gioia (eds), *The Thinking Organisation*. San Francisco: Jossey Bass.

Donovan, L.L., and Marsick, V.J. (2000) Trends in Literature: A Comparative Analysis of 1998 HRD Research. In K.P. Kuchinke (ed.), *Proceedings of the Academy of Human Resource Development Conference*. Baton Rouge: AHRD.

Douglas, M. (1986) *How Institutions Think*. Syracuse, NY: Syracuse University Press.

Dougherty, D. and Hardy, C. (1996) Sustained Product Innovation in Large, Mature Organizations: Overcoming Innovation-to-Organization Problems. *Academy of Management Journal*, 39(5), 1120–1153.

Drury, C. and Tayles, M. (1995) Issues Arising from Surveys of Management Accounting Practice. *Management Accounting Research*, 6(3), 267–280.

Drury, C., Braund, S., Osborne, P. and Tayles, M. (1993) *A Survey of Management Accounting Practices in UK Manufacturing Companies*. Chartered Association of Certified Accountants.

Dulewicz, V. and Higgs, M. (2004) Can Emotional Intelligence be Developed? *International Journal of Human Resource Management*, 15(1), 95–111.

Duncan, S.J. (1972) Some Signals and Rules for Taking Speaking Turns in Conversation. *Journal of Personality and Social Psychology*, 23, 283–292.

Duncan, W.J. (1984) Planning and Evaluating Management Education and Development: Why So Little Attention to Such Basic Concerns? *Journal of Management Development*, 2(4), 57–68.

Dunning, J.H. (1993) *The Globalisation of Business*. London: Routledge.

Durkheim, E. (1954) *The Elementary Forms of Religious Life*. Chicago, IL: The Free Press.

Dye, R.W. (2003) Keeping score. *CMA Management*, December/January, 18–23.

Dzinkowski, R. (2000) The Measurement and Management of Intellectual Capital. *Management Accounting*, February, 32–36.

Easterby-Smith, M. (1986) *Evaluation of Management Education, Training and Development*. Aldershot: Gower.

Easterby-Smith, M. and Araujo, L. (1999) Organizational Learning: Current Debates and Opportunities. In M. Easterby-Smith, J. Burgoyne and L. Araujo (eds), *Organizational Learning and the Learning Organization* (pp. 1–21). London: Sage.

Edvinsson, L. and Malone, M. (1997) *Intellectual Capital: Realising your Company's True Value by Finding its Hidden Brainpower*. New York: HarperCollins.

Edwards, J.S., Collier, P.M. and Shaw, D. (2005) *Knowledge Management and its Impact on the Management Accountant*. CIMA Research Report. http://www.cimaglobal.com/cps/rde/xbcr/SID-0AAAC56413E1E22A/live/Knowledge_Management_Full_Report_06-05.pdf

Edwards, T. and Ferner, A. (2002) The Renewed American Challenge: A Review of Employment Practices in US Multinationals. *Industrial Relations Journal*, 33(2), 94–11.

Egan, T.M. (2005) Factors Influencing Individual Creativity in the Workplace: An Examination of Quantitative Empirical Research. *Advances in Developing Human Resources*, 7(2), 160–182.

Ehigie, B.O. and Akpan, R.C. (2004) Roles of Perceived Leadership Styles and Rewards in the Practice of Total Quality Management. *Leadership and Organisation Development Journal*, 25(1), 24–41.

Ehrich, L.C. (2008) Mentoring and Women Managers: Another Look at the Field. *Gender in Management: An International Journal*, 23(7), 469–483.

Eisenberger, R., Fasolo, P. and Davis-LaMastro, V. (1990) Perceived Organisational Support and Employee Diligence, Commitment and Innovation. *Journal of Applied Psychology*, 75(1), 51–59.

Elangovan, A.R. and Karakowsky, L. (1999) The Role of Trainee and Environmental Factors in Transfer of Training: An Exploratory Framework. *Leadership and Organisation Development Journal*, 20(5), 268–275.

Elkjaer, B. and Wahlgren, B. (2005) Organizational Learning and Workplace Learning – Similarities and Differences. In E. Antonacopoulou, P. Jarvis, V. Andersen, B. Elkjaer and S. Høyrup (eds) (2005) *Learning, Working and Living. Mapping the Terrain of Working Life Learning*. New York: Palgrave Macmillan.

Elliott, C. (2003) Representations of the Intellectual: Insights from Gramsci on Management Education. *Management Learning*, 34(4), 411–427.

Elliot, R. (1996) Discourse Analysis: Exploring Action, Function and Conflict in Social Texts. *Marketing Intelligence and Planning*, 14(6), 12–26.

Elsbach, K.D. and Kramer, R.M. (2003) Assessing Creativity in Hollywood Pitch Meetings: Evidence for a Dual-Process Model of Creativity Judgments. *Academy of Management Journal*, 46(3), 283–301.

Engle, A.D., Mendenhall, M.D., Powers, R.L. and Stedham, Y. (2001) Conceptualising the Global Competency Cube: A Transnational Model of Human Resources. *Journal of European Industrial Training*, 25(7), 346–353.

Eraut, M. (2004) Transfer of Knowledge between Education and Workplace Settings. In H. Rainbird, A. Fuller and A. Munro (eds), *Workplace Learning in Context.* London: Routledge.

Eraut, M., Alderton, J., Cole, G. and Senker, P. (1998) *Development of Knowledge and Skills in Employment.* Final report of a research project funded by The Learning Society Programme of the Economic and Social Research Council: Institute of Education, University of Essex.

Ernst and Young (1997) Measures That Matter. http://www.corporatesunshine.org/measuresthatmatter.pdf

ESC Toulouse (2003) *Call for Papers.* For the UFHRD Conference for HRD Research and Practice Across Europe. June 27th–29th.

Etherington, K. (2004) *Becoming a Reflective Researcher.* London: Jessica Kingsley.

Eustace, C. (2000) *The Intangible Economy – Impact and Policy Issues, Report of the European High Level Expert Group on the Intangible Economy.* Brussels: European Commission, Enterprise Directorate-General, October. http://ec.europa.eu/enterprise/services/business_related_services/studies_brs/intangible_economy_hleg_report.pdf

Evarts, T.M. (1998) Human Resource Development as a Maturing Field of Study. *Human Resource Development Quarterly*, 9(4), 385–391.

Faifua, D. (2008) Democratic Reason and Practice: Repositioning Community Aspirations. *Journal of Organisational Change Management*, 21(4), 511–518.

Farmer, S.M., Tierney, P. and McIntyre, K.K. (2003) Employee Creativity in Taiwan: An Application of Role Identity Theory. *Academy of Management Journal*, 46(5), 618–630.

Feldman, D.H. (1999) The Development of Creativity. In R.J. Sternberg (ed.), *Handbook of Creativity.* Cambridge: Cambridge University Press.

Fenwick, T.J. (2003) Professional Growth Plans: Possibilities and Limitations of an Organizationwide Employee Development Strategy. *Human Resource Development Quarterly*, 14(1), 59–79.

Fenwick, T.J. (2004) Towards a Critical HRD in Theory and Practice. *Adult Education Quarterly*, 54(3), 193–209.

Fenwick, T.J. (2007) Rethinking Processes of Adult Learning. In *Understanding Adult Education and Training* (3rd edn), Forthcoming.

Ferraro, G.P. (1990) *The Cultural Dimension of International Business*, New Jersey: Prentice Hall.

Fiedler, F.E. (1964) A Contingency Model of Leadership Effectiveness. In L. Berkowitz (ed.), *Advances in Experimental Social Psychology* (Vol. 1). New York: Academic Press.

Fiedler, F.E. (1967) *A Theory of Leadership Effectiveness.* New York: McGraw-Hill.

Fiedler, F.E. (1971) Validation and Extension of the Contingency Model of Leadership Effectiveness: A Review of Empirical Findings. *Psychological Bulletin*, 76(2), 128–148.

Fiedler, F.E. (1996) Research on Leadership Selection and Training: One View of the Future. *Administrative Science Quarterly*, 41(2), 241–250.

Financial Accounting Standards Board (FASB) (1978) Objectives of financial reporting by business enterprises", *Statement of Financial Accounting Concepts,* no 1, November.

Fitz-enz, J. (2000) *The ROI of Human Capital: Measuring the Economic Value of Employee Performance.* American Management Association, USA.

Flamholtz, E.G. (1974) *Human Resource Accounting.* Encino, CA: Dickenson Publishing.

Flamholtz, E.G. (1985) *Human Resource Accounting* (2nd edn). San Francisco, CA: Jossey-Bass.

Fleishman, E.A., Harris, E.F. and Burtt, H.E. (1955) *Leadership and Supervision in Industry.* Columbus, OH: Bureau of Educational Research, Ohio State University.

Forbes, B.J. and Domm, D.R. (2004) Creativity and Productivity: Resolving the Conflict. *S.A.M. Advanced Management Journal*, 69(2), 4–11.

Forster, N. (2000) Expatriates and the Impact of Cross-cultural Training. *Human Resource Management Journal*, 10(3), 63–78.

Foucault, M. (1979) *Discipline and Punish – The Birth of the Prison*. Harmondsworth: Penguin.

Foucault, M. (1984) Nietzsche, Genealogy, History. In P. Rabinow (ed.), *The Foucault Reader* (pp. 76–100). New York: Pantheon.

Fournier, V., & Grey, C. (2000) At the Critical Moment: conditions and prospects for critical management studies. *Human Relations*, 53 (1), 7–32.

Fraser, N. (1994) Rethinking the Public Sphere: A Contribution to the Critique of Actually Existing Democracy. In P. McLaren (ed.), *Between Borders: Pedagogy and the Politics of Cultural Studies*. New York: Routledge.

Freire, P. (1970) *Pedagogy of the Oppressed*. New York: Seabury.

Friedman, T. (2005) *The World is Flat*. New York: Farrar, Straus and Giroux.

Froiland, P. (1993) Industry Report. *Training*, 49–59.

Garabaldi de Hilal, A.V. (2006) Brazilian National Culture, Organizational Culture and Cultural Agreement: Findings from a Multinational Company. *International Journal of Cross Cultural Management*, 6(2), 139–168.

Garavan, T.N. (1991) Strategic Human Resource Development. *Journal of European Industrial Training*, 15(1), 30–45.

Garavan, T.N. (1997) The Learning Organisation: A Review and Evaluation. *The Learning Organisation*, 4(1), 1–16.

Garavan, T.N. (2007) A Strategic Perspective on HRD. *Advances in Developing Human Resources*, 9(1), 11–30.

Garavan, T.N. and McGuire, D. (2001) Competencies and Workplace Learning: Some Reflections on the Rhetoric and the Reality, *Journal of Workplace Learning*, 13(4), 144–163.

Garavan, T.N., McGuire, D. and O'Donnell, D. (2004) Exploring Human Resource Development: A Levels of Analysis Approach. *Human Resource Development Review*, 4(4), 417–441.

Garavan, T.N., O'Donnell, D., McGuire, D. and Watson, S. (2007) Exploring Perspectives on Human Resource Development: An Introduction, *Advances in Developing Human Resources*, 9(1), 3–11.

Garcia-Morales, V.J., Matias-Reche, F. and Hurtado-Torres, N. (2008) Influence of Transformational Leadership on Organizational Innovation and Performance Depending on the Level of Organizational Learning in the Pharmaceutical Sector. *Journal of Organizational Change Management*, 21(2), 188–212.

Gardner, H. (1993) *Creating Minds: An Anatomy of Creativity Seen through the Livers of Freud, Einstein, Picasso, Stravinsky, Eliot, Graham and Gandhi*. New York: Basic Books.

Garrick, J. (1998) *Informal Learning in the Workplace: Unmasking Human Resource Development*. London: Routledge

Garvey, B. (2004) The Mentoring/Counselling/Coaching Debate. *Development and Learning in Organisations*, 18(2), 6–8.

Gedro, J.A. (2010) Lesbian Presentations and Representations of Leadership, and the Implications for HRD. *Journal of European Industrial Training*, 34(6), 46–54.

Gedro, J.A., Cervero, R.M. and Johnson-Bailey, J. (2004) How Lesbians Learn to Negotiate the Heterosexism of Corporate America. *Human Resource Development International*, 7(2), 181–195.

Geertz, C. (1973) Thick Description – Towards an Interpretive Theory of Culture. In C. Geertz (ed.), *The Interpretation of Cultures – Selected Essays* (pp. 3–13). New York: Basic Books.

Georgenson, D.L. (1982) The Problem of Transfer Calls for Partnership. *Training and Development Journal*, 36(10), 75–78.

Gergen, K.J. (1985) The Social Constructionist Movement in Modern Psychology. *American Psychology*, 40, 266–275.

Gergen, K.J., Gergen, M.M. and Barrett, F. (2004) Dialogue: Life and Death of the Organization. In D. Grant, C. Hardy, C. Oswick and L. Putnam (eds), *The Sage Handbook of Organizational Discourse* (pp. 39–59). London: Sage Publications.

Gherardi, S. and Nicolini, D. (2001) The Sociological Foundations of Organizational Learning. In A.B.A.M. Dierkes, J. Child and I. Nonaka. (eds), *The Sage Handbook of Organizational Learning* (pp. 35–60). Oxford: Oxford University Press.

Ghoshal, S. and Nohria, N. (1993) Horses for Courses: Organizational Forms for Multinational Corporations. *Sloan Management Review*, 34, 23–35.

Gibelman, M. (2000) The Nonprofit Sector and Gender Discrimination. *Nonprofit Management and Leadership*, 10(3), 251–269.

Gibson, E.J. (1941) Retroactive Inhibition as a Function of the Degree of Generalisation and Differentiation to Verbal Learning. *Psychology Review*, 28, 93–115.

Gibson, R. (1986) *Critical Theory and Education*. London: Hodder and Stoughton.

Gibson, S.K. (2004) Social Learning (Cognitive) Theory and its Implications for Human Resource Development. *Advances in Developing Human Resources*, 6(2), 193–210.

Gill, A., Fitzgerald, S.P., Bhutani, S., Mand, H.S. and Sharma, S.P. (2010) The Relationship between Transformational Leadership and Employee-Desire for Empowerment, *International Journal of Contemporary Hospitality Management*, 22(2), 1–19.

Gillespie, N.A. and Mann, L. (2004) Transformational Leadership and Shared Values: The Building Blocks of Trust. *Journal of Managerial Psychology*, 19(6), 588–607.

Gilley, J., and Eggland, S. (1989) *Principles of Human Resource Development*. Reading, MA: Addison-Wesley.

Gilley, J. and Maycunich, A. (2000) *Organisational Learning, Performance, and Change: An Introduction to Strategic Human Resource Development*. Cambridge: Perseus.

Ginzburg, S. and Dar-El, E.M. (2000) Skill Retention and Relearning: A Proposed Cyclical Model. *Journal of Workplace Learning*, 12(8), 327–332.

Giroux, H.A. (1997) *Pedagogy and the Politics of Hope: Theory, Culture and Schooling*. Boulder, CO: Westview Press.

Githens, R.P. (2007) *Critical Action Research in Human Resource Development*. Presented at the Academy of Human Resource Development Conference, Indianapolis, Indiana. February 28–March 4th 2006.

Goffee, R. and Jones, G. (2008) Bright Sparks, *People Management*, 14(3), 28–31.

Gold, J. and Smith, V. (2003) Advances Towards a Learning Movement: Translations at Work. *Human Resource Development International*, 6(2), 139–154.

Goldberg, L.R. (1990) An Alternative Description of Personality: The Big-Five Factor Structure. *Journal of Personality and Social Psychology*, 59, 1216–1229.

Goleman, D. (1995) *Emotional Intelligence: Why It Can Matter More Than IQ*. New York: Bantam Books.

Goleman, D. (1999) *Working With Emotional Intelligence*. London: Bloomsbury.

Goleman, D., Boyatzis, R. and McKee, A. (2004) *Primal Leadership: Learning to Lead with Emotional Intelligence*. Boston: Harvard Business Press.

Good, T.L., and Brophy, J.E. (1990) *Educational Psychology: A Realistic Approach*. White Plains, NY: Longman.

Gourlay, S. (2000) *Knowledge Management and HRD*. Presented at the First Conference on HRD Research and Practice across Europe. London: Kingston University. 15 January.

Grant, A.M. (2007) Enhancing Coaching Skills and Emotional Intelligence through Training. *Industrial and Commercial Training*, 39(5), 257–266.

Grey, C. and Mitev, N. (1995) Management Education: A Polemic. *Management Learning*, 26(1), 73–90.

Grimes, D. (2001) Putting your own House in Order: Whiteness, Change and Organization Studies. *Journal of Organisational Change Management*, 14(2), 132–150.

Grojer, J.E. and Johanson, U. (1998a) Current Development in Human Resource Costing and Accounting. *Accounting, Auditing and Accountability Journal*, 11(4), 495–505.

Grojer, J.E. and Johanson, U. (1998b) Human Resource Costing and Accounting – Time for Reporting Regulation? Workshop Scientific Report – The Value of Investing in the Workforce. http://www.fek.su.se/home/bic/meritum/download/BRYH.rtf

Groves, K.S. (2007) Integrating Leadership Development and Succession Planning Best Practices. *Journal of Management Development*, 26(3), 239–260.

Groves, K.S., McEnrue, M.P. and Shen, W. (2008) Developing and Measuring the Emotional Intelligence of Leaders. *Journal of Management Development*, 27(2), 225–250.

Gunnarsson, B.L., Linell, P. and Nordberg, B. (1997) *The Construction of Professional Discourse*. New York: Longman.

Guest, D. (1987) Human Resource Management and Industrial Relations. *Journal of Management Studies*, 24(5), 503–521.

Gustavsson, B. (2001) *Vidensfilosofi*. Århus: Klim.

Guthrie, J.P. (2001) High-involvement Work Practices, Turnover, and Productivity: evidence from New Zealand. *Academy of Management Journal*, 44(1), 180–190.

Habermas, J. (1987) *The Theory of Communicative Action, Volume 2, Lifeworld and System: A Critique of Functionalist Reason*. Boston, MA: Beacon Press.

Habermas, J. (2001) *On The Pragmatics of Social Interaction: Preliminary Studies in the Theory of Communicative Action*. Cambridge: MIT Press.

Hafeez, K. and Essmail, E.A. (2007) Evaluating Organisation Core Competences and Associated Personal Competencies Using Analytical Hierarchy Process. *Management Research News*, 30(8), 530–547.

Hakanson, L. (1990) International decentralization of R&D – the organizational challenges. In Bartlett, C.A., Doz, Y.L., Hedlund, G. (Eds), *Managing the Global Firm*. London: Routledge.

Hales, C. (2005) Rooted in Supervision, Branching into Management: Continuity and Change in the Role of First-line Manager. *Journal of Management Studies*, 42(3), 471–506.

Hall, R.I. (1979) Wittgenstein and Polanyi – The Problem of Privileged Self-Knowledge. *Philosophy Today*, 267–278.

Hamel, G. and Prahalad, C. (1994) *Competing for the Future*. Boston, MA: Harvard Business School Press.

Hamblin, A.C. (1974) *Evaluation and Control of Training*. London: McGraw-Hill.

Hamlin, B. (2002) Towards Evidence-Based HRD Practice. In J. McGoldrick, J. Stewart and S. Watson (eds), *Understanding Human Resource Development: A Research Based Approach*. London: Routledge.

Harbison, F. and Myers, C.A. (1964) *Education, Manpower and Economic Growth*. New York: McGraw-Hill.

Hardy, C. & Clegg, S.R. (1996) Some dare call it power. In S.R. Clegg, C. Hardy and W.R. Nord (Eds.), *Handbook of organization studies* (pp. 622–641). London: Sage.

Harris, L., Dougwoy, D. and Kirk, S. (2002) The Devolution of HR Responsibilities – Perspectives from the UK's Public Sector. *Journal of European Industrial Training*, 26 (5), 218–229.

Harrison, R. (2000) Learning, Knowledge, Productivity and Strategic Progress. *International Journal of Training and Development*, 4(4), 244–258.

Harrison, R. and Kessels, J. (2004) *Human Resource Development in a Knowledge Society: An Organisation View*. London: Palgrave Macmillan.

Hassan, A. (2007) Human Resource Development and Organizational Values. *Journal of European Industrial Training*, 31(6), 435–448.

Hatcher, T.G. (2006) An Editor's Challenge to Human Resource Development. *Human Resource Development Quarterly*, 17(1), 1–4.

Hayes, J. and Allinson, C.W. (1996) The Implications of Learning Styles for Training and Development: A Discussion of the Matching Hypothesis. *British Journal of Management*, 7(1), 63–73.

Hays, R.D. (1974) Ex-patriate Selection: Insuring Success and Avoiding Failure. *Journal of International Business Studies*, 5(1), 25–37.

Henderson, J. (2001) *Transformative Learning in the Executive Suite: CEOs and the Role of Context in Mezirow's Theory.* Unpublished Doctoral Dissertation, George Washington University, Washington DC.

Hennart, J.F. and Larimo, J. (1998) The Impact of Culture on the Strategy of Multinational Enterprises: Does National Origin Affect Ownership Decisions. *Journal of International Business Studies*, 29(3), 515–538.

Henriksen, L.B. (1992) *Etablering af virksomhedsnetværk (Establishing Business Networks)* Aalborg: Aalborg University.

Henriksen, L.B. (2004) *Dimensions of Change: Conceptualising Reality in Organisational Research.* Copenhagen: Copenhagen Business School Press.

Henriksen, L.B., Nørreklit, L., Jørgensen, K.M., Christensen, J.B. and O'Donnell, D. (2004) *Dimensions of Change – Conceptualising Reality in Organisational Research.* Copenhagen: Copenhagen Business School Press.

Henriques, D.B. (1991) Piercing Wall Street's Lucite Ceiling. *New York Times*, 11 August.

Hershey, P. and Blanchard, K.H. (1969) *Management of Organizational Behavior.* Englewood Cliffs, NJ: Prentice Hall.

Hershey, P. and Blanchard, K.H. (1988) *Management of Organizational Behaviour: Utilizing Human Resources.* New Jersey: Prentice-Hall.

Higgins, M.C. (2000) The More The Merrier? Multiple Developmental Relationships and Work Satisfaction. *Journal of Management Development*, 19(4), 277–296.

Hill, J. and McGowan, P. (1999) Small Business and Enterprise Development: Questions about Research Methodology. *International Journal of Entrepreneurial Behaviour and Research*, 5(1), 5–18.

Hillman, D.C. and Willis, D.J. (1994) Learner Interface Interaction in Distance Education: An Extension of Contemporary Models and Strategies for Practitioners. *American Journal of Distance Education*, 8(2), 30–42.

Hilton, B. and McLean, G.N. (1997) *The Status of Human Resource Development in French Companies.* Paper presented at the Academy of Human Resource Development 1997 Conference Proceedings, Baton Rouge, Louisiana.

Hinton, M., Francis, G. and Holloway, J. (2000) Best Practice Benchmarking in the UK. *Benchmarking: An International Journal*, 7(1), 52–61.

Hite, L.M. (1996) Black Women Managers and Administrators: Experiences and Implications. *Women in Management Review*, 11(6), 11–17.

Hite, L.M. (2007) Hispanic Women Managers and Professionals: Reflections on Life and Work. *Gender, Work and Organisation*, 14(1), 20–38.

Hite, L.M. and McDonald, K.S. (2006) Diversity Training Pitfalls and Possibilities: An Exploration of Small and Mid-Size US Organisations. *Human Resource Development International*, 9(1), 365–377.

Holbeche, L. (2008) Performance Management. In CIPD (ed.), *CIPD Recipe for Success*, London: CIPD.

Holland, J. (2001) *Corporate Value Creation, Intangibles and Disclosure.* Department of Accounting and Finance, University of Glasgow, Working Paper Series, Number 3. http://www.accfin.gla.ac.uk/Accfin/UploadedDocs/WorkingPapers/2001/2001-3.pdf

Holladay, C.L. and Quinones, M.A. (2008) The Influence of Training Focus and Trainer Characteristics on Diversity Training Effectiveness. *Academy of Management Learning and Education*, 7(3), 343–354.

Holman, D. (2000) Contemporary Models of Management Education in the UK. *Management Learning*, 31(2), 197–217.

Holman, D. and Pavlica, K. (1997) Rethinking Kolb's Theory of Experiential Learning in Management Education: The Contribution of Social Constructionism and Activity Theory. *Management Learning*, 28(2), 135–148.

Holmes, L. (2004) Challenging the Learning Turn in Education and Training. *Journal of European Industrial Training*, 28(8/9), 625–638.

Holton, E.F. (1996) The Flawed Four-Level Evaluation Model. *Human Resource Development Quarterly*, 7(1), 5–21.

Holton, E.F. III (2002) Defining HRD: Too much of a good thing? *Human Resource Development Review*, 1(3), 275–276.

Holton, E.F. and Bates, R.A. (2000) Development of a Learning Transfer System Inventory. *Human Resource Development Quarterly*, 11(4), 333–360.

Honey, P. (1998) The Debate Starts Here. *People Management* (October), 28–29.

Horkheimer, M. (1972) *Critical Theory*. New York: Herder and Herder.

Horkheimer, M. and Adorno, T. (1979) *The Dialectic of Enlightenment*. London: Verso.

Horwitz, F.M., Bowmaker-Falconer, A. and Searll, P. (1996) Human Resource Development and Managing Diversity in South Africa. *International Journal of Manpower*, 4(5), 134–151.

House, R.J. (1971) A Path-Goal Theory of Leadership Effectiveness. *Administrative Science Quarterly*, 16, 321–338.

House, R.J. (1977) Theory of Charismatic Leadership. In J.G. Hunts, and L.L. Larson (eds), *Leadership: The Cutting Edge*. Carbondale, IL: University Press.

House, R.J. (1996) Path-Goal Theory of Leadership: Lessons, Legacy and a Reformulated Theory. *The Leadership Quarterly* 7(3), 323–352.

House, R.J. and Mitchell, T.R. (1974) Path-Goal Theory of Leadership. *Journal of Contemporary Business*, 3, 81–97.

Howe, M.J. (1980) *The Psychology of Human Learning*. New York: Harper Row.

Humphreys, L.G. (1979) The Construct of General Intelligence. *Intelligence*, 3, 105–120.

Huo, Y.P. and Von Glinow, M.A. (1995) On Transplanting Human Resource Practices to China: A Culture-driven Approach. *International Journal of Manpower*, 16(9), 3–15.

Hviid, M.K., Keller, H.D., Rasmussen, A., Rasmussen, P., Stoustrup, L. and Thøgersen, U. (2006) *Practice-related General Adult Education. An Overview of Research in the Project 'Competence Development in Fringe Areas'*. Aalborg University: Department of Education, Learning and Philosophy.

Hwang, A. (1996) Positivist and Constructivist Persuasions in Instructional Development. *Instructional Science*, 24, 343–356.

Hymowitz, C. and Schellhardt, T. (1986, March 24) The Glass Ceiling: Why women can't seem to break the invisible barrier that blocks them from top jobs. *Wall Street Journal – A special report: The corporate woman*. p. 1, 4–5.

Iles, P. and Hayers, P.K. (1997) Managing Diversity in Transnational Project Teams: A Tentative Model and Case Study. *Journal of Managerial Psychology*, 12(2), 95–117.

Iles, P. and Yolles, M. (2003) International HRD Alliances in Viable Knowledge Migration and Development: The Czech Academic Link Project. *Human Resource Development International*, (3), 301–325.

International Federation of Accountants. (1998) *The Measurement and Management of Intellectual Capital: An Introduction*. Study 7, England.

Isen, A.M. (1999) On the Relationship between Affect and Creative Problem Solving. In S. Russ (ed.), *Affect, Creative Experience and Psychological Adjustment*. Philadelphia: Brumner/Mazel.

ITD (1992) *Human Resource Development: Diploma in Training Management – Syllabus Regulations and Approved Centres*. Marlow ITD.

Itami, H. (1987) *Mobilizing Invisible Assets*. Cambridge, MA: Harvard University Press.

Ittner, C.D. and Larcker, D.F. (2001) Assessing Empirical Research in Managerial Accounting: A Value-based Management Perspective. *Journal of Accounting and Economics*, 32(1–3), 349–410.

Jackson, T. (2002) *International HRM: A Cross-Cultural Approach*. London: Sage.

Jacques, P.H., Garger, J. and Thomas, M. (2008) Assessing Leader Behaviours in Project Managers. *Management Research News*, 31(1), 4–12.

Jaffee, D. (2001) *Organisation Theory – Tension and Change*. Boston, MA: McGraw-Hill.

James, C. and Roffe, I. (2000) The Evaluation of Goal and Goal-Free Training Innovation. *Journal of European Industrial Training*, 24(1), 12–20.

James, W. (1880) Great Men and their Environment. *Atlantic Monthly*, 276, 441–459.

Jankowicz, D. (1999) Editorial: Putting the 'I' into HRD … Why do we do it?, *Human Resource Development International*, 2(3), 171–174.

Jarvis, P. (1992) *Paradoxes of Learning. On Becoming an Individual in Society*. San Francisco, CA: Jossey-Bass Publishers.

Jaussi, K.S., and Dionne, S.D. (2003) Leading for Creativity: The Role of Unconventional Leader Behavior. *The Leadership Quarterly*, 14, 475–498.

Javidan, M. and Waldman, D.A. (2003) Exploring Charismatic Leadership in the Public Sector: Measurement and Consequences. *Public Administration Review*, 63(2), 229–242.

Johanson, U. (1998) The Answer Is Blowing In The Wind – Investments in training from a Human Resource Accounting perspective. *European Journal for Vocational Training*, 14, May–August, 47–55.

Johnson, G., Scholes, K. and Whittington, R. (2009) *Exploring Corporate Strategy – Text and Cases*. London: Prentice Hall.

Jones, C. (2007) Friedman with Derrida. *Business and Society Review*, 112(4), 511–532.

Jones, J. (1981) The Organizational Universe. In J. Jones and J. Pfeiffer (eds), *The 1981 Annual Handbook for Group Facilitators*. San Diego, CA: University Associates.

Jones, R. and Kriflik, G. (2005) Strategies for Managerial Self-change in a Cleaned-up Bureaucracy: A Qualitative Study. *Journal of Managerial Psychology*, 20(5), 397–416.

Jones, R.A., Rafferty, A.E. and Griffin, M.A. (2006) The Executive Coaching Trend: Towards More Flexible Executives. *Leadership and Organization Development Journal*, 27(7), 584–596.

Jørgensen, K.M. (2002) The Meaning of Local Knowledges. *Scandinavian Journal of Management*, 18(1), 29–46.

Jørgensen, K.M. (2004) Creating Value-based Collaboration – Life Forms and Power in a Change Project. *M@n@gement*, 7(3), 85–107.

Jørgensen, K.M. (2005) Serieproduktion eller kundeorientering – organisatorisk læring på en produktionsvirksomhed. In K.M. Jørgensen and P. Rasmussen (eds), *Forandringsprojekter som organisatorisk læring*. Aalborg, Aalborg Universitetsforlag: 169–194.

Jørgensen, K.M. (2006) Conceptualising Intellectual Capital as Language Game and Power. *Journal of Intellectual Capital*, 7(1), 78–92.

Jørgensen, K.M. (2007) *Power without Glory – A Genealogy of a Management Decision*. Copenhagen: Copenhagen Business School Press.

Jørgensen, K.M. and Boje, D.M. (2009) Genealogies of Becoming – Antenarrative Inquiry in Organizations. *Tamara Journal for Critical Organization Inquiry*, 8(1), 32–47.

Jørgensen, K.M. and Boje, D.M. (2010) Resituating Narrative and Story in Business Ethics. *Business Ethics: A European Review*, 19(3), 253–264.

Jørgensen, K.M. and Keller, H.D. (2008) The Contribution of Communities of Practice to Human Resource Development – Learning as Negotiating Identities. *Advances in Developing Human Resources*, 10(4), 525–540.

Jørgensen, K.M and Palle, R. (eds) (2005) *Forandringsprojekter som organisatorisk læring*. Aalborg: Aalborg Universitetsforlag.

Jørgensen, K.M. and Rasmussen, P. (eds) (2005) *Forandringsprojekter som organisatorisk læring*. Aalborg: Aalborg Universitetsforlag.

Judge, T.A. and Bono, J.E. (2000) Five Factor Model of Personality and Transformational Leadership. *Journal of Applied Psychology*, 85, 751–765.

Judge, T.A., Ilies, R., Bono, J.E., Gerhardt, M.W. (2002) Personality and Leadership: A Qualitative and Quantitative Review, *Journal of Applied Psychology*, 87, 765–780.

Kaplan, R.S., and Norton, D.P. (1996) *Translating Strategy into Action: The Balanced Scorecard*. Boston: Harvard Business School Publishing Corporation.

Kaplan, R.S. and Norton, D.P. (2004) Measuring the Strategic Readiness of Intangible Assets. *Harvard Business Review*, 82(1), 52–63.

Karp, H.B. and Sutton, N. (1993) Where Diversity Training Goes Wrong. *Training*, 30(7), 30–34.

Keegan, A.E. and Den Hartog, D.N. (2004) Transformational Leadership in a Project-Based Environment: A Comparative Study of the Leadership Styles of Project Managers and Line Managers. *International Journal of Project Management*, 22, 609–617.

Keller, H.D. (2004) *Læring i arbejdet. Om kompetenceudvikling i socialt arbejde*. Aalborg: Institut for Læring, Aalborg Universitet, Ph.d.-afhandlinger nr. 1.

Keller, H.D. (2005) *Undervisning som støtte til virksomhedens forandringsprocesser. Analyse af VUC-forløb på N. Graversens Metalvarefabrik A/S*. Forskningsrapport 8, Aalborg Universitet: Institut for Uddannelse, Læring og Filosofi.

Kelly, H.K. (1982) A Primer on Transfer of Training. *Training and Development Journal*, 36(11), 102–106.

Kerka, S. (1999) *Self-Directed Learning: Myths and Realities*. Columbus, OH: ERIC Clearinghouse on Adult Career and Vocational Education.

Kerr, S. (1975) On the Folly of Rewarding A, while Hoping for B. *Academy of Management Journal*, 18(4), 769–783.

Kessels, J. (2007) HRD Research in a Diversified Field. *Human Resource Development International*, 10(1), 83–89.

Kessels, J. and Harrison, R. (2004) *Reaching Knowledge Productivity*. Fifth European Conference on Human Resource Development Theory and Practice, University of Limerick.

Kidger, P.J. (2002) Management Structure in Multinational Enterprises: Responding to Globalisation. *Employee Relations*, 24(1), 69–85.

Kim, J.H. and Lee, C. (2001) Implications of Near and Far Transfer of Training on Structured On-The-Job Training. *Advances in Developing Human Resources*, 3(4), 442–452.

King, I.W. (1995) Learning? I've got no Time for That? *Management Learning*, 26(2), 249–257.

Kipp, P.H., Artiles, A.J. and Lopez-Torres, L. (2003) Beyond Reflection: Teacher Learning as Praxis. *Theory into Practice*, 42(3), 248–264.

Kirkpatrick, S.A. and Locke, E.A. (1991) Leadership: Do Traits Matter?, *Academy of Management Executive*, 5(2), 48–60.

Kirby, S. (2006) American Gay and Lesbian Student Leaders' Perceptions of Job Discrimination. *Equal Opportunities International*, 25(2), 126–140.

Klausen, K.K. (2003) *Offentlig organisation, strategi og ledelse*. Odense: Syddansk Universitetsforlag.

Kline, S. and Harris, K. (2008) ROI is MIA: Why are Hoteliers Failing to Demand the ROI of Training? *International Journal of Contemporary Hospitality Management*, 20(1), 45–59.

Knowles, M.S. (1998) *The Adult Learner: The Definitive Classic in Adult Education and Human Resource Development*. Houston, TX: Gulf Publishing Company.

Knowles, M.S. (1998) *The Modern Practice of Adult Education: From Pedagogy to Andragogy*. Cambridge: Cambridge Book Company.

Knowles, M.S., Holton, E.F. and Swanson, R.S. (2005) *The Adult Learner*. New York: Butterworth-Heinemann.

Kolb, D.A. (1984) *Experiential Learning. Experience as the Source of Learning*. Englewood Cliffs: Prentice Hall.

Kondrat, M.E. (1999) Who is the Self in Self-Aware: Professional Self-Awareness from a Critical Theory Perspective. *Social Service Review*, 73(4), 451–475.

Kouzes, J.M. and Posner, B.Z. (1995) *The Leadership Challenge: How to Keep Getting Extraordinary Things Done in Organizations.* San Francisco, CA: Jossey-Bass.

Kouzes, J.M. and Posner, B.Z. (2002) *The Leadership Challenge* (3rd edn). San Francisco, CA: Jossey-Bass.

Kram, K.E. (1985) *Mentoring at Work: Developmental Relationships in Organizational Life.* Glenview, IL: Scott Foresman.

Kramlinger, T. and Huberty, T. (1990) Behaviorism versus Humanism. *Training and Development Journal,* 44(12), 41–46.

Krinks, P. and Stack, R. (2008) The Talent Crunch. *People Management,* 14(13), 30–31.

Kuchinke, K.P. (1998) Moving Beyond the Dualism of Performance and Learning: A Response to Barrie and Pace. *Human Resource Development Quarterly,* 9, 377–384.

Kuchinke, K.P. (2004) Theorising and Practicing HRD: Extending the Dialogue over the Roles of Scholarship and Practice in the Field. *Human Resource Development International,* 7(4), 535–540.

Kuchinke, K.P. (2007) Kaleidoscopes and Multiplicity of Perspectives in Human Resource Development. *Human Resource Development International,* 10(2), 117–121.

Kumar, S. and Chandra, C. (2001) Enhancing the Effectiveness of Benchmarking in Manufacturing Organizations. *Industrial Management and Data Systems,* 101(2), 80–89.

Kunnanatt, J.T. (2004) Emotional Intelligence: The New Science of Interpersonal Effectiveness. *Human Resource Development Quarterly,* 15(4), 489–495.

Kur, E. and Bunning, R. (2002) Assuring Corporate Leadership for the Future. *Journal of Management Development,* 21(9), 761–779.

Kustin, R. and Jones, R. (1995) The Influence of Corporate Headquarters on Leadership Styles in Japanese and US Subsidiary Companies. *Leadership and Organisational Development Journal,* 16(5), 11–15.

Lahteenmaki, G., Toivonen, J. and Mattila, M. (2001) Critical Aspects of Organisational Learning Research and Proposals for its Measurement. *British Journal of Management,* 12, 113–129.

Lanigan, M.L., and Bentley, J. (2006) Collecting Sophisticated Evaluations Even When Corporate Culture is Resistant. *Performance Improvement,* 45(1), 32–38.

Larsen, H.H. and Brewster, C. (2003) Line management responsibility for HRM. What is happening in Europe? *Employee Relations.* 25(3): 228–244.

Laursen, E. and Rasmussen, J.G. (2007) *Organisatorisk læring gennem udviklingsprojekter.* Aalborg: Aalborg Universitetsforlag.

Lave, J. and Wenger, E. (1991) *Situated Learning – Legitimate Peripheral Participation.* Cambridge: Cambridge University Press.

Lee, M. (1996) Holistic Learning in the New Central Europe. In M. Lee, H. Letiche, R. Crawshaw and N. Thomas (eds), *Management Education in the New Europe: Boundaries and Complexity* (pp. 249–266). London: Routledge.

Lee, M. (2001) A Refusal to Define HRD. *Human Resource Development International,* 4(3), 327–341.

Lee, M. and Smith, A. (2004, 27–28 May) *The National Agenda, Incidental Learning and Television as a Learning Medium: The Case of the Professional Development Channel.* Paper presented at the Proceedings of the Fifth UFHRD/AHRD Conference, University of Limerick, Ireland.

Lee, M. and Stead, V. (1998) Human Resource Development in the United Kingdom. *Human Resource Development Quarterly,* 9(3), 297–308.

Lefrancois, G. (1999) *The Lifespan* (6th edn). Belmont, CA: Wadsworth.

Leiba-O'Sullivan, S. (1999) The Distinction between Stable and Dynamic Cross-cultural Competencies: Implications for Expatriate Trainability. *Journal of International Business Studies,* 30(4), 709–725.

Lenaghan, J.A. and Seirup, H.J. (2007) Transition and Transparency in the Employment Contract. *Journal of Management Development,* 26(5), 459–467.

Leonard-Barton, D. (1992) The Factory as a Learning Laboratory. *Sloan Management Review,* 34(1), 23–38.

Leont'ev, A.N. (1981) The Problem of Activity in Psychology. In J.V. Wertsh (ed.), *The Concept of Activity in Soviet Psychology.* New York: Sharpe.

Leskiw, S.L. and Singh, P. (2007) Leadership Development: Learning from Best Practices. *Leadership and Organization Development Journal,* 28(5), 444–464.

Leung, S.L. and Bozionelos, N. (2004) Five-Factor Model Traits and the Prototypical Image of the Effective Leader in the Confucian Culture. *Employee Relations,* 26(1), 62–71.

Lev, B. (2000) *New Math for a New Economy.* Fast Company, January/February.

Lev, B. and Daum, J. (2003) *Intangible Assets and the Need for a Holistic and More Future-oriented Approach to Enterprise Management and Corporate Reporting.* Paper presented at the 2003 PMA Intellectual Capital Symposium, Cranfield University, England.

Lewis, P. and Thornhill, A. (1994) The Evaluation of Training: An Organisational Culture Approach. *Journal of European Industrial Training,* 18(8), 25–32.

Likert, R. (1961) *New Patterns of Management.* New York: McGraw-Hill.

Lim, B.C. and Ployhart, R.E. (2004) Transformational Leadership: Relations to the Five-Factor Model and Team Performance in Typical and Maximum Contexts. *Journal of Applied Psychology,* 89(4), 610–621.

Lincoln, Y.S., and Lynham, S.A. (2007) *Criteria for Assessing Good Theory in Human Resource Development and Other Applied Disciplines from an Interpretive Perspective.* Paper presented at the annual conference of the Academy of Human Resource Development, Bowling Green, OH. March 4th–7th.

Lindsay, C. (1994) Things that Go Wrong in Diversity Training: Conceptualization and Change with Ethnic Identity Models. *Journal of Organisational Change Management,* 7(6), 18–34.

Linstead, S., Folup, L. and Lilley, S. (2004) *Management and Organisation: A Critical Text.* London: Palgrave Macmillan.

Lippitt, G. (1969) *Organizational Renewal.* New York: Appleton Century Crofts.

Littrell, L.N., Salas, E., Hess, K.P., Paley, M. and Riedel, S. (2006) Expatriate Preparation: A Critical Review of 25 Years of Cross-Cultural Training Research. *Human Resource Development Review,* 5(3), 355–388.

Loan-Clarke, J. and Boocock, G. (1999) Investment in Training and Development by Small Businesses. *Employee Relations,* 21(3), 296–310.

Longenecker, C.O. and Fink, L.S. (2006) Closing the Management Skills Gap: A Call for Action. *Development and Learning in Organisations,* 20(1), 16–19.

Losert, A. (2008) Coping with Workplace Heteronormativity Among Lesbian Employees: A German study. *Journal of Lesbian Studies,* 12(1), 47–58.

Low, J. (2002) The Invisible Advantage: Getting A Grasp on Intangible Assets. *Perspectives on Business Innovation.* Issue 7: Valuing Intangibles, 7–14. http://www.cbi.cgey.com/journal/issue7/invisibleAd.html

Low, J. and Kalafut, P. (2002) *Invisible Advantage: How Intangibles Are Driving Business Performance.* Cambridge, MA: Perseus Publishing.

Lunnan, R., Amdam, R.P., Hennestad, B., Lervik, J.E., Nilsen, S. (2002) Standardised Leadership Tools in MNEs – Critical Reflections for the Conditions for Successful Implementations. *Journal of European Industrial Training,* 26(6/7), 274–283.

Luoma, M. (2000) Investigating the Link between Strategy and HRD, *Personnel Review,* 29(6), 769–790.

Lussier, R.N. and Achua, C.F. (2009) *Leadership: Theory, Application and Skill Development.* Mason, OH: Cengage Learning.

Lynham, S. (2000) *Leadership Development: A Review of the Theory and Literature,* Presented at the Academy of Human Resource Development Conference. Raleigh-Durham, NC, 8–12 March 2000.

Lynn, B.E. (1999) *The Management of Intellectual Capital: The Issues and the Practice.* Strategic Management Series, Emerging Issues Paper, The Society of Management Accountants of Canada.

Lytras, M.D., Pouloudi, A. and Poulymanakou, A. (2002) Knowledge Management Convergence – Expanding Learning Frontiers. *Journal of Knowledge Management,* 6(1), 40–52.

Mabey, C. and Finch-Lees, T. (2008) *Management and Leadership Development,* London: Sage.

MacLean, D. (2006) Beyond English: Transnational Corporations and the Strategic Management of Language in a Complex Multilingual Business Environment. *Management Decision,* 44(10), 1377–1390.

MacNeil, C. (2004) *The First-Line Supervisor as a Faciliator of Knowledge Sharing in Teams.* Fifth European Conference on Human Resource Development Theory and Practice, University of Limerick.

Madjar, N. (2005) The Contributions of Different Groups of Individuals to Employee Creativity. *Advances in Developing Human Resources,* 7(2), 182–206.

Maher, F.A. and Tetreault, M.K.T. (2001) *The Feminist Classroom: Dynamics of Gender, Race, and Privilege.* Lanham, MD: Rowman and Littlefield.

Majaro, S. (1988) *The Creative Gap: Managing Ideas for Profit.* London: Longman.

Malhotra, Y. (2000) Knowledge Assets in the Global Economy: Assessment of National Economic Performance. *Journal of Global Information Management,* 8(3), 5–15.

Malmi, T. (2001) Balanced Scorecards in Finnish Companies: A Research Note. *Management Accounting Research,* 12, 207–220.

Malnight, T.W. (2001) Emerging Structural Patterns Within Multinational Corporations: Toward Process Based Structures, *Academy of Management Journal,* 44(6), 1187–1210.

Maltz, A.C., Shenhar, A.J. and Reilly, R.R. (2003) Beyond the Balanced Scorecard: Refining the Search for Organisational Success Measures. *Long Range Planning,* 187–204.

Mankin, D.P. (2001) A Model for Human Resource Development. *Human Resource Development International,* 4(1), 65–85.

Mann, R.D. (1959) A Review of the Relationships Between Personality and Performance in Small Groups. *Psychological Bulletin,* 56, 241–270.

Marcus, M. (2004) Preparing High-potential Staff for the Step Up to Leadership. *Canadian HR Reporter,* 17(18), 11–12.

Marquardt, M.J. (1999) The Global Age and Global Economy. *Advances in Developing Human Resources,* v–viii.

Marquardt, M.J. and Engel, D.W. (1993) *Global Human Resource Development.* Englewood Cliffs, NJ: Prentice Hall.

Marr, B. and Gray, D. (2002) *Measuring Intellectual Capital – The internal and external drivers for measuring and reporting the intangibles of an organisation.* Paper presented at 'The Transparent Enterprise. The Value of Intangibles'. Madrid, Spain.

Marsick, V. (1988) Learning in the Workplace: The Case for Reflectivity and Critical Reflectivity. *Adult Education Quarterly,* 38(4), 187–198.

Marsick, V. and Watkins, K. (1990) *Informal and Incidential Learning in the Workplace.* London: Routledge.

Marsick, V. and Watkins, K. (1999) Envisioning New Organisations of Learning. In D. Boud and J. Garrick (eds), *Understanding Learning at Work.* London: Routledge.

Martin, W.J. (2004) Demonstrating Knowledge Value: A Broader Perspective on Metrics. *Journal of Intellectual Capital,* 5(1), 77–91.

Marx, R.D. and Frost, P.J. (1998) Toward Optimal Use of Video in Management Education: Examining the Evidence. *Journal of Management Development,* 17(4), 243–250.

Matheson, B. (2006) A Culture of Creativity: Design Education and the Creative Industries. *Journal of Management Development,* 25(1), 55–64.

Mavin, S. (2008) Queen Bees, Wannabees and Afraid to Bees: No More 'Best Enemies' for Women in Management? *British Journal of Management*, 19, S. 75–84.

Mavin, S., Wilding, P., Stalker, B., Simmonds, D., Rees, C. and Winch, F. (2007) Developing 'New Commons' between HRD Research and Practice: Case Studies of UK Universities. *Journal of European Industrial Training*, 31(1), 4–18.

Mavrinac, S. and Seisfeld, G.A. (1997) Measures that Matter: An Exploratory Investigation of Investors' Information Needs and Value Priorities. In *Enterprise Value in the Knowledge Economy: Measuring Performance in the Age of Intangibles*, Ernst and Young Center for Business Innovation, Cambridge, MA.

Maxwell, G. and Watson, S. (2004) Quality Service in the International Hotel Sector: A Catalyst for Strategic Human Resource Development? *Journal of European Industrial Training*, 28(2/3/4), 159–182.

McCauley, C.D. and Douglas, C.A. (1998) Developmental Relationships. In C.D. McCauley, R.S. Moxley and E. Van Velsor (eds), *The Center for Creative Leadership Handbook of Leadership Development*. San Francisco, CA: Jossey-Bass.

McClelland, D. (1973) Testing for Competence rather than Intelligence. *American Psychologist*, 28(1), 1–14.

McCracken, M. (2005) Towards a Typology of Managerial Barriers to Learning. *Journal of Management Development*, 24(6), 559–575.

McCracken, M. and Wallace, M. (2000) Exploring Strategic Maturity in HRD – Rhetoric, Aspiration or Reality. *Journal of European Industrial Training*, 24(8), 425–467.

McFadzean, E. (2001) Supporting Virtual Learning Groups. Part 1: A Pedagogical Perspective. *Team Performance Management: An International Journal*, 7(3/4), 53–62.

McGaughey, S. and DeCieri, H. (1999) Reassessment of Convergence and Divergence Dynamics: Implications for International HRM. *International Journal of Human Resource Management*, 10(2), 235–250.

McGoldrick, J., Stewart, J. and Watson, S. (2002a) Researching HRD: Philosophy, Process and Practice. In J. McGoldrick, J. Stewart and S. Watson (eds), *Understanding Human Resource Development: A Research Based Approach*. London: Routledge.

McGoldrick, J., Stewart, J. and Watson, S. (2002b) Understanding HRD: A Research Approach. *International Journal of Human Resources Development and Management*, 1/2, 17–30.

McGraw, P. (2004) Influences on HRM practices in MNCs: A Qualitative Study in the Australian Context. *International Journal of Manpower*, 25(6), 525–546.

McGuire, D. and Cseh M. (2006) The Development of the Field of HRD: A Delphi Study. *Journal of European Industrial Training*, 30(8), 653–667.

McGuire, D., Garavan, T.N., O'Donnell, D. and Watson, S. (2007) Metaperspectives and HRD: Lessons for Research and Practice. *Advances in Developing Human Resources*, 9(1), 120–139.

McGuire, D., O'Donnell, D. and Cross, C. (2005) Why Humanistic Practices in HRD won't work. *Human Resource Development Quarterly*, 16(1), 131–137.

McGuire, D., O'Donnell, D., Garavan, T.N., Saha, S.K. and Murphy, J. (2002) The Cultural Boundedness of Theory and Practice in HRD?. *Cross Cultural Management: An International Journal*, 9(2), 25–44.

McGuire, D., Stoner, L. and Mylona, S. (2008) The Role of Line Managers as Human Resource Agents in Fostering Organisational Change in Public Services. *Journal of Change Management*, 8(1), 73–84.

McIntosh, P. (1988) White Privilege and Male Privilege: A Personal Account of Coming to See Correspondences Through Work in Women's Studies. In M.L. Andersen and P.H. Collins (eds), *Race, Class and Gender: An Anthology*. Belmont, CA: Wadsworth.

McIntosh, P. (1993) White Privilege and Male Privilege: A Personal Account of Coming to See Correspondences through Work in Women's Studies. In A. Minas (ed.), *Gender Basics: Feminist Perspectives on Women and Men* (pp. 30–38). Belmont, CA: Wadsworth.

McIntosh, P. (1998) White Privilege and Male Privilege: A Personal Account of Coming to See Correspondences through Work in Women's Studies. In M.L. Andersen and P.H. Collins (eds), *Race, Class and Gender: An Anthology*. Belmont, CA: Wadsworth Publishing.

McIntosh, P. (2002) White Privilege and Male Privilege: A Personal Account of Coming to See Correspondences through Work in Women's Studies. In C. Harvey and M. Allard (eds), *Understanding and Managing Diversity: Readings, Cases, and Exercises* (2nd edn). Upper Saddle River, NJ: Prentice-Hall.

McKenna, S. (1998) Cross-Cultural Attitudes towards Leadership Dimensions. *Leadership and Organisation Development Journal*, 19(2), 106–112.

McKinney, F. (1933) Quantitative and Qualitative Essential Elements of Transfer. *Journal of Experiential Psychology*, 16, 854–864.

McLagan, P. (1989) *Models for HRD Practice*. Alexandria, VA: ASTD Press.

McLean, L. (2005) Organizational Culture's Influence on Creativity and Innovation: A Review of the Literature and Implications for Human Resource Development. *Advances in Developing Human Resources*, 7(2), 226–246.

McLean, G.N. and McLean, L. (2001) If We Can't Define HRD in One Country, How Can We Define It in an International Context?. *Human Resource Development International*, 4(3), 313–326.

McLean, G.N., and Wang, X. (2007) *Defining International Human Resource Development: A Proposal*. Paper presented at the Academy of Human Resource Development International Research Conference in The Americas (Indianapolis, IN, Feb 28–Mar 4, 2007).

Megginson, D., Joy-Matthews, J. and Banfield, P. (1993) *Human Resource Development*. London: Kogan Page.

Mele, D. (2003) The Challenge of Humanistic Management. *Journal of Business Ethics*, 44(1), 77–88.

Merriam, S.B. (2001) Andragogy and Self-Directed Learning: Pillars of Adult Learning Theory. In S.B. Merriam (ed.), *New Directions for Adult and Continuing Education* (Vol. 89). San Francisco, CA: Jossey-Bass.

Merriam, S.B., Johnson-Bailey, J., Lee, M., Kee, Y., Niseane, G. and Mazanah, M. (2001) Power and Positionality: Negotiating Insider/Outsider Status within and across Cultures. *International Journal of Lifelong Education*, 20(5), 405–416.

Merx-Chermin, M. and Nijhof, W. (2004) *Factors Influencing Knowledge Creation and Innovation in an Organization*. Fifth European Conference on Human Resource Development Theory and Practice, University of Limerick.

Messick, S. (1984) The Nature of Cognitive Styles: Problems and Promises in Educational Research. *Educational Psychologist*, 19, 59–74.

Metcalfe, B.D. and Rees, C.J. (2005) Theorizing Advances in International Human Resource Development. *Human Resource Development International*, 8(4), 449–466.

Mezirow, J. (1990) *Fostering Critical Reflection in Adulthood. A Guide to Transformative and Emancipatory Education*. San Francisco, CA: Jossey-Bass.

Michalski, G.V., and Cousins, J.B. (2001) Multiple perspectives on training evaluation: Probing stakeholder perceptions in a global network development firm. *American Journal of Evaluation*, 22(1), 37–53.

Michelfelder, D.P. and Palmer, R.E. (1989) Introduction. In D.P. Michelfelder and R.E. Palmer (eds), *Dialogue and Deconstruction – The Gadamer–Derrida Encounter*. New York: State University of New York Press.

Miles, R. (1988) *The Women's History of the World*. London: HarperCollins.

Miller, P.B. and O'Leary, T. (1987) Accounting and the Construction of the Governable Person. *Accounting, Organization and Society*, 12(3), 235–266.

Miller, R.L., Butler, J. and Cosentino, C.J. (2004) Followership Effectiveness: An Extension of Fiedler's Contingency Model. *Leadership and Organisation Development Journal*, 25(4), 362–369.

Mintzberg, H. (2004) *Managers not MBAs*. San Francisco, CA: Berrett-Koehler.

Mintzberg, H., Ahlstrand, B. and Lampel, J. (1998) *Strategy Safari – A Guided Tour Through the Wilds of Strategic Management*. New York: The Free Press.

Miroshnik, V. (2002) Culture and International Management: A Review. *Journal of Management Development*, 21(7), 521–544.

Monserrat, S.I., Duffy, J.A., Olivas-Lujan, M.R., Miller, J.M., Gregory, A., Fox, S., Lituchy, T.R. and Punnett, B.J. (2009) Mentoring Experiences of Successful Women Across the Americas. *Gender in Management: An International Journal*, 24(6), 455–476.

Mooraj, S., Oyon, D. and Hostettler, D. (1999) The Balanced Scorecard: A Necessary Good or an Unnecessary Evil? *European Management Journal*, 17(5), 481–491.

Morgan, G. (1986) *Images of Organization*. London: Sage Publications.

Morgan, G.A. and Smircich, L. (1980) The Case for Qualitative Research. *Academy of Management Review*, 5(4), 491–500.

Morrison, M. (2009) *Leadership and Learning: Matters of Social Justice*. New York: Information Age Publishing.

Morson, G.S. (1994) *Narrative and Freedom – The Shadows of Time*. New Haven: Yale University Press.

Mostovicz, E.I., Kakabadse, N.K. and Kakabadse, A.P. (2009) A Dynamic Theory of Leadership Development. *Leadership and Organisation Development Journal*, 30(6), 563–576.

Mumford, M.D., Scott, G.M., Gaddis, B. and Strange, J.M. (2002) Leading Creative People: Orchestrating Expertise and Relationships. *The Leadership Quarterly*, 13(6), 705–750.

Mussig, D.J. (2003) A Research and Skills Training Framework for Values-Driven Leadership, *Journal of European Industrial Training*, 27(2/3/4), 73–79.

Myers, I.B. and McCauley, M.H. (1986) *Manual: A Guide to the Development and Use of the Myers-Briggs Type Indicator*. Palo Alto, CA: Consulting Psychologists Press.

Nadkarni, S. and Perez, P.D. (2007). Prior conditions and degree of internationalization: The mediating role of domestic mindsets. *Journal of International Business Studies*, 38(1), 160–176.

Nadler, D.A. and Tushman, M.L. (1990) Beyond the Charismatic Leader: Leadership and Organizational Change, *California Management Review*, 32(2), 77–97.

Nadler, L. (1970) *Developing Human Resources*. Houston, TX: Gulf.

Nair, P.K., Ke, J., Al-Emadi, M.A.S., Conser, J., Cornachione, E., Devassy, S.M. et al. (2007) *National Human Resource Development: A Multi-Level Perspective*. Paper presented at the Academy of Human Resource Development Conference, Indianapolis, Indiana, February 26th–March 3rd 2002.

Nam Cam Trau, R. and Hartel, C.E.J. (2004) One Career, Two Identities: An Assessment of Gay Men's Career Trajectory. *Career Development International*, 9(7), 627–637.

National Skills Task Force (2000) Third Report of the National Skills Taskforce: Tackling the Adult Skills Gap: Upskilling Adults and the Role of Workplace Learning, London: DfEE.

Naylor, J.C. and Shine, L.C. (1965) A Table for Determining the Increase in Mean Criterion Score Obtained by Using a Selection Device. *Journal of Industrial Psychology*, 3, 33–42.

Neely, A., Gregory, M. and Platts, K. (1995) Performance Measurement System Design – A Literature Review and Research Agenda. *International Journal of Operations and Production Management*, 15, 80–116.

Nelson, R.R. and Winter S.G. (1982) *An Evolutionary Theory of Economic Change*. Cambridge, MA: Harvard University Press.

Newall, A., Shaw, J.C. and Simon, H.A. (1979) The Processes of Creative Thinking. In H.A. Simon (ed.), *Models of Thought* (pp. 144–174) New Haven, CT: Yale University Press.

Newby, T. (1992) *Training Evaluation Handbook*. Aldershot: Gower.

Nickerson, R.S. (1999) Enhancing Creativity. In R.J. Sternberg (ed.), *Handbook of Creativity*. Cambridge: Cambridge University Press.

Nietzsche, F. (1974) *The Gay Science – With a Prelude in Rhymes and an Appendix of Songs*. New York: Vintage Books.

Nijman, D.J., Nijhof, W.J., Wognum, A.A.M. and Veldkamp, B.P. (2006) Exploring Differential Effects of Supervisor Support on Transfer of Training. *Journal of European Industrial Training*, 30(7), 529–549.

Nitsch, K.E. (1977) Structuring Decontextualized forms of Knowledge. *Unpublished Doctoral Dissertation*. Nashville: Vanderbilt University.

Noble, C. (1997) International Comparisons of Training Policies. *Human Resource Management Journal*, 7(1), 5–18.

Nonaka, I. (1991) The Knowledge-creating Company. *Harvard Business Review*, 69(6), 96–104.

Nonaka, I. and Takeuchi, H. (1995) *The Knowledge-creating Company: How Japanese Companies Create the Dynamics of Innovation*. New York: Oxford University Press.

Nørreklit, L. (1983) Aktørsmetoden: en indføring i erhvervsøkonomisk projektarbejde. Aalborg: Aalborg Universitetsforlag.

Northouse, P.G. (2010) *Leadership: Theory and Practice*. Thousand Oaks, CA: Sage.

Nyhan, B. (2002) *Human Resource Development in Europe – at the Crossroads*. Paper presented at the UFHRD Conference for HRD Research and Practice across Europe, Edinburgh, Scotland. January 29th–February 3rd 2002.

Oakes, D.W. and Ferris, G.R. (2001) Cognitive Ability and Personality Predictors of Training Program Skill Acquisition and Job Performance. *Journal of Business and Psychology*, 15(4), 523–548.

O'Connell, G. (2008) Crystal Clear. *People Management*, 14(5), 40–41.

O'Donnell, D. (2004) Theory and Method on Intellectual Capital Creation: Addressing Communicative Action through Relative Methodics. *Journal of Intellectual Capital*, 5(2), 294–311.

O'Donnell, D., McGuire, D. and Cross, C. (2006) Critically Challenging Some Assumptions in HRD. *International Journal of Training and Development*, 10(1), 4–16.

O'Donnell, D., Porter, G., McGuire, D., Garavan, T.N., Heffernan, M. and Cleary, P. (2003) Creating Intellectual Capital: A Habermasian Community of Practice (CoP) Introduction. *Journal of European Industrial Training*, 27(2/3/4), 80–87.

OECD (2001) *Economics and Finance of Lifelong Learning*. Paris: OECD.

Office for National Statistics (2008) *Annual Survey of Hours and Earnings*. London: Office for National Statistics.

Office for National Statistics (2009) *Labour Market Statistics*. London: Office for National Statistics.

Oldham, G.R., and Cummings, A. (1996) Employee Creativity: Personal and Contextual Factors at Work. *Academy of Management Journal*, 39(3), 607–634.

Olivares, O.J., Peterson, G. and Hess, K.P. (2007) An Existential–Phenomenological Framework for Understanding Leadership Development Experiences. *Leadership and Organizational Development Journal*, 28(1), 76–91.

O'Neil, D.A. and Bilimoria, D. (2005) Women's Career Development Phases: Idealism, Endurance and Reinvention. *Career Development International*, 10(3), 168–189.

Olve, N., Roy, J. and Wetter, M. (1999) *Performance Drivers: A Practical Guide to Using the Balanced Scorecard*. West Sussex: Wiley.

Ormond, J.E. (1999) *Human Learning*. Upper Saddle River, NJ: Prentice Hall.

Othman, R. (2006) Balanced Scorecard and Causal Model Development: Preliminary Findings. *Management Decision*, 44(5), 690–702.

Othman, R. (2008) Enhancing the Effectiveness of the Balanced Scorecard with Scenario Planning. *International Journal of Productivity and Performance Management*, 57(3), 259–266.

Owen, H. (1999) *The Spirit of Leadership: Liberating the Leader in Each of Us*. San Francisco, CA: Berrett-Koehler.

Palmer, J. and Smith, P. (1999) Turning to Learning. *Canadian Underwriter* (August), 62.

Pangarkar, A.M. and Kirkwood, T. (2008) Strategic Alignment: Linking your Learning Strategy to the Balanced Scorecard. *Industrial and Commercial Training*, 40(2), 95–101.

Parker, S.K. and Axtell, C.M. (2001) Seeing Another Viewpoint: Antecedents and Outcomes of Employee Perspective Taking. *Academy of Management Journal*, 44(6), 1085–1102.

Parker-Gore, S. (1996) Perception is Reality: Using 360-degree Appraisal against Behavioural Competences to Effect Organizational Change and Improve Management Performance. *Career Development International*, 1(3), 24–27.

Patel, N.V. (2003) A Holistic Approach to Learning and Teaching Interaction: Factors in the Development of Critical Learners. *International Journal of Educational Management*, 17(6), 272–284.

Patriotta, G. (2003) On Studying Organizational Knowledge. *Knowledge Management Research and Practice*, 2, 3–12.

Pearce, C.L. and Conger, J.A. (2003) All Those Years Ago: The Historical Underpinnings of Shared Leadership. In C.L. Pearce and J.A Conger (eds), *Shared Leadership: Reframing the Hows and Whys of Leadership* (pp.1–18). Thousand Oaks, CA: Sage Publications.

Pendry, L.F., Driscoll, D.M. and Field, S.C.T. (2007) Diversity Training: Putting Theory into Practice. *Journal of Occupational and Organizational Psychology*, 80, 27–50.

Perry, E.L. and Kulik, C.T. (2008) The Devolution of HR to the Line: Implications for Perceptions of People Management Effectiveness, *International Journal of Human Resource Management*, 19(2), 262–273.

Perry-Smith, J.E. (2006) Social Yet Creative: The Role of Social Relationships in Facilitating Individual Creativity. *Academy of Management Journal*, 49(1), 85–101.

Pershing, J.A. and Pershing, J.L. (2001) Ineffective Reaction Evaluation. *Human Resource Development Quarterly*, 12(1), 73–90.

Peters, T. and Waterman, R. (1982) *In Search of Excellence: Lessons From America's Best-Run Companies*. New York: Harper and Row.

Peterson, L.A. (1997) International HRD: What we Know and Don't Know. *Human Resource Development Quarterly*, 8(1), 63–79.

Pettigrew, A.M. (1979) On Studying Organisational Culture. *Administrative Science Quarterly*, 24, 570–581.

Phillips, J. (1991) *Handbook of Training and Evaluation and Measurement Methods* (2nd edn). Houston, TX: Gulf Publishing.

Phillips, T. (2009) *Stephen Lawrence Speech: Institutions must catch up with Public on Race Issues*. Delivered on the Tenth Anniversary of the Stephen Lawrence Inquiry, 19 January 2009.

Piaget, J. (1952) *The Origins of Intelligence in Children*. New York: International University Press.

Piaget, J. (1970) *Structuralism*. New York, Basic Books.

Pierce, J.L. and Newstrom, J.W. (2008) *Leaders and the Leadership Process: Readings, Self-Assessments and Applications*. Boston, MA: McGraw-Hill.

Pilch, T. (2000) *Dynamic Reporting for a Dynamic Economy*. London: The Smith Institute. http://www.academyofenterprise.org/downloads/smith_for_web.doc

Ployhart, R.E., Lim, B.C. and Chan, K.Y. (2001) Exploring Relations between Typical and Maximum Performance Ratings and the Five Factor Model of Personality. *Personnel Psychology*, 54(4), 809–843.

Poell, R.F. and Van der Krogt, F.J. (2003) Learning-Program Creation in Work Organisations. *Human Resource Development Review*, 2(3), 252–272.

Polanyi, M. (1958) *Personal Knowledge – Towards a Post-Critical Philosophy*. London: Routledge.

Polanyi, M. (1966) *The Tacit Dimension*. Glouchester, MA: Peter Smith.

Polanyi, M. (1969a) Knowing and Being. *Knowing and Being – Essays by Michael Polanyi*. London: Routledge and Kegan Paul.

Polanyi, M. (1969b) Sense-Giving and Sense-Reading. *Knowing and Being – Essays by Michael Polanyi* (pp. 181–207). London: Routledge.

Polkinghorne, D.E. (1988) *Narrative Knowing and the Human Sciences.* New York: State University of New York Press.

Pondy, L.R., Frost, P.J., Morgan, G. and Dandridge, T.C. (1983) *Organisational Symbolism.* Greenwich, CT: JAI Press.

Porter, M.E. (1990) *The Competitive Advantage of Nations.* London: Macmillan.

Posner, B.Z. and Kouzes, J.M. (1988) Relating Leadership and Credibility, *Psychological Reports*, 63, 527–530.

Post, H.A. (1997) Building a Strategy on Competencies. *Long Range Planning,* 30 (5), 733–740.

Power, W.T. (1973) *Behavior, the Control of Perception.* Chicago, IL: Aldine.

Prahalad, C.K. and Hamel, G. (1990) The Core Competence of the Corporation. *Harvard Business Review*, 79–91.

Preskill, H. (2007) *Building an Organization's Evaluation System: A Case Example of Using Appreciative Inquiry.* Presented at the Academy of Human Resource Development Conference, Indianapolis, Indiana. February 28–March 4th 2006.

Preskill, H. and Russ-Eft, D. (2005) *Building Evaluation Capacity: 72 Activities for Teaching and Training.* Thousand Oaks, CA: Sage.

Preskill, H. and Torres, R.T. (1999). *Evaluative inquiry for learning in organizations.* Thousand Oaks, CA: Sage.

Pritchard, C., Jones, D. and Stablein, R. (2004) Doing Research in Organizational Discourse – The Importance of Researcher Context. In D. Grant, C. Hardy, C. Oswick and L. Putnam (eds), *The Sage Handbook of Organizational Discourse* (pp. 213–236). London: Sage Publications.

Pullen, A. (2005) *Managing Identity.* Basingstoke: Palgrave Macmillan.

Purdy, M. (1997) Humanist Ideology and Nurse Education. 2. Limitations of Humanist Education Theory in Nurse Education. *Nurse Education Today*, 17, 196–202.

Rainbird, H. (1995) The Changing Role of the Training Function: A Test for Integration of Human Resources and Business Strategy. *Human Resource Management Journal*, 5, 72–90.

Rajan, A. and Martin, B. (2001) *Harnessing Creativity to Improve the Bottom Line.* London: CIMA Publishing.

Ralston, D., Wright, A. and Kumar, J. (2001) Process Benchmarking as a Market Research Tool for Strategic Planning. *Market Intelligence and Planning*, 19(4), 273–281.

Rappe, C. and Zwink, T. (2007) Developing Leadership Competence of Production Unit Managers. *Journal of Management Development*, 26(4), 312–330.

Ray, T. and Clegg, S.R. (2005) Tacit Knowing, Communication and Power – Lessons from Japan. In S. Little and T. Ray (eds), *Managing Knowledge – An Essential Reader.* London: Sage Publications.

Reber, A.S. (1993) *Implicit Learning and Tacit Knowledge: An Essay on the Cognitive Unconscious.* New York: Oxford University Press.

Reynolds, M. (1998) Reflection and Critical Reflection in Management Learning. *Management Learning*, 29(2), 183–200.

Reynolds, M. (1999) Critical Reflection and Management Education: Rehabilitating less Hierarchical Approaches. *Journal of Management Education*, 23(5), 537–553.

Reynolds, M. and Trehan, K. (2003) Learning from Difference. *Management Learning*, 34(2), 163–180.

Rhode, J.G., Lawler, E.E. and Sundem, G.L. (1976) Human Resource Accounting: A Critical Assessment. *Industrial Relations,* 15(1), 13–25.

Ricoeur, P. (1984) *Time and Narrative – Volume 1.* Chicago and London: University of Chicago Press.

Robbins, S.P., Bergman, R. and Stagg, I. (1997) *Management.* Sydney: Prentice Hall.

Roberts, H. (2003) Management Accounting and the Knowledge Production Process. In A. Bhimani (ed.), *Management Accounting in the Digital Economy*. New York: Oxford University Press.

Robinson, A. and Stern, S. (1997) *Corporate Creativity: How Innovation and Improvement Actually Happen*. San Francisco, CA: Berret-Koehler.

Robotham, D. (2003) Learning and Training: Developing the Competent Learner. *Journal of European Industrial Training*, 27(9), 473–480.

Rock, A. and Garavan, T. (2006) Reconceptualising Developmental Relationships. *Human Resource Development Review*, 5(3), 330–355.

Rodgers, W.M. III (2006) Male White–Black Wage Gaps, 1979–1994: A Distributional Analysis. *Southern Economic Journal*, 72(4), 773–786.

Rojek, C. (2003) *Stuart Hall*. Cambridge: Polity Press.

Roslender, R. (2000) Accounting for Intellectual Capital – A Contemporary Management Accounting Perspective. *Management Accounting*, March, 34–37.

Roslender, R. (2003) Accounting for Intellectual Capital: A Discussion of its Theoretical Foundations. University of Stirling Working Paper Series, Scotland.

Roslender, R. and Dyson, J.R. (1992) Accounting for the Worth of Employees: A New Look at an Old Problem. *British Accounting Review*, 24(4), 311–329.

Roslender, R. and Fincham, R. (2001) Thinking Critically about Intellectual Capital Accounting. *Accounting, Auditing and Accountability Journal*, 14(4), 383–399.

Roslender, R. and Fincham, R. (2004) Intellectual Capital Accounting in the UK – A Field Study Perspective. *Accounting, Auditing and Accountability Journal*, 17(2), 178–209.

Rothwell, W. (2002) Putting Success into your Succession Planning. *Journal of Business Strategy*, 23(3), 32–42.

Rugman, A. (2005) *The Regional Multinationals: MNEs and Global Strategic Management*. Cambridge: Cambridge University Press.

Rummler, G. and Brache, A. (1995) *Improving Performance*. San Francisco, CA: Jossey-Bass.

Ruona, W.E.A. (2000) Core Beliefs in Human Resource Development: A Journey for its Profession and its Professionals. *Advances in Developing Human Resources*, 2(3), 1–27.

Ruona, W.E.A. (2001) The Foundational Impact of Training Within Industry Project on the Human Resource Development Profession. *Advances in Developing Human Resources*, 3(2), 119–126.

Ruona, W.E.A., Leimbach, M., Holton III, E.F., and Bates, R. (2002). The relationship between learner utility reactions and predicted learning transfer among trainees. *International Journal of Training & Development*, 6(4), 218–228.

Ruona, W.E.A., Lynham, S.A. and Chermack, T.J. (2003) Insights on Emerging Trends and the Future of Human Resource Development. *Advances in Developing Human Resources*, 5(3), 272–282.

Rusaw, A.C. (2000) Uncovering Training Resistance: A Critical Theory Perspective. *Journal of Organizational Change Management*, 13(3), 40–51.

Russ-Eft, D. and Preskill, H. (2005) In Search of the Holy Grail: Return on Investment Evaluation in Human Resource Development. *Advances in Developing Human Resources*, 7(1), 71–85.

Russell, C. and Parsons, E. (1996) Putting Theory to the Test at the OU. *People Management*, 2(1), 30–32.

Russell, D., Calvey, D. and Banks, M. (2003) Creating New Learning Communities: Towards Effective E-learning Production. *Journal of Workplace Learning*, 15(1), 34–45.

Ryan, M.K. and Haslam, S.A. (2004) *Introducing the Glass Cliff*. http://news.bbc.co.uk/1/hi/magazine/3755031.stm, online BBC article (accessed 6 August 2009).

Ryan, M.K. and Haslam, S.A. (2007) The Glass Cliff: Exploring the Dynamics Surrounding the Appointment of Women to Precarious Leadership Positions. *Academy of Management Review*, 32(2), 549–572.

Ryle, G. (1949) *The Concept of Mind*. London: Hutchinson of London.

Sackmann, S.A., Flamholtz, E.G. and Bullen, M.L. (1989) Human Resource Accounting: A State-of-the-art Review. *Journal of Accounting Literature*, 8, 235–264.

Sacks, H. and Schegloff, E.A. (1974) A Simplest Systematics for the Organisation of Turn-taking for Conversation. *Language*, 50(4), 696–735.

Sadler-Smith, E. (2006) *Learning and Development for Managers: Perspectives from Research and Practice*. Malden, MA: Blackwell.

Sadler-Smith, E., Allinson, C.W. and Hayes, J. (2000) Learning Preferences and Cognitive Style: Some Implications for Continuing Professional Development. *Management Learning*, 31(2), 239–256.

Salaman, G. and Butler, J. (1994) Why Managers Won't Learn. In C. Mabey and P. Iles (eds), *Managing Learning*. London: Routledge.

Sambrook, S. (2004) A Critical Time for HRD? *Journal of European Industrial Training*, 28 (8/9), 611–624.

Sambrook, S. (2008) People, Organisations and Development – Is HRD being stretched? *Human Resource Development International*, 11(3), 219–223.

Sambrook, S. and Stewart, J. (2000) Factors Influencing Learning in European Learning Oriented Organisations: Issues for Management. *Journal of European Industrial Training*, 24(2/3/4), 209–219.

Sambrook, S. and Stewart, J. (2002) Reflections and Discussion. In S. Trepkema, J. Stewart, S. Sambrook, M. Mulder, H. ter Horst and J. Scheerens (eds), *HRD and Learning Organisations*. London: Routledge.

Sanchez, J.I. and Medkik, N. (2004) The Effects of Diversity Awareness Training on Differential Treatment. *Group and Organization Management*, 29, 517–536.

Santos, A. and Stuart, M. (2003) Employee Perceptions and their Influence on Training Effectiveness. *Human Resource Management Journal*, 13(1), 27–45.

Sarros, J.C. and Santora, J.C. (2001) The Transformational-Transactional Leadership Model in Practice. *Leadership and Organization Development Journal*, 22(8), 383–394.

Saunders, M.N.K. and Skinner, D. (2005) Mismatched Perceptions and Expectations: An Exploration of Stakeholders' Views of Key and Technical Skills in Vocational Education and Training. *Industrial and Commercial Training*, 29(5), 369–382.

Scarpello, V. and Theeke, H.A. (1989) Human Resource Accounting: A Measured Critique. *Journal of Accounting Literature*, 8, 265–280.

Schein, E. (1992) *Organizational Culture and Leadership* (2nd Ed.) San Francisco: Jossey-Bass.

Schmidt, C.K. and Nilsson, J.E. (2006) The Effects of Simultaneous Developmental Processes: Factors Relating to the Career Development of Lesbian, Gay and Bisexual Youth. *Career Development Quarterly*, 55(1), 22–37.

Schmidt, F.L. and Hunter, J.E. (1992) Development of a Causal Model of Processes Determining Job Performance. *Current Directions in Psychological Science*, 1, 89–92.

Schön, D.A. (1983) *The Reflective Practitioner – How Professionals Think in Action*. New York: Basic Books.

Schultz, M. (1990) *Kultur i organisationer: funktion eller symbol*. Copenhagen: Copenhagen Business School.

Schulz, K.P. (2005) Learning in Complex Organizations as Practicing and Reflecting: A Model Development and Application from a Theory of Practice Perspective. *Journal of Workplace Learning*, 17(8), 493–507.

Scott, S.G. and Bruce, R.A. (1994) Determinants of Innovative Behaviour: A Path Model of Individual Innovation in the Workplace. *Academy of Management Journal*, 37(3), 580–607.

Senge, P.M. (1990) *The Fifth Discipline – The Art and Practice of the Learning Organization*. London: Century Business.

Sfard, A. and Prusak, A. (2005) Telling Identities – In Search of an Analytic Tool for Investigating Learning as Culturally Shaped Activity. *Educational Researcher*, 34(4), 14–22.

Shalley, C.E. and Gilson, L.L. (2004) What Leaders Need to Know: A Review of Social and Contextual Factors that can Foster or Hinder Creativity. *The Leadership Quarterly*, 15, 33–53.

Shalley, C.E., Gilson, L.L. and Blum, T.C. (2000) Matching Creativity Requirements and the Work Environment: Effects on Satisfaction and Intentions to Leave. *Academy of Management Journal*, 43(2), 215–223.

Shalley, C.E., Zhou, J. and Oldham, G.R. (2004) The Effects of Personal and Contextual Characteristics on Creativity: Where should we go from here? *Journal of Management*, 30(6), 933–958.

Sheppard, E. (2002) The Spaces and Times of Globalisation: Place, Scale, Networks and Positionality. *Economic Geography*, 78(3), 307–331.

Shore, L.M. and Wayne, S.J. (1993) Commitment and Employee Behaviour: Comparison of Affective Commitment and Continuance Commitment with Perceived Organizational Support. *Journal of Applied Psychology*, 78(5), 774–780.

Short, D.C., Bing, J.W. and Kehrhahn, M.T. (2003) Will Human Resource Development Survive? *Human Resource Development Quarterly*, 14(3), 239–244.

Shotter, J. (2005) Inside the Moment of Managing: Wittgenstein and the Everyday Dynamics of Our Expressive–Responsive Activities. *Organization Studies*, 26(1), 113–135.

Shuell, T.J. (1990) Phases of Meaningful Learning. *Review of Educational Research*, 60(4), 531–547.

Silber, K.H. (2002) Using the Cognitive Approach to Improve Problem-solving Training. *Performance Improvement*, 41(3), 28–36.

Silverman, D. and Jones, J. (1976) *Organizational Work – The Language of Grading the Grading of Language*. London, Collier Macmillan.

Simmonds, D. and Pedersen, C. (2006) HRD: The Shape and Things to Come. *Journal of Workplace Learning*, 18(2), 122–135.

Simmonds, K. (1981) Strategic Management Accounting. *Management Accounting*, 59(4), 26–29.

Sippola, A. (2007) Developing Culturally Diverse Organisations: A Participative and Empowerment-Based Method. *Women in Management Review*, 22(4), 253–273.

Sirotnik, K.A. (1983) What you See is What you Get: Consistency, Persistency and Mediocrity in Classrooms. *Harvard Educational Review*, 53, 16–31.

Skinner, B.F. (1953) *Science and Human Behaviour*. New York: Macmillan.

Slotte, V., Tynjala, P. and Hytonen, T. (2004) How Do HRD Practitioners Describe Learning at Work? *Human Resource Development International*, 7(4), 481–500.

Skoog, M. (2002) *Visualizing Calue Creation through the Management Control of Intangibles*. Paper presented at the 25th Annual European Accounting Congress, Copenhagen, Denmark.

Smircich, L. (1983) Concepts of Organisational Culture and Organisational Analysis. *Administrative Science Quarterly*, 28(3), 339–359.

Smith, E.A. (2001) The Role of Tacit and Explicit Knowledge in the Workplace. *Journal of Knowledge Management*, 5(4), 311–321.

Smith, I. (2005) *Different in Similar Ways: Making Sense of Learning Styles*. Paisley, Learning Unlimited.

Smith, I.W. (2004) Continuing Professional Development and Workplace Learning 9: Human Resource Development – Measuring Return on Investment. *Library Management*, 25(6/7), 318–320.

Smith, P.J. (2000) Preparedness for flexible delivery among vocational learners. *Distance Education*, 21(1), 29–48.

Smith, R. (1988) *Human Resource Development: An Overview*. Washington, DC: Office of Educational Research and Improvement.

Sofian, S., Tayles, M.E. and Pike, R.H. (2004) *Intellectual Capital: An Evolutionary Change in Management Accounting Practices*. Paper presented at the Fourth Asia Pacific Interdisciplinary Research in Accounting Conference, Singapore.

Sosik, J. and Megerian, L. (1999) Understanding Leader Emotional Intelligence and Performance: The Role of Self–Other Agreement on Transformational Leadership Perceptions. *Group and Organization Management*, 24(3), 367–390.

Sparrow, P. (2000) Strategic Management in a World Turned Upside Down: The Role of Cognition, Intuition and Emotional Intelligence. In P.C. Flood, T. Dromgoole, S.J. Carroll and L. Gorman (eds), *Managing Strategy Implementation*. Oxford: Blackwell.

Stead, V. and Lee, M. (1996) Inter-Cultural Perspectives on HRD. In J. Stewart and J. McGoldrick (eds), *HRD Perspectives, Strategies and Practices*. London: Pitman.

Stedham, Y. and Engle, A. (1999) *Multinational and Transnational Strategies: Implications for Human Resource Management*. Paper Presented at the 8th Biennial Research Symposium of the Human Resource Planning Society, Ithaca, NY, June.

Stein, D. (2000) *Teaching Critical Reflection: Myths and Realities No. 7*. Columbus, OH, Eric Clearinghouse on Vocational Education and Training.

Stein, D.S. (2001) Situated Learning and Planned Training on the Job. *Advances in Developing Human Resources*, 3(4), 415–425.

Stern, L.R. (2008) *Executive Coaching: Building and Managing Your Professional Practice*. London: Wiley.

Sternberg, R.J. (1996) *Successful Intelligence*. New York: Schuster.

Sternberg, R.J. (1997) *Successful Intelligence*. New York, Penguin.

Sternberg, R.J. and Lubart, T.I. (1999) The Concept of Creativity: Prospects and Paradigms. In R.J. Sternberg (ed.), *Handbook of Creativity*. Cambridge: Cambridge University Press.

Stewart, J. (1999) *Employee Development Practice*. London: Financial Times Management.

Stewart, J. (2002) Individual Learning. In J. Leopold (ed.), *Human Resources in Organisations*. Upper Saddle River, NJ: Prentice Hall.

Stewart, J. (2007) The Future of HRD Research: Strengths, Weaknesses, Opportunities and Threats. *Human Resource Development International*, 10(1), 93–99.

Stewart, J. and McGoldrick, J. (1996) *Human Resource Development: Perspectives, Strategies and Practice*. London: Pitman.

Stewart, M.M., Crary, M. and Humberd, B.K. (2008) Teaching Value in Diversity: On the Folly of Espousing Inclusion, while Practicing Exclusion. *Academy of Management Learning and Education*, 7(3), 374–386.

Stewart, T.A. (2001) Accounting Gets Radical. *Fortune*, 16 April, 184–194.

Stogdill, R.M. (1948) Personal Factors Associated with Leadership: A Survey of the Literature, *Journal of Psychology*, 25, 35–71.

Stogdill, R.M. (1971) *Handbook of Leadership*. New York: Free Press.

Stogdill, R.M. (1974) *Handbook of Leadership: A Survey of the Literature*. New York: Free Press.

Storberg-Walker, J. (2008) Wenger's Communities of Practice Revisited: A (Failed?) Exercise in Applied Communies of Practice Theory-Building Research. *Advances in Developing Human Resources*, 10(4), 555–577.

Streibel, M.J. (1991) Instructional Plans and Situated Learning: The Challenge of Suchman's Theory of Situated Action for Instructional Designers and Instructional Systems. In G. Anglin (ed.), *Instructional Technologies; Past, Present and Future* (pp. 117–132). Denver, CO: Libraries Unlimited.

Sveiby, K.E. (1998) Measuring Intangibles and Intellectual Capital – An Emerging First Standard. http://www.sveiby.com/

Svensson, L. and Ellstrom, P.E. (2004) Integrating Formal and Informal Learning at Work. *Journal of Workplace Learning*, 16(8), 479–491.

Swanson, R.A. (2005) Evaluation: A State of Mind. *Advances in Developing Human Resources*, 7(1), 16–22.

Swanson, R.A. and Arnold, D.E. (1997) *The Purpose of HRD is to Improve Performance.* Paper presented at the Annual Academy of Human Resource Development Conference. Atlanta, Georgia. February 28th– March 4th.

Swanson, R.A. and Holton, E.F. (2001) *Foundations of Human Resource Development.* San Francisco, CA: Berrett-Koehler.

Swart, J., Mann, C., Brown, S., & Price, A. (2005) *Human Resource Development: Strategy and Tactics.* Oxford: Elsevier Butterworth-Heinemann Publications.

Swieringa, J. and Wierdsma A. (1992) *Becoming a Learning Organisation.* Wokingham, Addison-Wesley.

Szendi, J.Z. and Elmore, R.C. (1993) Management Accounting: Are New Techniques Making In-roads with Practitioners? *Journal of Accounting Education*, 11(1), 61–76.

Taggar, S. (2002) Individual Creativity and Group Ability to Utilise Individual Creative Resources: A Multi-Level Model. *Academy of Management Journal*, 45(2), 315–330.

Tajfel, H. (1982) Instrumentality, Identity, and Social Comparisons. In H. Tajfel (ed.), *Social Identity and Intergroup Relations* (pp. 483–507). Cambridge: Cambridge University Press.

Takacs, D. (2002) Positionality, Epistemology, and Social Justice in the Classroom. *Social Justice*, 29(4), 168–182.

Tan, H. and Tan, C.S. (2000) Toward the Differentiation of Trust in Supervisor and Trust in Organization. *Genetic, Social, and General Psychology Monographs*, 126(2), 241–260.

Tannenbaum, R. and Schmidt, W.H. (1958) How to Choose a Leadership Pattern. *Harvard Business Review*, 36(2), 95–101.

Tayles, M., Bramley, A., Adshead, N. and Farr, J. (2002) Dealing with the Management of Intellectual Capital – The Potential Role of Strategic Management Accounting. *Accounting, Auditing and Accountability Journal*, 15(2), 251–267.

Tayles, M.E., Pike, R.H. and Sofian, S. (2005a) *Intellectual Capital, Management Accounting Practices and Corporate Performance: Perceptions of Managers.* Paper presented at the 1st Workshop on Visualising, Measuring, and Managing Intangibles and Intellectual Capital, Ferrara, Italy.

Tayles, M.E., Webster, M., Sugden, D. and Bramley, A. (2005b) Accounting 'Gets Real' in Dealing with Virtual Manufacturing. *Journal of Intellectual Capital*, 6(3), 322–338.

Teece, D.J. (2000) *Managing Intellectual Capital: Organizational, Strategy and Policy.* Oxford: Oxford University Press.

Terry, R.W. (1993) *Authentic Leadership.* San Francisco, CA: Jossey-Bass.

Tesluk, P.E., Farr, J.L. and Klein, S.R. (1997) Influences on Organizational Behavior and Climate on Individual Creativity. *Journal of Creative Behavior*, 31, 27–41.

Thagard, P. (1996) *Mind: Introduction to Cognitive Sciences.* Cambridge, MA: MIT Press.

Thomas, A., Gietzmann, M. and Shyla, A. (2002) Winning the competition for capital. *European Business Forum*, 9, 80–83.

Thomas, D.A. (2001) The Truth about Mentoring Minorities: Race Matters. *Harvard Business Review*, 79(4), 98–107.

Thomas, K.M., Willis, L.A. and Davis, J. (2007) Mentoring Minority Graduate Students: Issues and Strategies for Institutions, Faculties and Students. *Equal Opportunities International*, 26(3), 178–192.

Thompson, D.E. and Thompson, C. (2004) *Students' Perceptions of Human Resource Development Classes Presented By Distance Education.* Fifth European Conference on Human Resource Development Theory and Practice.

Thompson, L. (2003) Improving the Creativity of Organizational Work Groups. *Academy of Management Executive*, 17(1), 96–111.

Thomson, A. and Mabey, C. (2001) *Changing Patterns of Management Development.* Oxford, Blackwell.

Tichy, N.M. and Devanna, M.A. (1990) *The Transformational Leader.* New York: Wiley.

Tierney, P. and Farmer, S.M. (2002) Creative Self-Efficacy: Potential Antecedents and Relationship to Creative Performance. *Academy of Management Journal*, 45, 1137–1148.

Tollington, T. (2000) The Cognitive Assumptions Underpinning the Accounting Recognition of Assets. *Management Decision*, 38 (1–2), 89–98.

Tonge, J. (2008) Barriers to Networking for Women in a UK Professional Service. *Gender in Management: An International Journal*, 23(7), 484–505.

Torraco, R. (2004) Challenges and Choices for Theoretical Research in Human Resource Development. *Human Resource Development Quarterly*, 15(2), 171–188.

Tregaskis, O. (1998) HRD in Foreign MNEs. *International Studies of Management and Organisation*, 28(1), 136–163.

Trehan, K. (2004) Who is not sleeping with whom? What's not being talked about in HRD? *Journal of European Industrial Training*, 28 (1), 23–38.

Tseng, C.C., and McLean, G.N. (2008) Strategic HRD practices as key factors in organizational learning. *Journal of European Industrial Training*, 32(6), 418–432.

Tung, R.L. (1981) Selection and Training of Personnel for Overseas Assignments. *Columbia Journal of World Business*, 26(4), 68–78.

Ty, R. (2007) *Performance, Learning and Social Justice: Theorising HRD Practices in the International Training Office, Yesterday, Today and Tomorrow.* Presented at the Academy of Human Resource Development Conference, Indianapolis, Indiana. February 28–March 4th 2006.

Tziner, A. and Haccoun, R.R. (1991) Personal and Situational Characteristics Influencing the Effectiveness of Transfer of Training Improvement Strategies. *Journal of Occupational Psychology*, 64: 167–177.

Unsworth, K. (2001) Unpacking Creativity. *Academy of Management Journal*, 26(2), 289–297.

Utman, C.H. (1997) Performance Effects of Motivation State: A Meta-Analysis. *Personality and Social Psychology Review*, 1, 170–182.

Valentin, C. (2006) Researching human resource development: emergence of a critical approach to HRD enquiry. *International Journal of Training and Development*, 10(1), 17–29.

Van der Veen, R. (2006) Human Resource Development: Irreversible Trend or Temporary Fad? *Human Resource Development Review*, 5(1), 3–7.

Van Vianen, A.E.M. and Fischer, A.H. (2002) Illuminating the Glass Ceiling: The Role of Organizational Culture Preferences. *Journal of Occupational and Organizational Psychology*, 75(3), 315–337.

Van Woerkom, M. (2004) *The Value of Critically Reflective Work Behaviour.* Paper presented at the Academy of Human Resource Development Conference, Austin, Texas.

van Zolingen, S.J. and Streumer, J.N. (2001) Problems in Knowledge Management: A Case Study of a Knowledge Intensive Company. *International Journal of Training and Development*, 5(3)

Velada, R. and Caetano, A. (2007) Training Transfer: The Mediating Role of Perception of Learning. *Journal of European Industrial Training*, 31(4), 283–296.

Verdonschot, S. and Kwakman, K. (2004) *Borderless Learning Experiences – The Development of Design Guidelines for Collaborative Distance Learning Environments.* Fifth European Conference on Human Resource Development Theory and Practice, University of Limerick.

Vergauwen, P. and Van Alem, F. (2005) Annual report IC disclosures in The Netherlands, France and Germany. *Journal of Intellectual Capital*, 6(1), 89–104.

Vermeulen, R.C.M. (2002) Narrowing the Transfer Gap: The Advantages of 'as if' Situations in Training. *Journal of European Industrial Training*, 26(8), 366–374.

Vince, R. (2003) The Future Practice of HRD. *Human Resource Development International*, 6(4), 559–563.

Von Krogh, G. (1988) Care in Knowledge Creation. *California Management Review*, 40(3), 133–153.

Von Krogh, G., Roos, J. and Slocum, K. (1994) An Essay on Corporate Epistemology. *Strategic Management Journal*, 15(Summer Special Issue), 53–71.

Voss, C.A., Chiesa, V. and Coughlan, P. (1994) Developing and Testing Benchmarking and Self-Assessment Frameworks in Manufacturing. *International Journal of Operations and Production Management*, 14(3), 83–100.

Vrasidas, C. and Zembylas, M. (2003) The Nature of Technology-Mediated Interaction in Globalised Education. *International Journal of Training and Development*, 7(4), 271–286.

Waldersee, R. and Eagleson, G. (2002) Shared Leadership in the Implementation of Re-orientations. *Leadership and Organization Development Journal*, 23(7), 400–407.

Walker, J.W. (2001) Are We Global Yet? In M.H. Albrecht (ed.), *International HRM: Managing Diversity in the Workplace*. Oxford: Blackwell.

Wallman, S.M.H. (1998) *The Future of Accounting and Financial Reporting – Part II: The Colorized Approach*. The American Institute of Certified Public Accountants Twenty-Third National Conference On Current SEC Developments. http://www.sec.gov/news/speech/speecharchive/1996/spch079.txt

Walton, J. (1999) *Strategic Human Resource Development*. London: Financial Times Prentice Hall.

Wang, X., & McLean, G.N. (2007). The dilemma of defining international HRD. *Human Resource Development Review*, 6(1), 96–108.

Ward, J. and Winstanley, D. (2005) Coming Out at Work: Performativity and the Recognition and Renegotiation of Identity. *Sociological Review*, 53(3), 447–474.

Ward, T.B. (1995) What's Old about New Ideas? In S.M. Smith, T.B. Ward and R.A. Finke (eds), *The Creative Cognition Approach* (pp. 157–178). Cambridge, MA: MIT Press.

Warr, P., Bird, M. and Rackham, N. (1976) *Evaluation of Management Training*. London: Gower Press.

Watkins, K. (1989) Five Metaphors: Alternative Theories for Human Resource Development. In D.B. Gradeous (ed.), *Systems Theory Applied to Human Resource Development* (pp. 167–184). Alexandria, VA: ASTD.

Watkins, K.E. and Marsick, V.J. (1994) *Sculpting the Learning Organisation: Lessons in the Art and Science of Systematic Change*. San Francisco, CA: Jossey-Bass.

Watkins, K.E. and Marsick, V.J. (1997) Building the Learning Organisation: A New Role for Human Resource Developers. In D. Russ-Eft, H. Preskill and C. Sleezer (eds), *HRD Review, Research and Implications*. California: Sage.

Watson, E. (2007) Who or What Creates? A Conceptual Framework for Social Creativity. *Human Resource Development Review* (6), 419–441.

Wayne, S.J., Shore, L.M. and Liden, R.C. (1997) Perceived Organisational Support and Leader Member Exchange: A Social Exchange Perspective. *Academy of Management Journal*, 40(1), 82–111.

Weber, M. (1971) *Makt og Byråkrati – Essays om Politikk og Klasse, Samfundsforskning og Verdier*, Gyldendal, Norsk Forlag.

Weeks, K., Weeks, M. and Frost, L. (2007) The Role of Race and Social Class in Compensation Decisions. *Journal of Managerial Psychology*, 22(7), 701–718.

Weick, K.E. (1995) *Sensemaking in Organisations*. Thousand Oaks, CA: Sage.

Weick, K.E. and Westley, F. (1996) Organisational Learning: Affirming an Oxymoron. In S.R. Clegg, C. Hardy and W.R. Nord (eds), *Handbook of Organisation Studies* (pp. 440–458). London: Sage.

Weinberger, L. (1998) Commonly Held Theories of Human Resource Development. *Human Resource Development International*, 1(1), 75–93.

Weiss, C.H. (1987) *Evaluating Action Programs*. New York: Sage.

Weiss, J.W. (1996) *Organisation Behaviour and Change: Managing Diversity, Cross Cultural Dynamics and Ethics*. New York: West.

Wenger, E. (1998) *Communities of Practice – Learning, Meaning, and Identity*. Cambridge: Cambridge University Press.

Westhead, P. and Storey, D.J. (1997) *Training Provision and the Development of Smalll and Medium-Sized Enterprises.* Norwich: HMSO Department for Education and Employment.

Wever, R., Boks, C., Marinelli, T. and Stevels, A. (2007) Increasing the Benefits of Product-Level Benchmarking for Strategic Eco-Efficient Decision-Making. *Benchmarking: An International Journal*, 14(6), 711–727.

Wexley, K.N. and Latham, G.P. (1991) *Developing and Training Human Resources in Organisations.* New York: Harper Row.

Wexley, K.N. and Latham, G.P. (2002) *Developing and Training Human Resources in Organizations.* New Jersey: Prentice Hall.

Wexley, K.N. and Nemeroff, W. (1975) Effectiveness of Positive Reinforcement and Goal Setting as Methods of Management Development. *Journal of Applied Psychology*, 64, 239–246.

Widener, S.K. (2004) An Empirical Investigation of the Relation Between the Use of Strategic Human Capital and the Design of the Management Control System. *Accounting, Organizations and Society*, 29(3–4), 377–399.

Williams, C.L. (1992) The Glass Escalator: Hidden Advantages for Men in the 'Female' Professions. *Social Problems*, 39(3), 253–267.

Wilson, J.P. and Beard, C. (2002, 25–26 January). *Experiential Learning: Linking Theory and Practice.* Paper presented at the Paper presented at the Third conference on Human Resource Development: Research and Practice across Europe: Creativity and Innovation in Learning, Edinburgh.

Wilson, J.P. and Beard, C. (2003) The Learning Combination Lock – An Experiential Approach to Learning Design. *Journal of European Industrial Training*, 27(2/3/4), 87–97.

Wiltsher, C. (2005) Fundamentals of Adult Learning. In J.P. Wilson (ed.), *Human Resource Development: Learning and Training for Individuals and Groups.* London: Kogan Page.

Wittgenstein, L. (1983) *Philosophical Investigations.* Oxford: Basil Blackwell.

Wright, P.C. and Belcourt, M. (1995) Costing Training Activity: A Decision-Maker's Dilemma. *Management Decision*, 33(2), 5–15.

Woodall, J. (2003) The Common Underlying Assumptions of HRD? *Human Resource Development International*, 6(3), 281–283.

Woodall, J. (2005) Theoretical Frameworks for Comparing HRD in an International Context. *Human Resource Development International*, 8(4), 399–402.

Woodall, J., Alker, A., McNeil, C. and Shaw, S. (2002) Convergence and Divergence in HRD: Research and Practice across Europe. In J. McGoldrick, J. Stewart and S. Watson (eds), *Understanding Human Resource Development: A Research-based Approach.* London: Routledge.

Yang, B. (2003) Towards a Holistic Theory of Knowledge and Adult Learning. *Human Resource Development Review*, 2(2), 106–129.

Yasin, M.M. (2002) The Theory and Practice of Benchmarking: Then and Now. *Benchmarking: An International Journal*, 9(3), 217–243.

Zaccaro, S.J. and Klimoski, R.J. (2001) *The Nature of Organizational Leadership: Understanding the Performance Imperatives confronting Today's Leaders.* San Francisco, CA: Jossey-Bass.

Zhou, J. (2003) When the Presence of Creative Co-Workers is Related to Creativity: Role of Supervisor Close Monitoring, Developmental Feedback and Creative Personality. *Journal of Applied Psychology*, 88, 413–422.

Zuriff, G.E. (1985) *Behaviourism: A Conceptual Reconstruction.* New York: Columbia University Press.

Index

change *cont.*
   adapt to change 40, 43, 84, 172, 193
   change agent 8, 107–9, 158
   change programme 139–40
   culture change 25, 174
   continuous change 142–3, 147
   environmental change 36, 194
   organisational change 76, 97,
      116, 118, 137, 139, 155
Chartered Institute of Personnel and
   Development (CIPD) 29, 32, 40
classroom training 15, 41, 79
coaching 36, 42–3, 53, 153,
   162, 166, 168
cognitivism 13, 22, 65–7, 77
   cognitive ability 17
   cognitive approaches to creativity 56
   cognitive schema 14
   cognitive style 57, 59, 66
   cognitive theories of learning 65–7
commitment 40, 41, 43, 72,
   161, 176, 183
communication 88, 120, 130–2
communities of practice 110–4
competences 37, 80, 83,
   86, 142–3, 188
competencies 7, 8, 15, 31,
   37, 41, 92, 97, 100
   core competencies 6, 56, 188, 192
   leadership competencies 152, 164
   practice competencies 80
   sets of competencies 152, 195
competitive advantage 7, 30, 36,
   37, 49, 51, 55, 143, 184, 195
complexity 37, 59, 86–9, 135, 147, 155
computer-based training 181
constructivism 13, 22, 62, 87, 88
   constructivist ontology 26, 27
   social construction of reality
      73–4, 76, 130–3
conditioning 19, 67–8
   classic conditioning 67
   operant/instrumental conditioning 68
continuing education 85, 194
continuous improvement
   30–32, 55–6, 122
cost 21–2, 25, 29, 45, 172, 186
counselling 39–41, 170
creativity 55–64, 76, 161, 172
   barriers to creativity 56
critical theory 10, 72–6, 77
   critical HRD 10
   critical reflection 20, 72–4

culture 116–128
   cross-cultural 164, 182
   culture change *see* change
   cultural diversity 187
   cultural issues 187, 189, 190–1
   cultural norms 172, 185, 189
   cultural values 15
   masculine culture 175
   organisational culture 179
customer 9, 29, 33–8, 53, 55,
   117, 141–3, 146, 184, 187
cybernetics theory 96

D
decision-making 17, 24–5, 73, 166
declarative information 13
deconstruction 103, 134,
   136, 153, 155–6
deutero-learning *see* learning
developmental opportunities 77
developmental relationships
   39–43, 178
devolvement 36, 39, 41,
   43, 192–3, 195
dialectic thinking 14
dialogue 14–5, 18, 73, 82, 100–4
discourse 104–6, 114, 146–7, 155–6
discrimination 174–180
   equality 10, 74, 173
   exclusion 135, 139, 177
   gender discrimination 174–6
   glass ceiling 175
   isolation 176–7
   lucite ceiling 175–6
   marginalisation 10, 130, 140, 176
   oppression 10, 11, 76, 148, 156
   privilege 177
   'Queen Bee' concept 176
   race discrimination 176–8
   resistance to diversity 172–3
   sexual orientation
      discrimination 178–9
distance learning 13, 22
diversity and HRD 172–180
diversity training 173–4
double-loop learning 107–10

E
e-learning 19
education 19, 26, 61, 79–94
educationalists 74–5
emotion 42, 58, 72, 161
emotional intelligence 42–3, 161–2, 171

international HRD 181–193
  convergence-divergence debate 183
  framework 182–7
  multi-domestic organisation 187–8
  multinational organisation 189–190
  international organisation 188–9
  transnational organisation 191–192
internet 19
interpersonal relations 87, 163, 192
interpersonal skills 41, 87
investors in people 27

J
job commitment 180
job readiness 166
job satisfaction 176, 180

K
Kirkpatrick's four levels
    taxonomy 27–29
Kirton's adaption-innovation theory 59
knowledge 14–6, 91–5
  contextual knowledge 152
  explicit Knowledge 37, 93, 95
  forms of knowledge 146
  knowledge management 37, 52, 112
  knowledge sharing 14, 18, 20, 112, 114
  knowledge transfer 183–4, 192
  social knowledge 15
  tacit knowledge 14, 91–5
knowledge economy, 15, 20, 24,
    36, 44, 46, 48, 51, 195
knowledge-skills mix 14–6
knowledge society 84
Kolb's experiential learning cycle 71

L
language games 98, 102–106, 111, 130–3
leadership 41–2, 159–172
  behavioural leadership 162–4
  contingency leadership 164–5
  criticisms of leadership theories 159
  great man theory 161
  leadership development 41–42
  path-goal leadership 165–6
  role in performance management 41
  situational leadership 166–7
  trait leadership 160–2
  transformational leadership 167–8
learning
  adult learning 64–78
  behaviourist theories of learning 67–8
  cognitivist theories of learning 65–7

learning *cont.*
  critical theory approaches to
      learning 72–8
  deutero learning 108–10
  double-loop learning 107
  experiential learning theory 70–2
  formal learning 81
  humanist theories of learning 69–70
  incidental learning 65
  informal learning 65, 79, 81,
      86–88, 113
  learner interaction 18–9
  learning needs 13, 82, 86, 99
  learning organisation 37, 109–110
  learning styles 13, 66, 67, 70, 71
  learning theories 13
  learning versus performance
      debate 65, 98
  organisational learning 97–115
  self-directed learning 19, 65, 87
  single-loop learning 107
  social learning theory 68–9
  workplace learning 79–96
lectures 13
legal regulations 142, 173
LGBT (Lesbian, Gay, Bisexual,
    Transgendered) 178–9
lifelong learning 79, 84–6
line managers 38–9
locus of initiation 19, 20

M
management
  management development 39, 159
  management education 74,
      75, 147, 151
  management programmes 135
  participative forms of management 39
management accounting 50–2
mental models 109
mentoring 40
memory 66, 154–5
metrics 28–34, 44, 47, 52
mission of the organisation
    38, 105, 118, 140, 145
models of HRD
  Argyris and Schon model of
      organisational learning 109
  Baldwin and Ford's training
      transfer model 16
  CIPD model of evaluation
      and value 32
  creativity model 57

models of HRD *cont.*
  Easterby-Smith evaluation
    framework 32
  experiential learning and learning
    styles framework 71
  Hamblin's evaluation framework 32
  UK investors in people model 27
  Warr, Bird & Rackham evaluation
    matrix 32
motivation 17–8, 28, 42,
    56–9, 68, 139, 151
  extrinsic motivation 56, 58
  intrinsic motivation 58, 61
motivational disposition 165–6
multi-domestic organisation
    see international HRD
multidisciplinary nature of HRD 2
multifactorial approach to examining
    creativity 57–9
multinational organization
    see international HRD

N
narrative 102–5, 110–1, 119–121,
    131, 134–140, 144–151
national skills taskforce (UK) 39
national qualifications frameworks
    (NVQ and SVQ) 164
networking 21, 176, 178, 180
networks 19, 42, 60, 106

O
ontology 26–7, 33, 95, 149
  constructivist ontology 26–7
  realist ontology 26–7
on-the-job training 16, 41
oppression *see* discrimination
organisation culture 62, 110,
    117–122, 179,196
organisational change *see* change
organisational citizenship 69, 74
organisational development 108,
    114, 116–128, 192
organisational inquiry 107–8
organisational learning *see* learning
organisational structure 86, 191, 196
outsourcing 3, 81
overseas assignment 183, 189
overseas subsidiary 184–5, 188–9, 192

P
paradigm 9, 27, 195, 198
  critical theory paradigm 72

paradigm *cont.*
  learning paradigm 65, 98
  performance paradigm 9, 35–6, 65, 98
  situational leadership paradigm 166
participation 41–2, 81–2, 93,
    111–4, 119, 157, 174–5
pedagogy 90, 152
performance 35–43
  performance appraisal 124
  performance drivers 30–4
  performance indicators 31, 49
  performance needs 36
  performance targets 121, 127
  role of HRD in performance
    management 36
personal challenges 177
personal development 40, 152
personality 16, 17, 28, 56, 151,
    161, 165
perspective 59–60
  agency 68
  community of practice 112
  critical theory 10
  cultural 118
  educational 85
  humanist 70
  individual level 112
  Jungian personality 17
  language game 104
  organisational level 112
political 9–11, 20, 25, 72–4,
    134, 148, 151, 155, 173,
    177, 183, 189, 191, 198
power 9, 10, 20, 25, 72–7, 85,
    92, 101, 105–8, 111, 114,
    119, 139, 154, 177
practical skills 92
pragmatism 88–91
problem orientation 88–90
problem-solving 13, 15, 17, 38,
    59, 66, 70–1, 90, 97, 172
process
  creative 56–61
  emergent 142
  identification 112, 132–3
  innovation 56
  internationalisation 183, 192
  learning 13, 18–21, 64, 66, 74,
    76, 79, 81, 83, 85–7
  process consultant 99, 110
  strategy 153–4
professional bodies 8, 75–6, 182
professional practice 2, 89

professional values 101, 139
profit maximisation 142

Q
quality 36, 43, 186
quality systems 107, 133

R
race 176–8
reactions 27–8, 33
reality 61, 72, 73, 92, 96, 111, 119–120,
    122–23, 130–4, 136–8, 141, 150
reflection 7, 70, 90, 96, 100
    critical reflection 72–4
    degree of reflection 20–2
    function of reflection 147
    reflections on HRD 194–9
    types of reflection 146
reflexive 96, 114, 144, 149–153, 198
reinforcement theory 77
reliability 26, 147
results 28, 29, 34
return on expectations 29, 32
return on investment 24, 26, 29, 32
reward systems 55–6,
role of HRD practitioners 8, 9, 65

S
Scottish Vocational Qualifications
    (SVQ) 164
self-actualisation 10, 28, 70, 76–7
self-awareness 42, 75, 161–2
self-confidence 58, 176, 180
self-directed learning 19, 22, 65, 87
self-efficacy 17, 58, 68, 166
self-interest 28, 163, 170, 176
self-management 9, 161
self-regulation 42
sexuality 61, 178–9
shared identity 139, 143, 150–1
shared repertoires 112, 114
shared understandings 15, 138, 140
shared vision 109, 168
simulations 13, 22, 173
single-loop learning 107–8
situated learning 17, 87, 95, 105
situational leadership 164–7, 169, 171
skill acquisition 10, 17
skill development 12, 36, 174, 185
skill set 26, 29, 30, 39
skills 15
skills training 42, 195
social learning theory 68–9, 77, 110–4

socialisation 14–5, 40, 69, 72
stakeholders 7–8, 27, 33, 38, 48–9,
    148, 150, 153–4, 195
strategic capability 142–3, 185
strategic goals 33, 101, 142
strategic HRD 36–8, 144, 153
strategic learning 147, 151
strategic planning 8, 25, 35
succession planning 41, 164, 175
summative evaluation *see* evaluation
supervisory support 18, 58
systems theory 29, 109
systems thinking 37, 109

T
tacit knowledge *see* knowledge
talent 10, 18, 41, 157
team building 3, 170
team learning 109
technical competence 42
technology 11, 19, 30, 35, 37,
    94, 100, 110, 118, 127, 133,
    136–7, 139, 142–4, 155
theory
    contingency theory *see* leadership
    critical theory and HRD
        see critical theory
    cybernetic theory *see* cybernetic theory
    experiential learning theory *see*
        experiential learning
    finance theory *see* finance theory
    great man theory *see* great man theory
    human capital theory
        see human capital
    path-goal theory *see* leadership
    Polanyi theory of tacit knowing
        see tacit knowledge
    Kirton adaption-innovation theory, *see*
        Kirton adaption-innovation theory
    social learning theory *see*
        social learning theory
    trait theory *see* leadership
total quality management 135
training 12–23
    diversity training *see* diversity training
    outward-bound training 14, 22
    training and development 6,
        11–21, 31, 196
    training design 12, 16, 17, 28
    training dimensions 13
    training evaluation 24–35
    training interventions 13, 20–2,
        27, 42, 162, 170

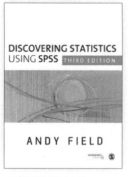
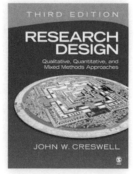
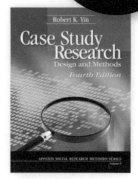

Research Methods
Books from SAGE

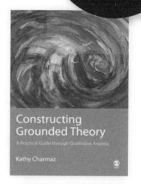

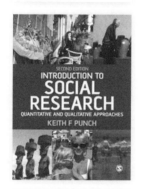

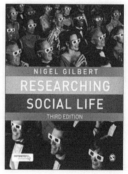

www.sagepub.co.uk

The Qualitative Research Kit

Edited by Uwe Flick

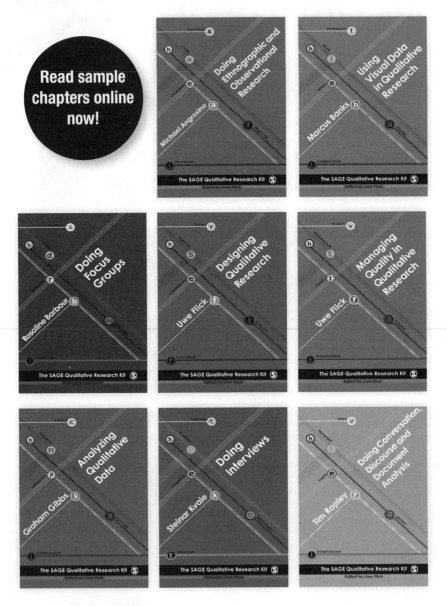

Read sample chapters online now!

Doing Ethnographic and Observational Research — Michael Angrosino
The SAGE Qualitative Research Kit — Edited by Uwe Flick

Using Visual Data in Qualitative Research — Marcus Banks
The SAGE Qualitative Research Kit — Edited by Uwe Flick

Doing Focus Groups — Rosaline Barbour
The SAGE Qualitative Research Kit

Designing Qualitative Research — Uwe Flick
The SAGE Qualitative Research Kit — Edited by Uwe Flick

Managing Quality in Qualitative Research — Uwe Flick
The SAGE Qualitative Research Kit — Edited by Uwe Flick

Analyzing Qualitative Data — Graham Gibbs
The SAGE Qualitative Research Kit — Edited by Uwe Flick

Doing Interviews — Steinar Kvale
The SAGE Qualitative Research Kit — Edited by Uwe Flick

Doing Conversation, Discourse and Document Analysis — Tim Rapley
The SAGE Qualitative Research Kit — Edited by Uwe Flick

www.sagepub.co.uk